FLORIDA STATE
UNIVERSITY LIBRARIES

JUL 1 2 2001

TALLAHASSEE, FLORIDA

Agricultural Marketing in Tropical Africa

Contributions from the Netherlands

H. Laurens van der Laan, Tjalling Dijkstra & Aad van Tilburg (Eds)

African Studies Centre Leiden
Research Series 15/1999

Ashgate

Agricultural Marketing in Tropical Africa
Contributions from the Netherlands

African Studies Centre
Research Series
15/1999

Agricultural Marketing in Tropical Africa
Contributions from the Netherlands

H. Laurens van der Laan
Tjalling Dijkstra
Aad van Tilburg
(Editors)

Ashgate

8. Maize and bean marketing in Benin *153*
    The peasant farmers' choice of marketing outlet
        Lineke van Bruggen and Aad van Tilburg

9. Horticultural marketing in Kenya *169*
    Why potato farmers need collecting wholesalers
        Tjalling Dijkstra

10. Cattle marketing in Zambia, 1965-1995 *185*
    Policies, institutions and cattle owners in Western Province
        Henk A.J. Moll and Désirée C.E. Dietvorst

11. Cross-border cattle marketing in Sub-Saharan Africa since 1900 *205*
    Geographical patterns and government-induced change
        Leo de Haan, Paul Quarles van Ufford and Fred Zaal

About the authors *227*

Index *233*

vii

List of maps

5.1 The cocoa regions of Ghana   89
5.2 The cocoa regions of Cameroon   91
7.1 Map of Sierra Leone showing the research area   134
8.1 Map of Benin showing the research areas   155
11.1 Main geographical patterns of cross-border cattle trade in West Africa since 1960   216
11.2 Main geographical patterns of cross-border cattle trade in East Africa since 1960   216

List of figures

2.1 Index of estimate maize production, area cultivated and yield (per capita)   32
2.2 State and market-dominated stages of Tanzanian marketing organisation and factors spurring organisational change, 1943-1998   40
3.1 Kenya: maize production in million tons (1976 - 1996)   49
4.1 Simplified food system   69
6.1 Index of unit value of export Côte d'Ivoire - Costa Rica   115
6.2 Growers' share of retail prices in consumer countries   125
7.1 Structure of the Annual Rice Account of rice-farming households in the research area   137
8.1 Assumed pattern of relations between actors and collection of information by household members involved in the selling of products   157
8.2 Characteristics of the farm, the farm household, and the environment, presumed to influence the choice of marketing outlet   161
9.1 Average marketing costs and marketing revenue per bag for Kinangop farmers taking potatoes to Nairobi market   178
10.1 Herd size and registered offtake in head of cattle in Western Province, 1965-1995   192

List of tables

1.1 Characteristics of agricultural production and their effect on marketing   2
1.2 Research coverage of major categories of crop   5
1.3 Research coverage of institutions in agricultural marketing   7
1.4 Research coverage of functions in agricultural marketing   8
1.5 Regions of the world, by strength of farmers' organizations and quality of publications on agricultural marketing   12
1.6 Categories of agricultural product, by marketing channel   13
2.1 Maize production and Strategic Grain Reserve (SGR) purchases   21
2.2 Sequence of economic liberalization measures   27
3.1 Maize: Official producer prices, consumer prices, 'price spread' and producer's share; 1980 - 1993   53
3.2 Maize prices in rural markets by province 1990-1996   54

3.3	Kenya: Post-reform official producer prices for maize (1993-1996; nominal prices)	59
4.1	Annual grain balance in Burkina Faso	73
4.2	Household 'expenditures' for different income classes	74
4.3	Annual grain balance per region of Burkina Faso	77
4.4	Average sorghum prices in some regional market centres	78
5.1	Cocoa bought by PBC and other LBCs in the Ashanti Region in percentages	100
5.2	Producer and FOB cocoa prices in Ghana and Cameroon, compared to world market prices, 1980 - 1996	101
5.3	Cocoa production in Ghana and Cameroon 1989 - 1997	103
6.1	Coffee area, output and yields Côte d'Ivoire and Costa Rica 1960-1995	111
6.2	Coffee farms by size	112
6.3	Share of gross value added in the retail price of roasted coffee in main importing countries	124
6.4	Indirect taxes on coffee in 1996	126
6.5	Income distribution in coffee chains 1994	127
7.1	Rice-farming households, by region and commercial orientation	133
7.2a	Average quantities of unthreshed rice (paddy) in kg, by sources, 1 November 1984 - 31 October 1985	141
7.2b	Average quantities of unthreshed rice (paddy) in kg, by uses, 1 November 1984 - 31 October 1985	142
7.3	Respondents (%) by sources of seed rice	143
7.4	Average quantities of rice, in kg, representing rents of land, labour and capital received and paid, 1 November 1984 - 31 October 1985	144
7.5	Respondents (%) using labour groups in rice-farming activities	145
7.6	Average quantities of rice purchased, in kg, 1 November 1984 - 31 October 1985	145
7.7	Number of transactions per respondent by type of buyer	146
7.8	Weighted average monthly prices of both free market transactions and transactions with creditors	148
7.9	Respondents (%) by access to services and products	149
7.10	Main formal institutions operating in the research area	149
8.1	Main market outlet chosen by peasant farmers for selected crops	156
8.2	Consultation of others by the head of household before products are sold	158
8.3	Results of the logistic regressions on the peasant farmer's choice of outlet for maize in 1990/91	166
8.4	Results of the logistic regression on the peasant farmer's choice of outlet for beans in the years 1990/91 and 1991/92	167
9.1	Average marketing costs per bag, incurred by potato farmers in Kinangop in 1990 under different marketing strategies	173
9.2	Direct and indirect transport costs, incurred by potato farmers in Kinangop in 1990 under different marketing strategies	174
9.3	Potato sales by potato farmers in Kinangop during the main harvesting period of 1990	179
10.1	Registered cattle purchases in Western Province by type of buyer, 1985-1995	189
10.2	Cattle herd size and registered offtake in Western Province, 1965-1995	193
10.3	Main characteristics of study areas, 1991	195
10.4	Household characteristics, mean values	196
10.5	Households by herd size and gender of household head	197
10.6	Sales decisions, actual and predicted by the binomial probit model	198
10.7	Respondents' reason for selling cattle	199
10.8	Respondents' reasons for not selling cattle	200

Preface

There has been surprisingly strong academic interest in the Netherlands in the subject of this book. It has come from three sources. The first is Wageningen Agricultural University (WAU) which was established in 1918, and testifies to the long-term involvement of the Dutch government in the agricultural sector. Marketing research with respect to agricultural and food products, always seen as a significant field of study at the WAU, qualified for a separate chair in the academic expansion of the 1960s. In the early 1980s, Prof. Matthew T.G. Meulenberg, the head of the department, introduced a new course entitled 'Agricultural Marketing in Developing Countries' in keeping with the WAU's growing desire to apply Western knowledge and expertise to non-Western problems. Aad van Tilburg, one of the authors of this preface, has taught this course since 1984.

The second group expressing interest in the topic is more diffuse. It consists of several universities that began to devote more resources to the study of 'economic development' in the 1950s and 1960s. In the Netherlands there has always been a great deal of idealism and a broad-based desire to help the Third World. At first, economists, for example Prof. Jan Tinbergen, were the pioneers but subsequently geographers also played a major role. For our purposes it is important to note that it has been easier for geographers than for economists to identify 'agricultural marketing' as a separate subject within the ever-widening field of economic development. Thus, two geographers at Utrecht University, Prof. Jan Hinderink and Jan Sterkenburg, initiated a teaching and research programme in agricultural commercialization in the 1970s.[1]

While the academic institutions just mentioned considered the whole of the Third World, the African Studies Centre in Leiden, the third source in our view, has confined its research to one continent. The ASC, as we now know it, was established in 1958. This was at the time when the relationship between the Netherlands and Indonesia was deteriorating and many tropical specialists urged the reallocation of Dutch manpower and resources to Africa. Since 1958, the African Studies Centre has been a stimulating and unifying force for academic research on Africa in the Netherlands. Laurens van der Laan, one of its researchers, has been instrumental in stimulating research on agricultural marketing in Africa since the mid 1970s.

In 1959, Laurens van der Laan started his academic career as a lecturer in economics at Fourah Bay College, Freetown, Sierra Leone. In addition to his teaching he carried out indepth research into the diamond industry and the Lebanese entrepreneurs working in Sierra Leone.[2] It was during his research that he became interested in agricultural marketing. Laurens returned to the Netherlands in 1971 and joined the African Studies Centre. He focused on Africa's export marketing boards, first pleading for a broader research perspective and then questioning their liquidation.[3] Tjalling Dijkstra, the other author of this preface, joined the ASC in 1988, cooperating with Laurens and strengthening marketing research at the Centre. Recently Laurens attempted a broad survey of Africa's export crop marketing, introducing the concept of the Trans-Oceanic Marketing Channel to model and unify his approach.[4]

Laurens has been a source of inspiration to many Africanists in the Netherlands and elsewhere. To mark his 65th birthday, a one-day symposium was held in his honour in November 1997. The theme was 'Agricultural Marketing in Tropical Africa'. It was jointly organized by the African Studies Centre and the Department of Marketing and Marketing Research of the WAU, where he had been a part-time lecturer since 1986. Researchers from several universities and research institutes in the Netherlands contributed papers and participated in the discussions.

The seven papers presented at the symposium, as well as four others, are to be found in this book. The call for papers was addressed to both Dutch and foreign researchers working in the Netherlands. Since some of those offering a paper collaborated with researchers in Africa or elsewhere, the total number of non-Dutch contributors to this volume is substantial, reflecting the cosmopolitan nature of the academic world in the Netherlands. Two African scholars were invited to act as discussants. Information on both the authors and the discussants is provided in the section 'About the authors'.

The book's chapters cover a wide range of commodities, countries and themes. Food crops such as maize, rice, sorghum, beans and potatoes are dealt with, as are export crops such as cocoa and coffee. In addition to crop marketing, cattle trading is also reviewed. The discussions focus on market liberalization, food security, global competitiveness, cross-border trade, farmers' transactions and the efficiency of private trade. Some of the papers are based on secondary data and have a historical perspective, others present primary data collected by the authors.

In the introductory chapter Laurens van der Laan explores how far the study of agricultural marketing with regard to Tropical Africa has progressed. He, as well as the other authors, show that a considerable amount of work has been done. This does not, however, imply that it is time to sit back and relax. Laurens proposes that the next step should be to work on a geographically specialized subdiscipline: Agricultural Marketing in Tropical Africa.

The editors of the book would like to thank the African Studies Centre and Wageningen Agricultural University for their contributions in time and money to, first, the symposium and, second, the publication of this book. They also thank Ann Reeves for correcting the English and Leontine van Dijl of the ASC for her work on the lay out.

Aad van Tilburg and Tjalling Dijkstra

Wageningen/Leiden, August 1999

1   J. Hinderink & J.J. Sterkenburg (1987) *Agricultural Commercialization and Government Policy in Africa*. London: Kegan Paul
2   H. Laurens van der Laan (1965) *The Sierra Leone Diamonds: An Economic Survey Covering the Years 1952-1961*. London: Oxford University Press. H. Laurens van der Laan (1975) *The Lebanese Traders in Sierra Leone*. The Hague: Mouton
3   Kwame Arhin, Paul Hesp & H. Laurens van der Laan (1985) *Marketing Boards in Tropical Africa*. London: KPI. H. Laurens van der Laan (1992) 'In defence of export marketing boards.' In: *APROMA Bimonthly Review,* December, no. 27/28/29, pp. 34-40
4   H. Laurens van der Laan (1997) *The Trans-Oceanic Marketing Channel: A New Tool for Understanding Tropical Africa's Export Agriculture*. Binghampton, NY: International Business Press (Haworth Press)

Agricultural Marketing in Tropical Africa
Obstacles to Systematic Study

H. Laurens van der Laan

Abstract

This chapter explores how far the study of agricultural marketing with regard to Tropical Africa has progressed. The exploration, which follows the academic discipline of agricultural marketing as it has developed in the West, surveys the literature on agricultural marketing in Africa, using first the commodity approach, then the institutional one and finally the functional one. In each case the conclusion must be that research coverage has been highly uneven. First, many crops have been neglected. Second, even with well-researched crops, some institutions and/or functions appear to have been overlooked.

At the end of the chapter doubts are expressed about the relevance for Tropical Africa of (a) publications on agricultural marketing in the West and (b) parallel publications for the non-Western world. These doubts reflect the author's conviction that Tropical Africa is different from Asia and Latin America and that this situation justifies a geographically specialized subdiscipline called 'Agricultural Marketing in Tropical Africa'.

1.1 Introduction

The study of agricultural marketing in Tropical Africa has made great strides since World War II. This should not, however, be a cause for complacency because on closer inspection we find that many topics have been neglected and some fundamental questions overlooked. In this chapter I want to review the achievements and shortcomings of research in this field.[1]

This chapter is arranged as follows. In the first section I sketch the academic discipline of agricultural marketing as it has developed in the West. This provides a matrix for the discussion in the next three sections, where I offer some comments on (a) the situation

---

[1] I am grateful to my coeditors and to Nana Arhin Brempong for their comments on earlier versions of this chapter.

regarding agricultural marketing in Tropical Africa and (b) the corresponding literature. In the final sections I formulate some fundamental questions which hopefully pave the way for a comprehensive publication project on this subject.

1.2 The academic discipline of agricultural marketing

Agricultural marketing has emerged as a separate discipline in many countries, notably in the countries of the West (for a definition, see below). This discipline is primarily distinguished by its subject matter and approach.

The subject matter of agricultural marketing is clearly demarcated. Scholars confine their attention to agricultural products.[2] They do so because they are convinced that these products have special features. While ready to remain within the general discipline of economics, they consider its general concepts of 'products' and 'services' too wide and therefore less useful.[3] Table 1.1 lists five major characteristics which distinguish agricultural production from production in general.

Table 1.1 Characteristics of agricultural production and their effect on marketing

Characteristics	Consequences for marketing activities
(1)	(2)
specific location	collection followed by distribution
small-scale activity	assembling and collecting, bulking
seasonality	seasonal storage, stock-holding
perishability of product	on-farm or nearby off-farm preservation
natural variation of product	sorting and standardization

Let me briefly elaborate on column 1. First, agricultural production is tied to specific locations because either the soils or the climate do not encourage or permit cultivation at other locations. Second, the scale of agricultural production tends to be small. Indeed, the majority of the world's agricultural enterprises are family farms with a limited labour force. Third, agricultural production tends to be seasonal. The product is not available throughout the year, but during the harvest season only.[4] Fourth, nearly all agricultural products are perishable: the quality deteriorates – quickly with some products, slowly with others. Fifth, agricultural products exhibit a natural variation: botanical units, even of the same variety, are not identical.

---

[2] The narrow definition of agriculture, which excludes livestock, is used here.
[3] I am an economist by training. Readers are reminded that my perspective on the relationship (and possible differences) between economics and agricultural marketing has been shaped by economics.
[4] In the temperate zones 'seasonal' refers to the alternation of summer and winter; in most parts of the tropics it refers to the rhythm of dry and wet seasons.

We now turn to column 2. The first two production characteristics combine to make the collecting or assembling aspect of agricultural marketing crucial. In particular if the scale of production is small and that of trade large, there is a strong convergence pattern in agricultural marketing. As a result the relationship (or nexus) between the farmer and the collecting trader[5] deserves special attention. Seasonality, the third characteristic, requires considerable storage for staple food crops, that is, crops which consumers want to eat as daily food throughout the year. This storage activity is only possible if the product is durable or storable (see below). Seasonal stocks explicitly introduce the time factor into the analysis. The same is true for perishability, but here time manifests itself in tight schedules to get the product preserved or transported from the farmer to the buyer.[6] Finally, since for those involved in agricultural marketing natural variation is a commercial disadvantage, they try to improve their economic position by adopting widely accepted standards (or grades) and by sorting their harvest accordingly. Sorting, which has been defined as "classifying a mixed lot of produce into homogeneous categories" (Kohls & Uhl, 1990, 534), is a useful and profitable activity, performed by either the farmers or the collecting traders. The five features presented in Table I (and some minor features not mentioned here) justify special teaching courses on 'agricultural economics' and 'agricultural marketing'. In my view they should be treated as subdisciplines within the discipline of economics.

Often 'food marketing' and 'agricultural marketing' are studied and taught together.[7] There are strong arguments for this combination. First, many agricultural products end up as food for human beings. Second, it creates a framework for studying both the producers and the consumers. They depend on each other, but they also have conflicting interests, for instance, with regard to prices. Third, when producers and consumers live in the same country, the government is often drawn into the role of referee. But there are also arguments against. For instance, while most agricultural products are 'unbranded', many food products are sold under a brand name.[8] Marketing of the latter normally involves 'marketing management' in the sense of sales promotion, advertising, monopolistic competition, etc. The marketing of unbranded products lacks these elements and takes place in competitive markets. As a result food marketing (of branded foods) tends to be interdisciplinary, combining psychology and sociology with economics, whereas agricultural marketing (of unbranded products) is more mono-disciplinary, using economics almost exclusively. We return to this point later.

The discipline of agricultural marketing is also shaped by its approach. It tends to take the farmer (or the farm)[9] as its starting point. This gives unity to the discipline, but also dictates priorities. The farmer's point of view and his interests come first. This explains the

---

[5] For the sake of brevity I use male pronouns in connection with 'farmer' and 'trader', but, of course, there are many female farmers and a few female collecting traders.
[6] The factor time, as encountered in seasonality and perishability, cannot easily be fitted into general economic theory.
[7] Kohls & Uhl (1990) do so in their standard textbook for the USA.
[8] The trend towards more branded food products is strong in the West, but weak in Africa.
[9] The word 'grower' is more precise as it includes plantations. When large-scale agriculture is meant, I mention it explicitly.

prevalence of pro-farmer feelings in this discipline. The views of the consumers, industrial buyers and the government take second place.[10]

Many farmers are aware of (a) the physical distance between producer and consumer and (b) the time interval between harvesting and consumption. This awareness is shared by scholars of agricultural marketing, most of whom recognize a 'product flow' which records how the agricultural product moves from the point of production to the point of consumption. These scholars favour analytical approaches based on the product flow, such as the marketing chain or the marketing channel (Stern, El-Ansary & Coughlan, 1996). These approaches are, however, marginal in general economic theory.

In studying the phenomena of agricultural marketing, three alternative approaches have proved useful: the commodity, the institutional and the functional approach. The commodity approach takes individual crops or groups of crops as its starting point. The institutional approach concentrates on the institutions and actors, that is, first of all, the enterprises which produce, process and distribute agricultural products. The legal status of these enterprises may vary. Thus, there are private, public and cooperative enterprises. Other institutions are the markets, in particular the physical markets where buyers and sellers meet face to face, and the trade associations whose aim is to organize markets and facilitate trade. In the functional approach we focus on the activities of the actors. Table 1.4 in Section 1.5 presents a list of functions. Here it suffices to say that in general the totality of the functions remains the same, even when the institutions in a marketing system are reorganized and the tasks reshuffled between the actors.[11]

Having surveyed the discipline as it has developed in the West, we have a working matrix for comments on the situation in Africa. Before offering my comments five preliminary remarks are appropriate. First, while I gained some firsthand knowledge of the situation during fieldwork in Sierra Leone and four other African countries, most of my knowledge is based on the literature. Second, I have not confined my reading to publications that carry the words 'agricultural marketing' in their title. (If I had done so, I would have missed a great deal of valuable information.) Third, much of the literature consists of inaccessible 'grey literature'. Those who commissioned research, both officials and businessmen, were often content with a simple publication because the intended readership was small. Fourth, the literature consists mainly of empirical material or case studies. There is as yet little theory that is specifically African. Fifth, references are given selectively and sparingly, in order to avoid an excessive list. For the same reason there are no references to the other contributions in this volume.

---

[10] This is less so in books which combine food marketing with agricultural marketing. In those books there tends to be a sector approach rather than a farmer approach. Kohls & Uhl (1990) may serve as example.

[11] This is due to the inherent relationship between the two approaches. Both pose the question: 'Who does what?' The functional approach focuses attention on the 'what' and the institutional approach on the 'who' (Kohls & Uhl, 1990, 23). One consequence is that the functional approach offers an independent framework for assessing the impact of a reorganization within a marketing system.

1.3 The commodity approach: comments

We must now turn to the situation in Tropical Africa. When considering the literature crop by crop we find that research coverage has been most uneven. Table 1.2 identifies four broad categories of crop.

Table 1.2 Research coverage of major categories of crop

export crops	well covered
staple food crops (durable)	well covered
staple food crops (perishable)	poorly covered
other crops	neglected

The fact that much research has been done on export crops undoubtedly has an economic explanation. During the colonial period it was thought that the best form of economic development consisted of stimulating exports. African farmers were encouraged (or forced) to grow export crops. After independence the academic climate changed and it became popular to associate export crops with distorted development or even economic decline. This fostered fresh, critical research on export crops and kept them in the limelight.

A subsidiary area of research has been the transport of export crops. In the early colonial period, lack of cheap transport was seen as the chief obstacle to export-oriented development. Since the study of transport was the special province of geography, this discipline was encouraged. Geographers have indirectly contributed a great deal of knowledge on agricultural marketing. Another subsidiary area of research has been the taxation of export crops. This has always been an important topic in Africa, both before and after independence. It should be noted that it was easier to levy a tax on exporters and traders than on small-scale farmers. Information about marketing systems for export crops was therefore valuable for governments. Many studies of government finance include sections on agricultural marketing.

Staple food crops have been a second focus of research. The African staple food crops consist of 'durable' grain crops (millet, sorghum, maize, rice, etc.) and 'perishable' crops such as tubers and roots (cassava, yam, etc.) and bananas and plantains. (There has been considerably more research on the former.) There was a great spurt of research on grain crops in the 1970s and 1980s, occasioned by droughts in the Sahel. At first research concentrated on the national availability of food, food deficit areas and urban food supplies, but Sen (1981) caused the research focus to shift to individual households and their 'food security'. Research on staple foods has often been prompted by a concern for the population or for special groups of people who might suffer as a result of food shortages. There is scattered evidence of this concern throughout the colonial period.

I put the adjectives 'durable' and perishable' in quotation marks because I use them to suit the marketing perspective. The words do not here refer to the condition of a product at the moment of harvesting. At that moment practically all products are perishable. In keeping with African usage, I use 'durable' for crops that can be preserved by simple and cheap means, such as drying in the sun or in the wind. The grain crops mentioned above are in this category. By contrast, I use 'perishable' for crops that cannot be preserved at all or only by expensive means such as refrigeration and canning. I do not suggest that the same distinction is useful in the West. But in Africa where temperatures and humidity levels are high and electricity supplies rare, expensive and often unreliable, the economic difference between drying and refrigeration is significant.[12] Put succinctly, the refrigeration threshold is high in Africa.[13] The staple food crops which I have called 'perishable' have in common the fact that their preservation is very difficult or impossible.[14]

We now turn to the 'other crops' of Table 1.2. Since vegetables and fruits predominate, a significant characteristic of this category is perishability, as defined above. The table suggests that inadequate research is generally associated with perishability. This association may be explained as follows. First, perishability limits (a) the storage period and (b) the distance over which a product can be transported. Hence, the trade in perishable products tends to be conducted on a small scale. Second, many researchers are reluctant to study small-scale economic activities because primary research is demanding and generalizations from local research findings are hazardous. Thus, perishability indirectly discourages research.[15]

Uneven research coverage is reflected in agricultural policies. A proper agricultural policy should be comprehensive and cover the entire agricultural sector and not certain subsectors only. Measured in this way most African governments (as well as the colonial authorities before them) have failed. For many crops they have completely failed to develop a policy. This often creates a vicious circle. When a government has no policy for a particular crop, it does not normally put money aside for research on it.

1.4 The institutional approach: comments

We now consider the institutions that play a role in agricultural marketing in Tropical Africa. Table 1.3 lists 12 institutions. Once again the research coverage is uneven.

Researchers, in particular European researchers, have been fascinated by those features that distinguished Africa from their home countries. This explains why so much research has been 'people focused' and has concentrated on the farmers and the traders. Even researchers with a preference for abstract concepts such as the agricultural enterprise tended to move their focus to the reality of the person of the farmer. The advantage of this move has been

---

[12] Shortage of capital is an additional factor. It thwarts investments to reduce the seasonal problems at either the production or the marketing stage.
[13] The parallel with livestock marketing is interesting. Since milk and meat spoil easily, refrigeration has often been advocated as the key to modernizing livestock holding. Unfortunately, refrigeration is expensive and there are very few public electricity plants in rural areas.
[14] There is scattered evidence of African resourcefulness in slowing down deterioration and in coping with seasonality.
[15] There is another side to the coin. Taxation on perishable crops is low or non-existent.

that anthropologists and sociologists were able to make valuable contributions to the study of agricultural marketing. Fascination also explains the research focus on traders. Many sociologists and anthropologists have been intrigued by them and have used or coined special terms for them.[16] Scholars of agricultural marketing have welcomed the information provided by outsiders,[17] even if it had to be 'translated' to fit their own theoretical framework.

Table 1.3 Research coverage of institutions in agricultural marketing

producers/farmers	well covered
traders	well covered
other entrepreneurs	poorly covered
consumers	neglected (until recently)
cooperatives	well covered
marketing boards	partly covered
export companies	moderately covered
farm input suppliers	poorly covered
physical markets	well covered
other markets	poorly covered
trade associations	poorly covered
commercial practices	poorly covered

As we saw, scholars of agricultural marketing tend to take the side of the farmers. This is reflected in pro-farmer feelings and the suspicion that farmers do not get a square deal in their transactions with collecting traders. Pro-farmer feelings have been strong in Africa and have been reinforced by the fact that many collecting traders and exporters have been overseas foreigners. One of the results of these feelings has been a considerable literature on marketing cooperatives.

Paid-for farm inputs have always been insignificant in African agriculture. This was especially true for the early years. After about 1960, with the trend towards modernization and the intensification of agriculture, these inputs became more important in certain areas, notably those specializing in export crops. The cotton sector should be singled out, partly because it uses relatively large quantities of inputs (fertilizers, pesticides, etc.) and partly because these inputs are supplied on credit by the owners of the cotton ginneries. One could say that practically all inputs in the cotton sector are supplied under monopoly. In most other sectors there has been somewhat more competition among the traders who supply inputs. Unfortunately, research on these traders and their operations has been rare. But interest in research grew in the 1980s because of the new structural adjustment policies, one of whose objectives was the removal of all elements of monopoly.

Much research has also been done into the physical markets of Africa, especially those of West Africa. These markets are rarely purely agricultural, but agricultural products form a

---

[16] The term 'mammy trader' seems to be found in Africa only. The terms 'stranger trader', 'foreign trading minority' and 'alhaji' are highly useful, but not exclusively African.
[17] In the West the contributions of geography, sociology and anthropology to agricultural marketing are normally negligible.

large part of the goods offered for sale, not only in rural but also in urban markets. Here again fascination fostered investigation but researchers soon found that the physical markets were also favourable research environments. Research was relatively easy to plan and to conduct. The researcher could see which products were offered for sale. He could interview the sellers and the (potential) buyers and observe the transactions.[18] He could see how much money was exchanged and record 'observed prices'. This is relevant for economists in the sense that they should realize that most African data on 'observed prices' have been collected at physical markets.

1.5 The functional approach: comments

Table 1.4 shows the research coverage with regard to functions. I identify 11 functions, slightly adapting the list provided by Kohls & Uhl (1990).

Table 1.4 Research coverage of functions in agricultural marketing

buying/assembling	well covered
selling	moderately covered
storage	moderately covered
transportation	well covered
processing (industrial)	well covered
processing (on-farm)	poorly covered
standardization	poorly covered
financing	poorly covered
risk bearing (physical)	moderately covered
risk bearing (commercial)	poorly covered
market intelligence	poorly covered

A fair amount of research has been done on buying and selling. For instance, the buying operations of collecting traders have been scrutinized by those researchers who wanted to protect farmers and justify cooperatives. When looking for information on the storage function, we must remember that it is limited to durable crops, that is, mainly export crops and food grain crops. To my surprise I found more information on the buildings than on the storage function. In most countries there are minimum requirements for the buildings in which export crops are stored and these stores are regularly inspected. Moreover, during my research in Sierra Leone I heard many complimentary remarks about traders in connection with the large modern stores they had built.

There is a great deal of information about the transportation function. As we saw, most of it has been contributed by geographers. There has also been much attention to industrial

---

[18] For an early, but substantial publication on African markets, see Bohannan & Dalton (1962). Research at farm level is less productive than that at market level because (a) there are so many farms and (b) questioning (with translation hazards) has to supplement or replace observation. Hence, data on farm-gate prices are less reliable than price data collected at physical markets.

processing, stimulated by a fascination for nascent industrialization. Any factory, even a simple cotton ginnery, has been a reason for pride among administrators and politicians. By comparison we know little about artisanal or on-farm processing. Incidentally, most of this has consisted of drying – a process we encountered above as the principal method of turning perishable crops into durable ones.

We now turn to the last five functions, all 'facilitating' functions (Kohls & Uhl, 1990). We begin with standardization. In agriculture, standardization has three dimensions: quality, weight and packaging. Natural variation in quality is partly remedied by sorting and grading, as we saw above. Grading makes handling and pricing easier. While this lesson is widely applied in agriculture in the West, in Africa it is only selectively applied. While in export crop and food grain marketing quality standardization is widespread (and partly backed up by legislation), it appears to be largely absent for perishable crops.[19]

The second dimension of standardization concerns weights. In Africa measurement by volume is more common than measurement by weight. (There are far fewer scales and weighing machines than in the West.) For economic research it is important to emphasize that data on prices, notably retail prices, are inherently inaccurate. As weights at the retail level are not standardized, a uniform price set by a seller is not truly uniform. It has to be corrected for weight variation among the quantities offered by him at this price. Reliable correction would require the actual weighing of all quantities by the researcher – a laborious task.

The third dimension of standardization concerns packaging. Because of low income levels packaging costs must be kept down in Africa.[20] A researcher has therefore to distinguish three situations: (a) far-reaching standardization and new containers, such as crates and jute bags, (b) moderate standardization based on 'used' (i.e. not new) containers such as jute bags and beer bottles, and (c) little or no standardization with miscellaneous containers or no containers at all. Apparently, the degree of standardization (in all dimensions) depends on the type of crop. Thus, for export crops shipped to industrial countries in the West, standardization is high. The international grading criteria and the rules and regulations for weighing and packaging are strictly adhered to. For domestic crops the degree of standardization is considerably lower.

The second facilitating function is finance. This function has been greatly neglected by researchers. This is a pity because, in view of the scarcity of capital in Africa, it is plausible that finance is more influential here than in the West or, conversely, lack of finance is more likely to be an obstacle to agricultural marketing. I single out the finance needed to hold stocks and therefore restrict my comments to durable or storable crops. First, export crops. In countries where large volumes are exported, considerable stocks accumulate. If, moreover, the price per ton is high, a great deal of finance is necessary. However, the period over which this finance is required may be relatively short. This is due to the practice of 'rapid evacuation from the country' which reduces the domestic storage period and the corresponding need for finance (Van der Laan, 1997, 155ff). Second, food grain crops for

---

[19] Of course, farmers and consumers are aware of many quality differences (for example in the kolanut trade), but these are rarely documented and hard to register in primary research.

[20] The low level of packaging is a significant reason why selling under a brand name is rare in Africa.

domestic consumption. Stocks of these crops are seasonal: they begin to increase during the harvest season, soon reach their peak and are afterwards gradually depleted. The funds needed to finance these stocks also show a seasonal cycle.

Stock-holding traders are crucial entrepreneurs in Africa. This is acknowledged by many people, but often in an unsophisticated manner. They focus on the stocks and the buildings in which the crops are stored, but not on the finance needed to hold the stocks. Indeed, few people realize that the traders' financial resources are essential for the continued operation of the export sector and for the year-round supply of grain to urban markets. Public opinion in Africa is well aware of the fact that the trade in storable crops is in the hands of big, wealthy traders, but it fails to recognize that their financial resources explain both their stock holding and their wealth. The popular view is that price manipulation provides the explanation. It is alleged that traders who hold stocks are able to control the market and thus grow rich. Then they strengthen their position with monopoly-type measures which further increase their wealth. Whatever the explanation, there is agreement that the stock-holding traders enjoy prestige and evoke envy. This social aspect cannot be isolated from the fact that overseas traders (from Europe and Asia) have long been important in these crops.

Two facilitating functions concern risk. When a trader holds stocks, he runs both physical and commercial risks. A fair amount has been published on the physical risks, notably those of export crops handled by European traders. Since they were acutely aware of the losses caused by spoiling, they sponsored research to prevent it. They also improved the design of their stores for this purpose. Much less has been published about the commercial or financial risks. These risks refer to the losses a trader incurs when prices fall during the storage period. This is a special feature of the stocks of food grains, part of which must be held until the new harvest, but it also occurs with export crops. Indeed, stock holding is always surrounded by worries about the commercial risk.[21] This risk has another side to it. Prices may also increase during the storage period in which case the traders make a large profit. It is this occasional large profit which has engendered envy and antagonism.

The last facilitating function concerns market intelligence. It consists of written and oral intelligence. With regard to the former we can be brief: it resembles that in the West, but, unfortunately, it is available for only a few crops. Oral intelligence deserves special academic interest in Africa because, for many crops, it is the only form of intelligence. Oral market intelligence may be defined as information that is passed on by word of mouth, and which is essential for people who read badly (or not at all). Since little research has been done in this area, I restrict myself to questions. How significant is oral market intelligence in agricultural marketing in Africa? Does it strengthen the bargaining position of farmers *vis-à-vis* collecting traders? Does it play a large part in ethnically homogeneous, successful marketing channels? Does it help explain why many primary cooperatives function better than the corresponding secondary cooperative unions? It is further interesting to recall that the colonial authorities had high expectations about the wireless in the 1950s. They hoped

---

[21] Since the abolition of the export marketing boards a decade ago much has been written about the 'price risk' for export crops. This term suggests that the market causes the problems. I would rather focus on the stocks because they expose the owner to the 'price risk'.

that commercial information, broadcast in vernacular languages, would be welcomed by farmers and would increase their bargaining power in the same way as traditional oral intelligence. It now seems that these expectations were not realistic.

The five facilitating functions seem to have been neglected in African research. Why is this so? My hypothesis is that these functions are more abstract and less visible than the other ones and are therefore more easily overlooked by public opinion and ignored by politicians and academics.[22] I came to this conclusion when I discovered how often the inherent link between the storage function (visible) and the finance function (invisible) was overlooked. One illustration is provided by the heated discussions prompted by occasional shortages of food grains. Attention nearly always focuses on the stocks and on the traders who 'hoard' them, but seldom on the financial aspect. The amount of finance involved is invisible and only measured on paper, and then only if financial accounts are kept! It is the duty of the scholar of agricultural marketing to point out that seasonal stocks of staple food crops are in the consumers' interest and that the borderline between stock holding and hoarding is arbitrary.

1.6 Fundamental questions

What I wrote above is hopefully useful in a practical way, but, on close inspection, it reveals a strong ambivalence in my thinking about the West. Apparently, I have enough confidence in the writings of the West to extract from them a matrix for my comments, but at the same time I am troubled by the great differences between the situation in the West and in Africa. Put differently, I am afraid to adopt the insights of the West because they may mislead me. But I also realize that I cannot do without these insights because many of them are universally applicable. Of course, my attitude is not exceptional. Presumably, it is typical of academics in the non-Western world.[23]

To cope with this ambivalence I have constructed Table 1.5. The relationship between the three regions is as follows: the West is contrasted with the non-Western world and Tropical Africa is part of the latter. As my interest is confined to agricultural marketing, I define the West in terms of agriculture. The West, as I see it, consists of countries in which farmers are well organized and able to defend their interests, both economically and politically. This is usually accompanied by a thorough knowledge of the problems of the sector and sufficient funds to finance up-to-date research. Moreover, most governments in the West grant various subsidies to their farmers. In the non-Western world, however, farmers are poorly organized with negative consequences for them.[24] The chances that publications satisfactorily describe the corresponding agricultural situation are high in the

---

[22] The same was true in Europe in the centuries before economics became a field of academic studies.
[23] The ambivalence is even stronger when the situation in the West is recommended as a model for other countries. The discussion then becomes political in nature.
[24] There are exceptions. In Africa the best-known exceptions were the European settler farmers in Kenya, Southern Rhodesia, etc.

West and low in the non-Western world – low because there are no farmers' organizations to scrutinize them.

Since countries are a more common unit of analysis in international debate than sectors, I should add that, in this chapter, the West is more or less synonymous with the developed countries and the non-Western world with the developing countries. It is fortunate that in the field of international cooperation and development assistance there have been numerous programmes to assist farmers in the developing countries. I mention the work of the FAO in this field and single out the work of its marketing division, long headed by John Abbott. While being grateful for what has been discovered and published about agricultural marketing in Asia, Africa and Latin America, I am troubled by the suspicion that there has been a bias in these writings.

Table 1.5 Regions of the world, by strength of farmers' organizations and quality of publications on agricultural marketing

	Farmers' organizations	*Pub. on agricultural marketing*
the West	strong	high quality
non-Western world	weak	fragmentary
Tropical Africa	very weak	very fragmentary

The bias I see is the following. In the 1960s and 1970s the goal of economic development was overriding in international cooperation. Moreover, the governments of the developing countries were then seen as the principal agents of development. This led to two dubious priorities. First, prescription (policy making) was seen as more urgent than description. Second, economic analysis was given a higher priority than agricultural marketing analysis. One consequence should be specifically mentioned. Many economists were satisfied with a high level of generalization and abstraction. It was too high, however, to satisfy scholars of agricultural marketing who wanted more empirical work and more attention paid to the institutions they encountered in the field.[25] I wholeheartedly concur with this wish. In the illustrations below I hope to show how agricultural marketing analysis refines and elaborates economic concepts, ties them to empirical evidence and leads to better, more instructive insights. The illustrations refer to Africa but are applicable to most of the non-Western world.

The first illustration concerns the terms 'subsistence crop' and 'cash crop', which (agricultural) economists have contributed to the literature.[26] Macroeconomists have made an additional contribution by subdividing the cash crops into export crops and domestic cash crops. Agricultural marketing analysis takes us several steps farther. It does so by considering the marketing channel which permits the distinctions shown in Table 1.6.

---

[25] Open criticisms from scholars of agricultural marketing have been few, mainly because most originally trained as economists.

[26] These adjectives are also used in conjunction with households and economies.

Some domestic crops are truly national in the sense of being produced and/or consumed throughout the country, while others figure in a small, often culturally homogeneous area only.[27] The gain in precision is even greater with export crops. They are divided into (1) inter-African crops and (2) intercontinental crops. The latter in their turn may be divided into 'traditional' seaborne and recent airborne ones. The export-oriented development of the colonial period was almost entirely based on the seaborne intercontinental crops, which I prefer to call 'trans-oceanic' crops. They are special because the trade in them was at first totally dominated by overseas foreigners. They organized the marketing channel even though the crop was cultivated by Africans (Van der Laan, 1997).[28] Today's channels still resemble the original ones.

Table 1.6 Categories of agricultural product, by marketing channel

Category of crop/product	Nature of marketing channel
subsistence crop	none (or intra-household)
local domestic cash crop	one culture, tribe or language
national domestic cash crop	more cultures, tribes or languages
inter-African export crop (by sea)	with destination within Africa
inter-African export crop (overland)	with destination within Africa
intercontinental crop (by sea)	with destination outside Africa
intercontinental crop (by air)	with destination outside Africa

The second illustration concerns the world market. Economists often postulate that there is a world market for each crop they consider and that most of these markets are free and highly competitive. Scholars of agricultural marketing are able to go further by pointing out that the world markets for agricultural products differ with regard to organization. There are at least three types of agricultural world market: (a) those that revolve around commodity exchanges, (b) those that include regular auction markets and (c) those that are held together by a network of brokers and merchants but lack a physical market (ibid.). Exporters need different skills for each type of market. These differences should be recognized by economists when they recommend export-oriented development.

The third illustration concerns the national market. Economists often imply that a national market exists for each national domestic cash crop (see Table 1.6). The national markets for maize, rice, millet, etc. are often discussed and it is the duty of scholars of

---

[27] This distinction presupposes national boundaries. For the precolonial period other adjectives must be used, possibly referring to boundaries between tribal and/or language areas. Most of the precolonial long distance trade crossed these boundaries as well as present-day boundaries. (Even if transport was organized and controlled by one tribe, the consumers belonged to a different one.) Scholars of agricultural marketing join historians in showing admiration for the long distance trade. But for them the main achievement of the traders was the coordination of a long marketing channel.

[28] The marketing channels for inter-African export crops were developed by African traders. In the case of kola nuts they were also the ones that organized the transition from overland trade to a combination of overland and seaborne trade in the first decades of this century.

agricultural marketing to ask persistently whether this market is fact or fiction. What can be observed on the ground? In some African countries there are a number of local physical markets scattered across the country. If researchers can find significant interdependence among the observed prices for, say, maize in these markets (by testing for spatial integration) they can take this as proof that a national market for maize exists. In other countries the physical markets do not exist or play only a minor role. But one knows that the principal traders in, say, millet form an informal network which facilitates trade in various ways (transport, information and credit). This network does not prove that a national market exists since the process of price formation is obscure. In general it is better if network markets become regular exchanges wherever possible. Well-functioning, transparent exchanges represent a real national market.[29]

The fourth illustration concerns the nexus of farmer and collecting trader. Economists tend to study this nexus in terms of market theory. They recommend a free market with unrestricted competition, to protect farmers against collecting traders. Accordingly, they warn against monopsony and/or collusion among traders. Scholars of agricultural marketing use marketing channel analysis as an alternative approach to study the nexus. Whether their analysis is superior to market theory depends on the circumstances. Relevant questions include: Do many collecting traders engage in the consolidation of (sections of) their marketing channel? Are they willing to sacrifice some immediate profits in order to strengthen the channel?[30] Do farmers object to these channels or do they themselves see advantages in them? Does personal loyalty play a role in these channels? In investigating these marketing channels I have found it useful to ask whether the collecting traders and the farmers deviate from the practice of cash-on-delivery. At least two deviations should be mentioned. One is the forward contract in which the farmer, some time before the harvest, makes a promise to sell his crop. Another is that of short-term pre-harvest credit granted by the trader to the farmer. In either transaction mutual trust is essential.[31] Most economists are critical of these practices because they put the farmer in a dependent position. They tend to forget, however, that a marketing channel relationship also imposes constraints on the trader.

The fifth illustration concerns the marketing boards. At first sight it appears that much has been written about the African export marketing boards (established in the 1940s) and the African grain marketing boards which began to attract a great deal of research in the 1970s (Hesp & Van der Laan, 1985). I nevertheless repeat what I indicated in Table 1.3: the boards have only been partly researched. Thus, while the export marketing boards have been thoroughly studied with regard to (a) the level of their official buying prices, (b) the way their monopsony harmed the farmers and (c) their role as fiscal instrument, very little is known about their international selling operations and the relationship between the board and

---

[29] African policy makers normally distrust network markets, especially those for food grains, and therefore favour government intervention which usually includes a grain marketing board. This distrust tends to disappear when an exchange comes into being and functions well. Policy makers may then agree that government dissolves the marketing board.

[30] A willingness to sacrifice immediate profits because of long-term considerations is also a feature of monopolistic competition. The concept of goodwill may therefore be employed in African research.

[31] The term 'trust' establishes a link with the New Institutional Economics, in which 'expectations' play a significant role.

the licensed traders who buy agricultural products on its behalf. Similarly, while the theoretical problems of the grain marketing boards have been well studied, publications on practical problems, including those that arise within the organization, tend to be rare and shallow.

1.7 Tropical Africa is special

My ambivalence towards publications on agricultural marketing in the non-Western world is reinforced by my conviction that Tropical Africa differs from the rest of the non-Western world. In fact, I am strongly in favour of a geographical specialization within the study of agricultural marketing.[32] Put differently, it is fruitful for me to study publications on Asia and Latin America but some of the conclusions do not apply to Tropical Africa. I must therefore read these publications with the same degree of vigilance as those on agricultural marketing in the West.

To win support for my plea for geographical specialization I have to show that Tropical Africa is different from Asia and Latin America. This is the last task I have set myself in this chapter. To keep my argument brief I mention three points only. The first point refers to geography. Because of its location and configuration Tropical Africa has a special pattern of international trade with an exceptionally high share of trans-oceanic trade (Van der Laan, 1997, 3). The second point is one of history. European colonialism came late to this area and was highly ambitious and overbearing. The third point concerns culture. Literacy was restricted in this area when colonialism came. As a result 'indigenous knowledge' was more inaccessible and less prestigious than elsewhere in the Third World.

These points had significant consequences for the way agricultural marketing was organized in practice. First, the marketing of trans-oceanic crops served as the principal model for other new forms of agricultural marketing. Second, Europeans imposed various commercial practices with no regard for indigenous practices. For example, measurement by weight was imposed on societies that were used to measuring by volume. Third, while the borderline between indigenous and foreign commercial practices was recognized by Europeans, their reaction tended to be one of exasperation rather than of adjustment and compromise.

The points on which Tropical Africa differs also affected the study of agricultural marketing in this region. First, disdain for indigenous commercial practices seriously restricted knowledge, whether published or not. Lack of published information, in its turn, promoted the interdisciplinary research approach in Africa. Unfortunately, this approach makes researchers reluctant to discard any part of the information they have laboriously

---

[32] Special attention has been paid to agricultural marketing in Africa at Stanford University (Food Research Institute), Michigan State University, the universities of Oxford and Reading, Wye College and the African Studies Centre in Leiden.

collected, including information from students of another discipline.[33] It may even be used as an excuse for not rigorously sifting one's data. A plea for more mono-disciplinary research seems to be particularly relevant for Tropical Africa.

Second, the combination of 'food marketing' and 'agricultural marketing' in one discipline is particularly unsuitable for Tropical Africa. This is primarily true for the trans-oceanic crops whose marketing channels happen to be intercontinental. The producers and consumers in these channels live thousands of miles apart. This separates agricultural marketing in Africa, geographically and politically, from food distribution in the countries of consumption.[34] For domestic crops it is important to remember that few agricultural products undergo processing in Africa (apart from drying). As a result the consumer, no less than the producer, sees them as agricultural products. When, in the future, processing and branding become more important in Africa, there will be scope for the systematic study of food marketing. But for the time being it causes needless confusion.

To sum up, I hope that sooner or later a book, preferably a textbook, will be written specifically for Tropical Africa. We cannot expect the FAO, the UNCTAD or other international organizations to take the lead in such a project because it is their task to treat the developing countries as a group and not to favour particular countries or regions. The initiative should instead come from the UN Economic Commission for Africa, the Organization of African Unity or CODESRIA. They should commission a team of scholars to carry out such a project. Such a team could certainly count on support from many quarters.

References

ABBOTT, J.C. (1987) *Agricultural Marketing Enterprises for the Developing World*. Cambridge: Cambridge University Press.
BOHANNAN, P. & G. DALTON (eds) (1962) *Markets in Africa*. Evanston: Northwestern University Press.
EICHER, C.K. & D.C. BAKER (1982) *Research on Agricultural Development in Sub-Saharan Africa: A Critical Survey*. East Lansing: Department of Agricultural Economics, MSU.
HESP, P. & H.L. VAN DER LAAN (1985) 'Marketing Boards in Tropical Africa: a Survey'. In K. Arhin, P. Hesp, & L. van der Laan, (eds) *Marketing Boards in Tropical Africa*. London: Kegan Paul.
HEYER, J. (1976) 'The marketing system'. In J. Heyer, J.K. Maitha & W.M. Senga (eds) *Agricultural Development in Kenya: An Economic Assessment*. Nairobi, Kenya: Oxford University Press, pp. 313-363.
HINDERINK, J. & J.J. STERKENBURG (1987) *Agricultural Commercialization and Government Policy in Africa*. London: Kegan Paul International.
JONES, W.O. (1972) *Marketing Staple Food Crops in Tropical Africa*. Ithaca: Cornell University Press.
KOHLS, R.L. & J.N. UHL (1990) *Marketing of Agricultural Products*. New York: Macmillan.
SEN, A.K. (1981) *Poverty and Famines: An Essay on Entitlement and Deprivation*. Oxford: Clarendon.

---

[33] There is a similar reluctance to discard past data. Often they are used to fill a gap in current data. To justify this the researcher has to assume that the situation has hardly changed since the period to which the past data refer. But Africa is less static than that!

[34] It is illuminating to ask at what stage a product loses its agricultural character. The consumer recognizes a banana as an agricultural product, but not a chocolate bar.

STERN, L.W., A.I. EL-ANSARY & A.T. COUGHLAN (1996) *Marketing Channels*. Fifth edition, Englewood Cliffs, NJ: Prentice Hall.
VAN DER LAAN, H.L. (1993) 'Boosting agricultural exports? A "marketing channel" perspective on an African Dilemma'. In *African Affairs*, Vol. XCII, no. 367, pp. 173-201.
VAN DER LAAN, H.L. (1997) *The Trans-Oceanic Marketing Channel: A New Tool for Understanding Tropical Africa's Export Agriculture*. New York/London: Haworth.
WHETHAM, E.H. (1972) *Agricultural Marketing in Africa*. London: Oxford University Press.
YOSHIDA, M. (1984) *Agricultural Marketing Intervention in East Africa*. Tokyo: Institute of Developing Economies.

Maize Marketing Policies in Tanzania, 1939-1998
From Basic Needs to Market Basics

Deborah Fahy Bryceson, Pekka Seppälä and Marja-Liisa Tapio-Biström

Abstract

According to the World Bank (1997), Tanzania ranks as the third poorest country in the world. It remains a primarily agrarian nation with roughly three-quarters of the population living on the land, engaged in low-yielding peasant agriculture. Not unlike other nations of the developing world, its policy makers must weigh economic development aims with political stability and welfare concerns. Nowhere is this more critically illustrated than in the arena of staple food policy. During the twentieth century, market demand has persistently expanded whilst peasant output has continued to fluctuate subject to climatic conditions. Shortfalls in marketed supply became an increasing, and not unfounded, fear. In this context, the organization of food marketing has preoccupied much of public policy debate until recently. Tanzania provides one of the most extreme examples of an about-face in food marketing. The present open market stands in stark contrast to the system of all-embracing state marketing for the preferred food grains that prevailed between 1973 and 1986. This chapter seeks to explore the tension between achieving marketing efficiency and ensuring an adequate national supply of the country's basic staple food.

2.1 Introduction: Features of maize supply and demand

For better or worse, white maize has become Tanzania's chief staple food during the twentieth century. It is cultivated on roughly one third of cultivated land (World Bank, 1994, 19).[1] Approximately one quarter of all food consumed by weight is maize. By value maize constitutes approximately 10 per cent of total household consumption in Tanzania (1976/77 and 1991/92 Household Budget Surveys). In a country where no less than three-quarters of

---

[1] The others ranked in terms of areal coverage are cassava, sorghum, rice, bananas, millet and wheat.

all consumption by value consists of food, maize, as the most important food item, is the quintessential 'basic need'.

Historically Tanzania was a nation of farmers geared to household food self-sufficiency, but urbanization and increasing non-agricultural activities in rural areas have caused farming households' self-provisioned food to be superseded by a proliferating network of staple food markets. Staple food marketing policy has become a strategic aspect of ensuring national welfare. The dilemma has been that the food marketing system, notably that of maize, must necessarily encompass an extremely wide variation in annual production. Table 2.1 provides indices of maize production fluctuation in the 1980s and 1990s. Between 1974 and 1989, preferred staples[2] availability per capita ranged between 99 and 154 kg (Sijm, 1990). Extremely bad harvests tend to appear every seven to ten years. But the fluctuation of marketed supplies is magnified by the continuing auto-consumption habits of farming households. In poor to average harvest years, the marketed supply of maize would be negligible, whereas in a good year, household maize surpluses would flood the market. Bearing in mind that Tanzanian farming households are dispersed throughout a large territorial area, the physical capacity and cost effectiveness of the marketing system is severely taxed by these fluctuations. If capacity is built up to accommodate bumper harvests, and all peasant surpluses are purchased, there is a glut of supply, whereas in average and bad years marketing capacity is underutilized.

Furthermore, the fluctuation of maize surpluses and deficits raises the problem of financial loss through import and export. White maize is thinly traded on world markets and Tanzanian production has not achieved international competitiveness due to high transport costs from surplus areas to the ports. In the 1980s, the price of domestic maize exceeded import parity, reflecting not only Tanzania's low agricultural productivity and high transport and marketing costs, but also the highly subsidized nature of European Union and American exports which prevailed at the time.

In contrast to the wild fluctuations of maize supply, maize demand has evidenced a relentless upward march since the 1920s. Maize consumption was encouraged by the British colonial government. Hitherto, rice had been the main staple food of the small numbers of urbanized Africans in what was then German East Africa (Bryceson, 1987). The staple food of rural dwellers varied from place to place depending on the climate. During the 1920s and 1930s as plantation agriculture was established, employers unwilling to cater to the multiple food tastes of their labourers sought to standardize their diet with maize (Bryceson, 1990). Maize is believed to have been introduced to East Africa in the sixteenth century by Portuguese traders, but was suitable only in the coastal strip. Not until centuries later did maize varieties developed by South African settlers start to displace the indigenous food crops of sorghum and millet in up-country areas (Acland, 1971). This process accelerated in the twentieth century when large numbers of African plantation workers grew accustomed to eating maize, and planted maize after returning to their home areas. During the 1940s, demand for maize accelerated with the onset of African urbanization. Since then, urbanization and maize demand have expanded in tandem.

---

[2] 'Preferred staples' refers to maize, paddy/rice and wheat.

Table 2.1 Maize production and Strategic Grain Reserve (SGR) purchases (Metric Tons)

Year	Production	SGR Purchases	NMC Purchases	Imports*	Aid
1970/71			175,000	- 24,000	0
1971/72			43,000	63,000	n.a.
1972/73			96,000	79,000	n.a.
1973/74			74,000	291,000	n.a.
1974/75	1,367,000		23,900	225,000	n.a.
1975/76	1,449,000		91,100	107,000	27,000
1976/77	1,664,000		127,500	42,000	7,000
1977/78	1,465,000		213,200	34,000	34,000
1978/79	1,720,000	77,000	220,400	- 49,000	0
1979/80	1,726,000	0	161,500	5,000	0
1980/81	1,839,000	0	104,600	275,000	87,000
1981/82	1,654,000	0	89,400	235,000	207,000
1982/83	1,651,000	0	86,000	123,000	106,000
1983/84	1,939,000	0	71,000	194,000	69,000
1984/85	2,093,000	0	90,000	129,000	18,000
1985/86	2,211,000	0	178,500	6,000	3,000
1986/87	2,359,000	0	173,000	94,000	9,000
1987/88	2,339,000	0	229,000	- 97,000	0
1988/89	3,128,000	142,000	124,000	0	0
1989/90	2,445,000	n.a.	149,000	2,200	-
1990/91	2,331,000	26,279	10,000	0	-
1991/92	2,226,000	84,863	10,000	24,500	0
1992/93	2,282,000	70,080		18,000	11,000
1993/94	2,159,000	27,798		27,000	14,000
1994/95	2,567,000	24,000		20,000	45,630
1995/96	2,638,000	73,006		100,000	19,500
1996/97	2,107,000	90,000		0	0

Sources: National Milling Corporation, cited in Tanzania, Ministry of Agriculture, 1988; Sijm, 1990; Tapio-Biström, 1996; Tanzania, *Food Security Bulletin*, 15/8/95, 20/8/96, 14/5/97; Tanzania, Marketing Development Bureau, 1988 and 1995.

* Import and export statistics from the statistics section of the Custom Department are considered unreliable. From 1991/92 onwards the Food Security Department provided figures on the basis of the permits they issued for food importation. Thus, these statistics are subject to private traders' permit evasion.

Over the years, with increasing demand and unpredictable, fluctuating domestic supply, Tanzanian food security came to prevail as a seemingly intractable problem in government policy. 'Food security' in this chapter is defined as the satisfaction of basic staple food requirements for the national population. In starch-based diets such as that which prevails in Tanzania, the FAO calculates an average intake of 180 kg per year of staple food grains. Given prevailing Tanzanian dietary habits, roughly half of annual staple food requirements are consumed in the form of maize (Tanzania, Bureau of Statistics, 1976/77). For the sake of understanding Tanzanian food security, it is necessary to differentiate two types of maize demand. The first, henceforth referred to as *Type I* demand, is the steadily increasing urban demand, locationally concentrated in Dar es Salaam, the country's major trading centre, as well as the regional administrative capitals. The second, *Type II*, is the sporadic but geographically widespread and more logistically difficult demand of rural dwellers in years of harvest failure. It is the intertwining of these two types of demand which have continually acted upon Tanzanian food policy formulation.

The following section traces the development of government maize marketing policies beginning with the onset of World War II until the present. Section 2.3 sketches the patterns of maize trading under recent market liberalization policies. Section 2.4 discusses the implications of market liberalization for food security in bad harvest years. This is followed by a concluding evaluation.

2.2 Balancing welfare with efficiency in colonial and post-colonial staple food marketing policies, 1939-present

Prior to the outbreak of World War II, rural food marketing policies were dominated by *Type II* demand considerations. The African population was overwhelmingly rural. The colonial government aimed to maintain this mass of peasant farmers as self-sufficient food producers and to prevent them from experiencing famine and food shortages when their harvests fell short of household, village or district needs. District officers had well worked-out procedures for famine prevention and relief measures embodied in the Native Authority Ordinance of 1921, the Native Foodstuffs Ordinance of 1924, and Circular No. 33 of 1930. The former two dealt with preventive measures including planting orders and restrictions on trade and beer-brewing, whereas the latter laid out detailed famine relief procedures beginning with precautionary measures for surveying village and regional food reserves, submission of annual district food reports, and advance identification of relief public works. Inevitably poor weather conditions did cause famine in some districts. In these cases, the export of staple foodstuffs beyond district borders was forbidden and there were well worked-out procedures for famine relief distribution, its financial accounting and for the submission of post-famine relief reports to the central government (Bryceson, 1980, 1981, 1990).

But all of these procedures were relevant only to the rural population, who comprised the vast majority of the population. As urbanization became a force during World War II, the colonial government had to devise new, more market-oriented measures to ensure urban food security. Over time a great deal of experimentation took place but it was clear that there was no one way to achieve food security. The post-colonial government inherited a policy tradition which had ranged from virtually no control to strict regulation and then back to free market conditions. Alterations to food marketing policy were often prompted by marked changes in supply as the following historical account shows.

Wartime price controls, 1939-48
Prior to World War II, maize market demand was primarily rural and dispersed amongst the country's plantations and mining centres which employed African labourers. Employers purchased supplies from farmers in adjoining areas. Restrictions on purchase were only imposed in cases of localized food shortages when grain trade and transport over district boundaries were temporarily banned (Bryceson, 1981). The war altered this. As in other

British territories, an Economic Control Board was set up which designated the Director of Agriculture as the Food Controller in Tanganyika. Retail prices for food were fixed on a locality-specific basis. In 1941, price control was extended to producer prices. Guaranteed minimum prices were set for maize which marked an increase for farmers, but the worldwide boom in commodity prices following the entry of the United States into the war would have brought increased returns to farmers anyway. The price controls were essentially seen as part and parcel of a planned war effort. East African grain was considered strategic for supplying troops stationed in the Middle East.

An East African Cereals Pool was established to organize grain movements within the region. Maize purchases and sales in commercial quantities were restricted to appointed selling places. Only those holding permits were allowed to purchase and move grain over district boundaries. These regulations were reminiscent of the district bye-laws temporarily enforced during food shortages with the difference being that they were now territorial and fixed for the foreseeable future.

Grain Storage Department (GSD), 1949-56
The war ended but territorial food insecurity continued. An international grain shortage and high world market prices for grain coupled with poor domestic harvests prompted the colonial government to continue food commodity controls. The aim was to keep consumer prices of staple foods as low as possible and to achieve territorial food self-sufficiency. 1949 was an extremely poor harvest. In the face of a widespread food shortage, the colonial government took the decisive step of establishing the Grain Storage Department (GSD) with the hope of levelling the fluctuations of supply by expanding territorial grain storage and rationalizing staple food marketing and transport throughout the country. Grain in 3-ton lots or over was considered a commercial quantity that had to be sold to the GSD. In so doing, the GSD purchased only from large-scale farmers and licensed traders in bulk at railheads. Private traders had space to buy smaller amounts or act as millers and retailers. They were however subject to all-embracing price control: the into- and ex-store prices of the GSD, as well as ex-mill and retail prices were specified by district commissioners through powers delegated to them by the country's Price Controller. Controlled prices varied regionally depending on local handling and transport costs.

The GSD was intended to be a break-even operation. Since world grain prices were exceptionally high at the time, territorial maize production and transport costs were below import parity. It was surmised that occasional marketed surpluses could be exported at a healthy profit to fund the Department's operational costs. As luck would have it, however, world prices declined during the 1950s, bringing domestic costs between import and export parity. In 1955/56, Tanganyika experienced a bumper harvest resulting in an unprecedented marketed surplus of 110,000 tons of maize and sorghum. The GSD had to dispose of the surplus on the world market at a great loss. The government decided to immediately disband the GSD, thereby marking the end of over 15 years of heavy government intervention in maize marketing.

Open market, 1957-62
For the remainder of the colonial period, a free market in grain trading reigned. The only stipulation on traders' activities was that their buying and selling should take place in Native Authority markets and should be subject to a market cess. Nonetheless it was estimated that over 75 per cent of produce sales took place outside Native Authority markets (IBRD, 1961). Even though over two-thirds of licensed traders were Africans, Asian merchants largely controlled the grain trade in their capacity as produce buyers, wholesalers, brokers, and millers. African trade was largely restricted to the retailing of extremely small amounts. Hawkins (1965) documents that, increasingly over time, large-scale Asian produce buyers specializing in foodstuffs began to dominate the regional grain trade. They tended to be oligopolistic, even monopolistic, with only one or two buyers operating in any one area. The buyers kept their overhead costs low by relying on the existing network of small Asian *dukawallah* retail shopkeepers who served as collecting agents, receiving remuneration on a salaried or credit arrangement. Despite monopoly conditions, wholesale and retail mark-ups on maize remained moderate which could be attributed to the fact that staple foodstuffs were fast-moving items and they sold at conventional price levels in accordance with the consuming public's notions of 'just prices' for its essential basic need (Economist Intelligence Unit, 1962). This was facilitated by the fact that in the run-up to independence Tanganyika was blessed with average and good harvests.

Amidst independence celebrations in late 1961 a drought hit the country, causing severe food shortages in the central regions. Maize prices rose, sparking a surge of ill-feeling towards Asian traders. The post-independent African government was alert to popular sentiment, already sensitive to the competitive threat Asian traders posed to the development of African marketing cooperatives for the country's major cash crops. The marketing cooperatives had been a major source of rural support to the newly elected government so, not surprisingly, one of the state's first priorities was staple food marketing reform.

National Agricultural Products Board (NAPB), 1963-1972
The objectives of the NAPB were identical to those of the GSD, namely national food security and price stabilization. The NAPB bore similarity to the GSD, though there were crucial differences. The NAPB was attempting far greater control. The weight of commercial quantities that had to be sold to the Board was lowered to 4 bags, i.e. 360 kgs, rather than 3 tons. Produce buying agents under the NAPB were almost exclusively regional marketing cooperatives whereas under the GSD they had been accredited private traders. The NAPB's pricing was pan-territorial as opposed to the GSD's into- and ex-store prices which had been region-specific.

African cooperatives had expanded during the 1950s on the basis of export crop marketing. Attempts to extend cooperatives into food marketing had not met with success. Now the way was cleared for them. Asian traders were no longer allowed to operate in food marketing by the government. The Cooperative Union of Tanganyika (CUT), the unions and primary societies formed a three-tiered system. The role of the NAPB, as a crop marketing board, was to purchase from the cooperative unions and provide extension advice to them.

Cooperative union staff and society members lacked training and were often engaged in operations of sub-optimal size. As cooperative marketing extended to food crops in the 1960s, peasants became all too aware of food crop margins, questioning low producer prices. Meanwhile, economic analysts, reviewing national economic performance, blamed the need for a high minimum wage on exorbitant consumer food prices. Thus, when Tanzania experienced a bumper harvest in 1968, the NAPB was in a quandary. The Ministry of Agriculture insisted on lowering the into-store price for farmers, whereas the NAPB, aware of farmers' views, refused.

The NAPB's wide margins arose from the inflated costs of cooperative produce buying, the implicit transport subsidies it extended to distant regions, and its fund to cover losses arising from grain imports and exports (Livingstone, 1971). It was clear by the early 1970s that the NAPB was becoming a serious drain on public revenues. Government subsidies were necessary to cover large export losses. The problem during this period was primarily glut, not shortage of supply. There were no serious food shortages in the country during the period of NAPB operations, despite the fact that peasants were growing increasing amounts of cash crops connected with the country's rural development strategy.

National Milling Corporation (NMC), 1973-85

In 1973 the Tanzanian government launched its extremely ambitious villagization programme in which peasant settlements were nuclearized into villages with social services, such as health dispensaries and schools, and productive services that included water supplies, agricultural input supplies and extension advice. In this context the government placed grain marketing under the control of the National Milling Corporation, destined to operate as a single-channel marketing system, providing services to peasant producers and urban consumers throughout the country. The logic was that agricultural marketing, particularly staple food marketing, was highly strategic, and should therefore be lodged firmly in the hands of the state.

In dismantling the National Agricultural Products Board and elevating the National Milling Corporation from an urban-based state milling complex to a single-channel state marketing agent for staple foodstuffs, the Tanzanian government had two main objectives: guaranteeing national food security and ensuring stable producer and consumer prices. The most immediate intention was to eliminate the wide marketing margins by abolishing inefficient agencies. With the introduction of pan-territorial producer pricing and the directive that the NMC could bypass inefficient cooperative unions and purchase directly from the cooperative societies, the marketing chain would be streamlined. Aimed at wiping out the cooperative movement's inefficiency and corruption, cooperative society and union margins were fixed and cooperatives functionally became the executing agents of the NMC.

The NMC quickly expanded to become the government's largest marketing parastatal, absorbing most of the personnel of the NAPB and many former cooperative staff. By 1978, NMC had 4,200 staff members, a third of these based in Dar es Salaam. Apart from the top management, most of the staff were relatively uneducated and poorly trained. Taking over from the NAPB, the NMC inherited a large bank overdraft. To compound matters, within its first years of operation, the prevalence of drought conditions in many parts of the country necessitated the distribution of free famine relief and heavy food importation. Over the following twelve years, adverse climatic conditions and poor harvests were the norm rather than the exception. Only the four-year period between 1976/77 and 1979/80 experienced net importation of maize of less than 100,000 tons (Tanzania, Marketing Development Bureau, 1988). Pan-territorial pricing, however, did create a maize boom in what became the 'Big Four' regions of Rukwa, Mbeya, Ruvuma and Iringa. These regions in the southern and south-western parts of the country had slumbered economically during the colonial period. Relatively fertile with reasonably reliable rainfall, this zone lacked good transport connections to Dar es Salaam, the main domestic and export market entrepôt. During the late 1960s and early 1970s, rail and road ties were built. Pan-territorial pricing, which embodied a government transport subsidy, gave farmers in this zone the green light to produce maize in abundance. Gradually over the years, they became the NMC's major source of supply.

Meanwhile, food demand in the towns (*Type I*) escalated, with a high urban growth of 10 per cent per annum between 1967 and 1978 (Bryceson, 1993). Satisfying urban food demand, specifically that of the capital, Dar es Salaam, increasingly preoccupied the NMC (Bryceson, 1992).[3] Low consumer prices, not just availability was at stake. *Type II* food demand was also in evidence. In poor harvest years, the NMC was obliged to supply grain to needy villages on the demand of a disaster relief unit of the Prime Minister's Office. Rarely did the NMC receive full payment from the government for these famine relief services.

The combination of a staple food producer price rise to encourage increased production during the years of shortage, the transport subsidy embodied in pan-territorial producer pricing, the impossibly tight fixed margins, shouldering rural famine relief costs, and Tanzania's over-valued currency exchange rate led the costs of the NMC's domestically procured maize to exceed import as well as export parity (Tanzania, Marketing Development Bureau, 1983, 1980 and 1977). The NMC could purchase imported maize for supply to Dar es Salaam more cheaply than it could deliver domestically procured maize. This was reinforced by the imported supplies that the NMC could obtain on concessional aid terms.

The NMC's operational difficulties and government-imposed welfare-oriented policies led to its spiralling bank overdraft. In 1973/74, the overdraft stood at Tsh 286.5 million, ballooning ten times by 1981, achieving notoriety as the biggest parastatal overdraft in the country. Audited accounts were in arrears by several years, so no one was certain of the true extent of the problem.

Beginning in 1979, Tanzania faced IMF demands for currency devaluation and measures to address the NMC overdraft. To offset criticisms, in 1980, the government began taking measures to reinstate marketing cooperatives as a way of relieving the NMC of its procurement constraints. The Tanzanian shilling was devalued four times between 1979 and 1984, but it was not until 1984, following two years of severe drought that NMC pricing was reformed with the partial removal of the subsidy on *sembe* (maize meal) for urban consumers. In a sense keeping urban food prices low was no longer so politically

---

[3] By 1983/84, 70 per cent of NMC *sembe* sales took place in Dar es Salaam and 30 per cent in the regions, whereas in 1974/75 these figures were reversed.

significant. Over the years, the NMC had increasingly failed to supply up-country towns with sufficient *sembe* such that urban consumers had come to rely on various supply channels, be it illegal markets, urban farming or supply from rural relations (Bryceson, 1992). With the reduction of the maize meal *sembe* subsidy came a rise in the minimum wage by 35 per cent. In fact, Dar es Salaam residents already had higher average incomes than elsewhere in the country. Most important for general acceptance of this measure and maintenance of political stability was the fact that national maize harvests beginning in 1984 and for the following five years were relatively good. This, in combination with further market liberalization measures to be described below, ensured adequate, reasonably priced supplies of maize for the general urban population.

Market liberalization, 1986-present
The government tentatively started introducing economic liberalization measures in 1984. Besides the partial lifting of the *sembe* subsidy in the national budget, the prime minister ordered the removal of inter-regional trade road blocks. 1985 was an election year. Nyerere stepped down from the presidency after almost a quarter of a century of service. Mwinyi was elected to take over. Mwinyi's consent to an IMF structural adjustment programme soon after he assumed the presidency was presented as the only way of securing a better livelihood for the Tanzanian population and relief for the economy. A train of liberalization measures followed as listed in Table 2.2.

Table 2.2 Sequence of economic liberalization measures

1984
- Removal of restrictions on movement of food grains intra- and inter-regionally in amounts of up to 500 kgs.
- Partial removal of the fertilizer subsidy.

1986
- Removal of government price control on all but 12 essential commodities.
- Consumer subsidies on maize removed.
- Presidential approval for the operation of the unregulated Tandale wholesale market in Dar es Salaam.

1987
- Lifting of restrictions on the transport and movement of any amount of food grains by the private sector. Private traders allowed to purchase maize and rice from the regional cooperative unions.
- Limitations on the role of the National Milling Corporation, designating it to work as a Strategic Grain Reserve, as well as food import and food aid distribution.
- Liberalization of inter-regional trucking rates.
- Import and marketing of agricultural inputs liberalized, excluding seeds and fertilizers.

1988
- Private traders allowed to purchase maize and rice from the National Milling Corporation.
- Unions free to sell cassava, sorghum and millet to any buyer. NMC free to buy anywhere.

1989
- Primary societies free to sell grains to any buyer.
- Export of all grains allowed except rice and wheat.*
- Announcement of phased removal of producer subsidies on fertilizers beginning in 1990/91.

Sources: Amani & Kapunda, 1990, 76-77; Bryceson, 1993, 101; World Bank, 1994, 178.
* Maize exporting required a permit which involved a complicated and time-consuming operation that could only be performed in Dar es Salaam.

2.3 Trading patterns under market liberalization

From the mid 1980s to the present, Tanzanian maize marketing has witnessed dramatic changes related to the declining importance of state marketing and the burgeoning number of private traders. The operations and viability of competing agencies are considered in turn.

The dwindling role of the National Milling Corporation
The NMC's functions were gradually curtailed both by conscious policy as well as financial exigencies determined by greater stringency on bank lending. By 1988, the NMC was reduced to being the 'buyer of last resort' and custodian of the nation's Strategic Grain Reserve (SGR). Staff and fixed assets were pruned. The only reminder of its once expansive grain empire was its large storage warehouses.

In the late 1980s, the government was still intent on keeping the NMC as a viable working structure on call in case of food emergencies. The experience of the 1981/82 drought was still fresh in the minds of policy makers. Over the period 1978-81, the SGR had consisted of approximately 80,000 tons of wheat and yellow maize from the USA, Canada, the UK and the World Food Programme. The adverse grain supply situation caused a decline in the reserve to the point of its exhaustion by 1981. The NMC was unable to replenish its stocks. In 1986, an FAO Food Security Mission recommended rebuilding and rationalizing the management of the reserve to serve as the government 'food security tool' in the face of liberalized grain markets. In the context of the late 1980s improved harvests, the NMC was charged with building up the SGR reserve to 100,000 tons by buying the maize surpluses of the 'Big Four' regions, especially Rukwa and Ruvuma, where it was anticipated private traders would not be so eager to buy, given the relatively high transport costs (Table 2.1). The reserve was calculated to tide the country over a major deficit while imports were arranged. In 1988, there was a wait-and-see approach:

> Greater liberalization in the movement of supplies coupled with improvements in the transportation network could reduce the need for large grain reserves. Nevertheless in the meantime Tanzania will need to safeguard against fluctuations in domestic production and limited capacity to import, by maintaining adequate stocks, for which the target is currently set at 100,000 tons (FAO, 1988).

The revived SGR was positioned in the Food Security Unit within the Ministry of Agriculture with the NMC acting as the executing agent to whom a management fee was paid. Obviously, the existence of a large national grain reserve required subsidy. Considerable budget resources were used to build up and operate the reserve. For example in 1991/92, the approved budget of the SGR was Tsh 5,400 million. Donors were unwilling to support it directly. However, during the late 1980s most of the food aid donated to Tanzania was monetized and sold through the NMC. The counterpart funds generated were made available to government as budget support. Such counterpart funds were below 2 per cent of central government expenditure in the period between 1978-88, and from this amount the costs incurred by the NMC to distribute, transport and administer food were deducted (FAO, 1988).

Despite this arrangement, the NMC remained financially unviable and collapsed in 1991 when the banks refused to lend it money. The Food Security Unit was reorganized and formed into a Food Security Department (FSD), which encompassed the SGR and the Early Warning Unit, and served as the agency for authorizing private traders to import and export staple food crops. At the same time, the size of the SGR was increased to 150,000 tons. The extra 50,000 was to be used for price stabilization while the original 100,000 tons remained as an emergency reserve. In practice there was no division between these two parts.

The new system was put to the test almost immediately. In 1991/92, Tanzania faced a relatively poor maize harvest. The SGR's supplies were obtained through its agents, the NMC and regional cooperatives. In that same year, the NMC ceased to buy food crops directly from farmers, and instead purchased from private traders who delivered to NMC godowns. In essence this lengthened the marketing chain. In 1992/93 and again in 1994/95, supplies for the SGR were directly procured through a tender system because it was deemed that the NMC and most regional cooperative unions were 'inefficient agents' (Tanzania, Marketing Development Bureau, 1995). But this method proved highly cumbersome and failed. The prices tendered in a deficit year were not competitive with those prevailing on the open market. Thereafter producers and traders delivering maize directly to SGR godowns became the major source of supply.

Private traders' ascendancy

The government's trade liberalization policies had prompted substantial numbers of people in towns and villages to become staple food traders. While the majority of staple food traders were men, women traders were evident in retailing and in areas where female produce trading was important traditionally.

The organization of maize trading throughout the country took on various regional forms making national generalizations difficult. Nonetheless, certain features were pervasive as revealed by a 1988 survey of traders in Dar es Salaam, Arusha, Mbeya and Songea (Bryceson, 1993). Maize trading was characterized by easy entry at the retail end. While all the towns had *in situ* retailers, the role of the mobile intermediary who brought maize from villages to the town was more developed in some localities than others. Short-distance intermediaries, operating intra-regionally or between neighbouring regions, were common in Mbeya and Mwanza. Retailers' progress into the ranks of the mobile intermediaries was not too financially taxing when bus and 'by-the-way' transport to rural locations was available, but viable operations required time, great mobility and a high level of risk-taking, which exceeded the capabilities of most retailers. The uncertainty surrounding transport arrangements, availability of supplies and destination markets and the need to cultivate good relations with suppliers and other traders for the purpose of gathering market and transport information made a resilient and gregarious individual most suitable for the role. The presence of specialized wholesalers, *dalali*, was restricted to the very large markets of Dar es Salaam and Mwanza. The position of a stationary wholesaler was difficult to achieve without having served as a mobile intermediary which not only gave the trader an acquaintance with various levels of the marketing chain, but provided contact with a wide circle of producers and traders. Some Dar es Salaam *dalalis* had trading experience in neighbouring countries or even further afield on the African continent.

Although traders were operating in a highly competitive environment, economic differentiation between traders seemed muted both within as well as between functional levels of the trading hierarchy. The actual transactions were generally characterized by the limited exchange of cash, i.e. the advance of stocks particularly to a *dalali* without full payment. The *dalali* then proceeded with the onward sale of maize stocks, paying the balance to the mobile intermediary after completion of the final sale. This practice occasionally caused delays or theft, but more generally it was based on a code of mutual cooperation.

Networks are often described as a means to stabilize forward and backward linkages. Amongst Tanzanian maize traders, networking was conducted within strict parameters. It included very limited or no sharing of capital and virtually no employment of subsidiary workers (Seppälä, 1996, 1998). It is widely believed, especially among male traders, that running a trading business with a partner will end in disaster. Deep-seated distrust in money affairs makes the pattern of trading very individualistic and inhibits the growth of the trading unit's size.

Wholesalers and mobile intermediaries were getting higher margins than retailers, yet accumulation was insufficient for them to invest in their own motor transport, storage or maize processing (Santorum & Tibaijuka, 1992; Bryceson, 1993; Parsalaw, 1996). Furthermore, competition between traders was tempered by the need for cooperation to overcome the constraints of a seriously inadequate physical infrastructure for trade with regard to transport and storage facilities as well as market information. In a sense their main strength was also their main weakness. Undercapitalized, they operated with extremely low overheads which kept their costs in check and made them flexible, but not even the large-scale wholesalers had grain storage capacity of any size or duration. They could keep their working stocks for no more than a couple of days. Without sufficient storage as a buffer, the system was liable to over- and under-supply as well as facing greater consumer price fluctuation in abnormal harvest years.

Emerging importance of the milling sector
One of the side-effects of the decline of National Milling Corporation was that a growing amount of consumer purchase of maize took place in the form of maize grain rather than maize flour. According to a 1995 Marketing Development Bureau (MDB) study (Mdadila et al., 1995), this began to change when a number of large-scale maize mills were installed in Dar es Salaam and major towns proximate to maize-growing areas (i.e. Arusha, Iringa and Songea), following the 1993 drought. Big private urban mills became a new and powerful node in the marketing chain. Their products were in particularly high demand during the rainy season when maize grain was in short supply and/or people could not afford to buy large 17 kg *debe* measures of maize grain. They sold a range of highly refined to less refined *sembe* flours.

The effects of a transition from public to private sector activity were still in evidence. The NMC, their competitor, had a storage advantage. NMC mills had difficulty using even half of their capacity, whereas private firms generally were woefully short of storage space relative to their production capacity. The NMC began renting out storage space to private mills.

The private firms refused to divulge information on their costs of production to MDB investigators, but the MDB estimated that large-scale maize processing was profitable at 70 per-cent mill capacity. As mill capacity levels increased, profits rose. The study found all the large private mills operating at full capacity, the medium-sized mills operating at 50 per cent capacity, whereas all the NMC mills except one operated at 25 to 35 per cent capacity.

Marketed maize in an average year was estimated at 550,000 tons. Total large- and medium-scale maize milling capacity, excluding the small hammer mills that are dotted around the country, was estimated at 217,500 tons per annum, but 40 per cent of this capacity was inoperative due to administrative and mechanical breakdown. Of the operative 60 per cent, the large-scale private sector accounted for 45 per cent while the NMC made up almost 15 per cent. Small local hammer mills and home processing accounted for the remainder.

Although information on the ethnic affiliation of owners of private mills was not collected, it is generally known that Asian and Arab capital are predominant in the private milling sector. It is possible that ethnic patterns of the 1950s are partially reasserting themselves. African maize wholesalers, even the very large-scale wholesalers in Dar es Salaam, were unable to accumulate enough to invest in transport or storage, let alone milling capacity. Nor were they in a position to import maize. Grain traders who imported supplies within the new liberalized markets had been restricted to a handful of traders mostly of Asian origin (Seppälä, 1998). The resurfacing of Asian and Arab capital in grain handling suggests that the highly competitive, open entry nature of liberalized maize trading made it very difficult for African traders to achieve the apex of private maize trading, whereas the large non-African private maize millers were able to make self-financed investments in milling thereby bypassing bank borrowing with interest rates exceeding 40 per cent.

2.4 Economic performance of liberalized maize marketing

In 1994 the World Bank ventured to proclaim that Tanzania's liberalized food market was successful based on:
> First, a sustained increase in grain supply has been maintained... Second, the average real maize price fell dramatically... Third, for maize, the main food crop, there has been a marked and sustained reduction in the price differentials between producing and consuming areas (World Bank, 1994, 143).

The prevailing wisdom in neo-liberal thinking is that the removal of state controls on the market will reduce marketing costs, causing a decrease in consumer food prices, and an increase in producer prices which will stimulate the adoption of improved farm technology and agricultural productivity. Various studies are currently appearing which test the validity of these assumptions in African countries (Barrett, 1997; Jayne & Jones, 1997; Seppälä, 1998). It is useful to consider the Tanzanian evidence, bearing in mind that it is impossible to disentangle the effect of liberalized policies from the influence of climatic conditions. In

Tanzania's hoe-based, rain-fed agricultural system, the impact of exceptionally good or bad rainfall in any given year will override the influence of farmers' responses to relative prices.

Maize production

There is no evidence that maize production and the cultivated area per capita has increased. Sarris & Van den Brink (1993) note only a modest food supply response to market liberalization, which they explain in terms of the basic inelasticity of demand leading to decreasing real food prices that mainly benefit urban consumers and deter private traders from buying from distant areas with high transport costs. The FAO figures on estimated average yields show quite a marked declining trend during the first years of the 1990s before rains improved and brought yields back to the levels of the late 1980s (Figure 2.1).

Figure 2.1 Index of estimate maize production, area cultivated and yield (per capita)

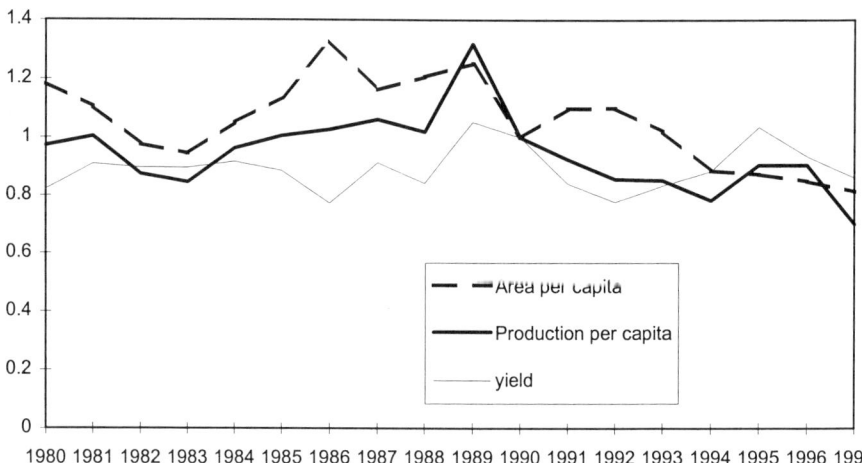

Source: FAOSTAT database.

In addition to adverse rainfall, the most likely reasons for a decline are twofold: first, farmers' inability to retain or increase fertilizer applications due to the removal of the fertilizer subsidy, and second, the disincentive effect of declining producer prices in the 'Big Four' regions which had formerly benefited from the transport subsidy embedded in the NMC's pan-territorial producer prices.

The comparative advantage of growing maize in different areas has altered. Climatic suitability for maize production is no longer so important and distance from main consumer markets and ease of transport have become major determinants. The Marketing Development Bureau (1995, 11) estimates that a Mpwapwa peasant producer proximate to the Dodoma town and Dar es Salaam markets gets a return of Tsh 1,905 per man-day of work in maize production as opposed to the Songea and Maswa peasants distant from consumer markets who only receive Tsh 1,150 and Tsh 631 respectively.

The Southern Highland areas of Iringa and Songea, beneficiaries of the government's earlier pan-territorial producer pricing and fertilizer subsidies, have lost their market share to northern production zones. Furthermore, an increasing amount of SGR supplies have been directly obtained from traders in Dar es Salaam rather than being procured in Rukwa and Ruvuma. There is field evidence that maize production in various Southern Highland areas has declined in terms of yields and area planted, a tendency that farmers attribute to the removal of the fertilizer subsidy and the contracting market (Airey et al., 1993; Mung'ong'o, 1998). These are areas where farmers enjoyed stable guaranteed prices for over a decade. Adjustment to fluctuating and indeed declining producer prices has demotivated many producers, particularly youthful farmers. Increased brewing for local village consumption of maize stocks has been noted in addition to the fact that many youth have reverted to an earlier pattern of labour out-migration from the area.

Despite these tendencies, the World Bank (1994) is confident that maize production will expand areally. It estimates that there are 9 million hectares of suitable land available for maize cultivation, even when the need for fallow (counted at 60 per cent of total cultivated area) is taken into consideration. The basis for such optimism is not clear.

Maize producer and consumer prices

Between 1984 and 1988, in the early stage of the liberalization process, indications were that the private staple food sector was highly competitive, operating with lower margins than those of the cooperatives (Bryceson, 1993). This good performance took place during a spate of reasonable to very good harvests (Table 2.1 and Figure 2.1). In general, the open market gave maize producers a higher percentage of the consumer sale price, ranging between 63 per cent (Mwanza) to 93 per cent (Songea) compared with 53 per cent under the official system.

Recent producer price data suggest that seasonal price changes are marked. In 1993/94, the lowest average price for a 90 kg bag of maize grain was Tsh 3,598 in the post-harvest month of July rising to more than three times that amount in the month of February (Tanzania, Marketing Development Bureau). The overall national average for the entire year was Tsh 5,797 which amounts to Tsh 64.42 per kg. Average real producer prices were on the increase from Tsh 41 in 1991/92 to Tsh 56 in 1992/93 to Tsh 64 in 1993/94 (Tanzania, 1995).

It is necessary to stress that these prices are 'producer prices' paid at urban wholesale markets. The prices that farmers actually receive are very sensitive to distance from market. Coulter & Golob (1992) found that the price paid by mobile intermediaries to producers 15 km off the main highway in Mbozi district, Mbeya, was Tsh 1,800/bag whereas the traders on the road who transported the maize paid Tsh 2,400, the Mbeya town wholesalers paid Tsh 3,200, while the Dar es Salaam wholesalers paid Tsh 5,500.

Urban consumer prices were low in the late 1980s reflecting the good harvests. The turning point was 1990/91 when staple grain prices began to rise. The open market maize consumer prices were about 100 per cent higher than in December a year earlier (FAO,

1990). Price volatility continued. Dar es Salaam had the lowest seasonal variation of prices due to it being supplied by several up-country locations. Consumer prices in up-country towns were heavily influenced by the harvest situation in the surrounding countryside. In 1997, when consumer food prices began escalating as a result of harvest failure in the northern and coastal parts of the country, variation in the nominal wholesale prices for a kilogramme of maize ballooned to 480 per cent (Marketing Development Bureau, reported in *Business Times*, 27/6/97).

Maize availability and market integration
Maize marketing is an easily accessible form of trade. Trade can begin by merely buying a 90 kg bag of maize. Improvement in bus transport throughout the country in the past ten years has made people more regionally mobile. Thus, the geographical coverage of the maize market is good and contrasts with the spotty coverage offered by the NMC in the past. Has increased market activity engendered market integration and a reduction in spatial price differentials in line with World Bank expectations? The large regional variations in both producer and consumer prices suggest that market integration is far from an accomplished fact. Analysis of maize price correlations amongst pairs of towns from the 1980s suggests that markets remained geographically segmented (Bryceson, 1993; Van Donge, 1994). Seppälä's (1998) recent analysis showed higher price correlations on average, suggesting a trend towards improved market integration. But averages mask the fact that market integration is not a uniform tendency. In Madagascar, Barrett (1997) found pockets of improved market interlinkages and another set of markets more segmented by market reform. This is also evident in Seppälä's (1998) study. Inaccessible maize deficit areas like Tunduru continue to have distinctive price levels and large fluctuations in comparison with other parts of the country related to the food demand exerted by the local diamond trade. Tapio-Biström (1996) cites the case of drought-induced high prices and food shortages in Mbinga district in 1993/94 despite large food surpluses just 150 km away in Mbeya region. The market is still very much in a state of flux.

Overall assessment
The evidence on balance suggests that marketing costs have been reduced. The combination of easy entry into staple food trading, the ability of traders to operate with extremely low fixed overheads, and the lack of integration of trading and transport enterprise has precluded excess profits. However, the lower margins are partly explained by the coincidence of the first years of liberalization of maize with good harvest years. The change in marketing arrangements and bountiful harvests combined to cause a decline in producer prices. In the 1990s, with less favourable harvests, producer and consumer prices have been rising, albeit not excessively.

For the producer, maize market liberalization has been a mixed blessing depending on location. Clearly, not only large territorial segments, but an area that had been fostered by earlier government policy for the mono-cropping of maize has suffered due to its distance from the main urban markets whereas other areas, less climatically suitable, but closer to the markets have benefited. Farmers in the remote areas are being forced to store their grain in the hopes that traders will later move in after supplies are exhausted elsewhere. If they have the capacity to do this, they may benefit substantially, since on-farm storage is reasonably efficient and seasonable price variation is high (FAO, 1994).

Interestingly, under market liberalization, the domestic producer price dipped considerably below import parity. 1994/95 was a subnormal harvest year when the government estimated import requirements of 350,000 tons. Nonetheless, private traders were not interested in importing maize because the cif price of maize imported into Dar es Salaam was US$196 per ton whereas the market selling price of domestic maize was only US$186. Maize may be consumers' most basic need and vital commodity, but from the perspective of traders it is simply a commodity with narrow margins, given the restricted purchasing power of the national population.

2.5 Weighing economic efficiency against political stability and humanitarian values

Few would dispute the efficiency gains of grain market liberalization in good and normal harvest years, but Tanzania regularly experiences bad harvests and the true test of the effects of market liberalization on consumers comes at these times. 1997/98 was a bad harvest year. Erratic rainfall, which some associate with the effects of global warming, persisted for more than a year. Already in mid 1996, eight out of the country's twenty regions were considered likely to face food deficits (Tanzania, Food Security Department, June/July 1996). The main rains in 1997 started exceptionally late and with fury. In several areas, the sudden flooding washed farmers' planted seeds away. In many places, inadequate commercial supplies of seeds or peasant purchasing power precluded farmers from replanting. Already the year before, farmers' problems in the commercial purchase of inputs had been detected by the Ministry of Agriculture's Food Security Department.

> Lack of adequate stockists in the districts, exorbitant prices paid by the farmers, risks of unfavourable weather and the availability of local cultivars as a substitute for improved seeds are among the factors that contributed to poor distribution and purchasing of the seeds. It is estimated that about 9,000 tonnes of improved seeds remained undistributed ...[however]... on reviewing the agricultural input situation for the past two seasons, the main concern has been more on the farmer's inability to purchase the input rather than availability (Tanzania, *Food Security Bulletin*, June/July 1996).

In March 1997, signs of widespread distress surfaced. The rate of inflation rose from 13.8 per cent to 17.5 per cent, pushed up by a rapid rise in staple food crops. President Benjamin Mkapa announced that an estimated four million Tanzanians faced a food shortage and needed about 150,000 tons of cereals to sustain them over the next five months until they harvested their crops. The deficit regions were primarily in the north and on the coast. By the end of May the estimate of import needs rose to 525,000 tons of grain. The 1996/97 harvest was reckoned to be short by over 1.3 million tons with 700,000 people in dire need of food assistance.

Relief food began to be distributed in June 1997. The government had nearly exhausted the SGR reserves. The World Food Programme donated 9,550 tons. In the first round of food relief, only the elderly, those in poor health or women recently widowed were assisted with food, a fact that villagers in affected areas bitterly complained about (Bryceson, 1997).

The overall responsibility of emergency assistance is vested in the Prime Minister's Office (PMO) and its Disaster Relief Coordination Committee. It is responsive to the appeals of district officials for food aid. The food aid can be distributed for sale, for public works or for free, depending on what is deemed necessary. The PMO finds that the districts tend to overestimate their needs. Since the PMO lacks transport capacity it is difficult for them to confirm actual levels of need. The PMO buys food from the SGR. The PMO has failed to pay the SGR for all the grain it has ordered and thus the financial situation and liquidity of the SGR is weak. This has led to difficulties in transporting grain from surplus to deficit areas.

The World Food Programme (WFP) is coordinating the NGO relief actions. There is an emergency relief committee which holds regular meetings. This committee consists of the major NGOs and WFP representatives. The meetings are chaired by a PMO representative. A number of mainly church-related NGOs (Caritas, World Vision, International Islamic Relief Organisation and Red Cross) have divided the major deficit areas among themselves according to their presence in the area and are the main channel of WFP emergency food aid. These NGOs do not cover the whole country, or even all the deficit areas. No agency has taken responsibility for the south-eastern part of the country.

Information on the amounts and destinations of the PMO/SGR's food relief deliveries is not readily available. This has led to deep suspicion among the donors about the PMO/SGR relief operations. The donors tend to express opinions indicating beliefs that the relief deliveries are made on political grounds and do not necessarily reach the intended beneficiaries, which has affected the donors' willingness to respond to government appeals for international food aid (Custodio 1996; Tapio-Biström, 1994; interviews with donor agencies). For example, in 1991/92, the Tanzanian government requested 218,000 tons of food aid. They received only 19,400 tons from donors. Mass hunger was averted by consumers substituting other staple foods for maize.

As time elapsed it became clear that the 1996/97 harvest deficit would not be so easily resolved. Tanzania's adverse climatic conditions and the consequent food deficit were part of a much wider food crisis embracing neighbouring countries like Mozambique, Malawi, Kenya, Uganda, Somalia and Ethiopia.

Donors began responding. The governments of Canada, Australia, Ireland, Germany and Belgium pledged $3.59 million to Tanzania through the World Food Programme (WFP) or food relief. When the WFP started distributing another 4,000 tons of maize in late August, the response revealed that they were just scratching the surface:

> Thousands of villagers in the affected areas of central and northern Tanzania are reported to be walking long distances in the hope of receiving even a minimum quantity of food. Lacking the purchasing power to acquire the limited amount of produce available in local markets, these populations are now consuming wild fruits or migrating

in search of assistance... The third and last tranche of WFP relief food was originally intended to assist some 100,000 persons. It is believed that this food will now have to be shared amongst thousands more, WFP reported (*Africa Online*, 27/8/97).

Alarmed, the government's estimates of food import requirements jumped to more than 900,000 tons. A special National Food Shortage (NFS) Committee was formed chaired by Ngombale-Mwiru, a long-standing party activist. The Prime Minister appealed to the business community to import more food, while the NFS Chairman had harsh words for traders continuing to export food. 'We cannot allow these people to starve our people because of their greed' (*Africa Online*, 28/8/97 and 4/9/97). The next harvest would not be until the spring of 1998. Thus the government faced more than half a year of escalating hunger. With only 17,000 tons remaining in the SGR, President Mkapa called on the donor community for emergency food aid of 103,600 tonnes of maize and pulses and $8 million financial support for food distribution. Stating that an estimated 1.5 million people would require relief until April 1998, he emphasized: 'This is a shortfall that is real and imminent, and one which has been verified from WFP, USAID and FAO. This is a shortfall that has to be met from external sources' (*Africa Online*, 17/9/97).

What can be gleaned from the above account of an unfolding famine situation? It is apparent that the government's crop monitoring programme within the Food Security Department does work effectively. Warning of a possible crisis was already on hand in July 1996. But the government's ability to act on such strategic information was lacking in several respects. Firstly, they reacted too late and in a curative rather than preventative manner. Not surprisingly, a wait-and-see policy was adopted by the government until the outcome of the 1996/97 harvest was evident, before any food relief was provided. But the irony of this food shortage is that, in many areas, the deficit might have been prevented with timely measures to assist peasants' seed purchase. Field observations and discussions with agricultural officers in Lushoto District of Tanga in June 1997 suggested this (Bryceson, 1997). The main rains of 1997 were quite good and extended into June. Had the farmers been able to afford the purchase of more seeds after their late start and flooding, the inadequate harvest might have been more than adequate. Certainly the lush appearance of the countryside supported this view.

Second, there are several fracture points in the country's famine relief machinery. Organizationally, the PMO relies on a political reporting network emanating from village governments through district councils to the PMO in Dar es Salaam. Regional government has undergone drastic streamlining over the past decade. Furthermore, the establishment of multipartyism has considerably undermined the neighbourhood ten-cell system that had operated as an effective information-gathering system at village level. Village government officials are still involved in identifying needy recipients as was the practice formerly, but with the dismantling of Tanzania's local ten-cell system and the increased mobility of people, village officials are no longer so aware of who is genuinely needy. Thus, in addition to the political bias that was always possible in situating a famine relief agency within a non-technical government ministry comes the effect of fragmentation in the political reporting network upon which the relief system depends at local level.

At national level, there are other hitches. The PMO does not have the confidence of donor agencies which jeopardizes the speed of appropriate aid responses. Donors would prefer to channel their contributions through the WFP and have the WFP coordinate releases to the participating NGOs and church organizations (Custodio, 1994; Tapio-Biström, 1996). Donors are worried about how the reserve stocks are utilized. They question how, where and to whom the stocks are released and whether the issued stocks really reach the needy. Donors have become increasingly partial to bypassing Tanzanian government famine relief machinery.

Third, more than ever, the government is financially unable to guarantee national food security. In line with market liberalization principles, the government expected the private sector to supply food deficit areas. Indeed the Tanzanian government itself reckoned on almost 90 percent of the deficit being met by trading activity. But a large deficit requires food importation, and local traders were reluctant to import for several reasons: very few African traders had experience in importing, importation procedures were bureaucratically cumbersome, and most importantly, there was very little if any profit to be made from it. Imported supplies continued to be more expensive than domestic prices traders were accustomed to paying, and the costs of transporting maize, particularly in areas of unusually heavy rain and bad road conditions, were considered to be too high.

Well aware of the legacy of colonial and post-colonial government intervention in famine situations and the political dangers of driving up prices, importers and traders refrained from heavy market involvement. Some firms expressed a willingness to import as long as they could sell their imports directly to the government. Demand for maize was not *effective* demand. 'Just price' principles, inherent in maize being the country's chief staple food and 'basic need' for a population with very low purchasing power, largely prevailed.

Considerable time elapsed between the appearance of food shortages and government and donor action to muster food relief, despite the fact that the SGR was being rapidly depleted. The SGR was short by 85,000 tons in May 1997. Numerous appeals by high-ranking government officials beginning in March 1997 elicited very little food aid from foreign donors burdened by requests from neighbouring countries as well. Nonetheless, by February 1998, 67 per cent of Mkapa's 103,600 ton request had been received. The Tanzanian government-donor relationship, however, was a delicate one. Prior to the 1997/98 famine, donors were increasingly of the opinion that Tanzania was essentially a food self-sufficient country which did not need food aid (Tapio-Biström, 1996). The Australian government and USAID had already bowed out of support for the SGR. The Tanzanian government contended with the reality that harvest failures were bound to occur amidst rising donor indifference and increasing international grain prices. The Uruguay round of trade negotiations had brought about a reduction in domestic and export subsidies on grain produced in developed countries.

The unfolding history of Tanzanian maize marketing organization illustrates the contradiction between market efficiency on the one hand and humanitarian concern and political stability on the other. Ranked as the third poorest nation in the world, the standard of living of the broad masses of the Tanzanian population lies very close to the limits of physical survival. In the long run, the market economy can serve to raise that standard of

Maize marketing policies in Tanzania 39

living and thereby remove the population from critical levels of food insecurity, but it is abundantly evident that when climatic conditions cause below-average harvests, the market may either exacerbate or in effect evaporate rather than alleviate life-threatening food insecurity.

2.6 Conclusion

This chapter has provided a broad historical overview of Tanzanian government policy regarding the basic staple food, maize. Through the decades, policy changes have been prompted by three main factors: climatic circumstances, national economic performance and political security. Figure 2.2 attempts to schematically show the interaction of variables related to the oscillation between state and market-dominated marketing policies.

There has been a tendency for major state intervention in maize marketing to take place following drought and famine conditions, e.g. the establishment of the Grain Storage Department in 1949 and the National Agricultural Products Board in 1963. In contrast, a spate of good harvests giving rise to an economic upturn can generate a feeling that national food self-sufficiency has been achieved once and for all and encourage more liberalized policies, such as the deregulation of the market from 1956 to 1961 as well as the optimism of the late 1980s when the NMC was delinked from the Strategic Grain Reserve. Finally, political security considerations of both an endogenous and exogenous nature have played a major role in policy formulation. This is exemplified by the NMC's increasing attention to Dar es Salaam's supply at the expense of regional supply during the late 1970s and early 1980s, and most recently, the implementation of market liberalization, which the Tanzanian government accepted under external pressure from the IMF and the World Bank.

The significance of market liberalization for Tanzanian food marketing policy and food security has been explored in this chapter. It has marked an historic change in several respects: first, by overturning state control; second, by triggering massive African as opposed to Asian private trader participation in maize marketing; and third, by unravelling key aspects of the country's national food security policy and institutional organization, which had evolved over decades of colonial and post-colonial government. In this way the response of external donors to food shortages has become more critical, both in humanitarian and political terms.

Throughout most of Tanzania's colonial and post-colonial history, the priority of rural production and marketing policies has been to ensure basic staple food security. Before World War II, emphasis was placed on retaining peasant households' food self-sufficiency and providing readily mobilizable famine prevention and relief when needed. Since World War II, state and market-led policies have been directed primarily at facilitating supply of maize at reasonable prices to the ever-growing, non-food producing, urban population, i.e. meeting a *Type I* maize demand. The state-led policies which dominated the 1940s and early 1950s and the post-colonial period until the late 1980s were characterized by state marketing organizations which incorporated *Type II* rural demand considerations while meeting *Type I* demand. In other words, the lack of purchasing power characteristic of famine-stricken

Figure 2.2 State and market-dominated stages of Tanzanian marketing organisation and factors spurring organisational change, 1943-1998

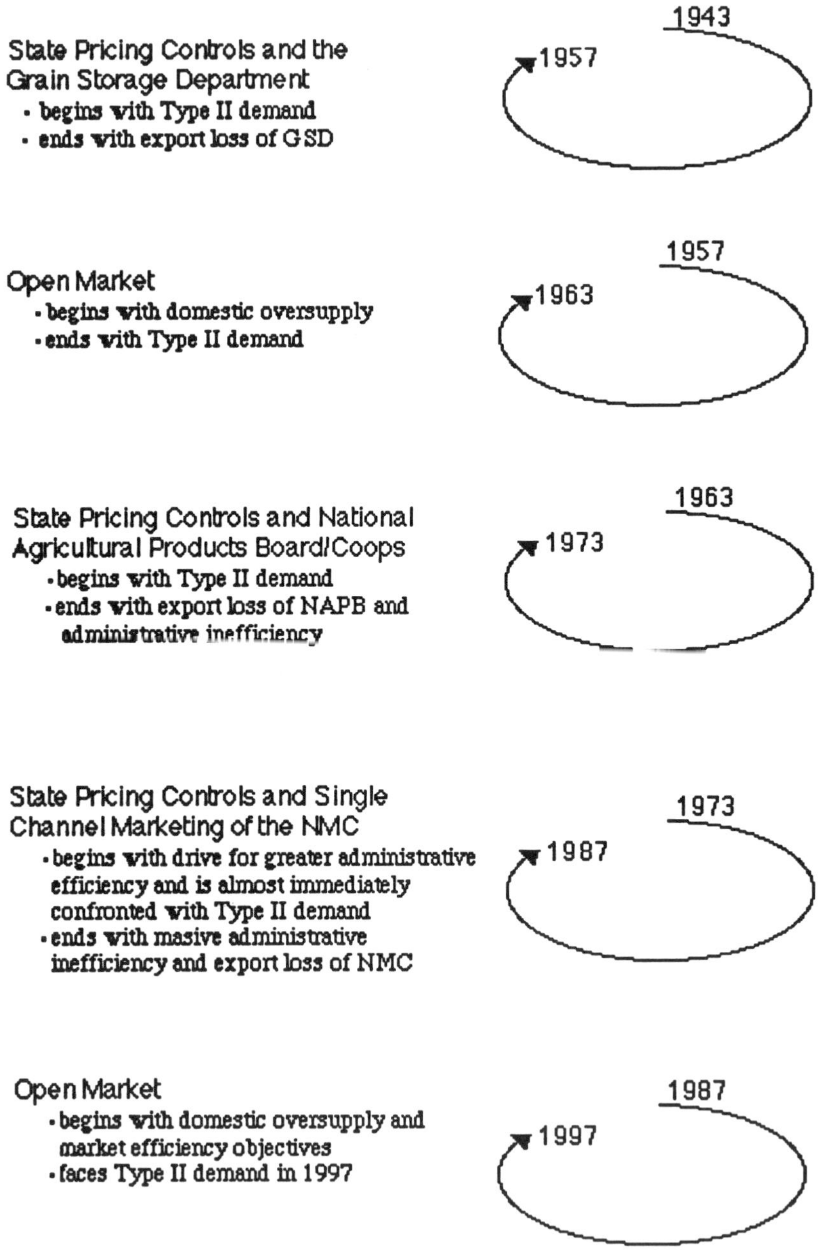

State Pricing Controls and the Grain Storage Department
- begins with Type II demand
- ends with export loss of GSD

1943 → 1957

Open Market
- begins with domestic oversupply
- ends with Type II demand

1957 → 1963

State Pricing Controls and National Agricultural Products Board/Coops
- begins with Type II demand
- ends with export loss of NAPB and administrative inefficiency

1963 → 1973

State Pricing Controls and Single Channel Marketing of the NMC
- begins with drive for greater administrative efficiency and is almost immediately confronted with Type II demand
- ends with masive administrative inefficiency and export loss of NMC

1973 → 1987

Open Market
- begins with domestic oversupply and market efficiency objectives
- faces Type II demand in 1997

1987 → 1997

peasants was accommodated in coordinated measures taken by government and parastatal agencies.

Most recently, market-led policies under Tanzania's structural adjustment programme have fundamentally altered the national policy balance, introducing an anti-rural bias which is most dramatically illustrated in the widespread rural famine conditions of 1997/98. An 'efficient market' bypasses these critical moments of basic needs provisioning since consumers lack sufficient purchasing power to participate in the market. Market basics override basic needs, necessitating international humanitarian intervention to patch up the gap between need and effective demand.

References

ACLAND, J.D. (1971) *East African Crops*. London: Longman.
AFRICA ONLINE, various issues.
AIREY, A., H. BANTJE, J. BURTON & E. WADE-BROWN (1993) *Final Impact Evaluation of Tanzania's Songea-Makumbaku Road Project*. London: Overseas Development Authority of the United Kingdom, ODA Evaluation Report EV 527, Vol. II.
AMANI, H.K.R. & S.M. KAPUNDA (1990) 'Agricultural Market Reform in Tanzania: The Restriction of Private Traders and Its Impact on Food Security'. In M. Rukuni, G. Mudimu & T.S. Jayne (eds) *Food Security Policies in the SADCC Region: Proceedings of the Fifth Annual Conference on Food Security Research in Southern Africa, October 16-18, 1989*. University of Zimbabwe and Michigan State University.
BARRETT, C.B. (1997) 'Liberalization and Food Price Distributions: ARCH-M Evidence from Madagascar'. In *Food Policy*, Vol. 22, no. 2, pp. 155-173.
BRYCESON, D.F. (1980) 'Changes in Peasant Food Production and Food Supply in relation to the Historical Development of Commodity Production in Pre-colonial and Colonial Tanganyika'. In *Journal of Peasant Studies*, Vol. 7, no. 3, pp. 281-311.
BRYCESON, D.F. (1981) 'Colonial Famine Responses'. In *Food Policy*, May 1981.
BRYCESON, D.F. (1987) 'A Century of Food Supply in Dar es Salaam: From Sumptuous Suppers for a Sultan to Maize Meal for a Million'. In J. Guyer (ed.) *Feeding African Cities*. London: Manchester University Press.
BRYCESON, D.F. (1990) *Food Insecurity and the Social Division of Labour in Tanzania, 1919-1985*. London: Macmillan.
BRYCESON, D.F. (1992) 'Urban Bias Revisited: Staple Food Pricing in Tanzania'. In C. Hewitt de Alcántara (ed.) *Real Markets: Social and Political Issues of Food Policy Reform*, in *The European Journal of Development Research*, Vol. 4, no. 2, pp. 82-106.
BRYCESON, D.F. (1993) *Liberalizing Tanzania's Food Trade*. London: James Currey Publishers.
BRYCESON, D.F. (1997) 'Lushoto's Slippery Slopes: Field Observations, June 1997', Leiden.
BUSINESS TIMES, Dar es Salaam weekly, 27 June, 1997.
COULTER, J. & P. GOLOB (1992) 'Cereal Marketing Liberalization in Tanzania'. In *Food Policy*, Vol. 17, no. 6, pp. 420-30.
CUSTODIO, E.L. (1994) *Review of the Operation and Management of the Strategic Grain Reserve*. Rome: FAO, URT/91/024.
DUMONT, R. (1969) *Tanzanian Agriculture after the Arusha Declaration*. Dar es Salaam: Ministry of Economic Affairs and Development Planning.
ECONOMIST INTELLIGENCE UNIT (1962) *A Survey of Wholesale and Retail Trade in Tanganyika*. London.
FAO (Food and Agriculture Organisation) (1988) 'Tanzania's Approach to Food Security: An Analysis of Policies and Achievements'. Rome: Paper presented at the FAO Committee on World Food Security, 13th Session.
FAO (Food and Agriculture Organisation) (1990) *Mid-Year Review in 1990*. Rome: FAO.

FAO (Food and Agriculture Organisation) (1994) *Annual Report, June 1993-July 1994 for United Republic of Tanzania.* Dar es Salaam: FAO.
FAO (Food and Agriculture Organisation) (1996) *Food Grains Marketing Improvement in Tanzania.* Dar es Salaam: FAO and Republic of Indonesia (Bulog).
HAWKINS, H.D.G. (1965) *Wholesale and Retail Trade in Tanganyika: A Study of Distribution in East Africa.* New York: Frederick A. Praeger Publisher.
INTERNATIONAL BANK FOR RECONSTRUCTION AND DEVELOPMENT (IBRD) (1961) *The Economic Development of Tanganyika.* Baltimore: Johns Hopkins Press.
JAYNE, T.S. & S. JONES (1997), 'Food Marketing and Pricing Policy in Eastern and Southern Africa: A Survey'. In *World Development,* Vol. 25, no. 9, pp. 1505-27.
KILLICK, T. (1981) *Policy Economics.* London: Heinemann.
LIVINGSTONE, I. (1971) 'Production, Price and Marketing Policy for Staple Foodstuffs in Tanzania'. Economics Research Bureau Paper 71.16, University of Dar es Salaam.
MDADILA, J.M. & ASSOCIATES (1995) *Maize Milling Industry in Tanzania: Present Position and Prospects.* Dar es Salaam: Marketing Development Bureau, Tanzanian Ministry of Agriculture, October 1995.
MUNG'ONG'O, C. (1998) 'Coming Full Circle: Agriculture, Non-Farm Activities and the Resurgence of Out-Migration in Njombe District, Tanzania'. Leiden: Afrika-Studiecentrum/Institute of Resource Assessment, University of Dar es Salaam Working, Paper, vol. 26.
PARSALAW, W. (1996) 'Liberalization of Maize Marketing in the Arusha Region in Tanzania'. In C. Harvey (ed.) *Constraints on the Success of Structural Adjustment Programmes in Africa.* Houndsmill: Macmillan Press.
PINCKNEY, T.C. (1993) 'Is Market Liberalization Compatible with Food Security?' In *Food Policy,* Vol. 18, no. 4, pp. 325-333.
SANTORUM, A. & A. TIBAIJUKA (1992) 'Trading Responses to Food Market Liberalization in Tanzania'. In *Food Policy,* Vol. 17, no. 6, pp. 431-42.
SARRIS, A.H. & R. VAN DEN BRINK (1993) *Economic Policy and Household Welfare during Crisis and Adjustment in Tanzania.* New York: New York University Press.
SEPPÄLÄ, P. (1996) 'The Politics of Economic Diversification: Reconceptualizing the Rural Informal Sector in South-east Tanzania'. In *Development and Change,* Vol. 7, no. 3, pp. 557-78.
SEPPÄLÄ, P. (1998) 'Tanzania - Decisive Liberalization Path'. In P. Seppälä (ed.) *Liberalized and Neglected? Food Marketing Policies in Eastern Africa.* Helsinki: UNU/WIDER, World Development Series 12, pp. 15-62.
SIJM, J. (1990) *Food Security and Policy Interventions in Tanzania.* Rotterdam: Tinbergen Institute, November 1990.
TANZANIA (1989) *Emergency Social Action Programme, July 1989-June 1992: Preliminary Draft for Discussion.* Dar es Salaam, April 1989.
TANZANIA, Bureau of Statistics, (1976/77) *1976/77 Household Budget Survey.* Dar es Salaam.
TANZANIA, Bureau of Statistics, (1995) *1994 (January to June) Prices and Price Index Numbers for Twenty Towns in Mainland Tanzania.* Dar es Salaam: Bureau of Statistics, January 1995.
TANZANIA, Food Security Department, *Food Security Bulletin.* June-July 1996.
TANZANIA Government of, (1991/92) *1991/92 Household Budget Survey: Methodology Report.* Dar es Salaam.
TANZANIA, Marketing Development Bureau (1988) *Annual Review of Maize, Rice and Wheat.* Dar es Salaam: Ministry of Agriculture and Livestock Development.
TANZANIA, Marketing Development Bureau (1995) *1993/94 Industry Review of Maize, Rice and Wheat.* Dar es Salaam: Marketing Development Bureau R.1/94.
TAPIO-BISTRÖM, M-L. (1996) *Food Aid in Tanzania: from Dependence to Independence?* Helsinki: University of Helsinki, Institute of Development Studies Working Paper 12/96.
TEMU, P. (1975) 'Marketing Board Pricing and Storage Policy with Particular reference to Maize in Tanzania'. Ph.D. thesis, Stanford University.
VAN DONGE, J.K. (1994) 'The Continuing Trial of Development Economics: Policies, Prices and Output in Tanzanian Agriculture'. In *Journal of International Development.* Vol. 6, no. 2, pp. 157-84.
WORLD BANK (1994) *Tanzania: Agriculture. A World Bank Country Study.* Washington D.C.

3

Maize Marketing in Kenya, 1976-1996
Liberalization and Food Security

Henk Meilink

Abstract

This chapter reviews Kenya's experiences with policy reforms in the staple food maize market. Escalating fiscal costs associated with intensive government involvement in the grain markets motivated the World Bank and the IMF to promote the 'liberalization' of marketing and pricing systems in the food market as a central component of the 'structural adjustment programmes' (SAP) implemented throughout Africa in the 1980s. As maize trade and pricing greatly affect Kenya's food security, this chapter attempts to trace the implications of maize market reforms for the various actors in the maize sector: producers, traders, millers, consumers and the state itself. There are five parts. Section 3.2 discusses the theoretical basis of SAPs and the anticipated consequences for food security. Section 3.3 describes the characteristics of Kenya's maize market prior to the reforms. Section 3.4 analyses the politics of the reform process and the emerging new setting of the maize market. Decisive reform implementation only commenced in 1994 when the maize trade was fully liberalized and private traders began to participate in the market. This period is analyzed in Section 3.5 and is followed by the conclusions in the final section.

The Kenyan government has long been reluctant to 'leave the maize market to the workings of the market forces'. The state marketing board, the NCPB, still holds a dominant position continuing to set the annual maize price for producers and to purchase a substantial part of the marketed maize.

From a food security point of view, the major beneficiaries of the reforms have been the urban consumers. Maize flour prices in the urban areas have dropped considerably, largely as the outcome of increased competition in the maize milling industry. Unfortunately, knowledge of the consequences of market reforms for Kenya's rural consumers and smallholder maize producers is still unsatisfactory. A tentative analysis of recent price developments in rural maize markets in various provinces in Kenya shows, for instance, no signs of diminished (regional or seasonal) price instability.

3.1 Introduction

The international financial institutions (IMF and World Bank) responsible for the design of 'structural adjustment programmes' (SAPs), and other donors involved in Africa's development, have reached the conclusion that African governments, through their interventions in the agricultural and food sector, have failed to secure reliable food supplies at stable and affordable prices for their populations (with the exception of the urban population to which food policies were often heavily biased). State food marketing boards in particular, which were granted a monopoly position in their food procurement and pricing activities, have been blamed for their inadequate performance, operating at high costs and causing a serious drain on the state budget. Their inefficiency and ineffectiveness are also thought to have contributed to low producer prices and a generally ill-functioning domestic food marketing system.

Consequently, 'structural adjustment' called for the end of government involvement in the pricing and marketing of agricultural produce. This policy reform would pave the way for ultimately 'liberalized' (or rather privatized) markets.[1] The replacement of the state boards by private marketing agents was expected to result in not only a better fulfilment of the marketing tasks but also in substantially lower costs. This would allow for positive incentive margins for both traders and processors and a higher price for food producers, thus stimulating the growth of food output. But consumer food prices were also expected to rise, as existing food subsidies were being reduced or entirely removed. This effect, however, was believed to be offset by a counter move to lower consumer prices made possible by the lower operating costs of the private marketing system.

This chapter seeks to confront SAP theory with the Kenyan experiences of food market reforms. It concentrates on the marketing of maize for two reasons. First, maize is the staple food of the large majority of the Kenyan population. It provides some 45 per cent of calorie intake of the average Kenyan household and over 90 per cent of Kenya's farmers are involved in maize production (Smith, 1992, 2). Second, Kenya has a long tradition, stemming from the colonial period, of extensive government price control and market regulations in its maize sector. Since the early 1980s the World Bank and other donors have been pressing the Kenyan government to reduce its role in the pricing and marketing of its staple food.[2]

As maize represents a crucial commodity in the food security record of the majority of the Kenyan population, it is important to examine how a de-controlled maize market impacts on the factors that determine food security at different levels. At the level of individual households a relevant question is if maize market liberalization helps (1) to increase a

---

[1] The term 'liberalized' conveys a positive message. It suggests that a market 'freed' from government intervention and regulation performs better! In the literature the term 'liberalization' refers to the relaxation of regulatory controls on private marketing, whereas 'privatization' implies a withdrawal of state agencies from pricing and marketing (Jayne & Jones, 1997, 1505).

[2] Marketing arrangements and price formation processes are closely interrelated and are therefore often discussed simultaneously.

household's ability to produce more food for self-consumption or (2) to enhance its capacity (purchasing power) to buy the required food in the market. And as the price of food is a crucial determinant of food security for consumers and producers alike, questions about how far food prices are affected by market reforms become of central importance.

Furthermore, at the sectoral level, relevant issues include: the effect of market liberalization on the level of, and the yearly fluctuations in, overall maize production (national food security). And finally, from a regional point of view, the question of whether market liberalization will facilitate the flow of maize from surplus to deficit areas in the country (regional food security) needs attention.

For a proper understanding of the factors at work it is argued that next to a 'technical-economistic' orientation a 'political-economic' approach is necessary. This is because in African conditions, food systems are highly politicized and 'patronized' by the politically powerful. Often political interests and considerations in the food policy-making process tend to overrule sound economic arguments. This makes an analysis in strict economic terms (which is typical for most of SAP design and theoretical reasoning) largely miss its mark.

The chapter is organized as follows. Section 3.2 briefly outlines the theoretical basis of SAP reforms and the anticipated effects on food security. In Section 3.3, the focus is on the long-term characteristics of Kenya's maize market. It discusses the motivations of heavy government intervention and the resultant outcomes and tries to explain the reluctance of the Kenyan government to comply with SAP 'market liberalization' demands. Sections 3.4 and 3.5 look at the period starting in December 1993, when the Kenyan government finally gave in to the World Bank/IMF conditionalities. Here the various actors involved in the market (producers, traders, millers, consumers and government itself) who have all responded differently to reforms are considered in an attempt to pinpoint the 'winners and losers' in the new maize market setting.

3.2 Structural adjustment: theoretical framework and rationale

The World Bank (WB) and the International Monetary Fund (IMF) are the originators of the 'structural adjustment programmes' in Africa. The general diagnosis of the IMF/WB involves the notion that macro imbalances and domestic supply constraints are at the root of Africa's ongoing crisis. Excessive deficits in the balance of payments (external imbalance) and the government's budget (internal disequilibrium) were caused by a combination of external and internal developments.

External shocks in the 1970s included the two oil crises, the recession and tariff protection in the industrialized western countries, the terms of trade deterioration, the higher interest rates and an overall diminished demand for Africa's traditional exports on the world markets. These events gave rise to a rapid worsening of the balance of payment position in a great number of African countries at the beginning of the 1980s.

Internally the situation was exacerbated by the consequences of mistaken development policies. These included: inappropriate exchange-rate policies (overvaluation of the local currency), disincentive trade policies, heavy taxation of farmers' output and an overextended and inefficient public and parastatal sector. Soon, government expenditures began to far exceed revenues and led to serious budget deficits, impeding the growth of domestic supplies of goods and services. Constraints on growth of production were also thought to emanate from excessive government regulation of, and participation in, economic transactions and decision making. This caused 'distortions' in the market and price formation processes and led to the unproductive allocation of scarce resources.

Not surprisingly the proposed remedy involved a substantially reduced role for African governments in the functioning of the economy. Financial resources were to be switched from the public to the private sector and from consumption to productive investments. More funds in the hands of private producers, accompanied by a proper price incentive structure, would lead to increased output, more employment and rising incomes for the African population. A move towards market-driven economies was also expected to produce internationally competitive goods and services, which would contribute to the foundation of a sustained, export-led growth of production. Correct price signals are crucial and are anticipated to effectively work their way through all (monetized) sectors of the economy where markets of different types (for products, inputs, labour, land and capital) are well integrated and operate efficiently and smoothly. These are the characteristics of the type of economy envisaged by international bankers to be the best guarantee for sustained economic growth and welfare improvement (World Bank, 1989 and 1994). Economic price signals and well-integrated, efficiently operating markets are the essential building blocks of standard SAP reasoning.

The agricultural sector, and small farmers in particular, are expected to benefit from three types of reforms: a) an end to past policies of high export taxes and overvaluation of the national currency. Devaluation (and the subsequent producer price rises) combined with internal decontrolling of price formation is assumed to enhance agricultural output; b) improved domestic marketing of agricultural produce. The replacement of inefficient parastatal marketing boards by private traders tends to lead to substantially lower operating costs of marketing activities. Gains resulting from more efficiency in the marketing system are assumed to translate into higher producer prices and c) reforms in international trade regulations. Liberalization of import/export regulations, in the form of reduced (or completely removed) tariffs, quotas and subsidies are also expected to clear the way for increased export trade and production in the agricultural sector.

It must be remembered that from the outset SAPs were not designed with the explicit goal of improving the food security conditions of the African population. Indeed, food security considerations did not rank high on the list of SAP priority objectives. The focus was first and foremost on exportable agricultural commodities which were expected to earn badly needed export revenues. Nevertheless market and related price reforms (as central elements of SAPs) have consequences for the food security of different socio-economic groups. The main analytical task is then to assess how food markets (and other types of markets in which households operate) are altered under the process of SAP implementation and how these changes in market conditions in turn affect the crucial determinants of household (and other levels of) food security. In particular, changes in: a) producer and consumer prices and b) food availability in urban and rural markets should be the subject of analysis.[3]

Food price rises may result in higher incomes for food producing households, at least if there is a production surplus that can be sold on the market. But a substantial proportion of the food producing households in sub-Saharan Africa are also food buyers on the market (when household stocks are depleted).[4] Households are then confronted with the adverse effect of higher retail prices. The net outcome depends on the household's own-produced food to food purchased ratio. Furthermore a devaluation of the national currency (a priority measure in SAP implementation) tends to increase farmers' costs of imported agricultural inputs (fertilizer, fuel, etc.) and consequently partly to offset the advantages of a food price rise.

So much for theory and the (sometimes hidden) assumptions incorporated in the theoretical framework. The remainder of the chapter will concentrate on the actual workings of Kenya's maize marketing system and our knowledge of the consequences of the changes brought about by the reforms.

3.3 Maize marketing and pricing in Kenya: before the reforms

Maize like any other commodity traded in a marketing system increases in value as it moves through the marketing channel from the farmer to the retail selling point. The value also increases when it is stored between harvests and if it is processed (milled and packaged). Different marketing functions are performed by different actors in the market chain. The operations of the actors are in turn affected by policies pursued by the state and a range of non-policy, agri-technical and socio-cultural variables (Thorbecke, 1992, 4). A proper understanding of each of the participating actors' roles and their behavioural determinants is a prerequisite for a meaningful analysis. But before focusing on the actor groups in the maize market, a brief overview of the trend in national supplies of maize over the years is called for.

---

[3] These are but two factors determining household food security. A host of other factors play a role including community support mechanisms and kinship and lineage relations, nutrition knowledge and eating habits, food storage and processing facilities, market infrastructure, health and sanitary conditions, decision making on the allocation of household expenditures, women's work load and time use, wars and conflicts, and droughts and environmental degradation. These complex inter-acting factors make an SAP-food security analysis a difficult exercise.

[4] The percentage of farming households unable to produce enough food to last from one harvest to the next varies with time and place, but is often surprisingly high according to empirical findings. Sijm (1997, 63ff) notes that in Mali during the 1980s 'probably one half of the farm households did not produce enough to meet their consumption requirements'. Corresponding figures for Malawi and Tanzania reach as high as 80 per cent! (Ibid., 64). For Zimbabwe, Tagwireyi (1991, 64) quotes a figure of 40 per cent.

Production

In Kenya almost all farmers (large- and small-scale) are involved in the cultivation of maize. But under the prevailing rain-fed conditions, harvests have shown great variation in the last 20 years (Figure 3.1). The serious declines in the drought years of 1979/80, 1984/85, 1992/93 and 1996 are well recorded. Production levels fluctuated from a low 1.4 million tons in the drought year of 1984/85 to over 3 million tons in the record year of 1994. It seems that in the fifteen-year period (1975/76 - 1989/90) maize production more or less kept up with the rate of population growth. In this period the five-year average rose from 1.8 million tons per year in 1975-1980 to 2.0 million tons in 1981-1985 and 2.5 million tons yearly in 1986-1990 (see Appendix). This volume of 2.5 million tons was assumed in 1990 to be enough to attain self-sufficiency (World Bank, 1991, 1). However, in the 1991-1996 period the yearly average dropped slightly to 2.46 million tons. Taking into consideration an average population growth rate of 3 per cent, this would indicate that the country slipped back to a maize output level lower than the self-sufficiency benchmark. As is clearly shown in the diagram, variations in maize production in the 1993-1996 period were extremely high: from a record harvest of 3 million tons in 1994 – a rise of 46 per cent! compared to the 2 million tons of the preceding year – to 2.2 million tons in 1996. This kind of variation causes considerable price fluctuations and has serious implications for national food security and the workings of the maize marketing system.

Variability in maize output is also reflected in the occurrence of exports and imports. During the nine-year period 1980-1988, Kenya exported 923,000 tons of maize and in the same period imported 1,021,000 tons, resulting in a net-inflow of around 100,000 tons (World Bank, 1991, 2). In the first half of the 1990s the net inflow increased dramatically to over 520,000 tons which may also be interpreted as a sign of lagging domestic production.

The planted acreage increased steadily (due to the introduction of hybrid maize) until the end of the 1980s when it levelled off at 1.4 million hectares (see Appendix). Statistical analysis indicates that the relationship between planted areas and production levels is strong.[5] Nearly two-thirds of the variation in production was explained by variation in the planted area. This implies that the area cultivated, rather than the yield, has been the determining factor for maize output growth. Maize yields stabilized at levels between 1,500 and 2,000 kg per hectare throughout the 1976-1996 period (see Appendix). Stagnation in land productivity is another worrying feature of Kenya's food sector. Given Kenya's overall shortage of good quality agricultural land, it is beyond any doubt that a radical intensification of maize production through increased use of agricultural inputs and the adequate provision of agricultural services is an absolute *sine qua non* for future food security.

---

5 The Pearson correlation coefficient is 0.80.

Figure 3.1 Kenya: maize production in million tons (1976-1996)

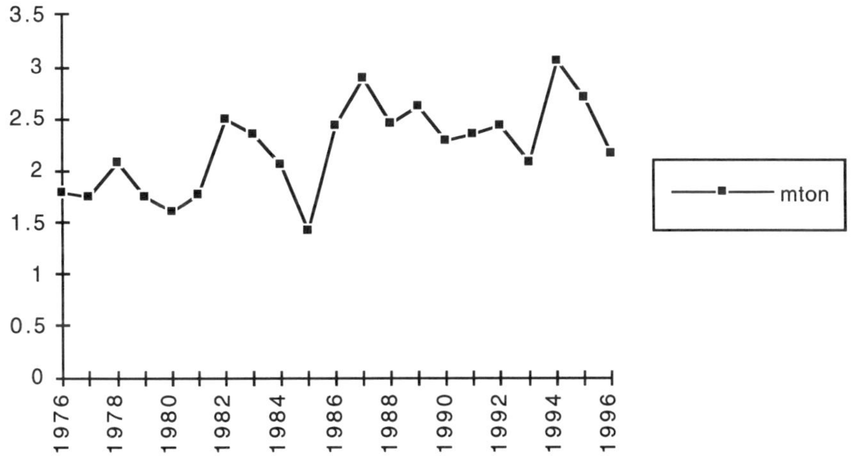

[Line chart showing maize production (mton) from 1976 to 1996, with values fluctuating between approximately 1.4 and 3.0 million tons]

Note: Data are in the Appendix.

Marketing
A large proportion (70 per cent) of Kenya's maize production is provided by small-scale producers with the remainder being produced by medium- and large-scale farmers (Karanja, 1992, 139).[6] But when *marketed* maize output is considered the situation is reversed: large maize farmers market around 75 per cent of their production and smallholders only 25 to 30 per cent. Smallholder producers often intercrop maize with beans whereas large maize producers grow maize in pure stand. The latter in most cases own farm machinery and have access to formal credit institutions. Smallholders are generally self-financing and have to rely on (more expensive) informal credit sources when they have to pay for services or inputs. Large farmers deliver their maize surplus directly to the National Cereals Produce Board (NCPB) depots. Most of these depots are situated near railway stations. (The railway runs through the heart of the large-scale farm region, the former White Highlands.) Many large farmers have their own vehicles or can easily hire them in order to transport maize to the depots.

Significantly, only a small portion of Kenya's total maize production finds its way into the marketing system. For the 1983-1989 period an average share of 41 per cent was estimated (Argwings-Kodhek, 1993, 333). The remainder is retained for seed and home-consumption. This relatively small proportion of marketed maize reflects the predominantly

---

[6] Kenyan statistics define smallholders as farmers with 8 ha or less, medium-scale farmers have between 9 and 20 ha and large-scale producers more than 20 ha.

subsistence nature of maize cultivation in Kenya. Obviously, a situation of thin food markets reduces the scope for 'economies of scale' in marketing and transport.

Prior to the market reforms, Kenya had a dual maize marketing system consisting of an officially regulated, state-controlled sector which predominantly served the large-scale, commercial maize farmers and a parallel, unofficial sector where smallholders traded small quantities at local markets.

In theory, nearly all marketed maize[7] was to enter the state-controlled NCPB marketing board (founded in 1979 after the merger between the Maize and Produce Board and the Wheat Board). This government parastatal was granted a legal monopoly to purchase, distribute and import maize. By 1987 the NCPB operated 60 depots and over 600 buying centres throughout the country (Government of Kenya, 1988, 42). But by far the largest part of the NCPB's purchases (85 per cent) came from the two western provinces of Rift Valley and Western which form the major maize producing areas of Kenya. Rift Valley alone provided two-thirds of the total NCPB maize purchases (World Bank, 1991, 14; Kliest, 1985, 43).

The official NCPB system predominantly served the large-scale producers and Kenya's urban population. Most (80 to 90 per cent) of the NCPB's sales of maize went to large millers[8] in the three major urban areas: Nairobi, Mombasa and Kisumu (Ikiara, 1998, 102). The neglect of rural consumers was largely due to the implicit assumption that the rural population produced enough to meet its own requirements (Jayne & Jones, 1997, 1512).

Essentially the pre-reform maize marketing system was characterized by a circuitous, expensive flow of maize from the NCPB depots in surplus regions to large-scale millers in urban areas, where it was milled at subsidized margins and then sent back as maize meal to the rural areas (Jayne & Jones, 1997, 1515). The margins granted to the large roller mills were much higher than those for the small *posho* mills which mainly operate in rural areas.

It is not clear how much of Kenya's total *marketed* maize under this system flowed into the official system, that is, into the NCPB depots. The World Bank estimated this share at 80 per cent in 1981/82 (World Bank, 1991, 14). But another WB publication puts the figure at 50 per cent (World Bank, 1986, 148). Maritim, in his comprehensive study on Kenya's maize sector, concluded that in 1974/75 no more than 40 per cent of all *marketed* maize entered the NCPB depots (Maritim, 1982, 21). And Jabara estimated a figure of 45-50 per cent for marketed maize sold to the official marketing system (Jabara, 1985, 615). Most likely, the NCPB share has fluctuated over time. Moreover, in years of abundant harvests the NCPB was often unable to absorb the maize that farmers offered for sale.

Nevertheless, there is no doubt that a great deal of Kenya's marketed maize was handled not by the controlled, official marketing system but in the parallel marketing subsystem. Maritim (1982, 21) estimated that 60 per cent of all marketed maize in Kenya was

---

[7] Movements of up to two bags of maize across district boundaries and 10 bags within districts were free, and did not require a transport permit issued by the NCPB.

[8] Maize is overwhelmingly consumed in milled (flour) form. In urban areas large mills produce refined 'sifted meal' maize while in the rural areas (and to a limited extent also in urban areas) so-called hammer mills produce a whole or *posho* type of maize meal.

traded in rural local markets where prices and the volumes exchanged were determined by the supply and demand conditions prevailing in that specific locality. Here the official prices set by the government, as part of its food price policy, were largely ineffective. Likewise, government regulations to restrict movement of maize across district and provincial boundaries (as the second characteristic of the official food policy) were generally evaded. Bribery of police and local administrators and 'smuggling' were common practices.

The unofficial marketing sub-system served in particular the large number of small-scale maize producers (up to 70 per cent of their *marketed* production was handled in this sub-system) and by far the majority of rural consumers (World Bank, 1986, 148). Unfortunately, the significance of the parallel market sub-system in Kenya is often underestimated in writings on marketing issues. The excessive attention paid to the merits and shortcomings of the official, government-controlled maize marketing sub-system is misplaced. It tends to ignore the market conditions faced by the larger part of the Kenyan population living in rural areas and often in locations beyond the reach of official marketing regulations. Here, food markets need not be 'liberalized' as they have never been subject to a firm 'government policy grip' (especially with regard to price formation).

Pricing
As a result of the dual marketing system, prices paid to farmers differed. Official prices were especially relevant to large-scale maize producers as they delivered directly to the NCPB depots. The policy of official pricing did not, however, affect the majority of Kenya's small-scale farmers. Here producers (and consumers) had to rely on local markets and local traders as the main actors in the price formation process. It is estimated that of the total smallholder *marketed* output only 30 per cent found its way to the NCPB depots (Meilink, 1985, 26).

The objectives of the official producer pricing policy (prior to the SAP reforms) were formulated in the "Sessional Paper No. 4 of 1981" and included the following: a) to provide incentives to farmers in order to encourage them to expand food production and to attain broad national self-sufficiency; b) to achieve that goal, producer prices at the farm-gate would be related to longer-term import parity prices (Government of Kenya, 1981, 16).

Producer price setting by the government has always been a complex and delicate exercise. This is not only because conflicting interests are involved, but also because marketed supplies are highly unpredictable due to factors beyond the control of pricing policies. There is no direct relationship between the price offered to farmers and the level of maize production because a host of other influences combine to determine actual maize output besides the set price level. These include public and private investment in the agricultural sector, storage facilities, input availability and their pricing, agricultural technology research, land policy, credit arrangements, the proper functioning of markets, timely payments to farmers and above all sufficient and timely rainfall.

In fixing the producer price for maize, the government made less and less use of the 'cost of production' criterion and gradually moved to 'import and export parity prices' as guidelines. [9] In retrospect, the official prices paid were not unfavourable. Attractive pricing echoed the colonial policy which involved relatively high prices paid to settler grain producers (Heyer, 1976, 317). After independence this policy was continued. In the 1980s official nominal prices for maize producers rose from Ksh 86 per 90 kg bag in 1980 to Ksh 239 in 1990. After the 1991 drought, prices were pushed up from Ksh 275 in 1991 to Ksh 729 in 1993 (Table 3.1).

Taking 1982 as a base year, the index for agricultural input prices, on the other hand, rose from 222 in 1991 to 350 in 1993 (Government of Kenya, 1995, Table 8.6). Thus the increase in input costs for farmers in the 1990s was significantly less than the increase in their output prices. It can therefore be concluded that the producer price policy pursued by the Kenyan government acted as an incentive for maize producing farmers.

When applying the import parity price criterion, this conclusion is confirmed. The World Bank estimated that producer prices hovered around 75 per cent of import parity during the 1980s and were nearing import parity levels in the early 1990s (World Bank, 1994, 82; Swamy, 1994, 220).

During the 1980s official consumer prices[10] for milled maize (*posho* meal) increased rapidly from a nominal Ksh 1.65 per kg in 1980 to Ksh 5.14 in 1990, a rise of 212 per cent. When compared to the change in the 'consumer price index' in the same period, retail food prices rose more than the overall index (World Bank, 1991, 54).[11] Increases were even more rapid in the 1990s: from Ksh 5.14 in 1990 to Ksh 13.88 per kg in 1993, a rise of 170 per cent in three years (Table 3.1). Inflation during the same period showed an increase of only 127 per cent (Government of Kenya, 1996, Table 4.19).

These price developments underline the fact that, in contrast to elsewhere in Africa,[12] during the 1980-1993 period food consumers in Kenya were not protected from inflation.[13]

The last column of Table 3.1 indicates that maize producers received a share of the consumer price which fluctuated between 67 per cent (1983) and 42 per cent (1986 and 1992). Although the share was higher in the first half of the 1980s there is, however, no clear indication of the marketing sector[14] taking an increasing share of the consumer price during the 1980 - 1993 period. Rather the pattern is one of fluctuating shares.

---

[9] These prices are relevant for commodities (tradables) entering international trade. They represent a reference point in measuring the opportunity costs of a country's exports and imports. In a situation where imports and exports are completely liberalized, the 'parity maize pricing' policy is supposed to clear the market internationally. However, at the time the (official) producer price is fixed and announced, it is uncertain whether this price will eventually turn out to be the 'equilibrium price'. Another complicating factor in the process of setting the right (market clearing) price is the wide price range between import and export parity prices, due to the extremely high transport and handling costs of maize in Kenya.

[10] Consumer prices are the retail maize flour prices included in the Nairobi 'cost of living index' as published in the *Statistical Abstract*.

[11] The maize consumer price index during the 1980s rose from 100 (1980) to 303 (1989) while the total consumer price index increased to 241 in the same period.

[12] In Africa a policy of low, subsidized urban food prices was widely adopted.

[13] Maize consumer prices after 1993 were not available at the time of writing as the *Statistical Abstract* of 1994 was the latest issue to have been published.

[14] Defined here as encompassing all actors : traders, transporters and millers.

Table 3.1 Maize: Official producer prices, consumer prices, 'price spread' and producer's share, 1980-1993 (nominal prices)

Year	Producer price (Ksh per 90 kg bag)	Consumer price (Ksh per kg)	Price spread (Ksh per kg)	Producer share (% of Cons.price)
1980	86	1.65	0.70	57
1981	90	1.65	0.65	61
1982	96	1.92	0.86	55
1983	139	2.30	0.76	67
1984	158	2.78	1.03	63
1985	168	4.11	2.25	45
1986	178	4.65	2.68	42
1987	188	4.65	2.57	45
1988	193	4.77	2.63	45
1989	201	5.00	2.77	45
1990	239	5.14	2.49	52
1991	275	5.92	2.87	52
1992	428	11.25	6.50	42
1993	729	13.88	5.78	58

Sources: Producer prices are from *Economic Survey* 1987, 107 and 1997, 126. Consumer prices are from *Statistical Abstract*, 1991 and 1994 respectively, Tables 234 and 230. These are Nairobi retail prices for wholemeal *posho* maize.

Note: 'price spread' is the consumer price minus the producer price in Ksh per kg.

As we saw, the 'outreach' of official pricing was restricted to NCPB operations and urban millers and consumers. Maize prices in rural Kenya were largely unaffected by official pricing, but determined by the prevailing local market forces of supply and (effective) demand.

A review of studies analyzing food price movements in these rural markets reveals substantial price variations, both regional and seasonal, even between adjacent areas (Meilink, 1987, 24ff). This finding supports the widely held view that the government's policy of restricting private food transports, within and across districts, has only worked to aggravate seasonal and regional price fluctuations in Kenya's rural markets (Schmidt, 1979; Maritim, 1982; Booker & Githongo, 1983; Ateng, 1984; Food supply monitoring project seminar, 1985). The variation of (uncontrolled) local market prices is illustrated in Table 3.2.

Average provincial prices for a bag of maize (90 kg) in different markets in the same year show an erratic pattern of variation. Here we consider the variation in the pre-reform period, recorded in the first four columns. In 1990 the differential between the highest price (Coast) and the lowest price (Nyanza) amounted to Ksh 108. In 1991 there was a difference of Ksh 210 between the highest price (Rift Valley) and the lowest price (Eastern). In 1992 the difference was extremely large: Ksh 642(!) between the high (Central) price and the low (Eastern) price. And in 1993 the price differential of Ksh 489 between the high (Eastern) price and the low (Nyanza) price also indicates the wide range of regional price variation in maize traded in the same year in various local markets in Kenya's rural areas. Clearly towards 1993, prices in all rural markets increased very rapidly (in many cases threefold in three years).

Table 3.2 Maize prices in rural markets by province, 1990-1996 (Ksh per 90 kg bag)

Province		1990	1991	1992	1993	1994	1995	1996
Coast	March	338	342	743	918	1755	1636	1841
	September	342	405	855	1215	1649	2106	2139
Eastern	March	257	275	405	736	997	662	786
	September	270	333	995	1110	1132	622	1099
Central	March	310	324	513	700	1567	796	724
	September	297	430	1047	1094	1172	753	1071
Rift Valley	March	230	333	675	810	1305	737	693
	September	272	485	1022	1035	911	688	1047
Nyanza	March	260	279	468	621	1326	755	764
	September	234	349	675	932	803	615	984
Western	March	275	288	488	736	1219	709	748
	September	248	432	684	937	770	607	1182

Sources: Economic Survey, 1994, 122, derived from Table 8.10; Economic Survey, 1997, 129, derived from Table 8.10.
Note: These prices can be interpreted as either producer or consumer prices. Consumers bought in these markets and then took the maize to a hammer mill to obtain *posho* meal. The average milling fee was Ksh 1 per kg milled maize.

3.4 Towards a liberalized maize market

Proposals for the reform of the maize sector in Kenya have met with persistent resistance on the part of the Kenyan authorities. Part of the explanation lies in the fact that the authorities have often used the parastatals in general and the NCPB in particular for political patronage purposes. Appointments in high positions in these marketing boards have served to 'buy' political support from important political figures (Ikiara, 1993, 99). Appointments of local staff in NCPB depots especially in the surplus producing Rift Valley (and President Moi's home province) have also been highly politicized. Rent seeking from issuing permits for grain movements was widely practiced (Smith, 1992, 5; Swamy, 1994, 220). Furthermore a number of (very) large farms in western Kenya (in the former White Highlands) were acquired by the political and business elite (the president, ministers, senior police and military officers, civil servants and high-ranking KANU party officials). This also explains the generally favourable policies towards agriculture and the maize sector in particular.

But it must be added that socio-economic motivations have also played a role. The government, through a nationwide network of NCPB assembly depots, set out to offer remunerative prices to farmers and reasonable prices to consumers by fixing in- and off-depot prices and all wholesale and retail margins. Controls of the movement of marketed maize volumes were also thought necessary to ensure maize supply to urban areas (and deficit rural districts). There was a genuine fear (though largely unproved) of private traders exploiting producers and consumers alike and of maize (illegally) crossing borders to neighbouring countries leaving the country with an unnecessary shortage. Moreover, private sector activity was restricted to prevent private traders from selling directly to processors (large millers) which would undermine the NCPB's access to marketed maize.

These policy considerations go far towards explaining the persistent reluctance, throughout the 1980s, to give in to pressures for marketing reforms emanating from the IMF and the World Bank regarding 'structural adjustment' conditionalities. Over the years numerous attempts to liberalize food marketing have been unsuccessfully tried (Mosley, 1991, 109).

But in 1987, when once again a reform proposal was formulated in the 'Cereal Sector Reform Programme' (CSRP) initiated by European Community donors, the Kenyan government seemed prepared to take action. The conditions attached to the World Bank's 'sectoral adjustment loan' agreed with the government in 1986 and the escalating costs of the NCPB's operations in the first half of the 1980s had certainly contributed to the readiness of the government to implement the policy change.[15]

The reform's aim was to scale down the role of the NCPB in maize marketing through a series of measures: a) the creation of a network of 'licensed buying agents' (LBA's)[16] who were allowed to purchase maize on behalf of the NCPB (and could also engage in maize trade on their own account) and along with this the reduction of the number of NCPB depots in the rural areas; b) to raise the amount of freely transportable maize from 2 to 10 bags across district boundaries; c) large urban millers were allowed to purchase 20 per cent of their maize supplies directly from traders and cooperatives (the remaining part still had to be purchased from the NCPB); and finally d) the financial position of the NCPB was to be improved by writing off of its accumulated debts to the Treasury (financed by the European Community) and the full subvention of the NCPB's future functions by the Ministry of Finance. Furthermore a 'crop purchase revolving fund' was to be introduced in order to enable the NCPB to make timely payments to farmers and trader agents.

NCPB tasks were scaled down to: a market stabilization function (through floor and ceiling market prices); to maintaining a national food security stock; and finally (continued) commercial operations in the maize market, in full competition with private traders. It was expected that financial support from the Treasury would enable the NCPB to reduce its into-depot and ex-depot margin while still being able to compete with private traders (Smith, 1992, 13).

By mid 1992, five years after the introduction of CSRP reforms, the progress made was far from impressive. Although restrictions on inter-district maize movements were further relaxed to free transportation of 44 bags in 1991 and raised further to 88 bags in 1992 (Argwings-Kodhek et al., 1993, 333), mention is made of the 'reluctance' of the district level bureaucrats to adhere to this measure and of the continued practice by local police of harassing traders and demanding fines (Lewa & Hubbar, 1995, 576). Moreover, in October 1992 the movement of maize was entirely banned before the December 1992 elections and not lifted until the end of 1993 (ibid, 575). This exemplifies the strong involvement of 'Kenyan high politics' in food marketing issues.

---

[15] The European Community financed the Cereal Sector Reform Programme (CSRP) which was carried out in the period 1988-1992 . Other donors such as the World Bank, USAID and the IMF also participated.

[16] This was not a new phenomenon as in the early 1980s, prior to the establishment of the NCPB buying centres, LBAs were also appointed, They later gave way to the new NCPB depots.

Regarding the restructuring of the NCPB, progress was equally disappointing. Due to a combination of continued financial indiscipline and the meagre subventions to the board provided by the Treasury, the NCPB's balance sheet by 1992 had worsened again and led once again to delayed payments to farmers. Furthermore, the intended closure of many NCPB buying centres and depots did not materialize. Following increased pressure from politicians, the closure schedule was interrupted and, in fact, some new buying centres were opened (ibid, 577).

The quota of 20 per cent (in 1990/91 increased to 30 per cent) that large millers were allowed to procure directly from traders or cooperatives also met with implementation difficulties. Procedural confusion arose on such issues as to who would receive movement permits to transport maize to the large millers and how the 20 per cent ratio was to be measured (Smith, 1992, 14).

However, for the sake of a balanced view, it must be remembered that things were also made difficult for the Kenyan government when in 1992, the European Community donors withdrew their financial support for several components of the CSRP programme in an effort to force the government to accept a multiparty political system (Lewa & Hubbard 1995, 577). In November 1991 donors in their 'consultative group' meeting in Paris had already expressed their dissatisfaction with the Kenyan government's attitude towards reform implementation. The donors' discontent was further intensified as in the course of 1992 (which turned out to be a serious drought year) the president decided to reintroduce the system of maize movement control. Further undermining of reforms took place with the government's decision to increase the NCPB in-depot prices to 110 per cent of import parity and to reopen previously closed NCPB maize buying centres. Moreover, maize was (again) offered to millers at subsidized prices, which contradicted the reform objective to let millers buy some maize directly on the open market. The result was that the NCPB once again operated at high costs and incurred growing deficits.

The sudden reversal of reforms was justified by the government which argued that the disappointing harvest of 1992 and the subsequent maize shortages 'forced' it to intervene in the market in the interest of national food security.

A frustrated World Bank in reply cancelled the second tranche of the 1990 agricultural sector adjustment loan in December 1992: no money was to be released until pricing and marketing in the maize sector (along with conditions in other sectors of the economy) were fully de-controlled (Swamy, 1994, 195). In late 1993, the government gave in and decided to comply with the donor's conditions and restarted the implementation of reform measures -- this time in a radical fashion. President Moi announced the full liberalization of the maize trade in December 1993. Free importation of maize by private traders and large millers (in the context of the overall import liberalization) was also permitted. Consequently since 1994, the maize trade in Kenya has been officially 'fully liberalized'. Notwithstanding, the government has reserved the right to 'make selected targeted interventions where market forces may not be effective' (Africa South of the Sahara, 1998, 559).

3.5 A liberalized maize market?

Although only a few years have passed since the effective liberalization of the maize market (in 1994), a number of profound changes have occurred affecting the various actors in the maize marketing chain (the NCPB, farmers, traders, millers and consumers) in different ways. These changes must now be reviewed.

The NCPB
One of the pressing problems to be solved in the liberalized maize market is the new design of the state marketing agent (NCPB) now facing competition from the private sector. Events in the first years testify to the difficulties the Kenyan authorities had with accepting the new conditions. In particular, there was a growing fear that food policy objectives (that is ensuring food security, especially in urban areas) would be jeopardized under the new system.

The NCPB had actually lost ground in maize marketing in the early 1990s. In 1989 about 24 per cent of the total maize production was delivered to the board but by 1993 this had fallen to a mere 15 per cent (Ikiara, 1995, 37). In an attempt not to be outdone by the private traders, the government decided to raise the NCPB's buying price to Ksh 855 (per 90 kg bag) for the following agricultural year. However, in that year (1994/95) Kenya experienced a bumper maize harvest of over 3 million tons due to favourable rainfall. In addition, large volumes of maize (8 million bags) were imported after the drought of 1992/93. Private traders, responding to the liberalized import policy, imported 3 million bags themselves. As a result of this abundant supply, retail prices dropped spectacularly from Ksh 1,400 per 90 kg bag in June 1994 to Ksh 400 in January 1995 (EIU, 1995, 17).[17] Though favourable for consumers, the maize producers suffered from not being able to sell their surplus maize and complained bitterly.[18]

In 1995 the government reacted by instructing the NCPB to accelerate its purchases from farmers in order to secure their market outlets. This exercise added an estimated Ksh 3 billion ($ 8 million) to public spending (although farmers had to wait several months for their money) and also added to the irritation of the donors, who once again witnessed increased government intervention in the maize market.

In late 1995, President Moi, responding to renewed donor pressure, announced major changes with regard to NCPB operations. It was directed to buy and sell maize only at market prices from then on and to continue to keep a strategic reserve of 3 million bags for food security reasons. Furthermore he promised the donors that the board would be fully commercialized by the end of 1996 and that it would be free to export maize to fund its payments to farmers (in October 1995 the board still owed maize and wheat farmers an

---

[17] Since production costs were between Ksh 450 and Ksh 1000 per 90 kg bag depending on the region, farmers had to sell at a loss.
[18] The Minister for Agriculture, Mr Simeon Nyachae, imposed a 6-month ban on imports in August 1994 to ensure a market outlet for Kenyan producers. Soon, however, the ban was lifted and replaced by an import duty and a dumping tax (*The Daily Nation*, 29/11/1994).

estimated Ksh 1 billion in respect of purchases during the 1994/95 season). In the first few months of 1996 the NCPB exported some 4.5 million bags of maize, mainly to drought-affected Southern African countries (EIU, 1996, first quarter, 15).

However, the 1996 maize harvest turned out to be much lower than was expected. In January 1997 the Finance Minister Mr Mudavadi again waved levies and VAT on maize imports resulting in imports of 7.1 million bags, of which 4.1 million were brought into the country by private traders (EIU, 1997, third quarter, 20).

These events illustrate that the role of 'buyer and seller of last resort', envisaged for the NCPB, was far from being realized. Thus, the government's struggle (against donor demands) to maintain its position of stakeholder in maize marketing lingers on.

The foregoing discussion leads to three important conclusions: a) The Kenyan government has proved (for political and food security reasons) to be a 'weak supporter' of liberalization. Especially in 'abnormal times' (bumper harvests or droughts), there is little willingness to leave the maize sector to the workings of the market. Although it is understandable (and even required) that the Kenyan government is keen to intervene in the food sector when food security problems arise, policies should be coherent and much less precarious. b) Apparently, the reform measure to fully liberalize maize imports has had far-reaching negative consequences for maize producers (price declines and the inability to sell). Much blame must be put on the chaotic (import and export) policy pursued by the Kenyan government in 1995 when a bumper harvest and substantial cheap imports simultaneously flooded the market and in 1996 when exports were allowed in a year which later proved to have a serious shortage. c) The role of the NCPB in the maize sector suffers from policy ambiguity. One year it is instructed by the government to actively participate in the market, while the next, it is told to give the private sector more room to operate. Obviously, there is a need for a proper and sustained definition of the 'rules of the game' to which the NCPB has to adhere.

The farmers
A noticeable move for farmers occurred in 1990/91 with the decision to liberalize fertilizer imports and with the subsequent removal of the fertilizer subsidy. This led to a sharp increase in the price of this important agricultural input. Real fertilizer prices in 1993 were 33 per cent higher than in 1992. Much of this increase was due to the devaluation of the Kenyan shilling, as one of the priority SAP measures (Government of Kenya, 1994, 119). The index of input use dropped by 40 per cent in 1993 compared to the 1989/1991 average level, despite higher producer prices for maize in 1993. Farmers were also complaining about the activities of Asian businessmen (now controlling the farm input market) who allegedly increased fertilizer prices every time the official producer price was raised (Ikiara, 1995, 55). Farmers threatened to plant less maize in the following agricultural season unless the fertilizer subsidy was reinstated. Indeed, as the Appendix shows, the area planted with maize drastically decreased in 1995 and 1996 leading to a serious decline in national production. The erratic policy of producer price setting, combined with drastic import liberalization in the reform period, clearly contributed to these adverse developments (Table 3.3).

Table 3.3 Kenya: Post-reform official producer prices for maize (1993-1996; nominal prices)

Year	Ksh per 90 kg bag
1993	729
1994	855
1995	720
1996	950

Source: Economic Survey, 1997, 126, derived from Table 8.4.

For farmers (and consumers) in the local, rural markets, prices during the reform period showed quite a different pattern, as is illustrated by the last three columns of Table 3.2. Rapidly increasing prices in the structurally maize-deficit Coast province are striking. Throughout the reform period prices here were far higher than in any other province in Kenya. There is little evidence in Table 3.2 to suggest that farmers and rural consumers elsewhere (outside Coast Province) faced less regional price variability in the first years of trade liberalization than before. In 1994 the regional differential between the highest and lowest market price amounted to Ksh 792. In 1995 it was only Ksh 89 but in 1996 it went up to Ksh 489 per 90 kg bag.

The traders
The large majority of maize traders in Kenya are locally based retailers and small market traders who typically handle between five and ten bags a week with a working capital of no more than Ksh 10,000 ($200). Trade activities are not confined to maize only. Most traders combine it with the buying and selling of wheat, beans, millet, sorghum, rice, cassava and potatoes. The majority hire transport (*matatus* or minibuses, handcarts or pick-ups) to move the maize to the selling points. The latter may be a NCPB buying centre or alternatively a local market. Generally it has been felt that the most profitable activity was retailing, in contrast to buying maize at the farm-gate and transporting it further along the trade channel (Ikiara, 1995, 61).

The only traders involved in inter-district trade are the larger transporters/distributors. Most of them own lorries and trucks and many are involved in maize transports to and from the large mills and also in international trade with Tanzania and Uganda whenever price differentials allow profitable operations. As noted above, in 1993, large volumes of maize flour flowed into the country, mainly from Uganda as a result of import liberalization following the 1992 drought. Liberalization was generally welcomed by the larger traders who reacted by importing massive volumes of maize from Uganda (EIU, second quarter 1995, 15).[19]

Unfortunately, not much is known about the evolution of inter-district maize movements after the reforms. Therefore the important question as to whether small-scale traders have been able to expand their role in the maize trade remains largely unanswered.

---

[19] Later the Kenyan government reimposed a ban on maize imports after complaints by the large farmers.

Results from a survey among traders reveal that few traders foresee a swift replacement of NCPB activities by those of private traders. Apart from the usual list of stated reasons (lack of working capital, difficult access to credit, inadequate storage capacity, a dearth of transport means and poor infrastructure) traders also stressed that they were discouraged by the uncertainties surrounding the future division of tasks between the NCPB and the private sector and the inconsistent policy environment in general (Ikiara, 1998, 107). The government in turn has clearly failed to support private trade expansion. It has been generally reluctant to strengthen the capacity of the private sector through providing adequate public provisions.

The millers
The effects of market liberalization in Kenya have been most strongly felt in the milling sector (Egerton University, 1995, 10). Before liberalization the large mills were obliged to purchase their maize either from the state-controlled NCPB or from large farmers with an NCPB permit. This changed in 1993 when market reforms allowed millers to buy directly from farmers. Millers expected to benefit from liberalization through cheaper maize purchases. On the other hand by 1994 subsidies on roller milled maize had been eliminated. The effect was dramatic: within one month in early 1994 the consumer price of roller mill (sifted meal) maize rose by 53 per cent (Jayne & Argwings-Kodhek, 1997, 449). For *posho* wholemeal maize, this improved relative price ratio *vis-à-vis* sifted meal, combined with the complete deregulation of private maize movement across district boundaries, decisively strengthened its competitive power. The result was that the large millers quickly lost ground to the rapidly expanding small *posho* hammer mills in urban areas. Quite surprisingly[20] (despite their perceived strong preference for 'sifted flour'), urban consumers in large numbers turned to wholemeal maize that had become increasingly available at a price amounting to only 60 per cent of that of sifted flour (Mukumbu, 1994, 126; Jayne & Argwings-Kodhek, 1997, 454). This feature continued during the second half of 1994 and throughout 1995 when prices of both types of maize flour decreased sharply following good maize harvests. Clearly, the pre-reform monopoly position of the large roller mills in the urban centres had come to an end. The cheaper (and more nutritious) maize flour of the hammer mills has successfully taken over part of the large mills' sifted flour market.

The consumers
Increased competition at the milling stage has led to lower milling margins and subsequently lower prices for consumers. Findings of two surveys, one carried out in Nairobi in October 1993 just prior to the reforms, and one in October 1995, about 20 months after market

---

[20] Urban consumers had been thought to have a strong preference for sifted maize flour. But increased urban poverty during 'structural adjustment' may have caused urban consumers to switch to cheaper maize flour.

liberalization,[21] indicate that between the surveys, the price of sifted meal dropped from Ksh 20.70 per kg to Ksh 15.33 (-26 per cent) and for wholemeal even more, from Ksh 14.46 to Ksh 9.71 (-33 per cent). It was estimated that 40 per cent of this decline could be attributed to the lower milling margins and 60 per cent to lower maize grain prices resulting from the good 1995 harvest. Jayne & Argwings-Kodhek (1997, 451) estimate that the total gain to Nairobi's consumers amounted to Ksh 525 million (over $10 million) in one year. They conclude that the removal of subsidies on roller milled maize meal was largely compensated for by the lifting of restrictions on private maize movements and that urban food security improved as access to cheaper whole maize flour increased (ibid, 456).

But whether rural households have also been able to benefit from increased maize supplies at lower market prices remains uncertain due to a lack of empirical research. Table 3.2 provides an inconclusive picture. Although in all provinces (except the Coast) prices dropped considerably in 1995, they rose again in 1996 in most provinces.

3.6 Conclusions

Since the decision to fully liberalize the Kenyan maize market was taken as late as December 1993, the time period over which I have been able to assess the outcomes of the reforms has been rather short. Therefore my conclusions must be tentative. Despite profound changes in maize trade and maize processing, the reform process has not yet been completed. The maize marketing board, the NCPB, is still far from being 'commercialized'. This state body continues to set the annual maize price for producers and also continues to purchase a proportion of the total marketed maize. It seems that the government is still hesitant and lacks the political commitment to scale down the NCPB's role to one of 'buyer and seller of last resort'.

There is a need, on the part of the Kenyan government, to be more explicit and establish a consistent policy with regard to the future role of the NCPB in the maize sector. (The haphazard policies of the past have discouraged private investors.) There is also an urgent need for a balanced policy concerning external maize trade and local production stimuli. The events of 1993/1994 were a frustrating experience for Kenya's maize producers as they lost a substantial part of their market sales when private traders and large millers were allowed to import maize freely and cheap imports flooded the country. Although, later, measures were taken to restore market outlets for Kenyan farmers, it illustrates that a complete and swift liberalization of maize imports may undermine incentives for badly needed growth in domestic production. In this context the observed decline in planted maize hectares in 1995 and 1996 (see Appendix) is a disturbing signal. Clearly, market reforms need to generate a positive supply response among producers. If not, fully-fledged liberalization will merely end up jeopardizing national food security objectives.

---

[21] The two random household level surveys were organized by a joint team of Egerton University and Michigan State University. Details may be found in Jayne & Argwings-Kodhek (1997).

However, the reforms in the maize market have also yielded positive results. In the maize flour market, large millers are now facing stiff competition from 'informal sector' *posho* millers whose access to maize is no longer restricted. Resulting lower prices of whole and sifted maize flour have conferred substantial benefits on urban consumers and certainly enhanced their food security.

But, unfortunately, the important question of the impact of market reforms on the rural maize deficit and generally poorer regions remains largely unanswered. Are smallholders who produce limited amounts of maize for market sale or who are located in remote areas better served by private traders than they were by the state-controlled system? Have maize flows from surplus to deficit districts been facilitated after lifting maize movement controls? And what has happened to seasonal and regional price variability in rural markets? These questions, which were placed in a theoretical framework in the first part of this chapter, remain largely understudied. There is therefore an urgent need for detailed micro-field studies that take into account the widely differing characteristics of Kenya's population groups and the varying ways in which they are involved as actors in the maize market.

Donors, especially the World Bank and the IMF, should strive to make this type of data available[22] and incorporate the findings into the design of future policies for reform.

References

AFRICA SOUTH OF THE SAHARA (1998) (27th Edition) London: Europa Publications Ltd., England.

ARGWINGS-KODHEK, G., M. MULINGE, MONKE (1993) 'The Impacts of MaizeMarket Liberalization in Kenya'. In *Food Research Institute Studies*, Vol. XXII, no. 3.

ATENG, B. (1984) 'Towards a Food Policy for Kenya'. University of Nairobi, Unpublished Thesis.

BOOKER AGRICULTURE INTERNATIONAL LTD & GITHONGO AND ASSOCIATES (1983) *Grain Marketing Study*. Vol. 1 Main Report. Nairobi: GOK, Ministry of Finance.

CORNIA, A., R. JOLLY & F. STEWART (eds) (1987) *Adjustment with a Human Face*. Vol. 1 & 2. Oxford: UNICEF/Oxford: Oxford University Press.

ECONOMIST INTELLIGENCE UNIT (1995, 1996, 1997) *Country Report Kenya*. London, United Kingdom.

EGERTON UNIVERSITY (1995) 'Towards 2000: Improving Agricultural Performance'. Proceedings of the Conference held at Kenya Commercial Bank, Institute of Banking and Finance, September 1995, Policy Analysis Matrix.

FOOD SUPPLY MONITORING PROJECT SEMINAR (1985) Central Bureau of Statistics, Ministry of Finance and Planning / Oxford University: Oxford Food Studies Group.

GOULD, J. & A. VON OPPEN (eds) (1994) 'Of rhetoric and market: the "liberalization" of food trade in East Africa'. In *Sociologia Ruralis,* Vol. 34, no. 1.

---

[22] Useful work in this respect has been done by (Kenyan) researchers of the Egerton University Policy Analysis Team (see Egerton reference) largely funded by USAID. A continuation of these, highly policy-relevant studies is clearly called for.

GOVERNMENT OF KENYA (1981) 'National Food Policy'. Sessional Paper No. 4 of 1981. Nairobi: Government Printer.
GOVERNMENT OF KENYA (1988) 'Household Food Security and Nutrition Policy'. Ministry of Agriculture and Ministry of Livestock Development.
GOVERNMENT OF KENYA (1994) *Statistical Abstract.* Central Bureau of Statistics, Office of the Vice-President and Ministry of Planning and National Development.
GOVERNMENT OF KENYA (1994) *Economic Survey.* Central Bureau of Statistics, Office of the Vice-President and Ministry of Planning and National Development.
GOVERNMENT OF KENYA (1995) *Economic Survey.* Central Bureau of Statistics, Office of the Vice-President and Ministry of Planning and National Development.
GOVERNMENT OF KENYA (1996) *Economic Survey.* Central Bureau of Statistics, Office of the Vice-President and Ministry of Planning and National Development.
HEYER, J., J. MAITHA & W. SENGA (1976) *Agricultural Development in Kenya. An Economic Assessment.* Oxford: Oxford University Press.
IKIARA, G., M. JAMA & J. AMADI (1993) 'Agricultural Decline, Politics and Structural Adjustment in Kenya'. In P. Gibbon (ed.) *Social Change and Economic Reform.* Uppsala: Nordiska Afrikainstitutet, pp. 78-106.
IKIARA, G., M. JAMA & J. AMADI (1995) 'The Cereals Chain in Kenya: Actors, Reforms and Politics'. In P. Gibbon (ed.) *Markets, Civil Society and Democracy in Kenya.* Uppsala: Nordiska Afrikainstitutet.
IKIARA, G. (1998) 'Rising to the challenge: the private sector response in Kenya'. In P. Seppala (ed.) *Liberalized and Neglected? Food Marketing Policies in Eastern Africa.* The United Nations University, Wider, World Development Studies 12.
JABARA, C. (1985) 'Agricultural Pricing Policy in Kenya'. In *World Development,* Vol. 13 , no. 5, pp. 611-626.
JAYNE, T. & S. JONES (1997) 'Food Marketing and Pricing Policy in Eastern and Southern Africa'. In *World Development,* Vol. 25, no. 9, pp. 1505-1527
JAYNE, T. & G. ARGWINGS-KODHEK (1997) 'Consumer Response to Maize Market Liberalization in Urban Kenya'. In *Food Policy,* Vol. 22, no. 5, p. 447-458.
KARANJA, D., J. RUTTO & K. NJOROGE (1992) 'Research Opportunities for Maize Productivity Growth in Kenya'. In *Proceedings of the Conference on Maize Supply and Marketing under Market Liberalization,* held at the Kenya Commercial Bank, Institute of Banking and Finance, Karen- Nairobi 18-19 June 1992, Egerton University, Policy Analysis Matrix, pp. 139-147.
KLIEST, T. (1985) *Regional and Seasonal Food Problems in Kenya.* Nairobi: Food and Nutrition Planning Unit, Ministry of Finance and Planning, and Leiden: African Studies Centre, Food and Nutrition Studies Programme, no. 10.
LEWA P. & M. HUBBARD (1995) 'Kenya's Cereal Sector Reform Programme: Managing the Politics of Reform'. In *Food Policy,* Vol. 20, no. 6, pp. 573-584.
MARITIM, H. (1982) *Maize Marketing in Kenya: An Assessment of Interregional Commodity Flow Pattern.* PhD No. 112. Berlin: Technischen Universitat.
MEILINK, H. (1985) *Agricultural Pricing Policy in Kenya: Scope and Impact.* Nairobi: Food and Nutrition Planning Unit, Ministry of Finance and Planning; Leiden: African Studies Centre, Food and Nutrition Studies Programme, no. 11.

MEILINK, H. (1987) *Food Consumption and Food Prices in Kenya.* Nairobi: Food and Nutrition Planning Unit, Ministry of Finance and Planning, Leiden: African Studies Centre, Food and Nutrition Studies Programme, no. 21.

MOSLEY, P. (1991) 'How to confront the World Bank and get away with it: a case study of Kenya, 1980-87' In C. Milner & A. Rayner (eds) *Policy Adjustment in Africa.* London: Macmillan pp. 99-131.

MUKUMBU, M. (1994) 'Consumer and Milling Industry Response to Maize Market Reform in Kenya.' In *Proceedings of the Conference on Market Reforms, Agricultural Production and Food Security,* held at the Kenya Commercial Bank, Institute of Banking and Finance, Nairobi, June 22-23, 1994. Nairobi: Egerton University, Policy Analysis Matrix, pp. 114-139.

NCPB (1990) *Liberalization under the Cereals Sector Reform programme: An Evaluation.* National Cereals and Produce Board, Forward Planning Unit, July 1990.

SCHMIDT, G. (1979) 'Effectiveness of Maize marketing Controls in Kenya'. In Mukui, K. (ed.) *Price and Marketing Controls in Kenya.* Institute for Development Studies, Occasional Paper 32, University of Nairobi.

SEPPALA, P. (1998) *Liberalized and Neglected? Food Marketing Policies in Eastern Africa.* United Nations University, WIDER, World Development Studies no. 12

SIJM, J. (1997) *Food Security and Policy Interventions in Sub-Saharan Africa: Lessons from the Past Two Decades.* Rotterdam: Erasmus University.

SMITH, L. (1992) 'Problems of Liberalizing Cereal Markets: The Kenya Case'. Paper for Institute of Social Studies, Research Seminar, 22nd January 1992.

SWAMY, G. (1994) 'Kenya: patchy, intermittent commitment'. In I. Husain & R. Faruqee (eds) *Adjustment in Africa. Lessons from Country Case Studies.* Washington D.C.: World Bank.

TAGWIREYI, J. (1991) 'Zimbabwe: food access and nutrition linkages' In: M. Rukuni & J. Wyckoff (eds) *Market Reforms, Research Policies and SADCC Food Security.* Harare: UZ/MSU Food Security Research in Southern Africa project.

THORBECKE, E. (1992) 'The Anatomy of Agricultural Product Markets and Transactions in Developing Countries'. Paper prepared for the Institute for Policy reform, Washington D.C.

WORLD BANK (1986) *Kenya: Agricultural Sector Report.* Vol. II, Washington D.C.

WORLD BANK (1989) *Sub-Saharan Africa, From crisis to Sustainable Growth, A Long Term Perspective Study.* Washington D.C.

WORLD BANK (1991) *Kenya Food and Nutrition Policy.* A World Bank Sector report No. 8351-KE, Washington D.C.

WORLD BANK (1994) *Adjustment in Africa. Reforms, Results and The Road Ahead.* A World Bank Policy Research Report, Washington D.C.

Appendix on maize production in Kenya

Maize acreage, production and yield, 1976-1996

Year	Million hectares	Million tonnes	Kg/hectare
1976	0.950	1.800	1890
1977	0.853	1.743	2043
1978	1.002	2.080	2070
1979	0.875	1.740	1980
1980	0.839	1.604	1912
1981	1.120	1.768	1570
1982	1.208	2.502	2070
1983	1.236	2.340	1890
1984	1.200	2.070	1720
1985	1.130	1.411	1240
1986	1.370	2.430	1770
1987	1.430	2.890	2020
1988	1.440	2.450	1700
1989	1.420	2.628	1850
1990	1.449	2.290	1580
1991	1.471	2.340	1591
1992	1.470	2.430	1727
1993	1.308	2.089	1597
1994	1.500	3.060	2040
1995	1.380	2.699	1956
1996	1.300	2.160	1662

Sources: (a) Government of Kenya, *Statistical Abstract*, various issues.
(b) FAOSTAT database for the 1990-1996 period.

4

Food Grain Marketing in Burkina Faso
The Challenge of Food Security

Andries Klaasse Bos, Clemens Lutz and Boubié Bassolet

Abstract

Within the general framework of structural adjustment policies, market liberalization is the major policy instrument of the Burkinabé government for improving the functioning of the food grain market. A properly functioning grain market constitutes an important asset for a food security policy as it improves food availability. However, the market mechanism does not solve the food insecurity problems of households that lack the necessary food entitlements. At the household level the threats of chronic and transitory food insecurity persist. To reduce the severity of these problems, a government policy is required. General measures to improve food production, job creation and income diversification as well as government support for initiatives taken by non-governmental organizations may reduce the chronic food problem. However, when a famine occurs, a transitory food insecurity problem threatens most households. In these cases the government has an important role to play in coordinating the timely replenishment of the deficit. Early warning and early action are needed. In Burkina Faso the early action component is unsatisfactory. A policy blueprint should be prepared that accurately answers the major strategic questions: How can the food grain deficit be balanced efficiently? How can the market be used as an instrument to distribute food? and How can the poor obtain the required entitlements?

4.1 Introduction

In recent years the food security issue in drought-prone Sub-Saharan Africa has received less attention than it did in the 1970s and 1980s, as favourable climatic conditions have resulted in satisfactory harvests. However, climatic conditions are still variable, incomes are low, the population is increasing rapidly and production systems are unsustainable. The food security of the urban and rural poor partly depends on opportunities for their household members to find ways of diversifying their income. A close look at expenditure patterns of rural households shows that production for self-sufficiency is still a major source of food consumption. Crop failures make these households food insecure if they lack a sufficient cash income to purchase the additional food grains they need. Moreover, food shortages inflate prices during the lean season, which lowers a household's purchasing power.

Since independence the issue of government intervention in food grain markets has been continuously debated in many African countries. In the 1960s and 1970s, policies focused on alleged market failures. In Burkina Faso the successive governments decided to intervene in the grain market because of market imperfections and the important role that food markets play in provisioning the population. Particularly the low-income groups in the fast growing cities and many rural households in arid regions experience a grain deficit. By the end of the 1980s, experience with these policies showed that most interventions merely replaced market failures by government failures. Budget deficits and adjustment policies forced governments to liberalize and privatize the markets. However, during the 1990s many grain markets have still been hampered by market imperfections. The experiences of the past few decades are a useful input in the debate on market policies. This debate is no longer restricted to the two extreme alternatives (market only or government only), but instead focuses on a mix of institutional regulations and market mechanisms.

This chapter concentrates on food entitlements and the functioning of the grain market. Household food security in Burkina Faso is very much dependent on food grains.[1] Our objective is to show the interrelationships between the functioning of the market and government policies to improve food security. We argue that further improvements in the grain market are necessary and that complementary instruments should be used to mitigate household food insecurity. In Burkina Faso the threat of insufficient food availability is real. As a disruption of the food supply will have major consequences for the functioning of both the rural and the urban economies, a food security policy should be part and parcel of a sustainable adjustment programme.

The chapter is structured as follows. Section 4.2 introduces some essential concepts. Sections 4.3 and 4.4 present the case under study: Burkina Faso. The annual grain balance and various food entitlements are discussed first. This is followed by a review of the grain market. Section 4.5 offers some conclusions and consequences for food policy.

4.2 Food security and food entitlements: some concepts

The food system
The food system of a country is characterized by a complex series of relationships between producers, traders and consumers. Figure 4.1 presents our model of a simplified agro-food system, based on three types of actor who transfer the surplus offered by the producer via

---

[1] The term 'food grains' corresponds with the French term 'céréales' -- the common term in the literature on francophone Africa. The two terms cover both the locally produced food grains (mainly sorghum, millet and maize) as well as the imported grains (wheat and rice).

the trader to the food consumer. The food system encompasses all interactions and the underlying strategies of each of the actors involved in the food chain. Properly functioning food markets serve both the producers at the one end and the consumers at the other end; market failures or missing markets reduce opportunities for producers, as well as food availability for consumers.

Figure 4.1 Simplified food system

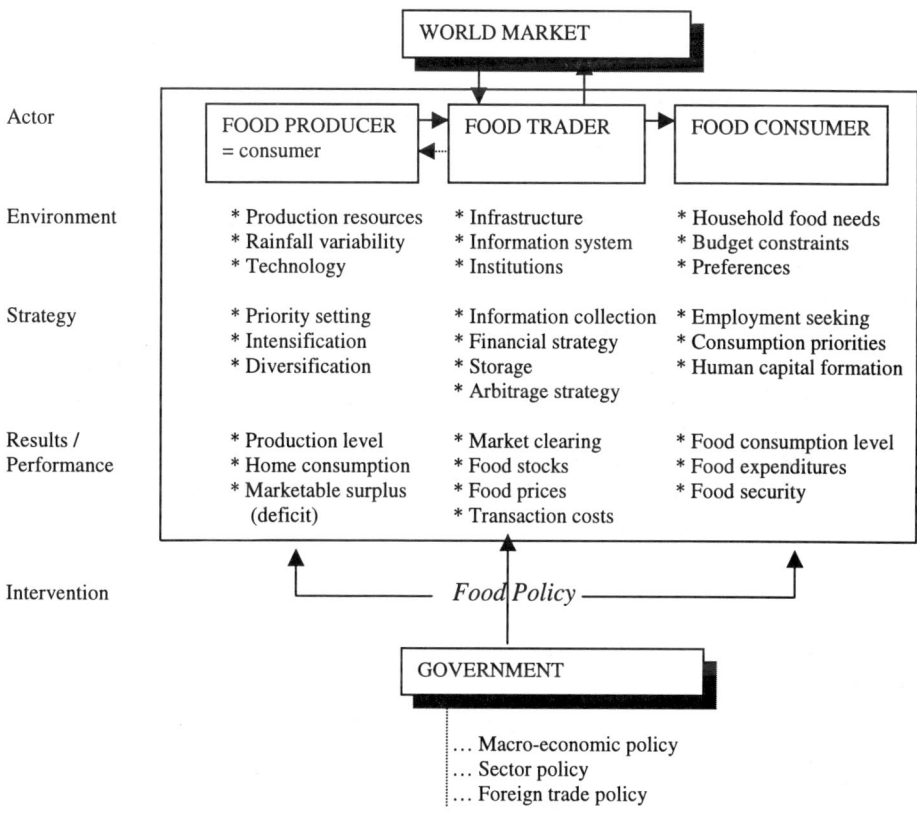

As the government is not necessarily an actor in the food system pictured above, we have placed it outside the system. However, the government can intervene at the level of each of the three types of actor. The intervention may consist of measures to encourage producers to increase food production; to improve the functioning of the food markets; or to improve the accessibility of food products to consumers. Other government policies may indirectly affect the private decision-making of any of the actors. These actions include various macroeconomic policies, e.g. external trade policies, exchange-rate policies, wage and tax policies or interest rate policies. We do not deal here with these types of indirect intervention, although their impact on the various elements of the food system should not be ignored.

We want to stress two important features of the system. First, the time patterns of food production and consumption do not coincide. In the semi-arid areas of Sub-Saharan Africa, there is only one harvest a year, while consumption is continuous. This seasonal aspect may cause large variations in seasonal stocks and substantial price fluctuations. Second, spatial arbitrage is crucial for the food system. Normally, the food chain goes from the rural producer towards the urban food consumer. In Burkina Faso the situation is more complex. Many food producers are constrained by variable seasonal agro-ecological conditions and appear to be net food buyers, particularly in structural deficit regions. This feature implies specific requirements for the functioning of trade within the food system.

Food security and the entitlements approach
During the 1970s, when serious concern arose with regard to grain imbalances in the Sahel countries, the term 'food security' was hardly used at all. It certainly did not have the connotation of food shortages at the household level which it has today. Food security had a supply-oriented meaning. It was based on a comparison between estimated national needs over the season (year) based on some FAO/WFO-developed norm of minimal caloric requirements per adult, and a national estimate of the net grain availability (after allowing for deductions due to losses and seed provision). These data provided an estimate of the national deficit. Efforts of food donors and Sahel governments focused on building up national and local grain security stocks. Thus, in most cases, public actions referred to increasing the total overall food grain supply situation at the national level.

Unfortunately, aggregated grain-availability statistics are quite uninformative about the causes of hunger. Prof. Amartya K. Sen forcefully argued: 'A food centred view tells us rather little about starvation. It does not tell us how starvation can develop even without a decline in food availability. Nor does it tell us - even when starvation is accompanied by a fall in food supply - why some groups had to starve while others could feed themselves.' (Sen, 1981, 154). He launched a radically different method for analyzing the food problem, particularly famines. He stressed the importance of the demand side, not at an aggregated level but at the household or individual level. He introduced the concept of 'exchange entitlements', by which he explained the starvation of millions of people during the famine in Bengal in 1943, a year in which total grain production had seriously fallen but was not below the level of two years earlier, when no famine occurred. The pioneering work of Sen is more important for our analysis of food security than the traditional grain balance approach.

A household has several 'entitlements' at its disposal which can be used to produce or buy goods and services. The bundle of entitlements consists of various components: income from employment, the assets owned, the food produced for home consumption, etc. If a farmer loses his crop due to some calamity like a drought, he loses entitlements. The same loss of entitlements occurs when he loses his job. The key to the explanation of the great many people starving in Bengal in 1943 was their sudden loss of exchange entitlements, mainly the loss of many jobs in certain employment categories (fishing, landless unskilled agricultural labour). The important element is that exchange entitlements 'are involved at a critical stage in the chain of causation' (ibid, 35).

The logical consequence of Sen's approach is that food security can only be analyzed at the household level. The definition as given by the World Bank report on Poverty and Hunger reads: 'Access by all people at all times to enough food for an active and healthy life' (World Bank, 1986). This nowadays widely accepted definition of food security contains three crucial elements:
- the accessibility of food resulting from exchange entitlements;
- the availability of food through market channels;
- the certainty of both accessibility and availability, at every moment and in the places where required.

Thus, food insecurity does not necessarily result, as is widely believed, from inadequate food supplies, but may also result from a lack of purchasing power.

The paradigm shift initiated by Sen has caused a lively debate on the entitlements concept, since the old food-availability idea seems to have lost much of its explanatory power. Maxwell has nicely worded the solution to the paradoxical position of food availability: 'it has been impossible since the early 1980s to speak credibly of food security as being a problem of food supply, without at least making reference to the importance of access and entitlement. In practice, it has been more usual to define food security as being first and foremost a problem of access to food, with food production at best a route to entitlement, either directly for food producers, or indirectly by driving market prices down for consumers.' (Maxwell, 1996, 157).

The World Bank's distinction between accessibility and availability helps to distinguish between chronic food insecurity and transitory food insecurity (World Bank, 1986). Chronic food insecurity is a continuously inadequate diet caused by the inability to acquire food. It affects households that persistently lack the ability either to buy food (lacking exchange entitlements according to Sen), or to produce their own. Transitory food insecurity is a temporary decline in a household's access to enough food. It results from a major shortfall in food production or household income - and in its worst form it ends in hunger. Famines are thus seen as the worst form of transitory food insecurity on a large scale. Similarly, Drèze & Sen (1989, 7) emphatically distinguish 'between chronic hunger (involving sustained nutritional deprivation on a persistent basis) and famine (involving acute starvation and a sharp increase of mortality)'. They point at important differences between policy instruments. To give one example: in the context of famine prevention the crucial need for timely intervention and the scarcity of resources often call for a calculated reliance on existing distributional mechanisms, supplemented by the logistic capability of relief agencies. Combating chronic hunger requires quite different actions, like institution building, entitlements protection, asset redistribution and provisioning in kind.

Interestingly, Drèze & Sen mention that in many countries famines have disappeared. However, chronic hunger is still widespread.

We conclude this section with three observations:

* The new terminology of exchange entitlements and food insecurity means considerable progress in the ways in which food problems can be analyzed when compared with the traditional views and food-balance approaches of the early 1970s. In particular it means a switch towards the individual or household food-security level, which depends to a large extent on the exchange entitlements that the poor have at their disposal.

* The narrow link between household food security and sources of income (exchange entitlements) implies that a person's degree of food insecurity is largely correlated with poverty. Since in low-income households food purchases constitute the largest part of total household purchases (see Table 4.2, Section 4.3), the degree of poverty together with the food price level and the price fluctuations are the main determinants of household food insecurity.

* Several authors who have studied food insecurity and hunger situations have particularly discussed the relationship between hunger and markets (Ravallion, 1987; Drèze & Sen, 1989). They have documented situations where market failures, thin markets and missing food markets have made hunger and famines more severe. Markets work badly during famines when scarcities are exacerbated by panic buying and excess hoarding. Food insecurity is aggravated by the seasonality of food production which causes food stocks to be at their lowest level during the hungry season. A comparison of the data for two consecutive years in Bangladesh demonstrates how the food security situation of households varied due to large price differences in the two years. At the same time it should be acknowledged that evidence on the Bangladesh famine also raises serious doubts about the performance of non-market food institutions and their effectiveness in the fight against hunger (Ravallion, 1987).

4.3 The grain balance and food entitlements in Burkina Faso

We begin with some national aggregated figures for annual food production, imports and food demand in Burkina Faso.

Food supply
Since the serious Sahel droughts of the early 1970s it has become customary to keep account of the annual food situation in each Sahel country and evaluate the food balance. Food donor countries have supported this because the results provide the basis for annual food-aid commitments. From these balances for Burkina Faso we learn that annual production fluctuations for food grains (sorghum, millet and maize) can be considerable (Table 4.1). Two out of twelve harvest years were extremely bad, leading to national deficits. (Increased imports and food aid partly covered these deficits; the balance was apparently met by depleting the stocks of farmers and probably also by lower consumption.)

Two successful harvests led to a large national surplus. There was a national surplus in most years. Unfortunately, total export figures from official and informal trade are not available. For our purposes it is sufficient to say that apart from the years 1985 and 1990, there has been no grain deficit.

Table 4.1 Annual grain balance in Burkina Faso (x 1000 tons)

Year	Production minus Consumption**	Imports	Food aid
1985	-581	202	n.a.
1986	-170	68	n.a.
1987	52	88	n.a.
1988	-194	126	n.a.
1989	146	126	n.a.
1990	-475	94	90
1991	277	189	44
1992	246	166	21
1993	186	149	n.a.
1994	148	104	25
1995	-69	99*	19
1996	69	94*	n.a.

Source: Direction des Statistiques Agro-Pastorales (DSAP), Burkina Faso.
* Estimates
** Computed on the basis of gross aggregate production statistics. Fifteen percent of gross production has been deducted for losses and seed use. Aggregate consumption is based on the total population with an average consumption of 190 kg per head.
n.a. = not available

The demand for food
From the 'INSD poverty study' we see that only 12.4 per cent of the farm households in Burkina Faso sold sorghum and only 10.5 per cent sold millet (INSD, 1996a, 161). Only a small part of total production is sold. Farmers consume a major part of the food produced: its average value accounts for 35 per cent of total rural household expenditure, with the highest percentage for the lowest income class (Table 4.2). Home consumption consists primarily of food grains and for the poorest income class this amounts to 70 per cent of total home consumption value (INSD, 1996a, 78).

These figures are only indicative. The 'INSD poverty study' arrives at an estimated average grain consumption of 141 kg per head (INSD, 1996b, 225). This is roughly 25 per cent below the standard of 190 kg of the official statistics of national food balances, which illustrates that the data from all poverty studies have to be interpreted carefully. For the rural deficit regions the poverty analysis lacks reliable data on a desaggregated level to reach meaningful conclusions. However, the microstudies that we shall refer to below show that, under average harvest conditions, most farmers do not produce enough to cover their annual food grain needs.

Table 4.2 Household 'expenditures' for different income classes* (in %)

Type of Expenditure	Income Class					
	I	II	III	IV	V	All Households
URBAN HOUSEHOLDS						
food purchases	31	36	39	41	34	36
food home-consumption	23	15	11	5	1	11
non-food purchases	28	29	33	40	56	37
non-food home-consumption**	19	20	18	14	9	16
total***	101	100	101	100	100	100
RURAL HOUSEHOLDS						
food purchases	20	21	22	25	27	23
food home-consumption	43	44	38	31	19	35
non-food purchases	17	18	23	32	47	27
non-food home-consumption**	21	18	16	13	7	15
total	101	99	101	100	100	100

Source: INSD, 1996a, Tableau III.7

* Household 'expenditures' include home consumption value. The data refer to the period October 1994 to January 1995.
** 98 per cent of these expenditures consist of imputed costs for housing.
*** Rounding leads to totals different from 100 per cent.

Food production, exchange entitlements and food security at the household level
It has been conventional wisdom to assume that farm households are subsistence units which produce a grain surplus. In line with this view the seasonality of food production leads to a harvest and post-harvest season of abundance during which farmers sell part of the harvest to obtain cash, to be followed by a lean season during which they consume the food stocks they have reserved. In years of drought, the available stocks will soon be depleted, and food grain shortages must be covered by food purchases. In the food policy debate concerning the semi-arid tropics policy-makers and researchers have tended to view sedentary rural households as almost exclusively dependent on their own production to ensure household food security; crop failure is therefore the only threat to their food security. Various recent research results have undermined this view and show that many farm households of different West African countries are net food buyers. Sometimes substantial quantities are involved.

Microstudies modify the picture of conventional wisdom. A study of grain marketing in five villages across three ecological zones in Burkina Faso (Ellsworth & Shapiro, 1989) shows that almost all households purchased grain. In contrast, there were significant numbers of grain sellers in only two of the villages. For the sample as a whole, about 15 per cent of the grain harvest was sold. Total grain purchases per village were considerable. The 'seasonal transaction patterns observed in the five sample villages provide some support for the conventional wisdom that African farmers sell low and buy high.' (ibid, 200). This study further shows that other transfers have elements similar to the seasonality of grain marketing: non-market grain transfers peak in the post-harvest season, with the pre-harvest season being next in importance. There is evidence of a substantial interhousehold non-market exchange of grains. This seasonal pattern of selling and buying, together with the characteristics of high self-sufficiency and net buying as explained earlier, may lead to a switch in the direction of intraregional trade flows and therefore has important consequences for the food trade.

Reardon et al. (1992) studied food security issues and compared household strategies in different agro-ecological zones of Burkina Faso. The study shows that coarse grains (sorghum, millet, maize) played a very small role in overall sales. The reason was that the marketable surplus was small in each region; no more than 8 per cent of total production for the period of 1982-85. Another important empirical finding has been that in the semi-arid tropics, a large number of farm households succeed in having enough livestock revenues and non-farm income to achieve food security. It has been called a paradox: 'despite recurrent crop failures, there is evidence that households are still able to assure their food security; even in zones where one would have expected famine, such as the Sahelian zone of Burkina.' (ibid, 265). Three-quarters of the average household income in the Sahel sample and two-thirds of the average income in the Sudan sample come from non-cropping sources (Reardon et al., 1988).

A process of income diversification may be observed in many West African regions (Reardon et al., 1992). It proves that farm households depend for their food security to a large (probably growing) extent on non-farm income sources. However, access to non-farm income sources appears to be unequal; in two out of the three zones studied non-farm incomes worsened interhousehold income distribution. The important finding is that the efforts towards income diversification and the degree of success with which household members find non-farm sources of exchange entitlements determine rural households' food security. Under difficult labour market conditions, many are unable to find such sources of additional income and suffer from chronic poverty. Consequently, malnutrition and chronic hunger prevail in their households. The food grain market is unable to serve them appropriately, unless non-farm income or cash money (e.g. transfers from migrated relatives) is available. This latter source, particularly from the large number of Burkinabè that have migrated to neighbouring countries, should not be neglected. The Burkina 'national poverty study' shows that for the lower two quintiles of the rural and urban population private transfers account for more than ten per cent of their total revenues (INSD, 1996a, 67/68). Those poor who also lack this particular social support do not have any entitlement. For them poverty alleviation can only be undertaken by the government and by non-government institutions.[2]

We conclude this section with three remarks:
* The greatest poverty at household level exists in the rural areas. Since a large share of the rural households are net buyers of basic foods, their failure to earn sufficient non-farm

---

[2] The sad story of chronic hunger can be traced through studies on poverty. Ravallion & Lipton state that in most developing countries the rural sector accounts for a substantially higher share of absolute poverty than the urban sector; a rural resident is also more likely to be poor, by almost any standards (Lipton & Ravallion, 1995).

income causes them to live below the poverty line. They are food insecure, not having continuous access to enough food for a healthy life.[3]

* Households in rural zones, having a low production potential and being drought prone, seem to have developed more and better mechanisms to cope with the threats of large-scale net food deficits than zones with better production potentials. Evidence, particularly from the Sahel zone, shows that the coping mechanisms in this area provide higher non-farm incomes than elsewhere. Therefore, no generalizations should be made with respect to the relationship between (a) the low and erratic level of food production and (b) the degree of food insecurity of the farm households in a particular zone.

* Food security of households is determined by two main factors: (a) entitlements creation within and outside the farm, and (b) an efficiently functioning food system. These factors can be influenced through the labour market and the food market of a country. However, if a famine occurs, threatening food insecurity for many households, government and other non-market institutions have to intervene. This field of public action (Drèze & Sen, 1989) is briefly discussed in the last section of this chapter.

4.4 The food grain market of Burkina Faso

Until the beginning of the reform policy in 1992, the food grain market of Burkina Faso had a dualistic character. The state represented by OFNACER, played an important role and was active as both a buyer and a seller (see below), while at the same time a large number of private traders were handling the major part of the marketable grain surpluses. Structural adjustment policies caused a change. Nowadays, private traders are playing a more important role, while OFNACER has been replaced by SONAGESS, which was given a more restricted task. Since the droughts of the 1970s the grain market has been studied many times: SEDES, CEDRAT & GOPA (1990), Déjou (1987), Sherman et al. (1987), Haughton (1986), and Lecaillon & Morrisson (1985).

The private market
The intermediaries in the market consist of a diverse set of private traders, supplemented by some farmers' organizations. Trading by farmers' organizations, like cooperatives and grain banks, was encouraged by the state. However, despite favourable policies, the market share of these organizations has been low and only a minority of them were successful (Yonli, 1997).

Most trade flows pass through a conventional marketing channel which relies heavily on regional spot markets. A distinction must be made between village, regional and urban spot markets. Each market-place ought to be cleared every market day so that no surpluses

---

[3] The country assessments of poverty that have been undertaken during the last decade, with technical and financial assistance of the World Bank, have practically without exception confirmed this fact. In a recent critical review of 23 poverty assessment reports of Sub-Saharan countries (Hanmer et al., 1996) it has been concluded that more than 75 per cent of the poor live in rural areas in all but two of the countries.

and deficits remain. This is quite a difficult task as the market is characterized by seasonal conditions and imperfect information. Depending on the regional supply and demand conditions markets can be deficit or surplus markets. In the South, the East, and especially in the Mouhoun area, most village markets are surplus markets, 'exporting' to urban centres (Table 4.3). During the hungry season most village markets in the Sahel region become deficit markets, 'importing' grain from other rural regions and transit markets. The large urban market of Bobo-Dioulasso, situated in a surplus region, is a centre for transit trade. Ouagadougou is the main consumer market, which explains the large deficits in the Centre region. The capital is provisioned by all surplus regions in the country and the Mouhoun region in particular. The highly fluctuating grain balances (Table 4.3) show the importance of an efficient market in order to bring regional balances into equilibrium.

Table 4.3 Annual grain balance per region of Burkina Faso (x 1000 tons)*

Year	Sahel	Centre	East	Mouhoun	South
1990	-164	-245	-135	62	7
1991	55	-41	-32	214	80
1992	22	-122	9	273	63
1993	-23	-128	103	215	18
1994	54	-164	44	157	58
1995	-86	-207	112	124	-11
1996	-63	-169	85	212	4

Source: Direction des Statistiques Agro-Pastorales (DSAP).
* (-) deficit, (+) surplus

Marketing channels are flexible. The shortest channel consists of farmers selling directly to consumers. When distances between producers and consumers are greater, the marketing channels become longer as well: farmers sell to local petty traders or agents, subsequently these sell to local wholesalers who provision urban deficit markets where urban wholesalers, brokers and retailers are involved in actually distributing grain. All actors provide specific services depending on the availability of capital, market information and the needs of potential clients. Most intermediaries are petty traders (retailers, small-scale wholesalers and agents) trying to earn some money for their daily needs. The number of large-scale traders is much smaller but they play a crucial role, for instance, in seasonal and regional arbitrage, as we must now discuss.

Seasonality in food production leads to a clear seasonal trading pattern. During the harvest season (October - December) consumers in rural regions are self-sufficient and the food supply is abundant: wholesale grain transactions are carried out between petty traders in the rural centres and wholesalers operating in Ouagadougou. In the post-harvest period (January - May) the collection of grain over greater distances is organized. Surplus regions in the South, East and the Mouhoun are accessible during this dry period.

During the hungry season (June-September) the opposite market situation emerges:

supply decreases and demand increases. Prices reach their highest levels. Due to the start of the rainy season many villages become inaccessible and the wholesale trade is confined to the regional centres that are linked to Ouagadougou by tarmac roads. These changing circumstances put great stress on the effectiveness of the market; thin or incomplete local markets could easily arise under such conditions with food insecurity as the result.

Most traders do not engage in storage activities. Capital is a limiting factor for the scale of their trade and, consequently, it has a high opportunity cost. A quick sequence of buying and reselling characterizes their behaviour. Credit facilities are not accessible for most traders as they do not meet the necessary conditions; they often lack collateral. The storage function is primarily carried out by farmers producing for their own consumption (this is the main source of supply, see Section 4.2). Some wealthier surplus farmers actively participate in seasonal arbitrage and sell during the hungry season (see Ellsworth et al., 1989). If they possess sufficient capital, traders may also decide to play an active role in storage.

Table 4.4 shows that local price variation during the year is limited. The coefficient of variation is below 15 per cent for most markets. This is surprising as the lean season is quite long. The harvest season is restricted to the months of October to December. An explanation may be found in the fact that most farmers stock maize primarily to guarantee their food security. During the lean season they start to sell when the new harvest is secured.

Table 4.4 Average sorghum prices in some regional market centres (Fcfa/kg)

Year	Market				
	Ouahigouya (Sahel)	Ouagadougou (Centre)	Fada (East)	Dédougou (Mouhoun)	Bobo-Dioulasso (South)
1990	76	80	66	83	98
cv	5%	8%	30%	24%	17%
1991	102	106	87	82	92
cv	2%	12%	9%	24%	21%
1992	65	84	72	64	64
cv	10%	6%	13%	22%	11%
1993	59	71	51	45	62
cv	11%	6%	14%	18%	13%
1994	59	73	52	43	55
cv	9%	8%	6%	12%	8%
1995	79	98	80	62	62
cv	16%	13%	14%	16%	13%

Source: Système d'Information du Marché (SIM).
cv = coefficient of variation (standard deviation divided by the average price)
Note: The average grain balance for the Sahel region shows a deficit, the Centre shows an important deficit, the East is more or less self-sufficient, whereas the Mouhoun shows a large surplus and the South a minor surplus.

However, price variation between the years is considerable. In 1991 a price increase followed the harvest failure in 1990. This shows the importance of a national balance policy to absorb shortfalls in production without major price changes.

We now turn to regional arbitrage. Sherman et al. (1987) reached the following conclusions about the grain markets in Burkina Faso: they seem to work quite well in urban centres and surplus regions, but less well in rural deficit regions, where transactions are more risky because markets are thin (see below) and information on local supply and demand conditions is deficient. An econometric analysis confirms the deficiencies in the market system (Bassolet & Lutz, 1999). Most price series of regional markets are not integrated with prices in Ouagadougou, indicating that serious price sluggishness exists, leading to divergent price patterns. The analysis concludes that the regional or spatial arbitrage system is deficient due to a general lack of information on regional price levels.

Food trade policy

Successive Burkinabè governments have tried to regulate trade in agricultural products through public and semi-public organizations. The goals were: improving the efficiency of the trade; making sufficient food available in the towns; protecting producers and consumers against traders making excessive profits; reducing inter-seasonal price fluctuations; and levying taxes on cash crops to finance investments.

Until 1970 state intervention in the grain market (sorghum, millet and maize) was limited to setting a minimum price for producers and a maximum price for consumers. Nevertheless, in practice the state was unable to guarantee the producer price (Lecaillon & Morrisson, 1985), which depended rather on supply and demand. Subsequently, with the drought of 1971-72, the grain trade was entrusted to local organizations (Organismes Régionaux de Développement, ORDs) and the National Grain Board (Office National de Céréales, OFNACER). OFNACER had a threefold mission: to stabilize intra-year prices, to decrease inter-year price fluctuations, and to manage a security food stock.

In order to supply OFNACER, the state granted a monopoly to the ORDs on the buying of food grains, on OFNACER's account, during the period 1974-77. The grain board OFNACER was further granted a monopoly for selling to consumers. The objectives of this policy were to reduce excessive speculation by private traders, and to facilitate the financial autonomy of the ORDs. However, the policy failed. The ORDs had neither the capital nor the experienced personnel to buy sufficient grain at harvest time (Haughton, 1986). This led to the termination of the statutory buying and selling monopoly of the ORDs and OFNACER (Filippi-Wilhelm, 1985).

From 1978 to 1981, the state accepted the dualism in the grain market. In the new situation OFNACER's objective was to obtain a sufficient share in the market (buying and selling) in order to guarantee a minimum producer price and a maximum consumer price. With the change in the political ideology and development policy in 1983, private trade was again heavily suppressed, by restrictions on inter-regional grain flows, the confiscation of stocks of traders suspected of having bought below the official price, and attempts to apply the official price in urban markets.[4]

In 1992 the government of Burkina Faso agreed to a structural adjustment programme. Pressured by the World Bank, the food policy was reformed and brought in line with the new economic development policy. These reforms included the withdrawal of the state and the liberalization of the food grain trade and food prices. The role of OFNACER in the grain trade was abolished. Prices were no longer set by regulations but determined by the market. A permanent market information system was created to enable producers, traders and consumers to reach rational decisions. SONAGESS (Société Nationale de Gestion de Stock de Sécurité alimentaire) was established to replace OFNACER and to manage a national security grain stock, to be used in case of famines.

The deregulation policy for the trade system aims on the one hand, to reduce certain marketing costs, and on the other hand to reduce price differences between deficit and surplus regions. Despite the liberalization policy, private traders still perceive local government regulations as constraints that hamper their activity. Trade policy has been changing continuously and the implementation of the regulations has been arbitrary, which makes the rules insecure and causes controls to be perceived as harassment. Traders are reluctant to visit new markets because of the risk of losses, transport delays, administrative rules and product confiscation (Déjou, 1987). Local traders on the other hand, especially those in the towns, maintain good relations with local market authorities and secretly try to influence prices (Sherman et al., 1987, the Manga case). The result is a limited transparency of the market which hampers competition.

This concise description of grain trade policies clearly reveals how difficult it is for a government to act in a fragmented market characterized by continuously changing supply and demand conditions. Moreover, government policy in Burkina Faso has inhibited the development of proper market institutions. Firstly, constantly changing regulations were a source of uncertainty and risk, especially for traders. Secondly, the arbitrary implementation of these regulations further reduced the transparency of the market.

Persistent difficulties for the private market
The failure of government interventions (discussed above) leads to the conclusion that the market should play a major role in grain distribution. However, the private market shows at least three deficiencies: imperfect information, incompleteness and 'thinness'. We discuss these in turn.

On a perfect market, ".... prices convey information from households to firms concerning what consumers want, and from firms to households about the resource costs associated with consuming each commodity" (Stiglitz, 1994, 8). The availability of proper information on prices, market regulations and seasonality, encourages potential competitors and improves the functioning of the market. However, one of the major constraints which hampers the functioning of a market is imperfect information on the opportunities offered by

---

[4] It should be noted that, in practice, the market evaded these policies. All these regulations proved to be unsuccessful: prices on the free market were dictated by the law of supply and demand, while OFNACER was kept functioning thanks to food aid, which represented 80 per cent of their total sales.

the market. Information on local supply and demand conditions is exchanged between individual traders on the basis of mutual interest (transporters also play an important role in this respect). Traders are reluctant to share their information with competitors. Due to the seasonality in production, the trade is a volatile business. Moreover, official regulations are not transparent and their implementation arbitrary. Asymmetric information between buyers and sellers may cause problems (e.g. adverse selection) which modify the nature of their transactions and, consequently, increase transaction costs (Hoff et al., 1993; Stiglitz, 1986).

In order to improve the situation, information services for the food grain markets have been established in several countries in transition (cf. FAO, 1997). In Burkina Faso, the market information system (Système d'Information du Marché céréalier, SIM) is one of the key instruments of the liberalization policy. The SIM collects data on prices and broadcasts them weekly on the radio. However, the influence of these broadcasts seems to be limited as no significant improvement in market integration can be observed (Bassolet & Lutz, 1999). On the contrary, traders neglect the information and doubt the correctness of the broadcasted prices.

Most of the commodity markets in Burkina Faso are highly incomplete. Imperfections in three related markets, providing essential services for the grain trade, significantly hamper the functioning of the food market and increase the marketing costs:

* Transport services are not always available. The small group of large-scale wholesalers have their own transport facilities, but the majority of the traders depend on public transport facilities, which are mainly oriented towards the urban centres. Rural areas are served to a limited extent and consequently the transport of commodities is less than optimal.

* Credit facilities constrain the commercial activities of traders and farmers, in particular the storage operations. The formal financial sector does not provide credit for trade activities and even if credit facilities exist, most traders and farmers lack the necessary collateral (Zeller et al., 1997).

* Finally, since a futures market does not exist, individual traders and farmers cannot hedge against price fluctuations. True, the recently opened auction (see below) offers this possibility to farmers' organizations, but its scope is still limited. The institutional structure to guarantee contract enforcement is still lacking.

Increasing urbanization and liberalization policies foster the development of market exchange. However, until recently most government policies were hostile to private trade. The ever-changing rules and the arbitrary implementation of regulations hampered the transparency of the market, which led to insecurity as to the rights of private traders and also destabilized the development of a sound institutional framework for the governance of market transactions. The actual market organization is still 'incomplete' and can be characterized as a 'young' market.

A final characteristic is the thinness of the grain market of Burkina Faso. Most farmers are highly self-sufficient with regard to grain and are only incidentally selling their surplus in the market. The grain stock is perceived as a liquid source that may be used for urgently needed household necessities. Consequently, poor farmers sell small quantities even when the quantity stored is insufficient for their household needs. The problem for the market is that most of these transactions concern small and highly variable quantities, and are scattered all over the country's territory. This fragmented structure inflates marketing costs as the quantities traded are small and the collection of grain (as its distribution by retailers) becomes a labour-intensive and thus high-cost activity. The development of a personal network of trade agents and farmers may provide traders with the necessary information on potential suppliers. However, the elaboration of such a network takes time and constitutes an entry barrier for new competitors.

In order to avoid high marketing costs, farmers may increase the number of non-market transactions and consequently aggravate the thinness of the market. Grain can be exchanged within the family and some services and goods can be paid for in kind. This exchange may be efficient if the transaction costs of trade coordinated by the market are high. Matthews (1986) formulated this problem as follows: 'Family production tends to make for high production costs because it restricts exploitation of scale economies and may create mismatches between talents and occupation. On the other hand it tends to reduce transaction costs, because if instead you have a lot of dealings with strangers you have to devote more resources to checking up on their personal characteristics and safeguarding yourself against opportunism' (see also de Janvry et al., 1991).

Alternative market institutions
We conclude this section with a brief description of two new institutions: the village grain banks and the grain auction market. Grain banks are a type of organization that may challenge the existing market structure (Saul, 1987; Yonli, 1997). They represent a communal village organization that coordinates the marketing and storage of grain. In general, grain is bought at harvest time and sold during the lean season to members of the community. The idea behind this institution is that poor farmers in rural areas have often been obliged to sell part of their production just after the harvest in order to settle debts. The same farmers then have to buy during the lean season to supplement the food deficit. Put differently, they sell low and buy high. The difference between these prices may be important for farmers in dry regions where grain has to be 'imported' from far away. Since the rural population density is low, the market is thin. As large-scale traders are not interested in provisioning these regions, supply may be lacking. Under these circumstances a farmers' organization (grain bank) may be useful; it may perform better than the market. However, until now most grain banks have failed. The objectives were too ambitious and there were serious organizational problems.

A more recent initiative is the development of a national grain auction market. The auction, which started in 1991 as an experiment, aims to facilitate the exchange between farmers' organizations, in particular grain banks. It simplifies the functioning of these banks as it provides the structure to directly link surplus and deficit banks, consequently limiting marketing costs (Yonli, 1997). Moreover, the auction may lead to a futures market as contracts can be concluded for delivery at a certain time, which could result in an effective instrument to protect farmers against price changes. However, a reliable and stable institutional environment is required to make these transactions successful.

The pervasive imperfections of private markets lead to high marketing costs and high food prices, which endanger the food security of the poor. To date, government interventions have been unsuccessful. However, government action is needed to facilitate improvements that decrease marketing costs and foster competition. The market is evolving, and the challenge is to develop market institutions that make exchanges less costly. A trade policy may facilitate this process: the market information system has to be improved, the national grain balance has to be monitored, and early action should be taken when severe shortages threaten. Finally, the implementation of the official regulations which govern the food grain trade (also with regard to West African regional imports and exports) should be unambiguous so as to improve the transparency of the market.

4.5 Market performance and food entitlements; consequences for policy

Sections 4.3 and 4.4 show the importance of the market mechanism for grain distribution in Burkina Faso. In normal years the country is more or less self-sufficient in the supply of staple food crops and a properly functioning market can provision deficit households that have sufficient purchasing power. For these target groups the food policy should focus on market imperfections; a more efficient market organization improves food security. However, households that lack the necessary entitlements are food insecure, even if the national grain balance is in equilibrium. These rural and urban poor suffer from chronic food insecurity. Market policies cannot provide them with the necessary food entitlements. To help these households, the government may decide to develop tailor-made interventions like income transfers, employment, and food-for-work programmes. Unfortunately, experience shows that the transaction costs of these programmes are high. How can the government detect those who are really food insecure and solve the problem of adverse selection? How can the administrative costs of food-for-work programmes be limited? What is the best way to prevent rent-seeking behaviour? Moreover, the government lacks the funds to establish structural programmes to reduce poverty and food insecurity. Taking into account these difficulties, it is not surprising that most governments limit their intervention to general policies that encourage job creation and the diversification of income sources. Consequently, to cover food deficits, most chronic food-insecure households have to depend on their social relationships.

Structural adjustment policies in Burkina Faso have led to a withdrawal of the state, also in the area of food provisioning. Food policy has been reduced to market liberalization and policies that reduce market imperfections: efforts have been made to make the regulations more transparent, to improve credit accessibility, to establish a market information system, to support the establishment of grain banks and the auction market. This food policy will be sufficient for normal years when no major shortfalls in production occur, but will be inadequate to cope with the serious harvest failures that Burkina Faso faces at irregular intervals. Food provisioning is now fully taken care of by private traders; SONAGESS only manages a small security stock, which is useful to settle some transitory shortfalls in supply. However, many inhabitants are facing the problem of chronic food insecurity.

The market mechanism is inefficient when famines occur. Speculation and hoarding then tend to inflate prices and reduce the purchasing power of existing exchange entitlements. At the same time, production shortfalls reduce the degree of self-sufficiency, which is a major food entitlement for rural and urban poor. Moreover, the loss of jobs due to economic decline after harvest failures implies a further loss of entitlements for many people. Consequently, a strong reduction in food production renders most of the poor food-insecure. This is a case of transitional (rather than chronic) food insecurity. The market cannot solve the problem as purchasing power is insufficient. Moreover, social relationships will not provide a solution for most households, as food insecurity will become a general phenomenon. Government action will be necessary to provide a safety net to cope with transitory food insecurity and possibly widespread famine. The action programme has to offer much more than just the channelling of food aid received from abroad. Reference should be made to the studies of Ravallion (1987) and Drèze & Sen (1989) on famines, markets and public action programmes.

With regard to food accessibility the following policies should be considered:
- income transfers and public works for vulnerable groups, and
- credit facilities for creditworthy households (Zeller et al. 1997).

With regard to food availability the following policies should be considered:
- a West African regional trade and import policy to profit from regional arbitrage opportunities
- an early warning and early response system, and
- the optimal use of food aid for the most vulnerable groups.

In the debate on food security it is regularly suggested that there is a conflict between market policy and food policy. The authors of this chapter hold the view that there is no such contradiction. The market is an important instrument in food security policies. However, it is not the panacea that the advocates of the market mechanism want us to believe. A food security policy is needed to protect vulnerable groups against potential shortages. The threat of insufficient food availability in Burkina Faso is real. A food security policy should be integrated in a sustainable adjustment programme, as major disruptions of the food supply have serious consequences for the functioning of the rural as well as the urban economies. A general lack of food entitlements provokes a collapse of the production system, which sustainable development policies aim to improve.

Food security is receiving insufficient attention in the current policies of the Burkina government. OFNACER has been liquidated and today the market allocates surpluses and deficits. SONAGESS is monitoring the national grain balance: it manages a food security stock and has established a market information system. However, these instruments are insufficient to cope with a major production shortfall. Moreover, in Burkina Faso, policy should also focus on the problem of chronic food insecurity. No active policy on food accessibility has been prepared. The new market institutions, like grain banks and auctions, are evolving too slowly. At the same time we observe that many market imperfections persist, and that a greater government determination is required to solve these problems. When food insecurity is transitory the government has an important role to play in coordinating the timely replenishment of the deficits. Early warning and early action are needed. In Burkina Faso the early action component is unsatisfactory. A policy blueprint is required to intervene efficiently while taking into account major queries like how the market deficit can be balanced, how the market can distribute the available food, and how the poor can obtain entitlements for the food they need.

References

BASSOLET, B. & C. LUTZ (1999) 'Information Service and Integration of Cereal Markets in Burkina Faso'. In *Journal of African Economies*, Vol. 8, no. 1, pp. 31-51.
DE HAAN, L., A. KLAASSE BOS & C. LUTZ (1995) 'Regional Food Trade and Policy in West Africa in Relation to Structural Adjustment'. In D. Simon, W. van Spengen, C. Dixon & A. Närman (eds.) *Structurally Adjusted Africa - Poverty, Debt and Basic Needs*. London: Pluto Press, pp. 57-76.
DEJOU, C. (1987) *Evaluation des systèmes de commercialisation des céréales dans les pays en développement: le cas du Burkina Faso*. Clermont Ferrand: Thèse de doctorat de l'Université de Clermont.
DREZE, J. & A. SEN (1989) *Hunger and Public Action*. Oxford: Clarendon Press.
EICHER, C.K. (1990) 'Africa's Food Battles'. In C.K. Eicher & J.M. Staatz (eds.) *Agricultural Development in the Third World*. Baltimore: John Hopkins University Press, pp. 503-530.
ELLSWORTH, L. & K. SHAPIRO (1989) 'Seasonality in Burkina Faso Grain Marketing: Farmer Strategies and Government Policy'. In David E. Sahn (ed.) *Seasonal Variability in Third World Agriculture. The Consequences for Food Security*. Baltimore: John Hopkins University Press, pp. 196-205.
FAO (1997) *Market Information Services, Theory and Practice*. Rome, FAO Agricultural Services, Bulletin 125.
FILIPPI-WILHELM, L. (1985) 'Traders and Marketing Boards in Upper Volta: Ten Years of State Intervention in Agricultural Marketing, 1968-78'. In K. Arhin, P. Hesp and L. van der Laan (eds.) *Marketing Boards in Tropical Africa*. London: Routledge and Kegan Paul, pp. 120-149.
HANMER, L., G. PYATT & H. WHITE (1996) *Poverty in Sub-Saharan Africa - What can we learn from the World Bank's Poverty Assesments?* The Hague: Institute of Social Studies.
HAGGBLADE, S., P. HAZELL & J. BROWN (1989) 'Farm-Nonfarm Linkages in Rural Sub-Saharan Africa'. In *World Development*, Vol. 17, no. 8, pp. 1173-1201.
HAUGHTON J. (1986) *La Réforme de la Politique Céréalière: le Burkina Faso*. Paris: Club du Sahel (OCDE/CILSS).
HOFF, K., A. BRAVERMAN & J. STIGLITZ (eds.) (1993) *The Economics of Rural Organization: Theory, Practice and Policy*. New York: Oxford University Press.
INSD (1996a) *Le Profil de Pauvreté au Burkina Faso*. Burkina Faso: Institut National de la Statistique et de la Démographie.
INSD (1996b) *Analyse des Résultats de l'Enquête Prioritaire sur les Conditions de Vie des Ménages*. Burkina Faso: Institut National de la Statistique et de la Démographie.
JANVRY, A. DE, M. FAFCHAMPS & E. SADOULET (1991) 'Peasant Household Behaviour with Missing Markets: some paradoxes explained'. In *The Economic Journal*, Vol. 101, pp. 1400-1417.
JAYNE, T.S. & S.JONES (1997) 'Food Marketing and Pricing Policy in Eastern and Southern Africa: A Survey'. In *World Development*, Vol. 25, no. 9, pp. 1505-1527.
LECAILLON, J. & C. MORRISSON (1985) *Politiques Economiques et Performances Agricoles. Le cas du Burkina Faso, 1960-1983*. Paris: OCDE.
LELE, U.(ed.) (1992) *Aid to African Agriculture: Lessons from two decades of donors' experience*. Baltimore: The Johns Hopkins University Press, World Bank.
LIPTON, M. & M. RAVALLION (1995) 'Poverty and Policy'. In *Handbook of Development Economics*, Vol. III B, chapter 41, pp. 2553-2638.

MATTHEWS, R.C.O. (1986) 'The Economics of Institutions and the Sources of Growth'. In *The Economic Journal*, pp. 903-918.
MAXWELL, D.G. (1995) 'Alternative Food Security Strategy: A Household Analysis of Urban Agriculture in Kampala'. In *World Development*, Vol. 23, no. 10, pp. 1669-1681.
MAXWELL, S. (1996) 'Food Security: a Post-Modern Perspective'. In *Food Policy*, Vol. 21, no. 2, pp. 155-170.
RAVALLION, M. (1987) *Markets and Famines*. Oxford: Clarendon Press.
REARDON, T. (1993) 'Cereals Demand in the Sahel and Potential Impacts of Regional Cereals Protection'. In *World Development*, Vol. 21, no. 1, pp. 17-35.
REARDON, T., C. DELGADO & P. MATLON (1992) 'Determinants and Effects of Income Diversification Amongst Farm Households in Burkina Faso'. In *Journal of Development Studies*, Vol. 28, no. 2, pp. 264-296.
REARDON, T. & P. MATLON (1989) 'Seasonal Food Insecurity and Vulnerability in Drought Affected Regions of Burkina Faso'. In D.E. Sahn (ed.) *Seasonal Variability in Third World Agriculture - The Consequences for Food Security*. Baltimore: Johns Hopkins University Press, pp. 118-136.
REARDON, T., P. MATLON & C. DELGADO (1988) 'Coping with Household-level Food Insecurity in Drought-affected Areas of Burkino Faso'. In *World Development*, Vol. 6, no. 9, pp. 1065-1074.
SAUL, M. (1987) 'The Organization of a West African Grain Market'. In *American Anthropologist*, Vol. 89, No. 1, pp. 74-95.
SEDES, CEDRAT SA & GOPA (1990) *Plan Céréalier du Burkina Faso*. Tome 1, Synthèse. Ouagadougou: Ministère de l'Agriculture et de l'Elevage, CILSS.
SEN, A. (1981) *Poverty and Famines - An Essay on Entitlement and Deprivation*. Oxford: Clarendon Press.
SHERMAN, J.R., K. H. SHAPIRO, & E. GILBERT (1987) *Analyse Economique de la Commercialisation des Céréales*. Tome 1. La Dynamique de la Commercialisation au Burkina Faso. CRED, Université de Michigan, IAP/Université de Winconsin.
STIGLITZ, J.E. (1994) *Wither Socialism?* Cambridge (Mass.): The MIT Press, Massachusetts.
STIGLITZ, J.E. (1986) 'The New Development Economics'. In *World Development*, Vol. 14, no. 2, pp. 257-265.
TIMMER, C.P., W.P. FALCON & S.R. PEARSON (1983) *Food Policy Analysis*. Baltimore: Johns Hopkins University Press.
WEBER, M.T., J.M. STAATZ, J.S. HOLTZMAN, F.W. CRAWFORD & R.H. BERNSTEN (1988) 'Informing Food Security Decisions in Africa: Empirical Analysis and Policy Dialogue'. In *American Journal of Agricultural Economics*, Vol. 70, no. 5, pp. 1044-1052.
WORLD BANK (1986) *Poverty and Hunger - Issues and Options for Food Security in Developing Countries*. Washington: The World Bank.
YONLI, E. (1997) *Stratégies Paysannes en Matière de Sécurité Alimentaire et de Commercialisation Céréalière: le rôle des banques de céréales dans le nord du Plateau Central du Burkina Faso*. PhD. Dissertation, University of Groningen, Netherlands.
ZELLER, M, G. SCHRIEDER, J. VON BRAUN & F. HEIDHUESS (1997) 'Rural Finance for Food Security for the Poor. Implications for research and policy'. *Food Policy Review* No. 4, IFPRI, Washington.

5

Cocoa Production and Marketing in Cameroon and Ghana
The Effects of Structural Adjustment and Liberalization

Ali de Jong and Annelet Harts-Broekhuis

Abstract

The West African countries of Ghana and Cameroon are important cocoa producers. Consequently their governments have pursued policies to control and stimulate this crop. Due to two severe economic crises, both countries were forced to implement structural adjustment programmes to reform their economies. This chapter explores the effects of the liberalization component of these programmes on cocoa production and marketing in (a) the Ashanti Region of Ghana and (b) Central Province of Cameroon. Before reform, the market situation in both Ghana and Cameroon was characterized by monopsony and the producers were forced into the role of price taker. Prices and marketing margins were fixed by the state. The liberalization measures in the two countries, and their results, differ a great deal. In Cameroon the economic reforms were implemented radically from 1989 onwards. The government stopped its intervention in cocoa collection as well as its policy of price stabilization and permitted the private sector to take charge of all marketing activities. By contrast, the restructuring of the cocoa sector in Ghana occurred gradually. Whereas reforms started to take place from 1983 onwards, the restructuring of the market system began only in the 1990s. In both countries the cocoa producers were faced with the reduction or even termination of subsidies on important inputs such as insecticides, sprayers and planting materials.

This chapter starts with an overview of the importance of the cocoa sector at the national and regional level, followed by a short review of the production circumstances at farm level. Before looking at what the country and its cocoa producers have gained from trade liberalization, considerations with respect to the role of the state are discussed. The market reforms and the changing market performance are presented separately for both countries. It is shown that the results of the reform measures are very modest in terms of production increase and producer prices. In particular in Cameroon, cocoa producers have been left completely alone and have had to face enormous uncertainties. The road to a perfect market has turned out to be a long one.

5.1 Introduction

The important role of cocoa in the national economies of Ghana and Cameroon explains why for many years after independence the governments employed all kinds of measures in order to control and stimulate the cocoa sector. This involvement, however, has come to an end or is diminishing as a result of what is generally called structural adjustment. After a period of relative prosperity and tranquillity both Ghana and Cameroon were confronted with great economic difficulties, political instability, and decreasing cocoa production. This period of unrest, culminating in a severe economic crisis, set in much earlier in Ghana (1973) than in Cameroon (1987). In Ghana the first structural adjustment measures to resolve the crisis were implemented within the framework of the Economic Recovery Program (ERP) in the period 1984-6, followed by a second ERP for the period 1987-9. In Cameroon a structural adjustment programme was implemented from 1989 onwards. For both countries part of the adjustment measures was meant to remedy the ailing agricultural export sector.

The liberalization component of the structural adjustment measures reflects the standpoint of the World Bank and the IMF that the economy should be based on autonomous producers who decide for themselves what and how to produce and market. In many African countries where the state was and sometimes still is deeply involved in the production and, even more, in the marketing of export crops, the implementation of liberalization policies means quite a break with the past. Liberalization of the important cash crop sector has met with opposition in the societies concerned. Besides, also on theoretical grounds liberalization is not always valued as an appropriate solution to the existing problems.

Structural adjustment programmes are often seen as blueprints imposed by the IMF and the World Bank. In reality large differences exist in the design and implementation of the policies. Ghana and Cameroon are countries where structural adjustment has been interpreted in different ways, especially with respect to the role of the state in export production and marketing. The adjustments undertaken in Ghana since 1984 and in Cameroon after 1989, in particular the liberalization measures, and their effects on cocoa production and marketing in both countries, are the focus of this chapter.

5.2 Cocoa in the economies of Ghana and Cameroon

After its introduction at the end of last century, cocoa production became of great importance to the economies of Ghana and Cameroon, as a source of government revenue and foreign exchange. In the areas studied, the Ashanti Region in Ghana and the Central Province in Cameroon[1] (Maps 5.1 and 5.2), cocoa is the most important export crop and an important source of revenue for rural producers.

---

[1] This study is based on (a) secondary data collected in Cameroon, Ghana and the Netherlands and (b), with respect to the regional aspects, secondary and primary data collected during fieldwork in the Ashanti Region of Ghana and Central Province of Cameroon by university students supervised by the authors. Participating students were: Nienke Boere, Marieke Hoorn, Johan Meijer, Hanneke van Mierlo and Bart

Map 5.1 The cocoa regions of Ghana

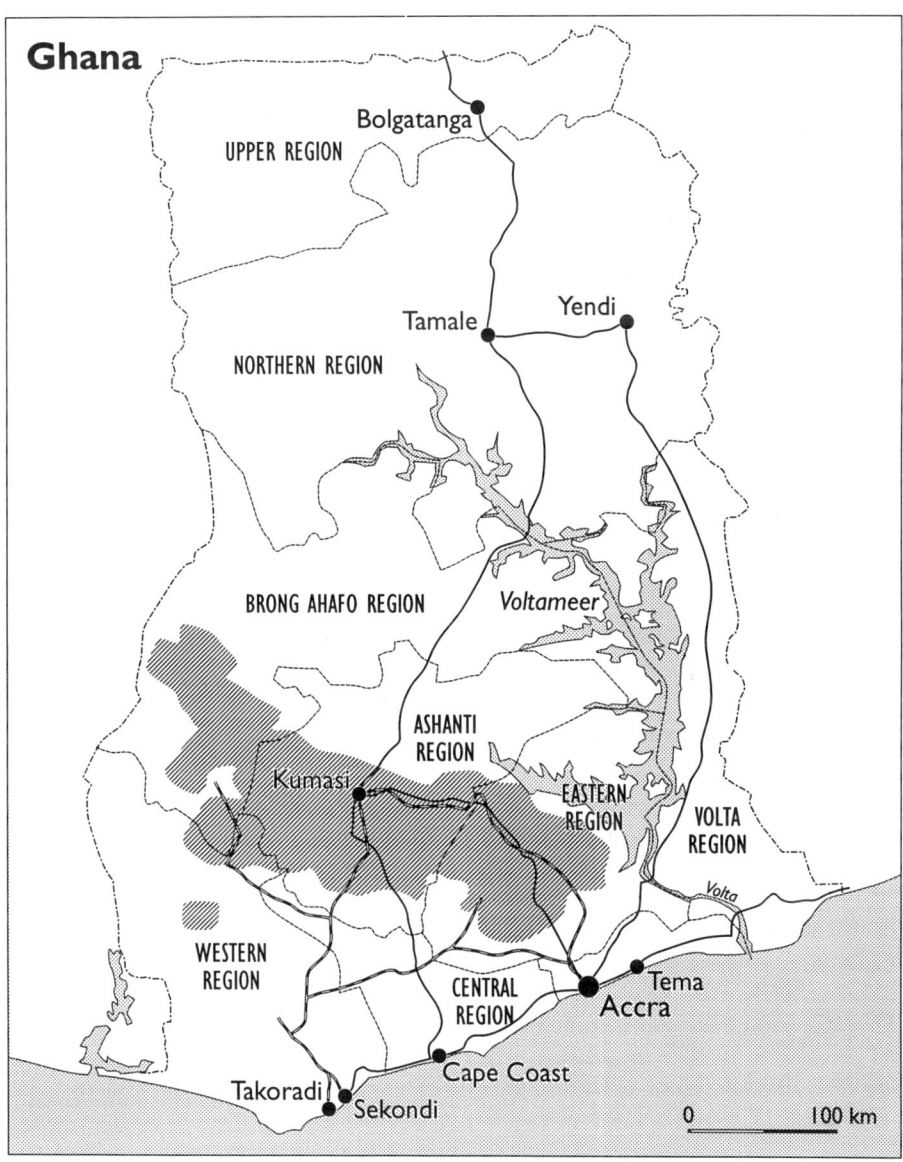

van Steenis. In Ghana as well as in Cameroon the students' fieldwork deliberately focused on the production and marketing of cocoa. In the text, references are made to the theses in which the students presented their results.

The Ashanti Region is one of the oldest cocoa producing regions of Ghana. In the 1940s it was the leading region, producing 30 per cent of all Ghana's cocoa and it held this position well into the 1980s. It is only recently that the Western Region has become the major cocoa producing region (Hoorn, 1998). The capital of the Ashanti Region is Kumasi. A number of surfaced roads from Kumasi make the hinterland accessible. Two railways link Kumasi with the ports of Tema and Takoradi, but bad maintenance of the railway and the absence of well-maintained feeder roads still hinder the efficient transport of cocoa from farm to port.

The physical conditions in the Ashanti Region with respect to temperature, rainfall and soil are ideal for cocoa production. The traditional cocoa variety has been Amelonado. In 1964 a new hybrid variety was introduced by the Ghana Cocoa Board. In a 1996 survey this hybrid variety appeared to be the most popular (Hoorn, 1998).[2] Cocoa producing households also grow other crops such as oil palm, coffee, food crops, and are sometimes engaged in non-agricultural activities.

Central Province of Cameroon is one of the oldest cocoa producing areas of the country, where smallholder cocoa production has been encouraged since French colonization. Within Central Province cocoa production shifted over time from the older districts such as Lekie to newer ones. The Mbam and Kim District in the northern part of the province, where unoccupied land is still available, is the fastest-growing cocoa region of Cameroon. The older production areas were accessible by way of feeder roads, which linked these areas to the cities and to the port of Douala, but the recently opened-up areas in the north of Central Province are less accessible because of inadequate infrastructure.

The physical conditions in Central Province are well suited to cocoa production. The secondary rain forest provides the shade under which the cocoa trees thrive. The soils in general are fertile and thick, although fragile, and rainfall is fairly reliable. Besides the traditional cocoa variety Trinitario, new hybrid varieties have been introduced. These hybrid varieties make higher demands on seedbeds and inputs (especially pesticides and fungicides), and are believed to be more drought resistant. For these reasons traditional varieties are sometimes preferred. Cocoa producing households always grow food crops alongside cocoa for their own consumption and sometimes also for the market. Some of these households engage in non-agricultural activities as well.

5.3 Cocoa production at the farm level

Cocoa production in Ghana and Cameroon takes place on small farms. Data from different sources show that farm sizes vary between 2 and 5 ha with 1 to 3 ha under cocoa.[3]

---

[2] In 1990/91 36 per cent of the total area under cocoa in Ghana was planted with hybrids, contributing 46 per cent to total production. In the same year in Cameroon only 16 per cent of the total area under cocoa was planted with hybrids, contributing 36 per cent to total production. Yields of hybrids in Cameroon were considerably higher (702 kg/ha) than in Ghana (550 kg/ha).

[3] The 1984 Cameroon agricultural census (Recensement agricole 1984, 1987) gives 1.6 ha as the mean size of a cocoa farm in Central Province, with 1.1 ha under cocoa. The MUCAM survey (Bergsma, 1996)

Map 5.2 The cocoa regions of Cameroon

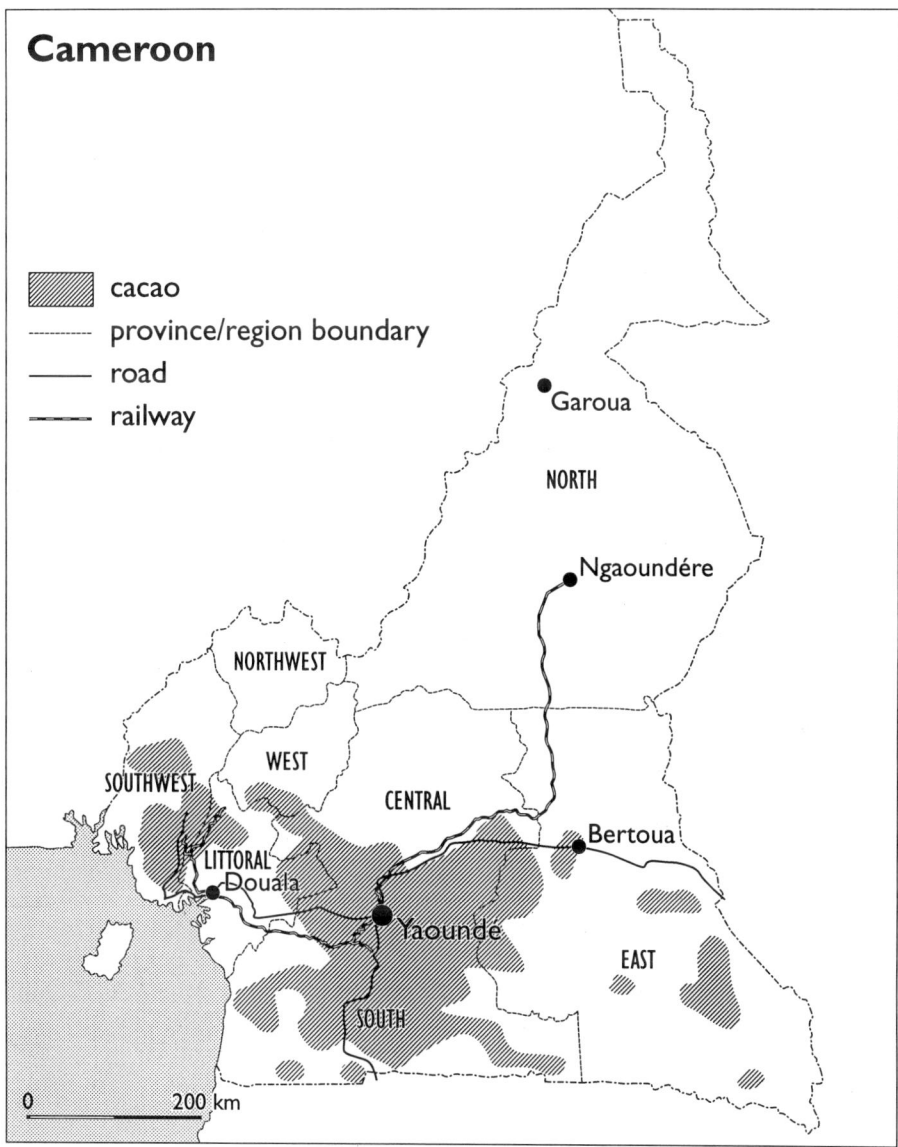

reports larger areas varying between 1.9 and 6.6 ha in the areas studied in Central Province. Alary et al. (1994) mention farm sizes between 3 and 5 ha for the Beti area (largely overlapping with Central Province). Nyanteng (1993) reports a mean size of 2.2 ha for cocoa farms in Ghana, but because many farmers have more than one 'farm', the total average holding was about 5 ha.

Cocoa production in both countries is extensive (Freud et al., 1996) and even has features of primitive gathering (Alary et al., 1994). Average yields are very low compared with most other major cocoa producing countries and vary between 200 and 400 kg/ha.[4] These low yields go hand in hand with a limited use of external farm inputs like fertilizer, pesticides and fungicides in general, the advanced age of a large number of the trees, and the cultivation of a low-yielding variety.

There are large differences in production levels among farms. Leplaideur et al. (1981) noted an extraordinary diversity in farm practices in Central Province ranging from quasi-abandonment to relatively intensive cultivation, while Weber (1977) noted that the harvest reflected the needs of the family and not the potential of the plantation. However, attitudes are changing and land is increasingly regarded as a factor of production instead of a nest egg (Ndembou, 1994).

Cocoa is not always planted for the purpose of production. Under insecure land tenure conditions perennial crops are planted to lay a claim to the land. Cocoa was often planted and maintained for this reason (Leplaideur et al., 1981). This also explains why low prices for cocoa do not lead to the cutting down of trees (which involves a lot of hard work) but result in neglect of the plantation. As a consequence production levels fall and the risk of diseases increases.

In the two regions studied it was found that generally cocoa trees grew old at the same rate as their owners (Nyanteng, 1993; Freud et al., 1996). Social organization in the Ashanti Region of Ghana and in the Pahouin society of Central Province, although very different from one another, confers a subordinate social position to youngsters. This explains the emigration of young people to urban centres or to other rural areas where land is available (Franqueville, 1987) and the relative old age of cocoa growers. But even when a plantation is inherited the new occupant does not always cut down the old trees out of respect and/or fear of the elders (Alary et al., 1996).

Due to the reasons mentioned above, the growth in cocoa production over the last hundred years was not the result of increasing yields but of the opening up of new land. The production of cocoa started in the more central areas of both countries with a relatively well-endowed infrastructure and shifted over the decades to more remote areas where unoccupied suitable land was available. In Ghana a gradual expansion took place from the Eastern Region, where cocoa production was introduced in the nineteenth century, to the neighbouring regions of Volta, Central and Ashanti, and later to the Brong Ahafo and Western regions. The major factors responsible for the decline of cocoa production in some areas and the rise of new production regions are the growing number of old farms, soil deterioration, and the spread of pests and diseases (Nyanteng, 1993).

---

4   As for Cameroon there are different estimates: 377 kg/ha (Recensement Agricole, 1984 and 1987); from 214 kg/ha to 328 kg/ha between 1960 and 1991 (Nyanteng, 1993, using the FAO production yearbook); between 100 kg/ha and 400 kg/ha with a mean between 100 kg/ha and 150 kg/ha (Alary et al., 1994). With respect to Ghana, Nyanteng (1993) provides averages between 1960 and 1991 of the same magnitude, that is, between 200 kg/ha and 330 kg/ha based on FAO production yearbooks but with a different chronology.

In Cameroon cocoa production was introduced in the South West and West as a plantation crop, became a smallholder crop in Central Province during French colonial rule and is now increasing in the South West. Within Central Province there is a new frontier in the northern district of Mbam and Kim.

This phenomenon of spreading into new areas is possible as long as new, sparsely populated and suitable land is available (and in the case of Ghana, is linked to the ports). In Ghana new, suitable land is becoming scarce. The latest region to be developed, the Western Region, has relatively poor soils and the decline of production will probably set in earlier and faster than it did in the older cocoa producing regions (Nyanteng, 1993). In Cameroon new, suitable land is still available, but it is questionable whether the rapidly vanishing equatorial forests should give way to extensive cocoa farms.

Cocoa producers have a choice as to the level of intensity of their production system, whether or not to upgrade, as well as the choice of whether to remain in cocoa production or engage in other types of production. This choice depends on the households' needs, and their resources with respect to capital and, more importantly, labour and land. This choice is also influenced by the price ratios between cocoa and other crops. As was mentioned before, an alternative to cocoa production in both study areas is the production of food crops. In both cases the presence of a large and growing market means a guaranteed outlet. With growing pressure on land and decreasing (relative) prices of cocoa, food crops have gained in importance. The maintenance costs and income of the cocoa plantation are considerations which will be compared with the investments and remuneration from other crops such as maize, oil palm, coffee, and non-agricultural activities locally or in town. The latter form an important source of income for many rural producers. The range of non-agricultural activities varies with local conditions and the distance to urban centres.

In a survey of the Ashanti Region non-agricultural activities were important in the villages near the tarred road and a gold mining site; in Central Province they were more important in the rural areas with good access to the capital than in the more remote frontier area. The contribution of non-agricultural activities to household incomes in the different research villages varied from 14 to 38 per cent (Hoorn, 1998; Bergsma, 1996).

5.4 Structural adjustment and the export crop sector

Structural adjustment always involves a reduction in the role of the state. Where agricultural marketing is concerned this implies a more limited role of the state with respect to the buying, transportation, processing and export or domestic distribution of agricultural produce, the fixing of prices and the supply of inputs. A larger role in these activities is now assumed by the private sector. At the same time structural adjustment envisages a reallocation of domestic resources to the more productive sectors, which for many African countries means the stimulation of export crops.

Although the prescriptions of the IMF and World Bank with respect to the structural adjustment measures were more or less similar, differences in implementation can be found between countries. In some countries changes were rapid, in others gradual. In some countries the state still has an important role to play, usually by way of marketing boards, in other countries marketing boards have been privatized or abolished. Within a country, structural adjustment may have been implemented differently for various crops.

Since structural adjustment became generally accepted and incorporated into national policy, the effects have been evaluated extensively (Ministry of Foreign Affairs, 1990; Duncan & Howell, 1992; Courade, 1994) and many criticisms have led to readjustments. The World Bank, being one of the main instigators of structural adjustment policies, and for that reason often accused of forcing the state to withdraw, takes the stand that the division of responsibilities between the state and the private sector should be a matter of pragmatism rather than a dogmatic choice for one or the other (World Bank, 1989). According to the World Bank the discussion is not solely about the division of responsibilities between the state and the private sector but also about the division between central government and local authorities. Empowerment of local people by stimulating grassroots organizations, notably farmers' cooperatives, is one of the options. In all circumstances the World Bank has insisted that the state create a favourable economic environment.

Many countries in Africa inherited a state system from the colonial period which was characterized by strong intervention in the agricultural export sector. Taxation of exports was, and often still is, a major source of state revenue. In Ghana the taxation of the cocoa sector was the major source of foreign-exchange revenue for a long time (Pearce, 1992; Nyanteng, 1993). To give up such an important source of revenue is clearly not the most attractive option for a government.

Economic arguments for state intervention in the marketing of agricultural produce (including export crops) in Africa were manifold: the scarcity of economic factors such as capital and entrepreneurship, the profit orientation of the traders at the expense of the farmers (Manu, 1992), the use of illegal practices by traders like cheating about weight and grade, and smuggling. Political arguments placed the state in the role of a development agent which (a) intervened in pricing (by fixing prices at the different stages of the marketing process and by fixing pan-territorial prices) in order to stimulate certain activities, certain crops, certain regions, or (b) protected the producers of export crops against the volatile world market prices by way of a stabilization fund or a buffer stock (Nzekio, 1973). Margins between the prices at the farm level and those at the port could be employed by the state not only for the stabilization of producer prices, but also for productive investments, and social and physical infrastructure.

Has the argument for state intervention been proved wrong after so many years of practice? Or did circumstances change so much that another framework for marketing was needed? In the past entrepreneurship was indeed lacking. The supervision of farmers by the marketing boards did not, unfortunately, contribute to the development of an enterprising and assertive population of farmers.

Private traders and producers have conflicting interests with respect to producer prices and prices for inputs. Nowadays producers are better educated and more able to avoid being cheated. Organization, on a voluntary basis, is still seen as a solution to counteract the influence of private traders. In regions where several traders are competing with each other, producers can demand better prices. In peripheral regions or in regions with a low production capacity, the organization of producers is more important. Traders and producers are not only opponents, they also have a common interest in stable and high production. Properly functioning institutions (e.g. chambers of commerce, local administration of justice) may contribute to an environment of trust and cooperation.

With respect to the arguments which concern the role of the government as a development agent, in the period leading up to the crises in the two countries the governments did not play this role to a satisfactory degree *vis-à-vis* the producers whose profits were skimmed off by low producer prices and large profits for the marketing boards. Production growth was more inhibited than it was stimulated. However, the argument that state intervention protected farmers from fluctuating world market prices merits more attention. World market prices for many tropical products still fluctuate as much as before. Without a stabilization fund these fluctuations cause huge problems for producers who depend on the sale of these products for a large part of their cash revenues, which is the case with many cocoa producers in the Ashanti Region of Ghana and Central Province in Cameroon. As Nzekio (1973) explains, the effectiveness of price stabilization by the state can be evaluated by the type of trade-off between (a) cocoa prices and cocoa price variation acceptable to producers, and (b) the benefits producers indirectly derive from the money deducted from their cocoa sales. In his study of the Cameroonian stabilization fund in the 1960s Nzekio found useful spending in the areas of cocoa disease control, research and extension, quality incentives and agricultural credit. He concluded that cocoa producers have undoubtedly benefited from these programmes and wondered if cocoa producers themselves would have been able, even if properly organized, to achieve the same results. This conclusion is important, but is only correct if funds are well managed and redirected to the cocoa sector. The problems of many marketing boards have been growing bureaucracy, mismanagement and inefficient functioning and the use of the stabilization funds outside the cocoa sector and even outside the agricultural sector, sometimes to line personal pockets. This has seriously damaged their credibility.

In most African countries the state has a record of compelling producers to form cooperatives in order to collect the local produce for the marketing board and to distribute farm inputs supplied by the board. Political control over the farmers probably was at least as important an objective as rural development. Different forms of cooperatives were tried, but many did not survive due to a lack of enthusiasm on the part of the farmers, a lack of organizational traditions or capacities and because of fraud. A characteristic feature of the era of structural adjustment has been the renewed interest in cooperatives. Again the official argument for cooperation is the participation of rural people in the economic development of the countryside (Penn & Ngenge, 1993). The cooperatives nowadays, however, are seen by the World Bank as true farmers' organizations and as a step towards empowering local people (World Bank, 1989).

The main conclusion of this short overview is that the production environment in both countries did not change in such a way as to justify the need for a radical change in rural economic policies. Did the arguments for state intervention prove wrong? Some arguments are false or misleading, but others still seem worthwhile. This does not mean that the way state intervention was realized was correct. But if that was the main problem, the new policies of market-led growth cannot be expected to offer a solution to farmers' problems. The advantages and problems of a market-led export crop sector based on small-scale farmers are examined below by comparing the situation in Ghana and in Cameroon, the former as an example of gradually changing practices, the latter as one of radically implemented policies.

5.5 Market reforms and changing market performance in Cameroon

After independence and up to the 1990s the marketing of cocoa in Cameroon was dominated by the activities of a state marketing board. The Ministry of Commerce and Industry was responsible for the internal and external marketing of cash crops and quality control. It operated through the National Produce Marketing Board (NPMB/ONCPB: *Office National de Commercialisation des Produits de Base*). The organization of the cocoa trade, however, differed from region to region.[5] For the purchase of cocoa in Central Province (part of francophone Cameroon) the NPMB/ONCPB cooperated with the Cocoa Development Agency (SODECAO), a semi-autonomous agency which was entrusted with rural development in designated areas by the Ministry of Agriculture. Apart from cooperation with the NPMB/ONCPB in the field of cocoa marketing and quality control, the SODECAO also developed programmes to stimulate and improve cocoa production through the supply of inputs, the maintenance of roads and the organization of cooperatives. During the period 1984-1989 it tried to create a system of marketing cooperatives and centres to collect cocoa at the village level. Except for the Lekie District, where five marketing cooperatives were active, other departments had one marketing cooperative each (SOCOODER), comprising nearly 2,000 village cooperative groups with about 50 members (150 in Lekie) in each group. Theoretically, cooperatives had local monopolies on cocoa buying and transport in their areas of operation. Exporters who bought from cooperatives and provided transportation to the port were allocated quotas and specific buying areas. In practice they also bought directly from farmers and therefore both competed and collaborated with the cooperatives (World Bank, 1988).

From the above, it can be seen that in the period before the restructuring of the marketing system, the market situation in Cameroon was characterized by monopsony, meaning that in general (with the exception of some parts of anglophone Cameroon) there was one official buyer in the market and the producers were forced into the role of price taker. Prices and margins were fixed by the state.

The legal framework for this situation changed drastically in 1989 as the Cameroonian government stopped its intervention in cocoa collection as well as its policy of price stabilization. It permitted the private sector progressively to take charge of the internal and

---

5   For the purchase of crops in anglophone Cameroon the NPMB/ONCPB made use of so-called Licensed Buying Agents (LBAs). These LBAs consisted of cooperative societies and private LBAs which, with some exceptions, were granted a buying monopoly in a certain region (Oosterlee, 1988).

external marketing of export crops. Market monopolies granted to certain exporters in certain regions were eliminated on a case-by-case basis.

The drastic changes in the market structure coincided with the collapse of the NPMB/ONCPB. This collapse resulted in the farmers not being paid in 1988-89 because the stabilization fund had run out of money (Courade et al., 1991; Courade & Alary, 1994). In the second half of 1991 the NPMB/ONCPB was replaced by a new supervisory body, the ONCC (*Office National du Cacao et du Café*). At the same time the development agency SODECAO had to transfer its tasks with respect to marketing assistance, the supply of inputs, the fight against diseases and pests, and the supply of credit, to existing and new farmers' organizations. The ONCC was given the following tasks: to supervise the marketing process, to fix a recommended producer price for cocoa and robusta coffee and to take care of quality control. Initially the government tried to influence the producer price by introducing a system of floor prices and intended to set up a system to share the surplus among producers, the government and the stabilization fund in years in which the sale price would be higher than the cost price, indicating that it hoped to continue with price stabilization in one form or another. In 1996, however, this policy was abandoned. Besides the ONCC another institution, the CICC (*Conseil Interprofessionnel des Cafés et Cacao*) was set up to organize all the actors in the market and to contribute to the professional conduct of the internal and export trade. The exporters, the manufacturers and the buyers each have their own division within the CICC, but the farmers are excluded although initially it was planned that they should have their own division as well. However, despite all good intentions this new organization has not yet had much impact.

The disengagement of the Cameroonian state meant that the organization of the marketing chain was left fully in the hands of the private sector and that price formation was left to market forces. The intention behind the market liberalization and the new institutional framework was to offer the producers the possibility of marketing their own cocoa in order to free themselves from the old system and its supposed disadvantages.

In the first few years after the liberalization of the market the number of buyers increased, but the liberalization of the internal cocoa trade also gave rise to many negative developments (Courade & Alary, 1994; SOCA'2, 1994) as summarized below.
- Lack of financial means (credit possibilities) hindered the participation of national companies in the early 1990s and resulted in an increasing number of foreign buyers on the Cameroonian markets. Courade and Alary (1994) state that 62 per cent of the farmers sold their cocoa to foreign traders in the first years after liberalization.
- In time the number of local buyers, however, increased. Generally these local buyers do not possess substantial working capital and as a result, despite increasing competition, they are unable to pay the farmers high prices. The buyer mentions his price and the farmer can accept it or reject it. In villages where more buyers visit, the farmer has the option of waiting for the arrival of a buyer offering higher prices. In the more remote villages the farmers often lack this choice. As a result the average prices paid to farmers in the more isolated villages of Mbam/Kim District were 5 (1994/95 campaign) and 3 per cent (1995/96 campaign) lower than in Lekie District (Van Steenis, 1998).

- Farmers who are in need of cash tend to sell their harvest in advance at very low prices, resulting in the return of a system of clientage and brokerage. The buyers in these cases are often unauthorized traders or richer farmers. Up to 40 per cent of the farmers were involved in these practices (Courade & Alary, 1994).
- The amount of cocoa (or coffee) per transaction diminished as a result of the farmers' wish to spread risk (secure payment) or to obtain other benefits such as access to inputs. For this reason farmers chose to sell (part of) their harvest to different buyers.
- Many cooperatives were unable to continue their activities because they had to compete with the private sector without the services formerly provided by the SODECAO such as input supply, on-farm collection, and technical and financial assistance. For this reason farmers' organizations in Central Province were more severely hit by liberalization than corresponding organizations in the western parts of the country (SOCA'2, 1994).
- With the collapse of the NPMB/ONCPB the quality control of cocoa at the organized periodic markets disappeared (Losch et al., 1992). Many new cocoa buyers and traders do not distinguish quality grades, pay one single price and mix the cocoa they buy (Van Steenis, 1998). Due to the improper handling of the cocoa during the marketing process and insufficient quality control, the grade of Cameroonian export cocoa dropped.

In 1996 and 1997 large quantities of cocoa (up to 30,000 tons) exported from Cameroon were classified *hors standard* (below export quality), as a result of which the good reputation of Cameroonian cocoa was severely damaged (Fotso Tchamekwan, 1997; CICC, Cacao-Café, Bulletin d'Information du Conseil Interprofessionel du Cacao et du Café, October 1996 and May 1997). The lack of professionalism among buyers was blamed for this shocking incident: they failed in many fields such as quality control, storage facilities, packing and transport. But the ONCC was also blamed for the catastrophe because it was responsible for the issue of trader permits and quality control.

5.6 Market reforms and changing market performance in Ghana

The conditions of the cocoa sector in Ghana before liberalization were quite similar to those in the region supervised by the SODECAO in Cameroon, with one big exception: in Ghana all policy measures and activities in the cocoa sector were coordinated by a single organization, the Ghana Cocoa Board (Cocobod), while in Cameroon the responsibilities were divided among several ministries and their agencies. The various divisions of the Ghana Cocoa Board were responsible for matters such as extension services, agricultural research, inputs supply, collection and quality control, price setting and trade. The internal buying arrangements, however, changed from time to time from monopsony to multiple buying. During the years 1977-1993 the Produce Buying Company (PBC) – one of the subsidiaries of the Cocoa Board – was the sole buyer of cocoa and operated from village-based collecting points. Each cocoa growing village had a PBC shed where cocoa could be sold, so over 4,000 buying centres had to be served (Boahene, 1995). After collection the cocoa was stored in regional warehouses and its quality graded by the Quality Control Division before it was transported by truck to the ports of Tema and Takoradi. As in

Cameroon three quality grades are distinguished, but only first-grade and second-grade cocoa are accepted for export.

In 1993 the Ghanaian government introduced competition in the internal cocoa market by licensing some private firms to buy cocoa alongside the Produce Buying Company. This meant a first step in the market liberalization process, but it was a minor step only because the Ghanaian state still exercised a strong influence on the cocoa market by setting the price the Cocoa Marketing Company (CMC) offered to private firms and the minimum price which these firms – like the PBC buyers – had to pay to cocoa farmers. The resulting profit margin was negotiated every year between the Cocoa Board and the Licensed Buying Companies. It increased in the first years after this system was introduced from 14 to 18 per cent (Hoorn, 1998).

The presence in the market of private firms alongside the PBC licensed buyers was expected to increase competition and as a consequence to lead to more efficiency in the market sector. Each private firm was obliged to set up cocoa buying points in at least three out of the six cocoa regions. The line of reasoning behind this policy was that in order to remain in business the PBC had to reduce its operational costs, while private firms through a higher degree of efficiency could increase their profits. It was assumed that part of this higher revenue would be passed on to the farmers because the PBC was expected to defend its market share and the newly licensed companies would extend theirs.

In Ghana the extent of the restructuring of the cocoa market system is as yet limited. Exports are still controlled by the government. Competition was introduced in the upstream segments of the marketing chain in order to improve market efficiency and effectiveness. One of the reasons why the Ghanaian government wants to continue its intervention is to safeguard the high quality of the country's cocoa.

In the first four years after competition was reintroduced the number of private firms grew slowly. Newcomers to the cocoa market have to obtain a permit from the Cocoa Board. The Board requires proof of creditworthiness (issued by a bank) as a guarantee that the new buyer is able to make sufficient investments. In 1993 five companies were licensed alongside the PBC to buy cocoa; most of them were existing firms trading in other products such as agrochemicals, cashew nuts and spices. The next year three new companies were added to the list and the same number again in 1996, making a total of 12 fully licensed companies. The market share these firms have won is still modest, but it did increase in the Ashanti Region between 1993 and 1996 as Table 5.1 illustrates. The PBC still accounts for more than three-quarters of all purchases in this region, a situation which is paralleled on the national market (Nyanteng, 1995). The next major buyer's share is less than ten per cent, and that of the third only three per cent. Per village, however, these percentages and the number and names of the operating buying companies vary substantially. New firms enter the fray but some of them are absent when the next buying season comes along. There are villages where besides the PBC no or only one other buyer operates, but there are also villages where four or five different buyers try to win a market share. Breaking up the established PBC-buying network and winning the farmers over have turned out to be difficult.

Table 5.1 Cocoa bought by PBC and other LBCs in the Ashanti Region in percentages

	1993/1994 Major season	1994 Minor season	1995/1996 Major season	1996 Minor season
PBC	84	81	78	76
Cashpro	7	16	13	8
Kuapa Kokoo	3	3	4	7
Others	6	1	6	10
Total	100	100	100	100
(tonnes)	(42,677)	(4,594)	(67,097)	(9,093)

Source: Hoorn, 1998.

Nyanteng (1995) mentions a range of factors which constrain new buyers from enlarging their market share, such as lack of finance, knowledge, facilities and infrastructure and also the advantages old companies hold over new ones in the market. The importance of this last-mentioned factor was confirmed by Hoorn's research. In her three research villages most farmers stuck to the PBC for reasons such as: "PBC is the oldest and most familiar company"; "PBC is controlled by the government"; "Unfamiliarity with new companies". Many farmers are still very suspicious of new buying companies and only want to sell to them if clear benefits are to be gained. An important incentive was prompt cash payment; a reason which turned out to be more important than higher prices or extra bonuses. This implies that new firms have to have access to sufficient capital during the harvest season to compete with the PBC on an equal footing and explains why existing trade companies have an advantage over newcomers. In addition to the financial aspect, lack of knowledge among the producers plays a role. The farmers' answers showed a misunderstanding of the new market situation.

Four years of competition show little progress towards the creation of a perfect market. In most villages farmers can sell their cocoa to only one or two buyers. However, the higher the production volume and the better the accessibility of the village, the more buyers are present. Remote locations in low production areas are less popular among the buying companies. Considering the investments these companies have to make, such as the building of sheds, the training of local employees who are responsible for the local trade, providing equipment for the local centres in the form of bags and scales, and the transport of the cocoa to the port, it is understandable that companies start their activities in regions with the lowest risks and costs, i.e. in regions with sufficient production and good transport linkages.

5.7 The consequences of liberalization for the cocoa producers

Cocoa is a commodity with highly fluctuating world prices. Changing production conditions in the different production regions and price speculation impact on cocoa prices.

Overproduction at the global level poses an even bigger problem in the long term. As far as the regions under study are concerned, these problems were acute from 1984 to 1992 with the fall in international cocoa prices (Table 5.2).

For many years the Cameroonian state fixed the cocoa buying price, the marketing margins and the export tax. In addition the government pursued a policy of heavy taxation on export crops. As a result cocoa farmers received on average only 52 per cent of the FOB price minus internal marketing costs in the period 1970-1985. Cocoa producer prices declined in real terms in all but one year after 1980 (World Bank, 1988). After the fall of the world market price the guaranteed producer price was kept above the world market price artificially. However, the under-financed stabilization fund soon became empty. As part of the SAP (and following the collapse of the NPMB/ONCPB) the cocoa price was lowered in 1989 from CFA franc 420 per kilogramme to CFA franc 250. The price reached rock bottom in the 1992/93 season when the farmers received CFA franc 200 (in Central Province even CFA franc 170 was recorded). After the 50 per cent devaluation of the CFA franc in January 1994 better producer prices were realized, as is illustrated in Table 5.2.

Table 5.2 Producer and FOB cocoa prices in Ghana and Cameroon, compared to world market prices, 1980-1996

Year	World price US$ (1980 = 100)	Ghana producer price		Cameroon producer price	
		cedi/kg	% of FOB price	fcfa/kg	% of FOB price
1980	100	4	67	290	58
1981	80	12	24	300	75
1982	76	12	29	310	70
1983	81	20	34	330	67
1984	92	30	28	370	56
1985	87	56	27	410	50
1986	79	85	27	420	52
1987	77	150	35	420	69
1988	61	165	40	420	82
1989	48	174	42	420	78
1990	49	224	46	250	64
1991	46	251	49	220	64
1992	42	258	42	200	59
1993	43	308	36	300	-
1994	54	700	53	495	-
1995	56	840	31	340	51
1996	62	1 200	44	425	65

Sources: EIU Country Profile Ghana, 1997-98; EIU Country Profile Cameroon, CAR, Chad, 1997-98.

As a consequence of the market reforms the cocoa producers in the SODECAO region faced enormous changes and were in fact left to fend for themselves. In the 1990s they had to contend with highly fluctuating cocoa prices, increasing prices for inputs, uncertainties concerning their income, and they had to learn to deal with private traders for their inputs and the selling of their produce. The possibilities of obtaining credit were reduced severely.

Feeder roads and storage facilities were no longer maintained. Part of the higher revenue from better cocoa prices after the devaluation in 1994 was indeed immediately spent on more expensive inputs. Prices of all kinds of basic needs increased at the same time. However, it cannot be denied that cocoa producers profited from the devaluation together with higher international cocoa prices in 1994, 1995 and 1996 and that their situation improved with respect to other population groups in Cameroon (urban groups especially).

In Ghana the economic restructuring of the cocoa sector was less radical than in Cameroon. It was and still is the Cocoa Board which, to a high degree, determines the producer price of cocoa. In the past any quantity of the highest two grades offered was bought and all over Ghana producers received the same price. Until the early 1980s the farmers were paid a fraction of the world market price, usually less than half of it. As a result much cocoa was smuggled to neighbouring countries where prices were considerably higher (Gibbon, 1992; Boahene, 1995). In the SAP framework the cocoa prices were readjusted in order to revitalize the cocoa sector. The Cocoa Board's marketing margins of about 37 per cent (reportedly the highest in the world) had to be lowered to the world average level of about 15 per cent in 1990 (Pearce, 1992). As a result the producer price of cocoa in Ghana rose against a steady decline in world market cocoa prices after the mid 1980s (Table 5.2). But despite these rising producer prices the income of cocoa farmers did not improve as much as did both urban incomes and wage incomes in rural areas; between 1987 and 1993 cocoa prices even declined in real terms (Gibbon, 1992).

From 1993 onwards, new firms have been allowed to buy cocoa from farmers, but the state still sets a minimum price. The internal cocoa market therefore is not yet a real 'free' market and sufficient (perfect) competition has yet to be attained. With one exception all new firms paid floor prices to the farmers (Hoorn, 1998). The exception was the Kuapa Kokoo, an LBC that differs from most other new buying companies in the sense that it operates on a cooperative basis and has managed to acquire foreign assistance. The Kuapa Kokoo consists of farmers' associations which sell their own cocoa. The company receives financial support from a Dutch semi-government organization SNV, a Dutch NGO Max Havelaar and a British organization TWIN. Due to this support the Kuapa Kokoo has been able to pay a margin of 500 cedis per bag and an extra bonus (of 700 cedis per bag). In comparison with the floor price of 75,000 cedis per bag this margin is modest. However, the fact that the number of participating associations increased from 57 to over 80 during the 1996/97 season indicates that this price difference was attractive to farmers.

The view that low producer prices were responsible for falling cocoa production (Herbst, 1993) and the shift to food crops and other sources of income, is generally accepted. It was confirmed by the upsurge in cocoa production from 1988 onwards, see Table 5.3, when cocoa trees planted after the increase of the official producer price in 1982 began production (Jacobeit, 1991).

Other measures which supported the price policy were a massive investment in infrastructure and rehabilitation, a devaluation of the overvalued currency, a reorganization of the marketing board and payment in cheques which producers could cash at all banks (Jacobeit, 1991). Counteracting these supporting measures was the reduction of subsidies on fertilizers, insecticides, sprayers and planting materials. Finally, local farmers' organizations have recently (1995/96) been given more freedom with respect to the purchase of inputs and the selling of cocoa.

Table 5.3 Cocoa production in Ghana and Cameroon, 1989 - 1997

Year	Cameroon			Ghana		
	Production in 1000 MT	Area harvested in 1000 ha	Yield in kg/ha	Production in 1000 MT	Area harvested in 1000 ha	Yield in kg/ha
1982	105	440	238	179	1 100	162
1983	90	425	209	160	1 000	160
1984	120	420	286	175	1 100	159
1985	119	420	283	219	1 000	219
1986	123	450	274	226	1 200	189
1987	131	450	291	188	1 200	157
1988	124	452	275	296	900	329
1989	126	420	299	300	900	333
1990	122	360	339	284	1 000	284
1991	105	350	300	243	1 000	243
1992	90	340	265	312	1 000	312
1993	101	340	284	240	1 000	240
1994	109	350	308	309	1 100	281
1995	137	360	380	400	950	425
1996	126	360	349	340	800	403
1997	125	360	347	370	850	435

Source: FAO Production Yearbooks 1985-1997.

Although structural adjustment and liberalization in Ghana had a positive reputation, particularly in the first few years, in Cameroon it was criticized almost unanimously. Even when the 50 per cent devaluation of the currency in 1994[6] raised their incomes, farmers were hesitant because they knew that there was no certainty of sustained price levels. However, the uncertain prices were not the main complaint of the cocoa producers in Central Province. They were very dissatisfied with being abandoned by an organization, the SODECAO, which had been set up and had functioned using their money. The whole structure collapsed rapidly from 1991 onwards, extension officers and monitors were dismissed, buildings and machinery were neglected. The fact that fertilizer, insecticides and fungicides were no longer distributed by the SODECAO may have had harmful consequences for the production of cocoa in the long run: the use of these inputs in general has diminished and sometimes they have been replaced by products of unreliable quality and even toxic ones (Nzegang, 1997).

The fact that both in Ghana and Cameroon cocoa is mainly cultivated by smallholders implies that the supply side of the market is made up of many sellers all of whom are offering small quantities. By combining forces in selling, cooperatives may contribute to a more

---

[6] Cameroon is a member of the CFA franc zone which comprises 16 francophone countries. The CFA franc was linked to the French franc at a ratio of 50:1, which changed to a ratio of 100:1 with the devaluation in January 1994.

efficient trade. At the same time the demand side has to consist of several buying firms to guarantee a competitive market. As we have seen, the number of buyers increased slowly in Ghana and substantially in Cameroon. Which changes occurred on the supply side? In Ghana collaboration among producers is still in its infancy, but in Cameroon, even before liberalization, it was suggested that farmers – in order to stand up to private traders – should organize themselves in cooperatives. Before its total retreat the SODECAO tried, in cooperation with the World Bank, to stimulate farmers to combine their forces in order to fill the vacuum left by the SODECAO with respect to the improvement of production, the purchase of inputs, the sale of produce and the chances of obtaining credit. One of the supporting institutions created in 1991 was the FIMAC *(Financements d'Investissements de Micro-Réalisations Agricoles et Communeautaires)* which has been active in assisting formal farmers' groups (for example the GICs, *Groupes d'Initiative Commune* and the GIEs, *Groupes d'Intérêts Economiques*) with credit (Boere & Van Mierlo, 1996). The number of farmers organized in formal groups is small, albeit growing. In 1993/94 19 per cent of the cocoa producers in Central Province were members of a *groupement*, but only half of them sold (part of their) cocoa together, i.e. 423 of the 904 *groupements* (SODECAO, 1994). Research conducted by Van Steenis (1998) and Meijer (1998) shows large differences, with respect to the *groupements* in three villages under study. In one of the villages the younger population headed by a dynamic village chief was much more organized and managed to obtain better prices from the traders compared with a more peripheral village whose chief was older.

The administration admitted grassroots organizations in its new 1990 law on organizations, thus revoking the law of 1967 which forbade all traditional organizations and allowed only state-controlled ones. Other laws followed in 1991 and 1992, differentiating between types of groupings. Various NGOs support these local organizations, among which SAILD is a very influential one (personal communication from B. Njonga, general secretary of SAILD *(Service d'Appui aux Initiatives de Développement)*.

Although most farmers see the advantages of cooperation it is not always easy for them to put it into practice because in the culture of, for instance, the Beti people, cooperation in larger contexts is a strange phenomenon. Many groups are formed but do not function or break up rapidly. Besides, past experiences with state-imposed cooperative organizations make people wary of cooperation.

5.8 Conclusions

Structural adjustment measures in Ghana and Cameroon have had significant consequences for the production and marketing of cocoa. With respect to production, the most important result seems to be the recovery of cocoa production levels. Higher production in both countries was a reaction to the higher price levels of cocoa, in Ghana the consequence of a changed price policy, in Cameroon the consequence of higher world market prices. However, success should not be overstated.

In Cameroon the production increase is the result of (a) more intensive harvesting and working on existing plantations, and (b) the opening up of new areas suitable for cocoa. New land is still available, and this land is (still) relatively fertile. For these reasons yields in this frontier area are relatively high and so are family incomes from cocoa production. The land use system, however, is labour and capital extensive and is not really different from the system in the older areas. Structural adjustment measures did not change this. Research has demonstrated that the farmers in the various areas apply the same low quantities of pesticides and fertilizer as before, or even less because of the high (no longer subsidized) prices of these inputs since liberalization.

In Ghana production began to increase impressively in 1988 and has fluctuated from then on at around the levels of the late 1970s, but is still much lower than in the 1960s and early 1970s. This production increase was caused by deliberate efforts by the national government to stimulate the cocoa sector: new plantations in the early 1980s, a massive investment in infrastructure, a devaluation of the overvalued currency and better payment practices for the producers. The provision of inputs did not really change until recently, but subsidies were reduced, increasing their prices. In Ghana new suitable land is scarce and the intensification of production at farm level seems necessary in the future.

The system of cocoa marketing changed more rapidly and more radically in Cameroon than in Ghana. In Cameroon state withdrawal from marketing and price fixing caused traders to reappear in the countryside where they competed with each other. However, for many reasons the buying system is not efficient and has not led to substantially higher producer prices than before the crisis. Even after having organized themselves, the cocoa producers were unable to negotiate for significant price increases. The relatively high world market prices, partly passed on to producers, worked out positively, but producers are no longer shielded from world price fluctuations and uncertainty has become an aspect of cocoa production and marketing.

In Ghana the marketing board retained a crucial role in cocoa marketing, quality control, research and maintenance of infrastructure. Only in 1993 were private firms licensed to buy alongside the state buying company. Because of the many restrictions competition among these private firms and between private and state buying companies is insignificant and the state is still by far the most important actor. Its importance may diminish in future, but it may also maintain itself with the risk of inefficient bureaucratic behaviour. The fluctuating real producer prices and their still low level relative to world market prices as well as the stagnation of national production could indicate a change in the latter direction.

In view of the discussion above, one wonders whether comprehensive liberalization is better than state intervention. The kind of questions posed by Nzekio (1973) are still important: Are individual cocoa producers, or organizations of producers, able to undertake investments (in quality control, disease control, cocoa research, education and training of farmers, maintenance of feeder roads, etc.) more effectively than a public organization? His answer was negative. For Cameroon after seven years of liberalization, and for Ghana after ten years of export stimulating policies, the answer is not yet clear.

Some conclusions may be drawn. The first is that structural adjustment measures can influence production levels in a positive way. In the long run, however, other factors such as land availability, production intensification, production and marketing costs as well as world market prices are more decisive factors. The second conclusion concerns the role of the state. Some state intervention seems necessary in the sphere of quality control and the maintenance of a minimal infrastructure. But when the state is unable to offer higher and/or more stable prices to small cocoa producers, better and more sustainable production results than under market-led conditions are hardly to be expected.

References

ALARY, V., G. COURADE & P. JANIN (1994) 'Permanence et flexibilité des cacaoculteurs Béti à l'heure des ajustements'. In G. Courade (ed.) *Le Village Camerounais à l'heure de l'Ajustement*. Paris: Karthala, pp. 170-183.
BATES, R.H. (1988) 'Governments and Agricultural Markets in Africa'. In R.H. Bates (ed.) *Towards a Political Economy of Development: a rational choice perspective*. Berkeley & Los Angeles, pp. 331-358.
BERGSMA, A.L. (1996) 'Commercialization of food crops in the Central Province of Cameroon'. MUCAM Research Report. Utrecht: Utrecht University, Faculty of Geographical Sciences.
BOAHENE, K. (1995) *Innovation adoption as a socio-economic process. The case of the Ghanaian Cocoa Industry*. Amsterdam: Thesis Publishers.
BOERE, N. & H. VAN MIERLO (1996) 'De rurale productiestructuur en commercialisatie van voedselgewassen in het arrondissement Mbagasinna. Onderzoek in de Province du Centre Cameroun'. Utrecht: Utrecht University, Faculty of Geographical Sciences, MA thesis.
CICC (1996, 1997) *Bulletin d'Information du Conseil Interprofessionnel du Cacao et du Café: Cacao - Café*. Douala: CICC
CHALFIN, B. (1996) 'Market reforms and the State: the case of shea in Ghana'. In *The Journal of Modern African Studies*, Vol. 34, no. 3, pp. 421-440.
COURADE, G., I. GRANGERET & P. JANIN (1991) 'La liquidation des joyaux du prince: les enjeux de la libéralisation des filières cafe-cacao au Cameroun'. In *Politique Afrique*, pp. 121-127.
COURADE, G. (ed.) (1994) *Le Village Camerounais à l'heure de l'Ajustement*. Paris: Karthala.
COURADE, G. & V. ALARY (1994) 'De la libéralisation à la dévaluation: les planteurs attendent leur réévaluation'. In G. Courade (ed.) *La village Camerounais à l'heure de l'ajustement*. Paris: Karthala. pp. 184-203.
DE JONG, A. (1994) 'The consequences of declining prices on the international cocoa market for the government and the producers in Cameroon'. In A. Harts-Broekhuis & O. Verkoren (eds) *No easy way out: essays on Third World development in honour of Jan Hinderink*. Utrecht: KNAG/FRW, pp. 220-227.
DUNCAN, A. & J. HOWELL (eds) (1992) *Structural Adjustment and the African Farmer*. London: Overseas Development Institute.
EIU Country Profile (1992-93) 'Cameroon, Central African Republic, Chad. Country Profile'. London: The Economist Intelligence Unit.
EIU Country Profile (1997-98) 'Cameroon, Central African Republic, Chad. Country Profile'. London: The Economist Intelligence Unit.
EIU Country Profile (1992-93) 'Ghana. Country Profile'. London: The Economist Intelligence Unit.
EIU Country Profile (1997-98) 'Ghana. Country Profile'. London: The Economist Intelligence Unit.
FOTSO TCHAMEKWAN, L. (1997) 'Libéralisation café-cacao: qui perd qui gagne?'. In *La Voix du Paysan*, no. 60, janvier 1997.
FRANQUEVILLE, A. (1987) *Une Afrique entre le village et la ville. Les migrations dans le sud du Cameroun*. Paris: Editions de l'ORSTOM.
FREUD, E.H., P. PETITHUGENIN & J. RICHARD (1996) 'Innovation in West African smallholder cocoa: some conventional & non-conventional measures of success'. Paper presented at the International

Symposium of Food Security and Innovations: Success and Lessons Learned. Stuttgart: University of Hohenheim.
GIBBON, P. (1992) 'A failed Agenda? African agriculture under structural adjustment with special reference to Kenya and Ghana'. In *The Journal of Peasant Studies*, Vol. 20 , no. 1, pp. 50- 96.
GUYER, J. I. (1984) *Family and Farm in southern Cameroon*. African Research Studies no. 15, Boston University.
HERBST, J. (1993) *The Politics of Reform in Ghana, 1992-1991*. Oxford: University of California Press.
HOORN, M. (1998) 'Cocoa production in the Ashanti region since the liberalization of the internal trade in 1992'. Utrecht: Utrecht University, Faculty of Geographical Sciences, MA thesis.
ICCO (1992, 1997) *Quarterly Bulletin of Cocoa Statistics*, Vol. XVIII and XXIII, no. 4. London: International Cocoa Organization.
JACOBEIT, C. (1991) 'Reviving Cocoa: Policies and Perspectives on Structural Adjustment in Ghana's Key Agricultural Sector'. In D. Rothchild (ed.) *Ghana, the political economy of recovery*. London: Lynne Rienner, SAIS African Studies Library.
LEPLAIDEUR, A., G. LONGUEPIERRE & A. WAGUELA (1981) 'Modèle 3C, Cameroun-Centre-Sud-cacaoculture'. Montpellier: SODECAO. IRAT.
LOSCH, B., B. DAVIRON, C. FREUD & N. GERGELY (1992) 'Relance régionalisée de la production paysanne de café et de cacao au Careroun'. Yaounde: CIRAD-SOFRECO.
MANU, F.A. (1992) 'The State and Marketing in African Countries: A case study of Ghana'. In *Journal of International Food and Agribusiness Marketing*, Vol. 4, no. 2, pp. 67-82.
MINAGRI (1992) 'Relance régionalisée de la production paysanne de café et de cacao au Cameroun. Etude de faisabilité. Phase 1: cadrage général de la relance'. Yaounde: Ministère de l'Agriculture.
MINISTRY OF FOREIGN AFFAIRS (1990) 'Sub-Saharan Africa beyond adjustment'. Africa Seminar, The Hague: Ministry of Foreign Affairs.
MEIJER, J. (1998) 'Respons op bevolkingsdruk. Veranderend landgebruik en migratie in de Centrale Provincie van Kameroen'. Utrecht: Utrecht University, Faculty of Geographical Sciences, MA thesis.
MUNTJEWERFF, C.A. (1982) 'The producers' price system and the coffee and cocoa trade at village level in West Africa'. Leiden: African Studies Centre, Working papers no. 6.
MUNTJEWERFF, C.A. (1982) 'Produce marketing co-operatives in West Africa'. Leiden: African Studies Centre, Working papers.
NDEMBOU, S. (1994) 'Les planteurs de café et de cacao du Sud-Cameroun dans le tourbillon de la crise, de la libéralisation et de la dévaluation'. Les Cahiers d'Ocisca no. 12, Yaounde: ORSTOM.
NYANTENG, V.K. (1993) 'Cocoa production in Ghana: a review of policies and impacts, 1890-1990'. Legon: Institute of Statistical, Social and Economic Research. University of Ghana.
NYANTENG, V.K. (1995) 'Market structure, conduct and performance of the international marketing system of cocoa in Ghana'. Paper presented at the West Africa Regional Seminar on Agricultural Sector Policy Analysis at Akosombo, Ghana, September 1995.
NZEGANG, M (1997) 'Relancer la production du café-cacao par la réhabilitation de la protection phytosanitaire'. In *La Voix du Paysan*, no. 65, juin 1997.
NZEKIO, E.P. (1973) *Stability export taxation, and economic development: The role of cocoa marketing boards and cocoa stabilization funds in Nigeria, Ghana, Ivory Coast and Cameroun*. Ann Arbor: University of Wisconsin.
OOSTERLEE, L. (1988) 'Marketing of export crops in Tropical Africa. A comparative analysis of cooperative societies and private licensed buying agents in the South West Province, Cameroon'. Utrecht: Utrecht University, Diskussiestukken van de vakgroep SGO, no 40.
PEARCE, R. (1992) 'Ghana'. In Alex Duncan & John Howell (eds.) *Structural Adjustment and the African Farmer*. London: Overseas Development Institute, pp. 14-43.
PENN, G.A.E. & W.A. NGENGE (1993) 'The evolution of cooperative legislation in Cameroon'. In *Verfassung und Recht Ubersee. Law and Politics in Africa, Asia and Latin America*, vol. 26, pp. 372-398.
RECENSEMENT AGRICOLE 1984 (1987) 'Secteur traditionnel. Résultats de la Province du Centre. DNRA'. Yaounde: Ministere de l'Agriculture.
REPUBLIC OF CAMEROON (1989) 'Statement of Development Strategy and Economic Recovery'. Yaounde: Republic of Cameroon.
SODECAO (1994) 'Bilan du processus de prise en charge par les groupement de producteurs de la fonction "Marketing du Cacao"', campagne 1993-1994. Yaounde: Société de Développement du Cacao.
SOCA'2 (1994) 'Etude d'un dispositif d'appui aux producteurs Camerounais pour leur implication dans la gestion des filières Café et Cacao'. Montpellier: Société de Réalisation et de gestion de projets Café &

Cacao. Etude executée pour Ministère de l'Agriculture , Yaounde, et le Ministère de la Coopération, Paris.

VAN DER LAAN, H.L. (1988) 'The Role of the Marketing Board in the South West and North West Provinces, 1978-1987'. Leiden: African Studies Centre, Working papers no. 11.

VAN DER LAAN, H.L. & W.T.M. VAN HAAREN (1990) 'African Marketing Boards under structural adjustment. The experience of Sub-Saharan Africa during the 1980s'. Leiden: African Studies Centre. Working Paper No. 13.

VAN STEENIS, B. (1998) 'Productie en verhandeling van Cacao onder Structurele Aanpassing in de departementen Lekie en Mbam/Kim in Kameroen'. Utrecht: Utrecht University, Faculty of Geographical Sciences, MA thesis.

WEBER, J. (1977) 'Structures agraires et évolution des milieux ruraux. Le cas de la région du Centre-Sud Cameroun'. Yaounde: ORSTOM-MIPAT.

WORLD BANK (1988) 'Staff Appraisal report: Cameroon, cocoa rehabilitation project'. Report number 6293-CM.

WORLD BANK (1989) *Sub-Saharan Africa, from Crisis to Sustainable Growth, a Long-Term Perspective Study*. Washington: The IBRD.

6

Coffee in Côte d'Ivoire and Costa Rica
National and Global Aspects of Competitiveness

Wim Pelupessy

Abstract

Comparative advantages are frequently considered as the main factor in re-establishing international competitiveness of primary commodities such as coffee. Using a comparative analysis between a stagnating producer such as Côte d'Ivoire and an efficient one like Costa Rica, this chapter demonstrates that competitive advantages, and especially the position in the global commodity chain, are more important. For the coffee sector in Côte d'Ivoire to really recover, land and farm prices should be reformed. Innovations should be introduced in infrastructure, productive organization and technology. But major improvements must further be realized in relationships with powerful international buyers and special segments of the world market. Côte d'Ivoire's coffee policy should foster product differentiation, specialization, upgrading of quality and the discovery of new market niches. The global commodity chain approach paves the way for a systematic and integral analysis of (a) the different markets and bargaining powers of the whole chain of international value creation and (b) the resulting (unequal) distribution of income among microeconomic agents and countries.

6.1 Introduction

For many Sub-Saharan economies, coffee is an important tradable that generates a substantial portion of their foreign exchange and tax revenues, as well as a large share of their agrarian GDP and employment. A natural monopoly of the tropics, available fertile land, cheap labour, and a relatively simple, locally developed technology give this mainly peasant-grown crop comparative advantages and make it an almost ideal vehicle for productive rural growth and income redistribution. In addition, international demand is stable and (slowly) growing, while producers have established access to world markets.

The long-term stagnation of the crop in Côte d'Ivoire, the fifth largest producer in the world and the first in Africa, has resulted in considerable decreases in output and productivity and is now a serious problem. The government has initiated a Coffee Recovery Plan for the rehabilitation and renovation of farms and the promotion of efficiency that will cost more than CFA franc 3 billion (Wheeler, 1995, 54). Urged on by the World Bank a reorganization of the marketing board and other structural adjustment policies for recovery have also been introduced.

At first sight the World Bank market-oriented approach seems to be the correct strategy for re-establishing comparative advantages to enhance the competitiveness of an export commodity. The approach basically focuses on the reform of the national productive structure and organization. International competitiveness seems to be primarily a matter of comparative advantages. However, the analysis can, and must, be refined because national coffee production and trade form part of a global commodity chain. This is an international socio-economic network of producers and traders, integrated in a sequence of value-added creation. The chain includes raw material exploitation, transformation, and trade till the final use of a product (Gereffi & Korzeniewicz, 1994, 1-14). Recent trends in international demand, technology, and product differentiation have increased the importance of global chains.

The purpose of this chapter is to compare the long-term or structural competitiveness of coffee production in Côte d'Ivoire with that in Costa Rica, in order to arrive at recommendations for the recovery of the first. It will be demonstrated that, to be competitive, Côte d'Ivoire should complement the enhancement of domestic productive and marketing efficiencies with an improvement of its position in the international chain. Competitiveness is seen as the ability of firms, sectors and countries to generate relatively high levels of factor income and employment on a sustainable base (OECD, 1992; Esser, et al., 1995).

As government measures to manage public goods and externalities play a key role in the creation of a competitive environment, the policies of both countries and their impacts should also be compared.

The intercontinental comparison with Costa Rica is justified because it is one of the most efficient producers in the world, in terms of both national advantages and its position in the global chain. The author has studied the Costa Rican coffee sector extensively (Pelupessy, 1998). It should also be noted that the explicit consideration of position in a global chain is a relatively new element in the discussion of competitiveness.

In this chapter, the national efficiency of coffee production and trade is dealt with in Section 6.2. Section 6.3 analyzes the effects of government coffee institutions and macro strategies for both countries. In Section 6.4 we discuss the importance of global commodity chains for the competitiveness of coffee. In the next section the position of Côte d'Ivoire and Costa Rica in their respective coffee chains is compared and related to national factors of competitiveness. Conclusions for Côte d'Ivoire's recovery strategy are presented in the final section of this chapter.

6.2 Comparing the competitive strengths of Côte d'Ivoire and Costa Rica coffees

Côte d'Ivoire produces one of the lower quality unwashed Robustas with a caffeine content of 2.27-2.70 per cent (Jobin, 1993, 241).[1] It is one of the most important suppliers of Robusta (about 16 per cent of the world market), with Indonesia and Uganda as main competitors. Vietnam, as a newcomer to this market, has recently made steady gains, partly at the expense of Côte d'Ivoire. In the 1990s, Côte d'Ivoire's apparent competitiveness (share of world exports) has declined.

In the same period, Costa Rica's share of high quality Arabica has been 11 per cent of the 'Other Milds' market and as the third supplier after Mexico and Guatemala, it has gained a bigger proportion of the export market of this class. Only Ecuador and El Salvador have done better.

Among the main reasons for the weak performance of Côte d'Ivoire are the age of most of the plantations (75 per cent of the trees are more than 15 years old and 40 per cent more than 35 years old), the extensive nature of cultivation (about 300 coffee trees per hectare), the reduction of care and maintenance on old plantations and low input use.[2] All these factors are interrelated and have brought about low and declining yields: from an average of 370 kg green coffee/hectare in the 1960s to 150 kg/hectare in the 1990s (Table 6.1).

Table 6.1 Coffee area, output and yields Côte d'Ivoire and Costa Rica, 1960-1995

Year	Area (1000 ha)		Output** (1000 MT)		Yield (kg/ha)	
	CI	CR	CI	CR	CI	CR
1961-63*	457	65	159	60	348	916
1987-89*	1291	96	226	154	175	1604
1990	1210	115	286	151	236	1314
1991	1215	106	199	158	164	1491
1992	1220	106	125	168	103	1585
1993	1225	105	139	148	113	1410
1994	1385	101	148	150	107	1480
1995	1385	101	194	153	140	1515

Source: Seudieu, 1996, 8; World Bank, 1990, 20; FAO Yearbooks 1992-95.
* 3 years weighted averages
** Green coffee

---

[1] In the world coffee market four main varieties are known, which in order of lower to higher quality and price are: 1) Robusta, with a 26 per cent world market share; 2) Unwashed or Brazilian Arabica (23 per cent); 3) Washed Arabica that is split into 'Other Milds' (33 per cent); and 4) Colombian Milds (18 per cent). In the 1990s the respective price differences with Robusta coffee have been 20-50, 25-60 and 30-80 per cent. Generally, Robusta coffee, with its higher caffeine content (1.7-4.0 per cent), is considered of lower quality than the Arabicas (0.8-1.4 per cent caffeine).

[2] Of the 1.4 million hectares under coffee only 1.2 million are actually harvested.

The Coffee Recovery Plan intends to introduce new varieties of Robusta with plant densities of more than 1,300 per hectare and to enhance the use of inputs and technical assistance. Actually, there are about 280,000 coffee farms with more than 0.5 million workers, of which 70 per cent are smallholders with less than 5 hectares. Only 4 per cent of the holdings have more than 10 hectares (Seudieu, 1996, 8).

Costa Rica, on the other hand, has achieved one of the world's highest coffee yields (1,500 kg/hectare), using technological packages of the new locally developed Arabica varieties Caturra and Catuai which have short high-density shrubs (up to 10,000 plants/hectare). In some regions, shade has been eliminated and the use of new varieties increased from 35 per cent in 1979/80 to 90 per cent in 1993/94 (ICAFE, 1995). In the early 1990s when world market prices were low, the use of agrochemicals declined by 50 per cent and yield growth stagnated somewhat (Table 6.1). However, coffee productivity remained approximately twice that of the nearest competitors El Salvador, Guatemala and Colombia.[3] More than 90 per cent of the 33,000 coffee farms, employing 64,000 workers, are smallholdings with less than five hectares and produce about 40 per cent of the national harvest. Only 3.2 per cent of the farms have areas of more than 10 hectares, and they also produce 40 per cent of the total crop. The average coffee farm size in Costa Rica and Côte d'Ivoire is 3 and 4.3 hectares respectively with 1.6 and 3.0 hectares per worker.[4]

Table 6.2 shows that the distribution of coffee land is more unequal in Costa Rica than in Côte d'Ivoire. Yields tend to be positively related to farm size in both countries (Pelupessy, 1998, 11; Ridler, 1988, 1524). In Côte d'Ivoire, however, large estates are disappearing due to labour shortages (Jobin, 1993, 239), and this may also have reduced average yields. The shortage of harvesting labour is also mentioned as a structural problem in Costa Rica (ICAFE, 1995, 65-76).

Table 6.2 Coffee farms by size

Farm size	Percentage of farms	
	Côte d'Ivoire	Costa Rica
< 2 hectares	26	70
2 - 5 hectares	47	22
5 - 10 hectares	23	5
> 10 hectares	6	3
	100	100

Sources: Ridler, 1988; Pelupessy, 1998, 11.

The long-term coffee output increase in Côte d'Ivoire (Table 6.1) is mainly explained by the occupation of new land and not by technological progress as indicated by the structural

---

[3] Costa Rican high quality Other Milds are a substitute for Colombian Milds.
[4] Real averages should be closer since the Costa Rican figures give the extension of coffee areas and those of Côte d'Ivoire register total farm areas.

decrease of the average yield figures. In Costa Rica, increasing yields accompanied by a moderate land increase explain the growth in output. In the 1960-95 period, the coffee area tripled in Côte d'Ivoire and increased by only 50 per cent in Costa Rica, while yields declined by 60 per cent in Côte d'Ivoire, but rose 65 per cent in Costa Rica.

The world price decline after 1989 affected the extension of coffee areas in both countries: a slower increase in Côte d'Ivoire and a decline in Costa Rica. It appears that the low prices reduced yields in Côte d'Ivoire more than those in Costa Rica. It is interesting to note that, in the 1990s, in particular small farms of less than 5 hectares have been successful in maintaining their productivity levels in Costa Rica. The price crisis seems to have affected primarily the investment and maintenance behaviour of existing growers and less the clearance of new land, which may be seen as a survival strategy of small peasants in this country.[5]

Another important determinant of competitiveness in the coffee industry is the integration and centralization of the first processing phase which converts berries into exportable green coffee. In Côte d'Ivoire, this process was at first carried out by the growers in the villages. In the second half of the 1970s, 16 hulling factories, with a total capacity of 332,000 tonnes, were put into operation, of which 12, with a capacity of 270,000 tonnes, are still functioning in the 1990s. Preliminary drying of the coffee berries is still done by the grower and the hulling plants have succeeded in increasing the conversion factor of dried berries to green coffee by 15 per cent and in raising overall efficiency (De Graaff, 1986, 265, 267). The process applied in Côte d'Ivoire is the dry method and due to the decline of the harvests in the 1990s, average hulling overcapacity has been 45 per cent, or 33 per cent if only the active factories are considered.

In Costa Rica the tradition of applying the wet method in small processing factories goes back to the nineteenth century, but these factories are more decentralized than in Côte d'Ivoire. However, there is a trend toward concentration: the number of factories has decreased from 256 to 129, of which 99 are still operating. With a coffee area equal to 7 per cent of that of Côte d'Ivoire, the number of processing factories is nevertheless eight times as high in Costa Rica. Wet processing is more vertically integrated and no drying is done by the grower. Growers deliver the picked berries directly to thousands of *recibideros* scattered around the countryside, to be transported to nearby factories.

In Côte d'Ivoire, where distances are larger, 200 authorized private buyers and their 15,000 agents collect the dried berries from the farmers for delivery to the factories. The Costa Rican factories are much smaller than those in Côte d'Ivoire. More than 100, that is, 85 per cent of the factories, have an annual capacity of less than 3,450 tonnes each. Together they account for about half of the national milling capacity, while only the five largest can process more than 6,800 tonnes each, about 20 per cent of the total capacity. Twenty-five factories are managed by cooperatives and operate as a federation, accounting for 40 per cent of the national output.

---

5 The sharp fall in growers' incomes in Côte d'Ivoire may have reduced the area of existing farms, but the increase of new coffee land has compensated for this.

In Côte d'Ivoire the capacity of the factories varies from 10,000 to 40,000 tonnes with the four largest providing 50 per cent of the used capacity. In Costa Rica processing overcapacity in the 1990s has averaged no more than 30 per cent and much less if only the 99 active factories are considered. Obviously, Côte d'Ivoire's coffee processing is more concentrated, but less efficient and may have lost competitive strength when compared with Costa Rica.

In both countries, only a small share of the coffee is consumed locally: about 5 per cent in Côte d'Ivoire and 10 per cent in Costa Rica. Domestic consumption in Côte d'Ivoire fell sharply in the 1990s to about one seventh of Costa Rican consumption in absolute terms (ICO, Sept. 1995, Tables I.2 and II.2). But even when earlier information is applied (De Graaff, 1986, 269) with annual consumption of 1.6 kg/person, it is well below the Costa Rican average of 5 kg. In addition, the local market in Costa Rica saw an increasing share of better quality coffee during the recent period of low world prices, while in Côte d'Ivoire, it is still lower grade Robusta and instant coffee that prevail. The big differences in real per capita income (300 per cent in the mid 1990s) undoubtedly play an important role in explaining the levels of local consumption.

Roasting is done in Côte d'Ivoire by three local companies, one of which is a Nestlé-owned instant coffee plant, which also exports. Costa Rica has some 35 roasters and traders of which three control 70-80 per cent of the domestic market. In both countries, local consumer markets have been liberalized. Exports of roasted coffee are still insignificant for both. Despite the very high effective rate of protection of Côte d'Ivoire roasting companies, exports are only allowed to WAEC countries (WTO, 1995, 85).[6]

The exportation of green coffee, the next stage in the chain, is organized by 43 and 49 authorized private exporters in Côte d'Ivoire and Costa Rica respectively. Foreign participation is high in the export stage. In Côte d'Ivoire the major French group Tardivat controls one quarter to one third of the coffee and cocoa exports (WTO, 1995, 82).

Figure 6.1 gives a comparison of the evolution of the unit values of exports of the two countries for the period 1987-94. Price fluctuations were smaller for Costa Rica and recovery was better. Both countries obtained better prices than the respective world averages for Robusta and 'Other Milds' coffee in this period. Summarizing the results of this section one may say that almost all stages of production and trade in Côte d'Ivoire are less competitive than those in Costa Rica. Outdated technology and unused capacity in both coffee cultivation and processing are serious problems in Côte d'Ivoire. It seems that neither the higher concentration ratio of land nor the smaller scale of processors has reduced Costa Rican efficiency. The export and domestic marketing structures are highly concentrated in the two countries, but Côte d'Ivoire performed worse in both the export and internal markets.

---

[6] In spite of duty-free access to the European, US, and Canadian markets.

Figure 6.1 Index of unit value of export Côte d'Ivoire - Costa Rica (June values)

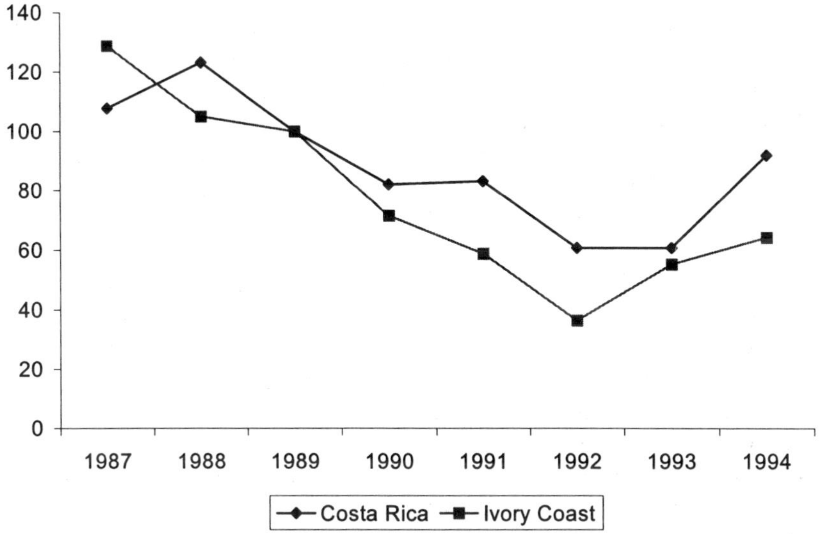

Source: ICO - statistics on coffee
Notes: - calculated from values in $/lb
- 1989 = 100

6.3 State intervention in Côte d'Ivoire and Costa Rica

State coffee institutions
Regulatory agencies are operating in the coffee sectors of both countries, to stabilize grower incomes, to preserve a certain income distribution within the sector, to provide public goods and to transfer resources to the public budget.

Côte d'Ivoire's Caisse de Stabilisation (CSSPPA) used to control all marketed coffee and to fix the payments to agents in the national chain, including the growers. The idea was to cover production costs and provide equal remuneration for all crops (Cárdenas, 1994, 355-6). The ratio of producer prices for coffee and cocoa, for instance, remained the same for a long time. However, cocoa gained the interest of smallholders because it required less labour. The CSSPPA also monitors the quality and sales of the crop and subsidizes a number of activities such as the rehabilitation of plantations, agricultural mechanization, coffee research, etc. Through SATMACI (Technical Assistance Company for Modernization of Agriculture), the Caisse provides technical assistance and extension services.

At times of high world prices, the Caisse received large financial surpluses, which were used for rural infrastructure projects, agricultural credit schemes, and state investment programmes in other sectors.

With the introduction of structural adjustment, state intervention in coffee marketing began to be questioned. The CSSPPA was thought to be primarily an instrument transferring resources from agriculture to inefficient state spending: prices were set too low to provide incentives to coffee growers, while they were not protected in periods of world price crises. Moreover, there have been inefficiencies because of bureaucracy and political favours. Since the mid 1980s, the government has been under pressure to reform the Caisse, but it resisted doing so until recently. Besides budgetary and political motives for resisting this pressure, there were also fears that liberalization would lead to a loss in quality, as it did in Cameroon and Nigeria (EIU, 1996-97, 22). Finally, in 1995, with the adjustment loan for agriculture from the World Bank, it was agreed that the producer price set at the start of the season by the CSSPPA should serve only as a guideline. After the 1994 devaluation, the government reformulated its economic programme, with flexible producer prices and improvements in the incentive system, lower export taxes, and less intervention, in order to stimulate recovery in the coffee sector. Producer prices in local money were increased several times from CFA franc 75/kg ($0.26) before the devaluation, to CFA franc 700/kg ($1.40) for the 1995/96 crop (EIU, 1996, 23; EIU, 1997, 1-16). However, with lower world market price perspectives, this was lowered again to CFA franc 500/kg ($0.98) for the 1996/97 season. Taxes on coffee were cut from CFA franc 200/kg ($0.26) in 1994 to CFA franc 110/kg ($0.22) in 1995 and CFA franc 10/kg ($0.002) for 1996/97. With an additional subsidy of $54.7 million from cocoa export revenues, total support to the coffee sector was $117.2 million for 1996/97 (EIU, 1997, 1-16).

Costa Rica's semi-autonomous Instituto del Café (ICAFE) originally regulated a number of coffee production and trade activities in order to maintain a more or less equitable income distribution within the chain. On its board are representatives of the growers, processors, (local) roasters, exporters and the government. In contrast to Côte d'Ivoire, it participated basically in establishing the rules of the game and raising taxes. International price fluctuations still affected the incomes of growers, processors, and traders. Because of ICAFE rules, growers carry the price risks and, when international prices are above a certain threshold, a tariff has to be paid to the National Coffee Stabilization Fund. This is used to subsidize growers when the sector's income is lower than its costs. Processors are guaranteed a fixed profit of 9 per cent of total sales and maximum profits for exporters are fixed at 1.5-2.5 per cent of the selling price.

Final prices are established at the end of the crop year by subtracting processing costs, the fixed profit margin and taxes from the export price. Thus, growers are forced to give credit to the factories until the coffee has been sold. Producer prices had normally been kept artificially low at a quarter of the FOB price. But since the world price decline of the early 1990s, the domestic market has been liberalized in Costa Rica and Côte d'Ivoire.

In the 1980s, coffee was taxed with ad valorem (production, export and other) taxes, absorbing, on average, 20 per cent of the output value (World Bank, 1990, 28-30). Most of these resources were used to cover ICAFE costs or transferred to the government budget. All taxes were eliminated during the crisis of the early 1990s to neutralize in part the fall in real producer prices. Credit costs approximated international opportunity costs of capital from 1984 onwards when a macroeconomic reform eliminated all domestic subsidized credit for the coffee sector. The price crisis of the early 1990s affected Costa Rican growers, but coffee cultivation did not regress as much as in Côte d'Ivoire.

International finance institutions like the World Bank argue that Costa Rican coffee growers should not bear the burden of price risk, margins should not be guaranteed or restricted, while controls on coffee flows and subsidies to domestic consumers and cooperative producers should be abolished (World Bank, 1990, 48).

However, one should be careful in judging ICAFE intervention as it has stimulated investment in technology intensive production and mitigated the effects of the price crisis after 1989. A comparison of the 1961-89 producer price evolution in the two countries shows that, before the crisis, prices were more stable in Côte d'Ivoire, but were fixed at lower levels. The elasticity of producer prices to world prices was close to one in Costa Rica and small or insignificant in Côte d'Ivoire, with stagnating output for the latter (Cárdenas, 1994, 364-78).

Macroeconomic policies
Macro policies affect international competitiveness for two reasons. First, the general stability of the economy should be guaranteed. Second, indirectly these policies may influence the economic position and coffee producers' incentives and may even contradict sectoral measures.

For more than 15 years, Côte d'Ivoire and Costa Rica have been influenced by World Bank and IMF-backed structural adjustment strategies, aiming at the recovery and growth of the tradable sectors. In the early 1980s, for different reasons, both countries suffered high public sector and current account deficits together with a huge foreign debt burden (Côte d'Ivoire 10%, 17% and 35% of GDP respectively; Costa Rica 10%, 19% and 48% of GDP). Traditionally overvalued currencies, falling foreign investment, adverse shifts in external terms of trade, and huge public sector wage bills made things worse in both cases.

In the early 1980s, a prolonged period of rapid growth (GDP increase of 7 per cent annually), mainly based on agricultural surpluses and some import substituting industrialization, came to an end in Côte d'Ivoire. Agricultural tradables were heavily taxed by low producer price setting and high export taxes. Revenues from world market price increases were used to finance (partly inefficient) public sector investments, which increased by 250 per cent in real terms in 1975-80 (Reed, 1992, 50). The country remained highly dependent on the export prices of its primary commodities: coffee, cocoa and timber. The serious economic destabilization caused by the fall of commodity prices and other external shocks in the early 1980s made adjustment necessary. Until 1991, support came from the Extended Fund Facility and six standby arrangements of the IMF, three SALs, and six sectoral loans from the World Bank and bilateral loans, mainly from France (Grootaert, 1996, 19).

The basic policy instruments used were a reduction in government spending, a limited trade reform, and the rescheduling of foreign debts, while exchange rate policy was not used because of membership of the West African Monetary Union. Devaluation did not occur till 1994 and then it coincided with rising international prices of agricultural commodities, among which was coffee. A restrictive wage policy was another policy instrument (World Bank, 1996, 132).[7]

The adjustment reforms of the 1980s had not been able to restore agricultural growth. Obviously, the sharp and continuing fall of world coffee prices after 1989 played a major role in this. An appreciation of the real exchange rate, labour market rigidities, the inability to raise real producer prices and to cut cost margins of the Caisse by downsizing its role gave no incentives to coffee growers to invest until 1994.

For Costa Rica, the early 1980s started with the worst recession in 30 years. In contrast to Côte d'Ivoire, exchange rate devaluation was applied immediately and recovery was relatively fast. Since 1982, different governments have implemented stabilization and adjustment measures that have reduced the macroeconomic imbalances, renewed growth, and attained some success in poverty reduction (World Bank, 1996, 127). A rapidly increasing external debt and extensive bilateral USAID support in response to social unrest and civil war in neighbouring countries, contributed a lot to this success. After some macroeconomic difficulties in 1990, the government took new steps to reduce fiscal and current account deficits. Higher indirect taxes and debt rescheduling were accompanied by considerable increases in private investment and exports. Public sector and financial system reforms were important instruments of the adjustment strategy in the 1990s. GNP per capita increased from $1,552 in the early 1980s to $2,590 in 1995, while it fell from $1,000 to $610 for Côte d'Ivoire in the same period (World Bank, 1996, 127, 131). Income distribution in Côte d'Ivoire became less unequal in the late 1980s showing a Gini coefficient decrease from 41.21 to 36.89 per cent, while Costa Rica's somewhat higher coefficient increased from 42.00 to 46.07 per cent in the same period. (World Bank, 1997, data base). It seems that the price of successful adjustment was more income inequality in Costa Rica. Its external debt had been $1,080 per capita in 1995; for Côte d'Ivoire, it was higher at $1,340 per head.

Summarizing the discussion about state influences in the chain, one must say first that developing countries' policies have only a limited influence on the chain's structure and functioning. (By contrast, the policies of developed countries often have far-reaching effects; see Section 6.5). Macro adjustment was less successful in Côte d'Ivoire, but poverty was distributed in a more equitable way there than in Costa Rica. Sector policies of Côte d'Ivoire were also less efficient in promoting productive investments and protecting growers' incomes from the international coffee crisis of the early 1990s. Intervention in producer countries should further consider the long-term supply elasticities of coffee growers, which are not insignificant.[8] These policies may affect both comparative and competitive advantages of coffee activities.

State coffee institutions are not only important for income stabilization and distribution, but also for the provision of public goods, and for handling externalities. It

---

[7] Government wages were 10.7% of GDP in 1993, 7.9% in 1994 and 6.9% in 1995.

[8] The World Bank (1990) gives estimates of significant long-term supply elasticities of coffee growers in three Latin American countries (including Costa Rica). Schiff & Montenegro (1997) show that agricultural supply responses in Sub-Saharan Africa are usually underestimated. Estimates for Côte d'Ivoire long-term supply elasticities vary from 1.06 to 1.99 (Berthélemy & Bourguignon, 1996, 40).

appears that in Côte d'Ivoire the Caisse was less efficient (McKay et al., 1997, 140-4). In the 1990s the coffee institutes in both countries lost influence because of structural adjustment strategies.

6.4 Global coffee chains and competitiveness

The general importance of global commodity chains for international competitiveness is explained in the first part of this section, while its application to the coffee case is discussed in the second. Dynamic competitive advantages may be obtained by segmenting and internationalizing production processes and looking for practices to improve productivity and profitability. With the global chain framework, we can specify the organizational features and changes in production systems in space and time that are basic to the competitive strategies of firms and states (Gereffi & Korzeniewics, 1994, 7). It should be emphasized that the processes may be developed at either intra- and interfirm level or industry level.

International commodity chains have three basic dimensions: an input-output structure for creating added value for goods or services, spatial dispersion or concentration of production and distribution networks, and a governance structure that determines the allocation and flow of resources within the chain (Gereffi, 1994, 97).

Agro-industrial chains usually include agricultural production, the initial processing that in most cases transforms commodities into exportables, one or more industrial transformations and the end-use or final disposition. Agro-food products normally maintain their original agrarian characteristics despite the transformations (examples are canned fruits, flour, and coffee).

The production of inputs and services from external sources and their eventual internalization in the chain depend on the governance dynamics. Each link or node in the chain is a group of producers or traders whose behaviour meets specific dynamic optimization criteria. In the absence of vertical integration the relationships between the links are often markets; the degrees of concentration and the entry barriers determine the distribution of value over the links. The link with the major economic weight in the chain or central nucleus is often protected by the highest entry barriers and controls the operation of the chain. The functional integration of activities and agents located in different countries is the outcome of strategic decisions to optimize investments, sales, etc. of big industrial or commercial enterprises situated in developed countries. This framework has some resemblance to a number of international production theories, for instance, Vernon's product lifecycle theory, Kojima's search for comparative costs advantages, internalization, and intra-industry specialization theories, the eclectic approach of Dunning, all of which intend to explain strategic decisions (for an overview see Kumar, 1997, 5-8). The internationalization process creates opportunities to obtain comparative and competitive advantages and to decentralize productive activities.

Developing economies are becoming progressively integrated into global chains because of the application of outward-looking development strategies, export-oriented industrialization processes and increasing specialization. This integration does not necessarily mean that the competitiveness of these economies will be enhanced (see below).

According to the nature of the nucleus and its governance structure, one may distinguish producer-driven from buyer-driven commodity chains (Gereffi, 1994, 97). In the first category, large integrated industrial enterprises take the central role in controlling the chain; these are capital and technology intensive industries, often producing durables, capital, and intermediate goods like cars, aircraft, machinery, etc. Control is commonly exercised by the headquarters of multinationals through their branches, the subcontracting of components, and international subsidiaries. Historically, these were the most frequently found international production chains, which concentrated international economic control in the industrialized world.

Recently, the second category of buyer-driven commodity chains has gained more importance. This fits a pattern of trade-led industrialization, where large trading houses, retailers, and sometimes manufacturers play the central role in creating a more decentralized productive network often with flexible specialization. These activities are generally labour, marketing, and service-intensive industries.

Many non-durable consumer goods industries belong to this category, and production, carried out in independent Third World factories, is organized and designed by large purchasers in the industrialized countries where most of the exclusive consumer goods markets are located. Maizels (1992, 163-4) argues convincingly that the erosion of the control by transnational corporations over primary commodity production in developing countries has been compensated for by the reinforcement of their dominance in downstream marketing, transport and distribution. In some cases, central control is still exercised by final stage manufacturing companies with good access to exclusive trading channels and brands, but merchandisers are progressively taking over.

In my opinion, coffee is a case in transition: concentrated coffee-roasting industries in developed economies still control a large part of the international chain, but big retailers, supermarkets, and specialized gourmet houses are gaining in prominence. Seven leading green coffee trading companies have accounted for about half of world imports in recent years (Wheeler, 1995, 15). Empirical research on the price spread between commodity and retail prices demonstrates that these companies dispose of substantial market power (Morisset, 1997). Some vertical integration of traders with roasters has also taken place. Sometimes big coffee roasters and traders merge with other activities forming powerful conglomerates. But decentralization due to the outsourcing of productive activities by big corporations can also be observed. An example is Sara Lee, the mother company of Douwe Egberts, which is the number three roasting firm in Europe and which has a 12 per cent market share in the EU (Wheeler, 1995, 70). The large US based food and consumer goods corporation Sara Lee recently announced the sale of its textile, meat and garment production units and the signing of delivery contracts with the new owners, while it will continue to manage the brand and its distribution (*Financial Times*, 1997). Outsourcing could release cash from low-margin activities, reduce future needs for capital expenditure, and transfer risks.

Modern coffee cultivation in tropical countries is closely related to the development of demand in the industrialized ones. Despite belonging to the category of half-channel crops with established world markets and price quotations (Van der Laan, 1997), coffee producers should consider the socio-economic changes that have caused the major segmentation and specialization of final markets, the emergence of new 'niches', and technologies that have led to specific long-term demand tendencies. Actually, high-quality gourmet coffee has already reached 30 per cent of consumer demand in the United States and may reach 70 per cent in the next century. Similar trends can be observed in Europe and Japan.

Large-scale multinational buyers are very much involved in the establishment, expansion or reduction of coffee cultivation, while the high concentration ratios of international markets make it difficult for producers to influence prices despite their comparative advantages mentioned in the introduction. The viability of coffee cultivation depends in many cases on external credit and related forward contracts with big buying companies, especially when government institutions withdraw from the market.

There seem to be few opportunities to change the international division of labour and localization patterns for coffee. Because of the nature of the raw material and the production processes, cultivation and initial processing should always take place together in tropical climates. On the other hand, changes might be possible in the relative position of producing countries because of technology, quality, delivery time, profitability and other factors. Countries or regions that exclusively depend on comparative advantages of available factors of production, such as cheap labour and raw materials, are at a disadvantage compared to those with such competitive advantages as technology, infrastructure, and specialized personnel. According to Porter (1990) the dependence on factor endowments is a first stage, while more advanced stages of competitiveness should be based on the capacity to innovate and the use of 'created' factors such as human capital, institutions, networks and services.

The position of large roasting companies in developed countries is protected by dynamic or creative competitive advantages such as access to final consumer markets, brands and consumer loyalty, blending skills and capital intensive technologies. This is strengthened by the increased concentration and scaling up of international coffee roasting and distribution. Four large companies, Jacobs (Kraft General Foods), Nestlé, Sara Lee D.E. and Proctor & Gamble account for more than half of total consumption in consuming countries (Heijbroek & Schoemaker, 1993, 28). They have significant market shares of roasted coffee in all important consuming countries. The position of a producer country or region in a global commodity chain is often weak in terms of bargaining power and the control of downstream activities, which is the main reason for the small share of the final price accruing to developing countries (Maizels, 1992, 164 for some examples). Coffee growing countries mostly depend on comparative advantages, while the position of Germany and Singapore (each without planting a single coffee tree) as fourth and eighth largest coffee exporters in the world is exclusively the result of created competitive advantages. The consideration of international markets in the competitiveness discussion is not new. However, the new approach proposes a systematic and integral analysis of the whole chain with its different markets and bargaining powers, which affect the (unequal) distribution of income and surplus among microeconomic participants and countries (Talbot,

1997). The effects of product differentiation, specialization, technology and market segmentation are normally not considered for largely homogeneous commodities like coffee. The importance of these aspects in connection with the competitiveness of Côte d'Ivoire coffee will be shown in the next section.

6.5 Global coffee chains in Côte d'Ivoire and Costa Rica

To compare the structure of the international coffee chains of the two countries one should identify the economic agents and look for the impact of the main governance unit or group on production and trade patterns. The functionally integrated stages and government interventions in developing countries were presented in the early sections of this chapter, while in the previous section it was argued that large roasters and traders in the main consuming countries generally control the coffee chains through to the final consumer.

With a combined share of 50 per cent, France and Italy are the most important markets for Côte d'Ivoire coffee, while Germany and the US together account for 40 per cent of imports of Costa Rican coffee. For historical reasons (see later) and because it is one of the largest customers, the French coffee industry and trade may be seen as the principal node for the Côte d'Ivoire coffee chain. In the Costa Rican case, it is the German market which has this role because of its growth prospects.

In the 1990s consumption per person in France averaged 2.7 cups a day while in Germany it was 3.7 cups. The vast majority of the population in the two countries drink coffee. With about 15 per cent of the French green coffee imports, Côte d'Ivoire is the second major supplier after Brazil. Costa Rica's share is barely 3 per cent of the German net imports. As in the rest of Europe, the concentration of roasting companies is high in the two countries and still increasing.

In France, there has been a sharp reduction from the 700 roasters who were operating ten years ago (Charpentier & Peters, 1988; EIU, 1991, 49). The share of the top four companies was at that time 65 per cent of the market while the largest five now control about 90 per cent (Wheeler, 1995, 71).

Europe's biggest coffee market, Germany, shows an even greater concentration. Within the last ten years, the number of roasters declined from about 160 to 75, while the market share of the biggest four increased from 75 to 86 per cent. Three of these were also among the largest four in 1986 and are no. 1 (Jacobs), no. 4 (Eduscho and Tchibo after their 1996 merger) and no. 7 (Aldi) in the European top ten. The higher retail prices and value-added shares in Germany cannot be explained by taxes and import prices only, but seem to be the result of a higher concentration of the industry in this country. In the 1990s, retail price differences have been more than 60 per cent between the two countries. Prices are relatively low in France due to competition among roasters (ECF, 1996, 14).

Concentration of coffee manufacturing has been related to that of coffee distribution. Wheeler (1995, 70) states: 'Since the single market was created in 1992, coffee industries and markets have drawn closer together'. Therefore, it is often difficult to find detailed economic data about the industry in specific countries.

Total employment in the EU roasting industry is estimated at 40.000 with an average annual turnover based on retail prices in the 1990s of about $500,000 per worker (EUCA, 1997, 8). Another source shows a turnover per worker of $600.000 for the Netherlands with gross profits of 9 per cent (EIM, 1995, 4). These are indicators of capital and technology intensive firms and may be utilized to approximate their relative bargaining power in the international chain (see Maizels, 1992, 165-7 for a similar reasoning in the case of TNCs and developing economies). Roasting and marketing technologies are very much the same in Germany and France, where the Jacobs company owns the largest roaster in the first and the two leading ones in the second case.

Price differences are not only explained by supply, demand and quality on spot markets. Some other factors are weather fluctuations in large producing countries, speculation on futures markets, policies, international agreements and substitution (EIU, 1991, 54-8).

The unstable nature of the world coffee market is partly caused by the futures markets in New York (for Arabicas) and in London (for Robustas), where expectations have important effect on prices. A recent study shows how the announcement of the coffee retention scheme, rather than its implementation, stimulated speculation that caused higher prices in 1993. The next year bond and equity market speculators affected price levels and volatility in the coffee futures market (Gilbert & Brunetti, 1997). But market segmentation may have stabilizing effects on the demand for coffee from a specific supplier. Stockholding used to affect prices. But the current inclination of large roasting companies to minimize stocks ('just-in-time' strategy) reduces its importance. Small producers such as Côte d'Ivoire and Costa Rica are unable to increase their export prices or to decrease the price risk in the futures market.

To obtain the final product, coffee varieties are generally blended by the roasters in the developed countries. This is done to suit consumer taste, to reduce costs and to decrease the roaster's dependence on specific providers of green coffee. Each variety has its own place in the so-called pyramid of blends. A small but high-priced segment consists of Colombian Milds and high quality 'Other Milds' which give the specific flavour to a blend. A higher percentage is the filler which contains Other Milds and Unwashed Arabica, while a major complementary part is the rest that consists of lower quality Unwashed Arabica and Robusta. Costa Rica operates in the upper, and Côte d'Ivoire in the lower segment of the international market.

Popular and cheaper blends use considerable proportions of Robusta coffee (30 per cent or more).[9] Because of consumer brand loyalty, substitution is limited, although there may be possibilities to substitute, for instance, Unwashed Arabica for cheaper Robusta, if this does not change the flavour of the blend. Roasters and traders spend a lot of money in advertising and other measures to strengthen customer relations.[10]

Today, however, there is a strong tendency in the main consuming countries to increase the quality by raising the shares of Colombian and Other Milds. It should be

---

[9] This is an approximate figure since exact proportions of blends are kept secret by the roasters.
[10] The use of consumer gift coupons is very much institutionalized in the Netherlands.

remembered that roasters use these varieties as the main flavour determinant in quality blends. Arabicas are also used for single-variety specialty coffee, while Robusta must always be mixed with others.[11] This is generally a disadvantage for Côte d'Ivoire and favourable for Costa Rican exporters. Because of its lower price, Robusta is preferred for instant coffee (6 per cent of the world market). Colombian Milds are preferred for their quality and the large quantities which can be guaranteed for special deals and security. Sometimes, however, substitution by Other Milds is considered because these may be 5-8 per cent cheaper. In France, Robusta is now used in half of the blends, while in the past this proportion was 75 per cent (Wheeler, 1993, 71).

Price elasticities for high quality varieties such as Costa Rica's may be higher than the usual values of -0.2 with respect to import prices and -0.34 for retail prices in industrialized countries. (EIU, 1991, 50). Income elasticities vary in Europe from 0.3 for the higher income countries to 0.5 for the lower ones (Pelupessy, 1993, 30). The difference is related to market saturation: the high income countries of northern and western Europe consume 7-13 kg per capita annually, while for southern European countries the figure is 2-4 kg. Cultural factors, substitution by soft drinks and health considerations, account for the similar low consumption figures per head in the UK, US and Japan. Again, all these aspects indicate that Côte d'Ivoire coffee has a weaker international position.

Table 6.3 Share of gross value added in the retail price of roasted coffee in main importing countries (%)

Country	1990	1991	1992	1993	1994	1995
USA	71	69	77	70	56	58
France	70	68	77	67	43	56
Germany	78	75	83	79	71	-
Italy	83	84	87	84	71	70
Sweden	68	67	78	63	58	-
UK*	82	81	86	78	67	73
Japan	90	92	94	94	88	89

Source: ICO, 29/3/96, Tables 5-6.
* Soluble coffee

The weight of the economic centres of gravity in the international coffee chains is given in Table 6.3, with high shares of gross value added in the retail prices of roasted coffee in the main consuming countries. The declining proportions for 1994/95 show the recovery of international coffee prices after the crisis. Large roasting and trading companies use their market power to obtain a major share in the generated economic surplus. Retail prices tend to be about nine times those that farmers get in producer countries (Figure 6.2). The gap between retail and growers' prices did not disappear in the period of declining world prices.

---

[11] Recently there have been trials with Robusta-only brands on the Dutch market.

Coffee in Côte d'Ivoire and Costa Rica

Figure 6.2 Growers' share of retail prices in consumer countries

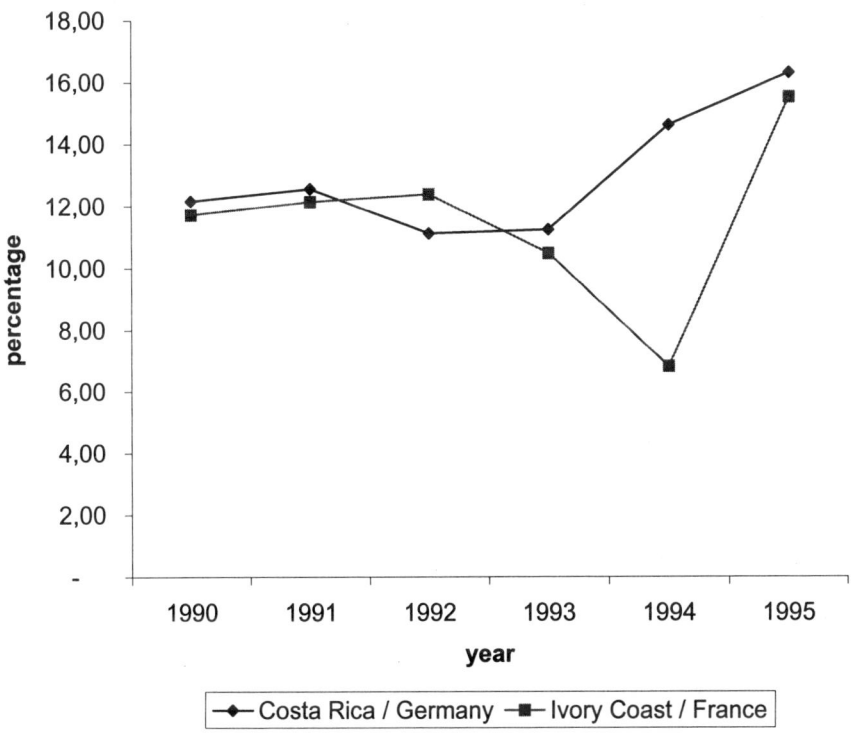

Source: ICO statistics on coffee
Notes: - calculated values in $/lb
 - retail prices of roasted coffee

In Third World countries state policies have a tendency to be of an interventionist nature to enhance competitiveness at the macro, micro, and sectoral levels. In the developed countries, however, tax policies can affect the structure of the chains and the distribution of the generated value.

In the EU, a common external tariff that varies between 4 per cent for green coffee to 12.5 per cent of the imported CIF value of roasted and decaffeinated coffee protects the European roasting industries. There are, however, many exemptions. Côte d'Ivoire, as a member of the Lomé agreement, does not pay any duty, while Costa Rica is exempted for green coffee exports. An overview of other European national taxes on coffee is given in Table 6.4.

Various taxes increase the retail price of coffee in Europe and may reduce consumption despite low elasticity values. There seem to be also certain threshold values for coffee consumers, where higher price increases cause considerable consumption declines. For the

Dutch market the threshold is calculated at $5.50 per pound of roasted and ground coffee (Charpentiers & Peters, 1988, 63).

Tabel 6.4 Indirect taxes on coffee in 1996

Country	VAT-rate on coffee	Consumption taxes on roasted coffee	Coffee extracts
Austria	10%	no taxes	
Belgium[1]	6%	BEF 10 per kilo	BEF 28 per kilo
Denmark[2]	25%	DKr 5.22 per kilo	DKr 13.0 per kilo
Finland	17%	no taxes	
France	5.5%	no taxes	
Germany	7%	DM 4.30 per kilo	DM 9.35 per kilo
Italy	19%	no taxes	
Luxembourg	6%	no taxes	
The Netherlands	6%	no taxes	
Norway*	23%	0.4% food tax	0.4% food tax + 0.3% research tax
Portugal	17%	no taxes	
Spain	7%	no taxes	
Sweden	12%	no taxes	
Switzerland*	2%	special national fees on coffee	
United Kingdom	0%	no taxes	

* as at 1995
Source: ECF, 1996, 28.
[1] Green coffee: BEF 8 per kilo
[2] Green coffee: DKr 4.35 per kilo

Government policies in consuming countries may also force substitution, as was the case of France which achieved an almost complete replacement of traditionally imported Latin American Arabicas by Robusta from its former colonies in the 1930-50 period (Daviron, 1994, 51). This result was obtained by the application of tariffs and quotas. Within 25 years coffee production increased 15 times in francophone Africa. This is an example of how interventions by the government of a developed country can affect the chain in producing countries. France and some other southern European countries are still important Robusta importers. Today Germany has much higher taxes on coffee than France, which may explain part of its higher gross value added.

Table 6.5 provides the income distribution along the international chain for Côte d'Ivoire/France and Costa Rica/Germany. The estimates refer to values in cents (US) of one pound of roasted, ground and packed coffee for consumption. The average retail price gives the total generated value, which is less for the Côte d'Ivoire/France chain. This is also the case for almost each category of participants, both in absolute figures and percentages. Roasting and trading companies in the consuming countries receive the biggest share of the retail price. This confirms the weight of the central nodes for the Côte d'Ivoire and Costa

Rica chains.[12] Côte d'Ivoire receives a smaller proportion of the retail price than Costa Rica and in US$ per unit end-product its income can even be 45 per cent lower. Government tax participation is in both cases much higher in the developed than in the developing countries. In Germany it is more than ten times the state participation of Costa Rica, while the French government receives twice as much as its counterpart in Côte d'Ivoire.

Table 6.5 Income distribution in coffee chains, 1994

	Côte d'Ivoire - France and Costa Rica - Germany			
	US$ cts per lb		% of retail price	
Agent	Côte d'Ivoire	Costa Rica	Côte d'Ivoire	Costa Rica
Grower	45.4	76.8	13.8	14.6
Processor/Trader[1]	13.2	31.8	4.0	6.0
Exporter[2]	12.5	22.7	3.8	4.3
Export Tax[3]	9.4	15.0	2.8	2.8
Export FOB (subtotal)	(80.5)	(146.3)	(24.4)	(27.7)
Freight, insurance	9.0	9.0	2.7	1.7
	France	Germany	France	Germany
Import CIF	89.5	155.3	27.1	29.4
Adjustment[4]	96.7	- 5.0	29.5	- 0.9
Roaster/Dealer[5]	62.0	112.2	18.9	21.5
Retailer[6]	62.5	99.7	19.0	19.0
Taxes	18.0	162.8	5.5	31.0
Retail price	328.7	525.0	100.0	100.0

Sources: Estimates based on: ICO-International Coffee Statistics; Wheeler, 1995, 16-7; EIU, 1996; ICAFE, 1995.
[1] Respectively dry- and wet-processed, incl. transport costs and local traders' margin
[2] Incl. grading, sorting and port costs
[3] Côte d'Ivoire CFA franc 110/kg. Costa Rica 10% FOB price
[4] Adjustment for blending and weight losses
[5] Incl. financial costs of importer
[6] Incl. advertising, etc. A fixed % of retail price is assumed.

6.6 Concluding remarks

From the comparative analysis in the preceding sections, one may conclude that a durable recovery of the coffee sector in Côte d'Ivoire needs more than market liberalization alone. At the national level Côte d'Ivoire coffee suffers from structural disadvantages as a consequence of the recurrent lack of investment and the use of outdated technology. Inappropriate land and producer price policies, where insignificant supply elasticities and the absence of scale economics at the farm level were erroneously assumed, should be reformed. The domestic market should be extended in terms of quantity and quality. Improved transport infrastructure may provide the possibility to modernize coffee

---

[12] Because of data problems the results are more reliable for roasters, dealers and retailers together than for each category separately.

processing, to introduce the wet method, and to use the existing overcapacity for processing coffee from neighbouring countries.

Structural adjustment policies have, after more than 15 years, achieved some success in the stabilization of Côte d'Ivoire's macro balances, but have neither brought the economy onto a higher growth path nor changed its production structure. This means that tradables such as coffee are still very necessary income generators with important local multiplier effects. Recovery requires sectoral policies and a state coffee institution to provide the necessary public goods and technical assistance, to improve the position of the crop in the international chain and to manage externalities. In this sense a reorientation of the CSSPPA and related institutes may be a better option than privatization or outright liquidation. The Caisse should be more oriented towards the strengthening of dynamic competitive advantages, innovations, and environmentally sound technologies. Meanwhile, most of the taxation and income distribution objectives could be realized by other institutions.

Traditional coffee producing countries should enter the more advanced stages of competitiveness by improving their position in the international chain using created advantages in the fields of technology and marketing. Côte d'Ivoire is no exception.

Global commodity chain analysis has added a useful dimension to the evaluation of competitiveness. It gives an explicit outcome of the spatial income distribution as a consequence of strategic actions of economic agents from raw material exploitation to the final use of transformed products. Côte d'Ivoire coffee has, in comparison with more advanced producers such as Costa Rica, major weaknesses due to its position within the chain. The African country produces a cheap variety of coffee for an inferior segment of the world market, which is now moving into high quality demand specialization. Côte d'Ivoire's marketing efforts could in the first place be directed at instant coffee and Robusta brand roasters, as well as 'special deals' by offering traders large quantities with special discounts. A specific strategy for southern European markets might be worthwhile. As most other coffee producing countries, Côte d'Ivoire faces a buyer's market with increasing downstream concentration which reduces its bargaining power. Core companies have sufficient market power to influence prices and non-price conditions to strengthen their position in the chain. Recent specialization and marketing tendencies will only reinforce this situation. A possible improvement for Côte d'Ivoire in the international chain might be obtained by significant quality upgrading to allow it to operate in a higher market segment. However, for the enhancement of its international competitiveness, strategic alliances will be more useful than trade at arm's length.

References

BERTHÉLEMY & BOURGUIGNON (1996) *Growth and Crisis in Côte d'Ivoire*. Washington: World Bank.
CÁRDENAS, M. (1994) *'Stabilization and Redistribution of Coffee Revenues: A Political Economy Model of Commodity Marketing Boards'*. In *Journal of Development Economics*, Vol. 44, pp. 351-80.

CHARPENTIER, J. & V. PETERS (1988) *Koffie uit Costa Rica, El Salvador en Nicaragua in de landen der Europese Gemeenschappen*. Afstudeerwerkstuk, Vakgroep Economie van Ontwikkelingslanden, Tilburg: KUB.
DAVIRON, B. (1994) 'La crisis del mercado cafetalero internacional en una perspectiva de largo plazo'. In *Samper Mario: Crisis y Perspectivas del Cafe Latinoamericano*. Convenio Instituto del Café de Costa Rica - Universidad Nacional, Heredia, Costa Rica.
DE GRAAFF, K. (1986) *The Economics of Coffee*. Wageningen: Pudoc.
ECF (EUROPEAN COFFE FEDERATON) 'European Coffee'. Report: 1995, 1996, 1997.
EIM (1995) *Koffiebranderijen en Theepakkerijen*, 6e Interim rapportage, Den Haag.
EIU (ECONOMIST INTELLIGENCE UNIT) (1991) *Coffee to 1995 Recovery without Crutches*. Special Report no. 2116.
EIU (1996) 'Country Report Côte d'Ivoire'. London.
EIU (1997) 'Country Report Côte d'Ivoire'. London.
ESSER, K., W. HILLEBRAND, D. MESSNER & JÖRG MEYER-STAMER (1995) *Systemic Competitiveness, New Governance Patterns for Industrial Development*. GDI Book Series no. 7, London: Frank Cass.
EUCA (1997) *The European Coffee Roasting Industry*. Brussel.
FAO (FOOD AND AGRICULTURAL ORGANIZATION) (1992-95) Yearbooks, Rome.
FINANCIAL TIMES, 19 September 1997.
GEREFFI, G. & M. KORZENIEWICZ (1994) *Commodity Chains and Global Capitalism*. Connecticut, London: Praeger, Westport.
GEREFFI, G. (1994) 'The Organization of Buyer-Driven Global Commodity Chains: How U.S. Retailers shape Overseas Production Networks'. In Gereffi Gary and Miguel Korzeniewicz (eds), London.
GILBERT, C.L. & C. BRUNETTI (1997) *Speculation, Hedging and Volatility in the Coffee Market, 1993-96*. Queen Mary and Westfield College, University of London.
GROOTAERT, C. (1996) *Analyzing Poverty and Policy Reform*. Hants: Avebury.
HEIJBROEK, A.M.A. & M.J. SCHOEMAKER (1993) *The World Coffee Market*. Utrecht: Rabobank.
ICAFE (INSTITUTO DEL CAFÉ DE COSTA RICA) (1995) *Informe sobre la Actividad Cafetalera de Costa Rica*. San José.
ICO (1996) Statistical Table 5 & 6, London.
JOBIN, P. (1993) *Les Cafés Produits dans le Monde*. S.A.A.A.A. Le Havre, France.
KUMAR, N. (1997) 'Multinational Enterprises and Globalization of Production'. Paper Development Economics Seminar, ISS, Den Haag, January 1997.
MAIZELS, A. (1992) *Commodities in Crisis*. Oxford: Clarendon Press.
MCKAY, A., O. MORRISSEY & C. VAILLANT (1997) 'Trade Liberalisation and Agricultural Supply Response. Issues and Some Lessons'. In *European Journal of Development Research*, Vol. 9, no. 2, 1997, pp. 129-47.
MORISSET, J. (1997) *Unfair Trade? Empirical Evidence in World Commodity Markets over the Past 25 Years*. Washington: The World Bank, Policy Research Working Paper no. 1815 .
OECD (1992) *Technology and the Economy: The key relationships*. Paris.
PELUPESSY, W. (1993) *El Mercado Mundial del Café*. San José: DEI.
PELUPESSY, W. (1998) 'La Cadena Internacional del Café y el Medio Ambiente' In *Economía Sociedad*, no. 7, pp. 1-20.
PORTER, M. (1990) *The Competitive Advantage of Nations*. New York: Free Press.
REED, D. (1992) *Structural Adjustment and the Environment*. London: Earthscan.
RIDLER, N.B. (1988) 'The Caisse de Stabilisation in the Coffee Sector of the Ivory Coast'. In *World Development*, Vol. 16, no. 12.
SCHIFF, M. & C.E. MONTENEGRO (1997) 'Aggregate Agricultural Supply Response in Developing Countries: A Survey of Selected Issues' In *Economic Development and Cultural Change*, Vol. 45, no. 2.
SEUDIEU, D.O. (1996) 'Impacts de la Production du Café sur l'Environnement en Côte d'Ivoire'. Seminar on Coffee and the Environment, ICO.
TALBOT, J. (1997) 'Where Does Your Coffee Dollar Go? The Division of Income and Surplus along the Coffee Commodity Chain' In *Studies in Comparative International Development*, Vol. 23, Spring 1997, pp. 56-91.
VAN DER LAAN, H.L. (1997) *The Trans-Oceanic Marketing Channel*. New York: The Haworth Press.
WHEELER, M. (1995) *Coffee to 2000*. Research Report, London: The Economist Intelligence Unit.
WORLD BANK (1990) *Policy Responses to the Collapse of World Coffee Prices: the Cases of Costa Rica, Mexico and El Salvador*. February 1990, Washington D.C .

WORLD BANK (1996) *Trends in Developing Economies*. Washington D.C.
WORLD BANK (1997) Data base (WEB page): Gini coefficients, Washington D.C.
WTO (1995) *Trade Policy Review, Côte d'Ivoire*. Geneva: October 1995.

7

Primary Rice Marketing in North-West Sierra Leone
Market and Non-market Transactions

Aad van Tilburg and Inge Hamming

Abstract

Unlike many other West African countries, in Sierra Leone rice is the staple food crop. It is widely cultivated in most parts of the country under a variety of ecological conditions. This study analyzes the types of rice transactions of rice-farming households (n=372) in north-west Sierra Leone by studying their 'Annual Rice Accounts'. An Annual Rice Account includes both the ways in which rice is obtained (sources) and the ways in which it is used and applied (uses). Several categories of operations and transactions are identified. They include subsistence operations (e.g. rice harvesting, rice consumption), social security transactions (e.g. giving rice as gifts), transactions compensating for resource use (e.g. rents in kind for the use of land or capital), and commercial transactions (e.g. sales or purchases of rice). Until now, little has been published about such transactions in this area.

Three types of rice-farming households are distinguished corresponding to the rice-farming system(s) they employ, and their geographical location: those in the upland area, those in the upstream area and those in the midstream area of the Great Scarcies River. Subsistence-oriented rice-farming households are mainly found in the upland area, whereas commercially-oriented households are primarily located in the upstream and midstream sections of the river. Finally, possible implications for decision makers regarding the institutional infrastructure in north-west Sierra Leone are discussed.

7.1 Introduction

Objective of the chapter
Rice has always been an important crop in the economy of Sierra Leone, not only as a staple food but also as a commodity that can be exchanged for other products and services. This

study[1] shows various aspects of the rice economy of rice-cultivating households in north-west Sierra Leone by analyzing their subsistence operations with respect to rice as well as several types of rice transactions with actors in their economic and socio-cultural environment. Insights derived from this analysis can help decision makers in the institutional environment improve the rice transaction infrastructure.

Rice production and marketing in Sierra Leone
Rice is a special commodity in Sierra Leone because of its high status as a staple food, its long-lasting qualities and its role in trade. The main rice surplus areas have traditionally been the delta of the Great Scarcies and Little Scarcies Rivers, the area between Makeni and Lunsar in Northern Province, and areas near Moyamba and Pujehun in Southern Province (Gwynne-Jones et al., 1978). In Sierra Leone, there are several rice-farming systems with the main ones being upland and swampland rice cultivation (Levi, 1976; Gwynne-Jones et. al., 1978).

The rice market in Sierra Leone was free until 1952, when the Sierra Leonean government started to implement a buying scheme with fixed prices. The government wanted to stimulate swamp rice production and constructed a rice mill in Mambolo in the Great Scarcies area. Unfortunately the mill's purchase price was usually lower than the market price. After the mid 1950s the government's main responsibility was to import and distribute rice. In 1979, the tasks of the governmental rice authority (then called the Rice Corporation) were taken over by the Sierra Leone Produce Marketing Board (SLPMB) which operated several buying stations in the early 1980s. The SLPMB also purchased domestic rice through its subsidiary the National Produce Company (NAPCO) (Borren, 1986; Van der Laan, 1975; Donnhauser, 1986). The rice trade in Sierra Leone is based on trade between surplus and deficit areas (e.g. large towns and the mining areas) and, increasingly, on rice imports.

Research area
The north-western part of Sierra Leone (Map 7.1) was suitable for our research because of its traditional role as a rice surplus area and because of the large variation in rice-growing conditions in this area. Two large rivers, the Great Scarcies River and the Little Scarcies River, intersect this area and flood the fertile riverbanks daily at high tide. Rice has been an important component of the rural economy of this area for a long time.

The economic value of many goods and services in the economy of north-west Sierra Leone was traditionally expressed in a volume measure, the 'bushel of rice' (about 27.3 kg). However, with the advent of the money economy, these values have been increasingly expressed in monetary terms. During the research period (August – December 1985), the

---

[1] Many institutions and persons have assisted in this study. They include the many rice-farming households in north-west Sierra Leone participating in the survey, staff of the Rice Research Station and the West African Rice Development Association both in Rokupr, eighteen interviewers in the Great Scarcies area, the staff of the Institute of African Studies, Fourah Bay College and Njala University College (both part of the University of Sierra Leone), Dr. H. Laurens van der Laan of the African Studies Centre in Leiden, my colleague Ab van Eldijk and several former students of the University of Sierra Leone and Wageningen Agricultural University.

money standard was still linked to the commodity standard. A general rule was that 20 Leones were equal to one bushel of rice. In times of high inflation, as was the case in the research period, it was safer to calculate amounts in bushels of rice rather than in money.

Our research area (shaded area in Map 7.1) consisted of three regions along the Great Scarcies River: the upland area, and the upstream and midstream sections of the river. We expected the rice-growing households in these three areas to differ with regard to rice operations and transactions. Villages within the three areas were subsequently selected reflecting variations in types of rice-farming system and distance to the nearest rice market centre. Consequently, the *ex ante* criteria to segment rice-growing households were (a) the type of farming system and (b) the distance to the nearest rice market centre.

An *ex post* segmentation of the rice-growing households, by means of a cluster analysis of household characteristics, confirms the relevance of the *ex ante* segmentation (Hamming, 1996). The majority (69 per cent) of the rice-farming households belonged to the subsistence-oriented segment and a minority (31 per cent) to the commercially-oriented segment. (For the effect of the severe drought during the 1984-85 cropping season, see below.) Subsistence-oriented rice-farming households were dominant in the upland region and commercially-oriented ones in the midstream area (Table 7.1).

Households and case studies
A (farming) household is a social and economic unit whose members engage in activities to satisfy the material needs of the group and create conditions to fulfil non-material needs (e.g. Spijkers-Zwart, 1980). Resources of the household may include land, labour, assets, savings and a social network. In traditional societies, rules of reciprocity (e.g. the obligatory giving of gifts among friends and kinsmen) and redistribution activities (e.g. the obligation to contribute money according to political or religious principles) tend to be important, whereas non-traditional societies are more often governed by exchange processes based on economic principles (Scott, 1978).

Farming systems in north-west Sierra Leone are complex, as is the case in many tropical countries. The case study method was used to obtain a better understanding of the various sources of rice in the households and the use of rice during the year. One case study is presented for each main type of farming system (rainfed shifting cultivation, inland valley swamp and tidal swamp). The names of key persons in the case studies have been changed to ensure privacy.

Table 7.1 Rice-farming households, by region and commercial orientation (n=371)

Orientation	Upland (%)		Upstream (%)		Midstream (%)		Total
Subsistence	98	86%	84	76%	74	50%	256
Commercial	16	14%	26	24%	73	50%	115
Total	114	100%	110	100%	147	100%	371

Map 7.1 Map of Sierra Leone showing the research area

Sample design
With the two sets of criteria in mind (location near the Great Scarcies River and distance to the nearest market centre), eleven villages and small towns were selected. The downstream section of the Great Scarcies River was excluded because, measured in travelling time by boat, it was too far from our research base at the Rice Research Station in Rokupr to allow adequate supervision of the enumerators.

The eleven villages and small towns consisted of five upland villages: Gbonkor Masesse, Masuri, Kamba, Sindugu and Funkuya, three upstream villages/towns: Robat, Rokupr and Rosino, and three midstream villages/towns: Mambolo, Mafufune and Kalenke. Rokupr, Rosino and Mambolo are all market centres. Mafufune is located about 4 km to the north and Kalenke about 6 km to the south of the Great Scarcies River.

In small villages all heads of farm households were listed to obtain a sample frame. In larger villages or small towns another procedure was followed: for every 25 households needed in the sample, 50 heads of farm households were listed in the sample frame (for more detail, see Van Tilburg, 1992). From the sample frame, 435 households were randomly selected: 395 of these households participated in all the surveys. After checking the questionnaires, 372 households were found to be actively involved in rice cultivation during the 1984-85 cropping season. Our research findings are based on these 372 households.

Relation to a larger study
This chapter is a smaller study belonging to a larger one (Van Tilburg, forthcoming). The latter includes the results of four surveys conducted between 17 October and 21 December 1985 which covered amongst others, the characteristics of the farming household, the (rice) farms, and aspects of various types of rice transactions during the 1984-85 cropping season.

In the first survey ('Inventory'), questions were asked about household composition, the types of land being cultivated, the quantity of seed rice used for the 1985-86 cropping season, the quantity of rice harvested during the 1984-85 cropping season, and other crops grown on the farm. In the second survey ('Sources and uses of rice'), questions were asked about the quantities of rice obtained from different sources and the way in which this rice was used. Other questions related to the purpose for which money was borrowed, the conditions of the loan, and participation in rotating savings and credit associations (*osusu*). The third questionnaire ('Post-harvest survey') contained questions on post-harvest operations with respect to rice, the farmers' knowledge of the official producer price for rice, and the price for which the farmer was willing to sell the next harvest's paddy. In the fourth survey ('Additional questions'), questions were asked about the role of various institutions operating in the area, the farmer's attitude towards farming and the main constraints experienced with rice farming. This chapter is primarily based on data from the second survey.

7.2 The Annual Rice Account

In this section, a new analytical tool is introduced. It is a list or account in which all sources and uses of rice in a rice-farming household (measured in kg) are entered. The account covers one year, a full rice-cropping and marketing season, in this case from 1 November 1984 to 31 October 1985. Since economic values have traditionally been expressed in bushels of unthreshed rice, the entries are expressed in kg.

What is new in this approach is that 'sources of rice' not only record the quantity of rice harvested but also the quantities purchased or received as payment for services rendered. In the same way, the 'uses of rice' not only record the quantity of rice consumed or sold but also the quantities stored as seed rice, and the quantities used as compensation for loans, or used for gift-giving (Figure 7.1). For each rice-farming household in the survey (n=372) we drew up an Annual Rice Account (ARA).

Rice transactions of a farming household can serve many purposes. Based on a literature review (e.g. Huijsman, 1986), rice transactions can be categorized as subsistence-oriented or exchange-oriented. The subsistence-oriented section consists of both subsistence operations and social security transactions, and the exchange-oriented section includes transactions compensating for resource use as well as commercial transactions (Figure 7.1).

Subsistence operations include rice obtained from the harvest, rice used for consumption in the household and transactions involving seed rice. Social security transactions include all types of activities in which rice is used in order to improve the household's economic position in the future. Rice may be given to relatives in the expectation that the household will receive support in times of illness, misfortune, etc. Rice is also given to the mosque as *zakat* to fulfil religious obligations. In many transactions involving land, labour or capital, the giving or receiving of rice is one of the contract conditions. Commercial transactions include not only sales of rice but also rice purchases to be used for consumption in the household or for trading purposes. Rice purchases during the (new) cropping season may be a consequence of repayment of loans in kind (with rice) just after the harvest of the previous cropping season. Loss of rice may occur during storage. One of the 'miscellaneous' entries is the unexplained variation in rice stocks when comparing the data for the beginning and the end of the year. The unexplained balance can be a result of inaccuracies in the collected data. (Part of the information which respondents gave concerned events that took place several months earlier.) The model Annual Rice Account of Figure 7.1 is used in Section 7.4 to analyze the household rice economy in north-west Sierra Leone. But first the various rice farming systems in the research area have to be discussed. Some case studies are added to demonstrate the context of rice operations and transactions.

Figure 7.1 Structure of the Annual Rice Account of rice-farming households in the research area

Sources of rice	Uses of rice
'Subsistence operations'	
S1 Harvest	U1 Consumption
S2 Seed rice:	U2 Seed rice:
harvested	used
exchanged	exchanged
purchased	
'Social security transactions'	
S3 Gifts in kind (received)	U3 Gifts in kind (donated)
	U4 Celebrations
'Transactions compensating for resource use'	
S5 Rents in kind of:	U5 Rents in kind of:
S 51 land	U51 land
S 52 labour	U52 labour
S 53 capital	U53 capital
'Commercial transactions'	
S6 Purchases of rice for:	U6 Sales of rice
S 61 consumption	
S 62 trade	
	U7 Loans in kind to:
	U71 Individuals
	U72 Participants in a *osusu*
'Miscellaneous'	
	U8 Losses
	U9 Other uses
S10 Unexplained balance	U10 Unexplained balance
Total of sources of rice	Total of uses of rice

7.3. Three rice-farming systems, with case studies

There are three dominant modes of rice farming in the Great Scarcies area: rainfed shifting cultivation, inland valley swamps and tidal swamps. Rice-farming households tend to spread their yield risk by using more than one farming system to cultivate rice.

Rainfed shifting cultivation
In the upland area, the main rice farming systems are rainfed shifting cultivation and inland valley swamps. In the rainfed shifting cultivation system, rice is sown at the beginning of the rainy season (June) often in combination with sorghum, millet and maize. After the rains begin to slacken, normally from September onwards, the rice matures and the harvest can take place in October or November. Many farmers then plant other crops such as cassava. After harvesting, the plot may be left fallow for several years.

The following case study illustrates this system. Bangali is a farmer of about 40 years of age. He is head of the household and has two wives and three children. The household had one rice meal in the late afternoon of 7 October 1985. Fish was purchased for 2 Leones (Le), as well as one pint of palm oil for Le 2.50, chillies for Le 0.40, Maggi cubes for Le 0.40, and balls of groundnuts for Le 0.80. Bangali explained that he is responsible for supplying food to the household. At the beginning of the rainy season Bangali broadcasts half a bushel of one rice variety and three-quarters of a bushel of another variety. Rice is intercropped with Guinea corn (sorghum) and benniseed. He intends to grow maize on the same piece of land the following year. In the period just before the harvest, he is in his rice field during the day (6.30 - 19.00 hours) to scare birds away. If Bangali has the opportunity, he will also cultivate rice in a tidal swamp along the river. He expects to pay about Le 350 a year for a two-bushels-of-seed-rice field and would hope to harvest 30 to 35 bushels from such a plot.

On 8 October 1985, Bangali harvested rice of the first variety. The yield was ten bushels. He sold two bushels to a female trader in the village for Le 50 each. He lent two bushels to a friend on the traditional condition 'two for two', and he put the remaining six bushels in his store for later consumption by the household. On 31 October, Bangali started to harvest rice of the second variety. This took him three days.

Formal institutional credit cannot be obtained in the village but Bangali is involved in three rotating savings and credit associations, called *osusus*. The first *osusu* had eight members contributing Le 10 every fortnight. Bangali is the *osusu* master, which means that he collects the money and pays the full amount to the participant who is entitled to it. Bangali is also a member of another *osusu* in which ten members contribute Le 10 every year. The third *osusu* has 20 members each contributing Le 10 when a member (or one of the members of his household) dies.

Cultivation in inland valley swamps
In north-west Sierra Leone, two types of swamp are used for the cultivation of rice: inland valley swamps in the uplands and tidal swamps along the rivers and creeks. Inland valley swamps can be found in valleys where streams and rivers provide water. When inland valleys have been sufficiently inundated during the rainy season, farmers transplant their paddy, sown in nurseries, in the swamp. The following case study illustrates this system.

Samura (32) lives in a household with his wife (20), his two brothers and their wives, and both his mother (50) and step mother (48). The majority of the women combine farming activities with activities in the household. Several are also engaged in petty trading. The household includes 21 children. The family operates an inland valley swamp (rice) and an upland field (rice, maize, millet, sorghum, cassava, and groundnuts). Fruits are also harvested from oil palms, orange trees and coconut trees. The rice harvest of the 1984-85 cropping season was 25 bushels from the upland field (October 1984) and 6 bushels from the inland valley swamp (January 1985). The upland rice was used for (a) gifts to relatives, (b) as seed for the next cropping season, and (c) for sales. In June 1985, seven bushels of rice were sold for Le 35 each and in July eight bushels for Le 44 each. The rice was sold to other farmers in the village and to somebody in Rokupr who used it for consumption purposes. The swamp rice was used (a) to 'pay' a labour group, (b) for seed rice, and (c) for consumption. Farmers attempt to store the best rice for seed, the next best for sales, and the rice with the lowest quality for consumption. In 1985, the upland field was harvested later than usual, at the beginning of November. Only two bushels were harvested whereas two and a half bushels had been sown. This disappointing result was due, according to Samura, to a short fallow period and a lot of weeds in the field.

Cultivation in tidal swamps
Tidal or mangrove swamps can be found on the plains near the rivers. During high tide the river floods the land along the river (twice a day). The water is more saline during the dry than during the rainy season, but fresh water dilutes and washes away the salt during the wet season. A 'pure mangrove' and an 'associated mangrove' cultivation system can be distinguished. Pure mangrove swamps are inundated at each high tide, whereas the associated mangrove areas, situated at some distance from the river, are only inundated during the rainy season or, occasionally, with the spring tide. The following case study (Van der Kamp, 1987) illustrates this system.

Osman, a 34-year-old farmer lives with fifteen people in the same house. He is married and has two wives with three and two children, respectively. Osman's mother (50) cooks the meals with the help of Osman's wives. A brother of his and a niece also belong to the household. All members participate in the farming operations. A labour group was invited on several occasions to plough a swamp or an upland plot and when such a group is working on the farm, other household members join it. Osman likes this form of cooperation because there is no cash payment involved. Normal household expenses are covered by money earned by household members. Money is borrowed for large expenditures such as rebuilding and Osman is worried because he will have to sell a lot of rice in order to be able to finish the house.

Osman cultivates two plots in the pure and one in the associated mangrove system, one plot in an inland valley swamp, and three pieces of upland. One plot in the pure mangrove was obtained from a farmer who needed Le 150 four years ago and pledged the plot in return for cash. Osman can use the plot until the farmer returns the money. Money to purchase plots of land was partly obtained through an *osusu* and the rest was borrowed from a rice trader. Osman is not satisfied with the local rice variety he uses for his upland plots. He wants to buy a few bushels of a better variety. Maize was sown after the rice harvest. Osman cultivates floating rice in the inland valley swamp during the rainy season. After the rainy season, the water level in the valley drops and after a few weeks the soil is dry and in November the rice can be harvested. The resulting 20 bushels were used for consumption.

The total quantity of rice harvested in the 1985-86 cropping season was 131 bushels: 72 bushels from the pure and 24 from the associated mangrove, 20 bushels from the inland valley swamp and 15 bushels of upland rice. The rice harvest obtained from the upland field was half the quantity usually obtained because of insufficient rainfall during the 1985 rainy season. Osman had to give 28 bushels of rice to three people who had lent him money. One is a friend with a rice mill who lent him Le 240 in return for 16 bushels of husk rice (paddy) after the harvest. This is about 11 bushels of clean rice and corresponds with the usual condition of borrowing Le 20 for every bushel to be given in return after the harvest. After the harvest, 7 bushels of CP4 swamp rice, an improved variety, were kept separately as seed rice. The rice was stored under the roof in bags and in two wooden boxes which contained 30 bushels (about 800 kg). After the harvest, two rice meals are eaten every day. This may be reduced to one rice meal in the rainy season.

These three case studies illustrate both the farming systems used by the households and the sources and uses of their rice.

7.4 The Annual Rice Account of rice-growing households

The data we collected were used to draw up an Annual Rice Account for each of the 372 farming households. The sources of rice are presented in Table 7.2a and the uses in Table 7.2b. The general data are followed by those for the three (regional) groups: the upland, upstream and midstream areas. The codes used in the Tables 7.2a and 7.2b correspond to those given in Figure 7.1.

The main source of rice was the harvest (S1). The purchase of rice was also important for other purposes (S62) – mainly trade. Rice purchases for consumption (S61) were considerable, probably higher than normal due to the drought. The next entry in order of importance was S5, the receipts of rice in return for renting out land and loaning money.

Since rice was not their only crop, the rice-farming households were asked to indicate which other crops, out of a list of 22, they were cultivating. Groups of crops that tended to be cultivated by the same household were obtained through a factor analysis. These groups are cereals and pulses (e.g. groundnuts, millet, maize, sorghum, and Guinea corn), tree crops (e.g. kolanut, coconut and orange) and root crops (e.g. sweet potato and cassava).

Columns 2-4 of Table 7.2a show that the quantities differ geographically. The harvest (S1) was the main source of rice in each of the three regions, notably in the upland and midstream villages where the harvest generated about two-thirds of total rice resources. Households in the upland villages tended to buy rice for subsistence purposes but in the upstream and midstream villages rice purchases were also used for trading purposes. These points are discussed below in more detail.

The main use of rice (Table 7.2b) was household consumption (U1) for daily meals. The quantity of 914 kg of unthreshed rice is equivalent to about 640 kg of clean rice, which is about 67 kg per adult consumer. If one adds to this the quantity of rice consumed at celebrations (10.7 kg), the annual rice consumption per adult consumer amounts to about 78 kg. Other important uses of rice were sales of paddy (U6), payments in kind (U5) and gifts to persons in the household's social network (U3).

Primary rice marketing in north-west Sierra Leone

Table 7.2a Average quantities of unthreshed rice (paddy) in kg, by sources, 1 November 1984 - 31 October 1985

Region	All	Upland	Upstream	Midstream
Number of respondents	372	115	110	147
S1 Harvested	1730	767	1491	2663
S2 Seed rice exchanged or purchased	41	30	54	35
S3 Gifts received from relatives or others	46	24	38	68
S5 Receipts in kind:				
S51 Rice for land	76	5	79	128
S53 Rice for credit	106	22	122	158
S6 Purchases:				
S61 for consumption	253	163	340	258
S62 for other purposes	555	169	993	528
S10 Unexplained balance	24	25	83	-2
Total	2831	1205	3200	3836

All: All eleven villages and towns in the survey
Upland: Five upland villages: Gbonkor Masesse, Masuri, Kamba, Sindugu. Funkuya
Upstream: Three upstream villages: Robat, Rokupr, Rosino
Midstream: Three midstream villages: Mambolo, Mafufune, Kalenke

Once again the uses of rice (Table 7.2b) differ among the three regions. Notably, the proportion of rice sold differs considerably: it was very low in the upland villages and relatively high in the upstream and midstream villages. Payments of rice in return for credit (U53) are relatively low in the upland area and relatively high in the other two areas. These points are discussed below in more detail.

Selected entries in the Annual Rice Account

In Figure 7.1 we identified five categories of transaction: subsistence operations, social security transactions, transactions compensating for resource use, commercial transactions and miscellaneous transactions. Below each of these categories is discussed in turn. We use the codes of Table 7.2a (sources) and Table 7.2b (uses).

We begin with the subsistence operations. The rice harvest (S1) of the 1984-85 season happened to be extremely low because of a serious drought during the cropping season (Adam, 1985).[2] This was confirmed when we compared the quantity of seed rice used for the 1985-86 season with the quantity harvested in 1984-85. Seed productivity was,

---

[2] The following quotation from Adam (1985) is relevant. 'Rainfall in 1984 was poor with an uneven distribution. Nurseries were affected by drought in July/August and swamps dried up earlier than usual. The trend from August 1984 onwards was to plant more cassava on the upland and associated swamp in anticipation of the shortfall.'

on average, only 10.4 whereas figures of 200 are quite normal (personal communication L. ten Have, Wageningen Agricultural University).

Table 7.2b Average quantities of unthreshed rice (paddy) in kg, by uses, 1 November 1984 - 31 October 1985

Region	All	Upland	Upstream	Midstream
Number of respondents	372	115	110	147
U1 Household consumption	914	666	941	1088
U2 Seed rice	209	79	180	332
U3 Gifts to chief, relatives, friends, mosque	242	136	250	321
U4 Rice for celebrations	152	84	160	196
U5 Payments in kind:				
U51 Rice for land	54	5	73	82
U52 Rice for labour	234	103	253	324
U53 Rice for credit	204	19	239	324
U6 Sold	683	65	976	949
U7 Loans in kind to:				
U71 Individuals	54	16	52	90
U72 Participants in an *osusu*	14	0	3	35
U8 Losses during storage	30	16	35	35
U9 Other uses (e.g. rice in stock)	41	16	38	60
Total	2831	1205	3200	3836

All: All eleven villages and towns in the survey
Upland: Five upland villages: Gbonkor Masesse, Masuri, Kamba, Sindugu. Funkuya
Upstream: Three upstream villages: Robat, Rokupr, Rosino
Midstream: Three midstream villages: Mambolo, Mafufune, Kalenke

The rice harvest was 1730 kg and the yield was 925 kg/ha. The yield was remarkably similar in the three regions: 924 kg/ha in the upland area, 909 kg/ha in the upstream area and 928 kg/ha in the midstream area. This was probably due to the practice of many farmers spreading their yield risk by simultaneously using the three different rice-farming systems.

Consumption (U1) was the main use of rice. More than 50 per cent of total rice used in the upland area was for consumption. This figure was about 30 per cent in the other regions. The quantity of rice consumed for daily meals was 914/9.6 = 95.2 kg per adult consumer. This was 78.4 kg in the upland area, 81.1 kg in the upstream area and 120.9 kg in the midstream area. Alternative food sources like cassava (n=300 households), yam (n=168), sweet potato (n=119), millet (n=158), maize (n=103), sorghum (n=73) and Guinea corn (n=60) were more readily available in the upland and upstream areas than in the midstream area. A regression analysis shows that rice consumption per adult consumer was significantly higher in households farming in the mangrove swamps than in those farming in the uplands or inland valley swamps.

Seed rice appears in Table 7.2a (S2) and in Table 7.2b (U2). The entry in Table 7.2b represents the use of part of the rice obtained as seed rice. The entry in Table 7.2a covers the (additional) acquisition of seed rice (e.g. from the Seed Multiplication Project in Mambolo or the NWIADP project) or the exchange of seed rice with other farmers to obtain better quality seed than that harvested in one's own fields. The various sources of seed rice are shown in Table 7.3. 'Own stock' (of previous harvest) and 'exchange' with other farmers were the main sources.[3]

We now turn to social security transactions. The quantities of rice received from relatives or others (S3) were low (46 kg), but the quantities donated to village chiefs, relatives, friends or as *zakat* to the mosque (U3) were substantial (242 kg). The proportion of the harvest allocated to these purposes was 14 per cent. There was some geographical variation: about 17 per cent in the upland and upstream areas and about 12 per cent in the midstream area.

Table 7.3 Respondents (%) by sources of seed rice (n=372)

Source	Percentage
Own stock	81.5
Exchange	17.2
Trader	7.0
Master farmer	4.0
NWIADP	9.1
SMP	5.4
Other source	12.4

NWIADP: North-Western Integrated Agricultural Development Programme
SMP: Seed Multiplication Project

Sierra Leone has, like other parts of Africa, a rich tradition of celebrating births, initiation rites, marriages and funerals. Many people are invited to these celebrations. Providing a meal with a lot of rice and a sauce containing meat, vegetables and groundnuts is an important aspect of the ceremony. Rice consumption at these celebrations was 15.8 kg per adult consumer. This figure was 9.9 kg in the upland area, 13.8 kg in the upstream area and 21.8 kg in the midstream area. The quantity of rice used at celebrations appeared to be

---

[3] Obviously, there is a strong relationship between the quantity of seed rice (on which we collected data) and the area sown. Using an econometric relationship derived by Ashante & Spencer (1986) we offer the following estimates of rice farm size: for the research area as a whole 1.87 ha, for the upland area 0.83 ha, for the upstream area 1.64 ha and for the midstream area 2.87 ha.

positively correlated with farm size, household size and borrowing capacity of the head of the household.

The third category consists of transactions compensating for resource use. The entries 'rents received' (S5) and 'rents paid' (U5) are shown in more detail in Table 7.4. Rents received represent predominantly compensation for renting out land and for lending paddy or money to other households. Rents paid are compensation for services rendered in the form of credit and farm labour. Rents in kind (received and paid) in relation to the volume harvested were greatest in the upstream area, followed by the midstream and upland areas. Rents paid in kind were higher than rents received. Rice received in return for credit was more important than rice received in return for renting out land. Rice used to provide meals for labour groups and rice given in return for credit were major uses of rice, especially in the upstream and midstream areas.

Table 7.4 Average quantities of rice, in kg, representing rents of land, labour and capital received and paid, 1 November 1984 - 31 October 1985

Region	All	Upland	Upstream	Midstream
Number of respondents	372	115	110	147
Rents received in kind:				
Rice for land	76	5	79	128
Rice for credit	106	22	122	158
Total	182	27	201	286
Percentage of harvest	10.5%	3.5%	13.4%	10.7%
Rents paid in kind:				
Rice for land	54	5	73	82
Rice for labour (groups)	234	103	253	324
Rice for credit	204	19	239	324
Total	492	127	565	730
Percentage of harvest	28.4%	16.6%	39.9%	27.4%

All: All eleven villages and towns in the survey
Upland: Five upland villages: Gbonkor Masesse, Masuri, Kamba, Sindugu. Funkuya
Upstream: Three upstream villages: Robat, Rokupr, Rosino
Midstream: Three midstream villages: Mambolo, Mafufune, Kalenke

Mutual assistance with labour (U52) is very common in north-west Sierra Leone. A labour group is a typical form of mutual assistance when heavy farm work has to be done. Usually, the participant does not obtain compensation in money but receives a good meal, cigarettes and a little money. Mutual assistance in the form of farm labour was particularly important in cultivating swamp rice (Table 7.5).

The fourth category consists of commercial transactions. A major source of rice was the purchase of rice (S6). Rice was purchased for consumption in the household or for trading. The quantity for consumption appeared to be negatively linked with farm size, but positively with household size and the borrowing capacity of the head of the household. Rice purchases were considerable when compared with the harvest, especially in the upstream area (Table 7.6).

Table 7.5 Respondents (%) using labour groups in rice-farming activities (n=372)

Farming activity	Use of labour groups (%)
Upland rice:	
Brushing	16.1
Clearing	10.2
Weeding	13.7
Harvesting	18.3
Swamp rice:	
Ploughing	57.0
Transplanting	49.5
Harvesting	54.8

In the upstream villages about 89 per cent of the quantity harvested was, on average, obtained by purchasing rice. This percentage was about 43 in the upland area and about 30 in the midstream area. Farm households living near rice mills tended to engage in rice trading as a sideline. This was especially true for households near the market centres of Rokupr and Rosino (upstream area). Farmers periodically purchased rice from other farmers in order to economize on transport costs to the rice mill or to qualify for a higher price by delivering a larger quantity.

Table 7.6 Average quantities of rice purchased, in kg, 1 November 1984 - 31 October 1985

Region	All	Upland	Upstream	Midstream
Number of respondents	372	115	110	147
Purchases of rice:				
For consumption	253	163	340	258
For other purposes	555	169	993	528
Total purchases	808	332	1333	786
Percentage of harvest	46.7%	43.3%	89.4%	29.5%

The quantity of rice sold (U6), as a percentage of the total of uses of rice (Table 7.2b), was highest in the upstream villages (about 30 per cent) and lowest in the upland villages (about 5 per cent). All respondents in the survey sold, on average, 39.4 per cent of the quantity of rice harvested. The percentage was 8.4 for upland households, 65.5 for upstream households and 35.6 for midstream households. These figures underline the subsistence character of the households in the upland area and the more commercial character of the households in the upstream and midstream areas. The quantity sold was positively associated with farm size and the quantity of rice purchased and negatively with household size.

Farmers selling rice were asked to supply information on individual transactions with rice buyers (Table 7.7). One to four transactions were reported by 247 of the 372 households, giving 425 transactions in total.

Table 7.7 Number of transactions per respondent by type of buyer

Type of outlet/buyer	Number of transactions per respondent		
	One	Two-four	Total
creditor	115	36	151
farmer	70	71	141
consumers	7	9	16
rice mill	0	2	2
trader	55	50	74
Total	247	178	425

Creditors (36 per cent), (neighbouring) farmers (33 per cent), and traders (27 per cent) appeared to be the main outlets for rice. The majority of the first (obligatory) transactions were concluded with the creditor indicating considerable debts during the lean season, possibly higher than usual due to the drought. Most subsequent transactions were concluded with other market parties. The 'interlocked' transactions with creditors were omitted from the analysis. Only transactions with either a trader or a (neighbouring) farmer were taken into account.

The following hypotheses about the choice of outlet – trader or (neighbouring) farmer who engaged in rice trading as a sideline – have been formulated and tested by means of logistic regression analysis using the data we collected in 1985 (Hamming, 1996). A significance level of $P<0.05$ was chosen as the criterion for accepting or rejecting a hypothesis.

Hypothesis 1:
The price level of rice was positively related to the probability of selecting a trader as outlet and negatively related to the probability of selecting a farmer as outlet. Traders tended to have more resources to buy rice than farmers in times of scarcity of rice. This hypothesis was accepted.

Hypothesis 2:
The quantity of rice sold was positively related to the probability of selecting a trader as outlet and negatively related to the probability of selecting a farmer as outlet. When farmers have a large quantity to sell, they will probably choose a trader, who is assumed to be capable of generating sufficient working capital. This hypothesis was accepted.

Hypothesis 3:
Sales transactions concluded in the months just before and during the harvest were positively related to the probability of selecting a trader as outlet and negatively related to the probability of selecting a farmer as outlet. In the period September - December the only outlet with enough working capital, and thus capable of buying rice, was the trader. This hypothesis was accepted.

Hypothesis 4:
Whether the transaction was a first or second sale of rice may influence the choice of outlet. This hypothesis was rejected.

These four hypotheses lead to the conclusion that traders tended to purchase larger quantities of rice and at higher prices than farmers, especially in periods of relative scarcity of working capital.

We found some information on prices obtained during individual transactions. First, the farmers in the survey were not always aware of the official producer price of the marketing board SLPMB or its subsidiary NAPCO. About 67 per cent of the respondents did not know the official producer price. Only 25 per cent mentioned the correct SLPMB buying price of Le 20. During the period of the survey (in the second half of 1985), the SLPMB hardly bought any rice because of the higher free market price (Borren, 1986; Donnhauser, 1986). Second, as Table 7.8 shows, paddy prices in 'interlocked' transactions with creditors were considerably lower than free market prices. The prices in the interlocked market generally reflected the traditional condition of exchanging one bushel of paddy for Le 20.

Credit played a major role in the research area, as the comments on Table 7.4 show. In this paragraph loans in kind, and not directly related to the production factors land, labour and capital, are discussed. Loans in rice to individuals (U71) belonging to other households were more important in the midstream and upstream areas than in the upland area. This is due to the fact that surpluses in the midstream and upstream areas were larger than in the uplands. Fifty per cent of the households participated in one or more *osusus*, for reasons such as saving for the maintenance of a house, starting a small business, repaying a debt, or paying funeral costs. We found that 26.3 per cent of the households (n=372) participated in one, 15.3 per cent in two and 8.4 per cent in three or more *osusus*. Households participate in *osusus* either in money or in kind (rice). *osusus* in kind were quite substantial in the midstream area where each household invested, on average, 35 kg of rice (U72).

The fifth category consists of miscellaneous entries. Losses during storage (U8) were, on average, only 30 kg per household, that is, less than two per cent of the quantity harvested. This low percentage was due to the fact that rice was highly valued (especially during the drought of 1985), and the good storage conditions in the houses either in sacks under the roof or in large wooden boxes. Other uses of rice (U9), e.g. rice in stock not yet allocated to a certain purpose was a minor item. The unexplained balance (S10) was relatively low, less than one per cent, on average, for all respondents. It was somewhat higher in the upstream area (2.6 per cent), probably due to the importance of rice trading in that area.

Table 7.8 Weighted average monthly prices (Leone per bushel of paddy) of both free market transactions and transactions with creditors

Month	Free transactions		Transactions with creditors	
	Price	Number	Price	Number
December 1984	48.90	10	20.00	5
January 1985	28.87	16	24.87	14
February	48.72	19	22.43	41
March	39.43	56	19.87	53
April	44.42	60	17.10	27
May	46.73	31	17.36	6
June	53.39	24	-	-
July	56.82	14	(60.00)	1
August	60.13	23	(59.27)	2
September	59.39	14	-	-
October	58.57	3	-	-
November	59.88	4	(36.00)	2
Total		274		151

Note: Averages based on only one or two transactions are given in brackets.

7.5 Rice transactions and rural institutions

One of the objectives of this study has been to help decision makers in the institutional environment of rice-farming households to improve the transaction infrastructure.

To improve insight into the transaction environment of the rice-farming households, the following question was asked (n=372): 'What are the main problems concerning your farming activities?' The main answers were: insufficient labour 31.5%; lack of farm inputs 20.2%; lack of farm machinery 16.4%; and pests and diseases 21.8%. It is hoped that the institutional environment of the rice-farming community will help households to solve or at least reduce these problems.

The sample population was further asked whether there was any formal organization operating in the village which helped them obtain access to credit, mechanization, new varieties, fertilizer or agricultural extension. Table 7.9 shows that about one fifth of the sample population had access to services such as agricultural extension and new varieties. About one seventh had access to fertilizers. The rice-farming population had hardly any access to mechanization services. Only one twelfth of the respondents had access to formal credit. However, obtaining small amounts of credit was not a problem because it was relatively easy to participate in rotating saving and credit associations (*osusus*).

Both formal (Table 7.10) and informal institutions were active in the research area. The main informal institutions were (mutual) labour groups, rotating savings and credit associations (*osusus*), factor markets for land, labour and capital, input markets for seeds and output markets for rice (often located near private rice mills along the Great Scarcies River). As we saw, the sample households used these informal institutions extensively.

Table 7.9 Respondents (%) by access to services and products (n=372)

Services	Percentage (%)
Credit facilities	8.1
Mechanization	1.1
Introduction of new rice varieties	20.4
Fertilizer supplies	14.8
Agricultural extension	21.5

Table 7.10 Main formal institutions operating in the research area

NWIADP	North-Western Integrated Agricultural Development Programme
RRS	Rice Research Station
SMP	Seed Multiplication Project
WARDA	West African Rice Development Association
SLPMB	Sierra Leone Produce Marketing Board
NAPCO	National Produce Company, subsidiary of SLPMB
SLDB	Sierra Leone Development Bank.

In the 1970s, the World Bank argued that the participation of small-scale farmers in Green Revolution technologies would increase if they were not constrained by lack of credit and limited physical access to inputs. To solve these problems the Bank promoted Integrated Agricultural Development Projects (IADPs). Typically, an IADP was a semi-autonomous regional development authority which supplied small-scale farmers with improved inputs (and credit for their purchase), provided extension services, and attempted to solve physical access problems by, for example, a programme of rural road construction or improvement. The first IADPs in Sierra Leone were inaugurated in the eastern (1972) and northern (1976) regions (Richards, 1985).

The national Rice Research Station in Rokupr was established before the Second World War in 1934. In 1976, the West African Rice Development Association (WARDA) started a regional project on swamp rice in the Great Scarcies area. Seed rice could be obtained from various sources including the Seed Multiplication Project and the NWIADP (Table 7.3).

The services of the formal institutions were only used to a limited extent by the sample population. The services of the NWIADP were used by 11.6 per cent, those of the RRS by 0.8 per cent, those of the WARDA by 3.8 per cent, those of the SMP by 0.8 per cent, those of the SLDB by 1.1 per cent and those of other rural institutions by 0.5 per cent. The services of a non-governmental organization operating in the area (ACRE) were used by 7.5 per cent of the sample households. The conclusion is that, in contrast to the informal institutions, only a small proportion of the sample population used the services of the formal organizations. Only the NWIADP had a 'market share' of more than 10 per cent. This result corresponds with the observation by Richards (1985) that many rice-farming households remained outside the direct reach of new technologies.

7.6 Concluding remarks

Our survey has increased our insight into various aspects of the rice economy of north-west Sierra Leone, notably concerning the following five points.

Subsistence operations
Rice-farming households were, in the period covered by the study, more subsistence oriented than expected, presumably due to the drought of that year. The rice yield per hectare was remarkably equal in the three regions, which was probably due to the fact that many farmers followed a practice of spreading their yield risk by using different rice-farming systems: rainfed shifting cultivation, inland valley swamps and tidal swamps. The quantity of rice consumed for the daily meals was 95.2 kg per adult consumer, with significant geographical variation.

Social security transactions
The quantities of rice received from relatives or others was low, 46 kg per household, on average, but the quantities donated to village chiefs, relatives, friends or as *zakat* to the mosque were substantial, 242 kg per household, on average. Sierra Leone has, like other parts of Africa, a rich culture of celebrating births, initiation rites, marriages and funerals. Many people are invited for these celebrations and providing guests with a rich meal is important. Rice consumption at these celebrations was, on average, 15.8 kg per adult consumer.

Transactions compensating for resource use
Quantities of rice used to pay for rents were higher than those received as rents. Rice received in return for credit was more important than rice received in return for renting out land. Rice used to provide meals for labour groups and that given in return for credit were major uses of rice, especially in the upstream and midstream area. Mutual labour assistance among farming households was common in the research area. A labour group is a typical

means of providing mutual assistance when heavy farm work has to be done. Mutual labour assistance was particularly important in cultivating swamp rice.

Commercial transactions
In the upstream villages about 43 per cent of the total rice resources were, on average, obtained by purchasing rice, mainly for trading. Farm households living near rice mills tended to engage in rice trading as a sideline. This was especially true for households in the market centres of Rokupr and Rosino. The proportion of rice sold was highest in the upstream villages (30 per cent) and lowest in the upland villages (5 per cent). All respondents in the survey sold, on average, 39.4 per cent of the quantity of rice harvested. The percentage was 8.4 for upland households, 65.5 for upstream households and 35.6 for midstream households. These figures underline the subsistence character of households in the upland area and the more commercial character of the households in other areas. Paddy prices in 'interlocked' transactions with creditors were considerably lower than free market prices. The prices in the interlocked market reflected the traditional condition of exchanging one bushel for 20 Leones. Traders tended to purchase larger quantities of rice and at higher prices than (neighbouring) farmers who engaged in rice trading as a sideline.

Services provided by rural institutions
We found that the households' access to formal institutions was low, sharply contrasting with access to informal institutions such as labour groups, *osusus*, and informal markets for inputs and outputs.

References

ADAM, J.M. (1985) *Assessment of technology for mangrove swamp rice in West Africa: A case study of the Great Scarcies river area of Sierra Leone.* Rokupr: Progress Report ODA-ESCOR-WARDA.
ASHANTE, K.P. & D.S.C. SPENCER (1986) *Mangrove swamp rice production in the Great Scarcies area of Sierra Leone: Socio-economic implications.* Rokupr: WARDA.
BORREN, C.E. (1986) 'Collecting rice trade in the Great Scarcies area of Sierra Leone'. M.Sc Thesis, Wageningen Agricultural University, Departments of Development Economics and Marketing and Marketing Research.
DONNHAUSER, F. (1986) *Agrarmaerkte und landwirtschaftliche Markt- und Preispolitik in Sierra Leone.* Giessen (Germany): Justus-Liebig Universitaet.
GWYNNE-JONES, D.R.G., P.K. MITCHELL, M.E. HARVEY & K. SWINDELL (1978) *A new geography of Sierra Leone.* London: Longman Group Ltd.
HAMMING, I. (1996) 'Rice farmers in North-West Sierra Leone: Choice of outlet, purchase channel and degree of commercialisation'. M.Sc. thesis, Wageningen Agricultural University, Department of Marketing and Marketing Research.
HUIJSMAN, A. (1986) 'Choice and uncertainty in a semi-subsistence economy. A study of decision-making in a Philippine village'. PhD thesis, Wageningen Agricultural University.
LEVI, J. (1976) *African agriculture: economic action and reaction in Sierra Leone.* Oxford (UK): Commonwealth Agricultural Bureaux.
RICHARDS, P. (1986) *Coping with hunger. Hazard and experiment in an African rice-farming system.* London: Allen and Unwin.

SCOTT, E.P. (1978) 'Subsistence, markets and rural developments in Hausaland'. In *The Journal of Developing Areas*, Vol. 12, pp. 449-469.

SPIJKERS-ZWART, S.I. (1980) 'The household and "householding", some conceptual considerations'. In C. Presvelou & S.I. Spijkers-Zwart (eds). *The household. women and agricultural development*. Wageningen: Veenman, pp. 97-74.

VAN DER KAMP, J. (1987) 'The production structure of rice in the Great Scarcies area of Sierra Leone'. Student thesis, Wageningen Agricultural University, Department of Rural Sociology.

VAN DER LAAN, H.L. (1975) *The Lebanese traders in Sierra Leone*. PhD dissertation, Tilburg University, the Netherlands. The Hague: Mouton.

VAN TILBURG, A. (1992) 'Tied and untied rice transactions of farm household in Northwest Sierra Leone'. Proceedings of the session on 'Commodity markets and institutional changes', EAAE Seminar on 'Food and agricultural policies under structural adjustment', Hohenheim (Germany), pp. 96-110.

VAN TILBURG, A. (forthcoming) *Transactions with rice of rice farming households in north-west Sierra Leone*. Wageningen Agricultural University

8

Maize and Bean Marketing in Benin
The Peasant Farmer's Choice of Marketing Outlet

Lineke van Bruggen and Aad van Tilburg

Abstract

In this chapter the peasant farmer's choice of marketing outlet for maize and beans is analyzed on the basis of a survey among large peasant farmers in Benin. Two main types of outlet are available: physical markets and buyers coming to the farmgate. Actors within and outside the farm household play a role in decisions relating to the choice of outlet. Variables related to the farm household as well as factors relating to the market environment appear to affect the choice of outlet. Hypotheses are formulated and tested by means of logistic regression analysis. The variables 'crop choice of the previous year', 'acreage cultivated with the crop', 'the number of sources used for market information', and 'preference for the farmgate as outlet' were found to have a positive influence on the probability of peasant farmers choosing buyers at the farmgate. A negative relationship was found for the variable 'number of markets in the evoked set' and the probability of choosing buyers at the farmgate.

8.1 Introduction

This chapter forms part of a larger research project aiming to obtain a better understanding of the relationship between 'crop choice' and 'market behaviour' of farm households in Benin.[1] For this purpose three choice levels are distinguished: crop choice, harvest allocation, and the choice of marketing outlet. For these sequential decisions the following questions are formulated:

a. crop choice. What crops do farm households select for cultivation and why?

---

[1] This is a PhD project, for which field work was carried out from 1990 to mid 1992 in two regions in Benin: Mono Province and Borgou Province. In total 187 large peasant farmers were included in the survey. Data were collected over two agricultural years, during a field period of 18 months.

b. harvest allocation. What happens to crops once they have matured? Given the outcome of the harvest, what are the uses to which it is put: household consumption or the fulfilment of social or economic obligations, or is it sold either immediately or after it has been stored for some time? What is the reason for this choice?
c. choice of marketing outlet. If a product is to be sold, and given the market environment, which marketing outlet is selected and why: a physical market or a buyer at the farmgate?[2]

These decisions influence each other. The first (crop choice) is a limiting factor for the second (harvest allocation) and the third (choice of outlet). The outcome of the harvest allocation may influence the choice of outlet. However, past experience and an assessment of the selected marketing outlet may influence the peasant farmer's choice of crop in the next cycle and in subsequent harvest allocations.

The aim of this research project was to study the interaction between the market environment or market incentives and the decisions of farm households with respect to crop choice, harvest allocation and choice of outlet. An important element of this research was the relationship of the farm household with the market. As a result, the selected households were the larger (largest) ones in their regions and they produced a considerable proportion of their crops for the market.[3]

After a preliminary survey, Mono Province in the south and Borgou Province in the north were selected as research regions (Map 8.1). In these two areas, we expected to find large entrepreneurial peasant farmers[4] engaged in production for the market. Since the two research areas are located at some distance from each other and because Mono Province has two agricultural seasons a year and Borgou Province has only one, it was decided that the Mono region should be the main research area and Borgou Province should be visited for a period of several weeks once a year. In this way sufficient data could be collected to compare our findings satisfactorily.

In Benin, a large variety of annual crops are grown including cotton, various kinds of cereals (maize, sorghum, millet), tubers (principally yam and cassava), leguminous crops (mainly beans and groundnuts) and horticultural crops such as tomatoes, red peppers, ladies' fingers and a variety of vegetables. Several of these crops are cultivated with a specific purpose. For example, cotton is grown for the market, sorghum and millet (in the north of Benin) are mainly grown for home consumption, while horticultural crops in the south are usually cultivated for sale. Other crops such as maize and beans are what can be called multi-purpose crops. They are used for home consumption as well as for market sales.

---

[2] In fact, transactions take place 'at the farm', since farmgates are hard to find in the African context! Among the buyers coming to the farmgate were traders, consumers and processors.
[3] We tried to include all the largest peasant farmers in a selected area in the survey. Their households cultivated at least five hectares each year, either in one or two crop cycles.
[4] Peasant farmers are defined as agriculturalists living in a more or less peasant society but producing a considerable proportion of their crops for the market, i.e. their production is partly commercialized.

Maize and bean marketing in Benin 155

Map 8.1 Map of Benin showing the research areas

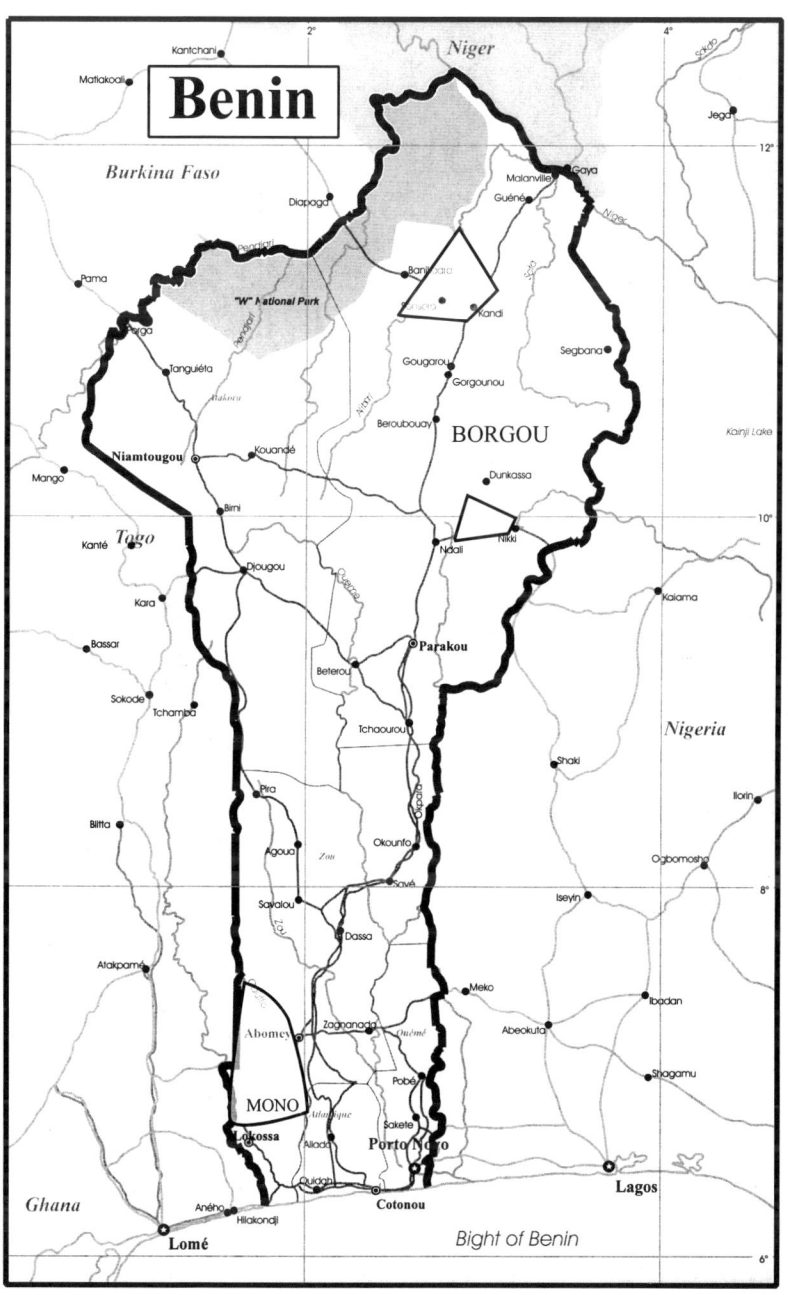

Three main marketing outlets can be identified in Benin: physical markets, buyers coming to the farmgate and the CARDER (Centre d'Action Régional pour le Développement Rural), a state-run organization that purchases mainly cotton. For all other crops there were only two real options for Beninese peasant farmers: the physical market and buyers coming to the farmgate.

In this chapter, we focus on the marketing outlets chosen by Beninese farm households for two important food crops: maize and beans. In both research areas these crops were produced by many peasant farmers and intended for both home consumption and the market. We limit ourselves here to these two crops and the choice between the two main marketing outlets.

The main outlets chosen by the peasant farmers in the survey are presented in Table 8.1. (Only one choice per peasant farmer was included.)

Table 8.1 Main market outlet chosen by peasant farmers for selected crops

	Physical market	*Buyers at farmgate*	*N**
Maize 1990	45	70	115
Beans 1990	53	35	88
Beans 1991	24	44	68

* The N value given here is the N value used in the analysis in Section 8.5. Due to missing values for several of the variables in the analysis, the values of N in this column are lower than the actual number of peasant farmers engaged in selling these crops. (The total number of peasant farmers selling maize in 1990 was 144, for 'beans 1990' the figure was 95, while for 'beans 1991' the number was 81. At the time of the survey some of the peasant farmers still had maize and/or beans in stock, which they may have sold later in the season.)

The table suggests considerable variation between crops and between years. For beans, for instance, in 1990 the sale conditions at the market seemed better, while in 1991 the sale conditions at the farmgate were more attractive. This conclusion is tentative because not all of the 1991 harvest had been sold at the time of the survey.

In explaining the choice of marketing outlet, we make a distinction between the characteristics of the farm household and those of the market environment. Opportunities or limitations of the market environment include: market conditions and risks, type and number of marketing outlets, costs and benefits of the use of these outlets, the distance to the main market, and the availability and cost of transport.

Factors that reflect the characteristics of the farm household include: habit or tradition (what people used to do in the past), preference for a particular outlet, the purpose for which the crop is grown and the (gathering of) market information and the exchange of this knowledge between household members. All of these factors are considered to be influential.

In Section 8.2, the actors involved in making decisions about product sales are discussed, while in Section 8.3, the characteristics of the farm household and those of the market environment are discussed. Hypotheses are developed and discussed in Section 8.4, and in Section 8.5 the results of the analysis are presented for the two products selected: maize and beans. In Section 8.6 the findings are summarized and conclusions drawn.

8.2 Actors: household members and other actors

Various actors can be distinguished in the decision-making process with regard to the choice of marketing outlet. Members within and outside the farm household may influence the decision, while within the household some members play a more important role than others. An important issue in this respect is household composition and the division of labour within it. Who makes the decisions in the household? Who is consulted? Who is collecting market information? Who is responsible for the actual crop sales?

In Figure 8.1, the assumed pattern of relations between the different actors and the gathering of information by members of the farm household is shown in relation to the (market) environment.

Figure 8.1 Assumed pattern of relations between actors and collection of information by household members involved in the selling of products

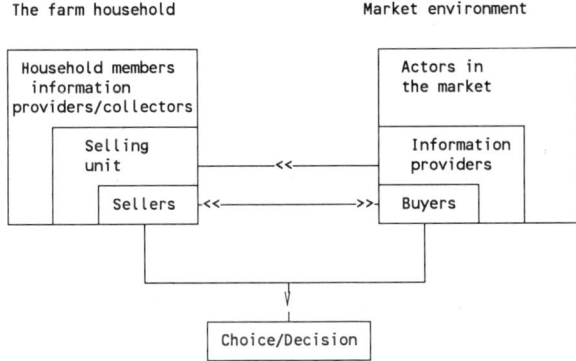

Cohesion is strong within farm households. Most members belong to a household for a long period of time and members have specific tasks or roles. Cohesion outside the household, in particular with actors in the market environment, may be weak because one buyer may easily be replaced by another.

The selling unit within the farm household
Members of the farm household may act as a 'selling unit', analogous to buying centres in industrial marketing theory.[5] Farm households in Benin are large and interaction between household members may be expected (see Kool, 1994, for instances of buying centres in farm households in the Netherlands).

The persons in the household may have different roles. We may distinguish producers, influencers, deciders, approvers, sellers and gatekeepers. The head of the household is the major actor, he[6] may play all these roles, or delegate some to other household members. Sometimes, actors from outside the household such as friends, other farmers, relatives, or buyers (traders) influence the decision to sell. Sometimes they may give market information or advice on whether to sell or not. These actors play a role as influencers or gatekeepers (for example traders may try to prevent particular information reaching the peasant farmer). The roles of producer, seller, decider and approver will only be played by members of the farm household. Producers are household members actively engaged in agricultural work. Sellers are members who go to the market with the product or negotiate at home with buyers at the farmgate. Deciders are the household members who decide on whether or not to sell a particular product at a certain time. Approvers are the members who are able to authorize a sale (Kotler, 1997, 209-210). In the survey, the decider and approver were often one and the same person: the head of the household. He took the final decision, generally after he had consulted others. In a limited number of cases other members of the farm household could veto the sale of a product, but in most cases, they could only (strongly) advise the head of the household.

Various actors influencing the head of the household
Market information can be obtained from sources within and outside the household. Table 8.2 shows how the head of the household receives market information.

Table 8.2 Consultation of others by the head of household before products are sold

	Consulting household members		*Consulting others*	*N*
	Wife/wives	*Children*		
Total	151 (85.3%)	83 (47.2%)	89 (50.3%)	177
Mono Province	107 (89.2%)	44 (37.0%)	40 (33.3%)	120
Borgou Province	44 (77.2%)	39 (68.4%)	49 (86.0%)	57

---

5 Kotler (1997, 209/210) defines a buying centre as including all members of the organization who play any of the following six roles in the purchase decision process: Users, Influencers, Deciders, Approvers, Buyers and Gatekeepers. Webster & Wind (1972, 6) define a buying centre as follows: 'all those individuals and groups who participate in the purchasing decision-making process, who share some common goals and the risk arising from the decisions'.
6 In our survey all heads of household were male which was probably due to he fact that (in size) the farm households in the survey were the largest in their areas.

Almost all household heads (over 96 per cent) consulted others before selling their products. Three main categories were distinguished according to the relationship with the head of the household: wife/wives having their own fields, children having their own fields and others. Most household heads consulted their wife or wives (more than 85 per cent). In Mono Province they consulted their wives more often than in Borgou Province. About half of those interviewed consulted their children. Here again there was a geographical difference. In the Borgou area more than 68 per cent of the farmers consulted their children but in Mono Province this figure was 37 per cent. About 50 per cent of the farmers in the survey also consulted 'others': in the Borgou region 86 per cent and in the Mono region 33 per cent. 'Others' were mostly friends (in more than 50 per cent of the cases), buyers (traders) or other relatives.[7]

In Mono Province, peasant farmers and their wife/wives participate more actively in trade than in Borgou Province. Apparently in Mono Province, the market information a peasant farmer and his wife/wives collect is sufficient to allow a decision to be made. In Borgou Province, the peasant farmer seemed to be less well informed. It was therefore useful for him to collect more information from various sources.

We may conclude that in Mono Province the role of wives in the decision-making process is more important than in Borgou Province, while in Borgou Province children and 'others' are more important. In Mono households, members are the main source of market information, while in Borgou Province information often comes from people outside the household.

8.3 Factors related to the choice of marketing outlet

In this section some characteristics of the farm household and the market environment are discussed. These characteristics are considered to be relevant factors in the decisions about the choice of marketing outlet. Most of these factors are included as variables in the model in Section 8.5. Unfortunately, some had to be excluded from the model because they were difficult (or impossible) to measure or estimate. However, for a better understanding of the context, these factors are also discussed here, albeit briefly.

Infrastructure: market information and transport
There are two important infrastructural factors: access to market information and access to transport. During the research period there were no public price information systems or public bodies collecting or disseminating market information. This is why the providers of market information, especially the various sources described in the previous section, played such an important role.

---

7   In both research areas, information providers from about two sources were used (1.9 sources to be exact). There is, however, an interesting geographical difference: in Mono Province the average was 1.6 and in Borgou Province 2.5 (the modus in Mono Province is 1 source and in Borgou Province 3 sources). Apparently, peasant farmers in the Borgou region generally use more sources to gather information than those in the Mono area.

The quality of the roads, the distance between the farmgate or field and the market, and the availability of transport all influenced transport costs. The quality of the roads during the survey was poor and some roads were impassable during the rainy season. The distance to the nearest or the most important market is assumed to be a proxy variable for transport costs. There are large differences between Mono and Borgou Provinces with respect to marketing infrastructure. The population density and the density of physical markets in the Borgou region are much lower than in Mono Province, which means that the average distance between farmgate and market is larger and access to marketing outlets poorer in Borgou Province.

Types of outlets, costs and proceeds
The two main types of outlet identified above – the physical market and the buyer purchasing at the farmgate – are now discussed in more detail. Physical markets are mostly periodic markets. Some are held every four days (as is the case with most markets in Mono Province), some every five days, others every seven days and a few once a month. There is, as we saw, a high density of physical markets in Mono, but a low density in Borgou Province. Mono peasant farmers are therefore relatively well-served by markets. Both market and price information are presumably easier to obtain there than in Borgou Province. Many types of buyers can be identified at these markets: wholesalers, collecting traders, retailers, processors as well as consumers (Fanou, 1994; Lutz, 1994).

The numerous markets in Mono Province differ in size. They range from small local markets to large interregional ones. Many traders operating at these markets also buy at the farmgate. This means that peasant farmers in Mono Province have a wider choice of marketing outlet: several physical markets, and buyers at the farmgate. The negotiating power of the average Mono peasant farmer is therefore greater.

In Borgou Province, the situation is different. There are not many physical markets and the nearest are mostly local or regional ones. Nevertheless, the Borgou peasant farmer is able to exercise the same sort of power as his Mono counterpart but costs are higher. For example, the decision to sell the product at a market far away may be very profitable, but it demands organizational skills and involves more risk.[8] We decided to use the variable 'Regio' (Borgou or Mono) to represent market density.

Relevant factors which, unfortunately, are difficult to measure or estimate, are the (expected) costs and benefits involved in the use of a (potential) outlet by peasant farmers. Various aspects may be taken into consideration: 1. the price offered (benefit), 2. the costs involved (for example market taxes), 3. the costs incurred in ensuring access to an outlet (e.g. transport costs), and 4. the costs of completing a transaction (time and remuneration of sellers). The cost of using the market (points 2 to 4) are relatively high, while the benefits (price offered) also tend to be high. The peasant farmer must take the different aspects into account when he decides where he will (try to) sell the product. Since it was impossible to measure all these factors in a satisfactory way, approximate indicators have been used. The

---

[8] Risk includes, for example, the chance that a product is transported to the physical market but is not sold because demand is not high enough or the price is not in line with the farmer's expectations.

region and the distance to the nearest market are used as such for estimating transport costs and the allocation of time by sellers.

Habit or tradition: knowledge and experience
Society's influence on the peasant farmer's choice of outlet may be great. Some categories of peasant farmers are supposed to be traditional: they tend to do what they always did and are reluctant to change. Peasant farmers may avoid changing their sales policy except when the risk is small. We expected that the peasant farmer's previous choices would influence his present decisions to a large extent. Tradition is the result of a combination of social and cultural values and economic factors. The habit factor will be partly captured in the variable 'choice of marketing outlet of the previous year'.[9]

The peasant farmer's market knowledge is assumed to be an important factor in the choice of type of outlet. This is reflected in the variable 'number of sources used to collect market information'. A 'Market Intention Code' indicates the purpose for which the crop is grown: market, household consumption or a combination of both. When crops are mainly produced for the market, presumably more market information is gathered and more alternative outlets considered. Also, the household's stated preference for a certain marketing outlet is considered to influence the actual decision on the outlet.

Figure 8.2 presents a summary of the farm household and market characteristics. All are assumed to be relevant to the farmer's choice of marketing outlet. The number of the hypothesis – see Section 8.4 – is given in brackets.

Figure 8.2 Characteristics of the farm, the farm household, and the environment, presumed to influence the choice of marketing outlet

Characteristics of the farm and the farm household	Characteristics of the environment
Factors of production: * area under cultivation (H3) Habit or tradition: knowledge and experience: * past choices/experiences and evaluation of past choices (H1) * purpose for which the crop was grown in the previous year (H2) * knowledge regarding market conditions and information gathering (H4) * preference for an outlet (H5)	Area/region: * Mono/Borgou (H9) Market environment: * infrastructure: transport and media; distance to the nearest market (H6) * costs and proceeds (prices) (H6/H9) * number of markets (H7) * number of buyers (H8)

---

[9] Habit and/or tradition is used as an indicator for a present decision in relation to past choices. It should not be confused with risk aversion (see for example Ellis, 1993).

8.4 Hypotheses regarding the choice of marketing outlet

Nine hypotheses were formulated relating the peasant farmer's choice of marketing outlet – market or buyer at the farmgate – to a set of variables. The variable to be explained is MC(t): choice of marketing outlet in year t.

Explanatory variables related to the farm household
Previous choice {MC(t-1)}: Beninese peasant farmers tend to make the same choice as they did in the recent past because of habit or tradition. This means that the previous choice of marketing outlet largely explains the present choice. The hypothesis is:

H 1: *There is a positive relationship between the choice of marketing outlet in year (season) t-1 and that in year (season) t, or MC(t)= f{MC(t-1)}.*

The intention to sell, reflected by a Market Intention Code (MIC), represents the proportion of the crop (0 - 100 per cent) that is intended for sale rather than for household consumption.[10] It is assumed that it is more profitable to sell large quantities at the farmgate (no transport organization or costs, and no transport risks).

H 2: *The higher the intention to sell a crop, the more likely it is that the product is sold to buyers at the farmgate.*

The area of the cultivated crop (ACR). A factor that is assumed to influence the choice of marketing outlet is the size of the area cultivated with a particular crop. The larger the area cultivated with a crop, the more likely it is that the crop is sold at the farmgate.

H 3: *There is a positive relationship between the area cultivated with a particular crop and the probability of selling it to buyers at the farmgate.*

Information gathering (NUMSRC): We described three categories of information providers: wives, children, and 'others'. Information was collected on the number of sources that a peasant farmer used in his information search. We assume that the more sources used for information gathering, the better informed the peasant farmer is. He will therefore have more countervailing power (negotiating possibilities) with respect to buyers at the farmgate.

---

[10] In the survey, the peasant farmers were asked what they intended to do with their crops. The reason for this question was that it can take a long time - sometimes more than a year – before the crop is actually sold or used for consumption. It was possible to compare intention with actual behaviour by analyzing the data from a one-year period. We found that there was hardly any difference between intention and what was actually done. Since the years of the survey were not exceptional, there was no need to make adjustments. This is the reason why intention is used as an indicator of actual behaviour.

Maize and bean marketing in Benin 163

H 4: *There is a positive relationship between the number of sources that are used for information gathering by the head of the household and the probability that the crop is sold to buyers at the farmgate.*

Preference for a certain outlet (PREFOUT): It is likely that the peasant farmer will sell a product at an outlet that corresponds with his overall (stated) preference. However, other factors such as market conditions may prevent this.

H 5: *There is a positive relationship between the peasant farmer's overall preference for a certain outlet and the choice of that outlet.*

Explanatory variables related to the market environment
The distance to the nearest market of importance (DM) is assumed to influence the choice of marketing outlet. If this market is near, there is less need to sell to buyers coming to the farmgate. (There are a few peasant farmers who prefer a distant market to one nearby.) The distance to the nearest market gives a good indication of (a) the effort involved in getting a product to a market and (b) the costs of marketing.

H 6: *There is a positive relationship between the distance to the nearest market of importance and the probability that the crop is sold to buyers at the farmgate.*

Number of markets in the peasant farmer's evoked set (NUMMAR): The markets that are visited by household members and/or are considered as possible outlets belong to the 'peasant farmer's evoked set'.[11] Most of these markets are visited at least occasionally. It may be that not all the markets close to the household belong to the evoked set. On the other hand, it is possible that distant markets may be included.[12]

H 7: *There is a positive relationship between the number of markets in the peasant farmer's evoked set and the probability that a market is chosen as an outlet.*

Number of buyers coming to the farmgate in the peasant farmer's evoked set (NUMBUY): In the same way as with the number of markets in the peasant farmer's evoked set, the number of buyers was determined. When there are several buyers coming to the farmgate, the peasant farmer can be said to have some countervailing power *vis-à-vis* the buyers.

---

[11] During the first visit to a peasant farmer (before the first growing season of the survey) we asked which physical markets he might visit. The response to this question forms 'the peasant farmer's evoked set'. At that time the crops of year t-1 of most peasant farmers were still in the fields.

[12] The number of markets in the evoked set differs from market density which is an objective way of measuring the number of markets in the vicinity of a farm household. By contrast, the number of markets in the evoked set is a subjective measure indicating the number of markets the household considers reasonable to use. (Some peasant farmers stated that the market at Cotonou belonged to their evoked set, while for one of them the distance to this market was almost 300 km.)

H 8:   *There is a positive relationship between the number of buyers coming to the farmgate in the peasant farmer's evoked set and the probability that a buyer at the farmgate is chosen as an outlet.*

The region of residence (REGIO) is assumed to influence the choice of marketing outlet, since the market situation differs considerably between the two regions. In Borgou Province, the number of physical markets is limited and more produce is sold to buyers at the farmgate. In Mono Province, there are more physical markets and presumably more produce is sold at markets than in Borgou Province.

H 9:   *There is a positive relationship between Borgou Province as a region of residence and the probability that the farmgate is selected as an outlet.*

The model
The hypotheses discussed above are reflected in the following equation:

```
MC(t) =  α  +  ß1{MC(t-1)}  +  ß2(MICt)  +  ß3(ACRt)  +  ß4(NUMSRC)  +
         ß5(PREFOUT) + ß6(DM) + ß7(NUMMAR) + ß8(NUMBUY) + ß9(REGIO) + U.
```

Variables related to the farm household are:
MC(t)	The choice of marketing outlet in year t; (MC=0 for 'market' and MC=1 for 'buyer at the farmgate')
MIC	Market Intention Code for the crop (purpose for which it was cultivated)
ACR	Area under cultivation with a particular crop
NUMSRC	Number of sources used for the gathering of market information
PREFOUT	Preference for a certain outlet

Variables related to the market are:
DM	Distance to the nearest market of importance
NUMMAR	Number of markets in the peasant farmer's evoked set
NUMBUY	Number of buyers at the farmgate in the peasant farmer's evoked set
REGIO	Region dummy: 0 for Mono Province and 1 for Borgou Province
U	Disturbance term

The model was tested for two main food crops: maize and beans. Only data for the year 1990/91 were used for maize.[13] This meant that the choice of outlet of the previous year could not be taken into account in the model. The same was true for the analysis of the

---

[13] The only relevant year for maize is 1990/91, since the harvest of 1991/92 remained partly unsold in mid 1992 at the end of the research period.

choice of outlet for beans in 1990/91. Data for all variables in the equation were available for beans for the year 1991/92.

8.5 Variables affecting the choice of marketing outlet

The dependent variable in the model is a binary variable. It represents the choice of marketing outlet for maize or beans: mainly using the market or mainly using buyers at the farmgate. The analysis was made at the level of the peasant farmer. The analysis for maize concerns the aggregation of data concerning both the improved and the local variety of maize. For maize the analysis was also carried out at the level of individual transactions. Depending on the number of transactions, one or two outlet choices per peasant farmer were possible.

The hypotheses were tested with logistic regression.[14] The interpretation of the results is similar, but not identical, to that of regression analysis. In logistic regression other tests are used to test the significance of the relationship (model Chi-square instead of F-test) or the parameters (Wald-statistic instead of the t-test).

Maize
For maize, the following equation was assumed (data for 1990/91):

$$MCt = \alpha + \beta_1(MICt) + \beta_2(ACRt) + \beta_3(NUMSRC) + \beta_4(PREFOUT) + \beta_5(DM) + \beta_6(NUMMAR) + \beta_7(NUMBUY) + \beta_8(REGIO).$$

Analysis of the correlation matrix of the variables showed that 'Regio' is relatively highly correlated with several other variables. For this reason, the analysis was carried out with and without this variable. Table 8.3 gives the results of the logistic regressions for maize. Results vary with the type of observation: the peasant farmer's predominant choice ('farmer') or the peasant farmer's choice related to an individual transaction ('transaction') and 'with Regio' or 'without Regio' as explanatory variable.

Most variables do not show a significant relationship. The coefficient belonging to the variable 'preference for an outlet (PREFOUT)' is significantly positive in all cases, indicating that a preference for buyers at the farmgate had a positive influence on the probability of selecting a buyer at the farmgate as an outlet. In the equations 'without Regio', the parameter belonging to 'number of sources used (NUMSRC)' is also positively significant, indicating that the more sources of market information used, the more likely it was that buyers at the farmgate would be chosen as an outlet.

---

[14] For a short description of this method, see, for example, Hair et al. (1992, 60-62).

Table 8.3 Results of the logistic regressions on the peasant farmer's choice of outlet for maize in 1990/91

| | Farmer | | Transaction | |
	With Regio	Without Regio	With Regio	Without Regio
- 2 Log Likelihood	136.79	137.77	242.09	243.57
Goodness of Fit	111.54	112.02	193.18	193.45
Model Chi-Square	17.15	16.18	15.66	14.18
Significance	0.0286	0.0235	0.0475	0.0481
N	115	115	196	196
Q	0.652	0.661	0.634	0.628
P	0.524	0.524	0.535	0.535
t_{N-1} [15]	2.753	2.940	2.781	2.6127
VARIABLES	B (WALD statistic)			
MICt maize	- 0.85 (0.46)	- 0.50 (0.18)	0.81 (0.87)	0.99 (1.44)
ACR maize	0.00 (0.15)	0.00 (0.01)	0.00 (0.00)	- 0.00 (0.05)
PREFOUT	1.36 (7.7)**	1.38 (8.03)**	0.82 (5.24)**	0.84 (5.53)**
NUMSRC	0.50 (2.11)	0.66 (4.87)**	0.23 (0.78)	0.38 (2.83)*
DISTANCE (DM)	- 0.00 (0.34)	- 0.00 (0.04)	- 0.01 (0.72)	- 0.00 (0.18)
NUMMAR	0.43 (3.24)*	0.35 (2.42)	0.19 (1.11)	0.10 (0.42)
NUMBUY	0.02 (0.01)	- 0.01 (0.00)	0.10 (0.64)	0.08 (0.44)
REGIO	0.77 (0.96)		0.72 (1.45)	
CONSTANT	- 2.25 (4.54)	- 2.28 (4.72)	- 1.47 (3.71)	- 1.49 (3.80)

** significance at 0.05 level   * significance at 0.1 level

Beans

Two equations were estimated for beans for the years 1990/91 and 1991/92.

Beans 1990/91: MCt = α + ß1(MICt) + ß2(ACRt) + ß3(NUMSRC) + ß4(PREFOUT) + ß5(DM) + ß6(NUMMAR) + ß7(NUMBUY) + ß8(REGIO).

Beans 1991/92: MCt = α + ß1(MCt-1) + ß2(MICt) + ß3(ACRt) + ß4(NUMSRC) + ß5(PREFOUT) + ß6(DM) + ß7(NUMMAR) + ß8(NUMBUY) + ß9(REGIO).

In the case of beans we are in a position to compare two agricultural years and can test the hypothesis that peasant farmers tend to select the same type of outlet as in the previous year. This is confirmed by the significantly positive coefficient for 'BEANS90' indicating that the choice of outlet in 1991/92 was strongly affected by the choice in 1990/91 (Table 8.4). For both 1990/91 and 1991/92 we find a significantly negative coefficient for 'the number of markets in the evoked set (NUMMAR)'. This means that the probability of choosing a buyer at the farmgate was positively affected when there were fewer markets in the evoked set.

---

[15] The t-value is calculated as follows: $t_{N-1} = (Q-P) / \sqrt{P(P-1)/N}$
  Where:
  $Q = (N_{11} + N_{22})/N$: proportion of correctly classified cases
  $P = (N_1^2 + N_2^2)/N$: result of random classification based on observed group sizes

Maize and bean marketing in Benin 167

Table 8.4 Results of the logistic regression on the peasant farmer's choice of outlet for beans in 1990/91 and 1991/92

	Beans 1990/91		Beans 1991/92	
	With Regio	Without Regio	With Regio	Without Regio
- 2 Log Likelihood	86.60	87.38	59.83	63.28
Goodness of Fit	97.47	92.99	55.35	56.32
Model Chi-Square	31.69	30.90	28.47	25.02
Significance	0.0001	0.0001	0.0008	0.0015
N	88	88	68	68
Q	0.773	0.784	0.779	0.765
P	0.521	0.521	0.543	0.543
t $_{N-1}$	4.728	4.934	3.907	3.675
VARIABLES	B (WALD statistic)			
MIC beans	- 0.52 (0.13)	- 0.75 (0.27)	0.37 (0.05)	0.78 (0.22)
ACR beans 90/91	0.01 (11.84)**	0.01 (11.77)**	- 0.01 (2.63)	- 0.00 (2.49)
BEANS90 (MC90)			2.22 (5.80)**	2.24 (5.94)**
PREFOUT	0.65 (0.73)	0.54 (0.53)	1.23 (2.30)	1.21 (2.40)
NUMSOURCE	0.26 (0.37)	0.50 (2.01)	0.26 (0.22)	0.07 (0.02)
DISTANCE (DM)	- 0.00 (0.01)	0.00 (0.00)	0.04 (1.32)	0.01 (0.11)
NUMMARKET	- 0.61 (3.59)*	- 0.74 (6.44)**	- 1.06 (5.89)**	- 0.88 (4.62)*
NUMBUYER	0.29 (2.07)	0.29 (2.08)	0.38 (1.92)	0.27 (1.14)
REGIO	0.94 (0.79)		- 4.25 (3.72)*	
CONSTANT	- 1.98 (1.44)	- 1.64 (1.08)	1.08 (0.29)	1.29 (0.44)

** significance at 0.05 level   * significance at 0.1 level

We find a significantly negative relationship with 'Regio' for 'Beans 1991/92' with 'Regio' as an independent variable, meaning that the probability of selling beans at the farmgate, contrary to expectations, was higher in Mono Province than in Borgou Province. In the case of 'Beans 1990/91', 'choice of outlet of the previous year (t-1)' could not be used as an explanatory variable. Here we found that 'area cultivated with beans (ACR)' had a significantly positive coefficient, meaning that the larger the area under beans, the more likely it was that the crop would be sold to buyers at the farmgate.

8.6 Concluding remarks

The results for maize and beans gave no significant coefficients with respect to three hypotheses (H2, H6 and H8). For the other six hypotheses, we found significant coefficients: five hypotheses were confirmed and one was rejected. The hypothesis (H1) that there is a strong relationship in outlet choice between period t-1 and t was confirmed when the data allowed for this test (beans in the year 1991/92). The positive relationship between the area cultivated with a particular crop and the choice for the buyer at the farmgate (H3) was confirmed for 'Beans 1990/91'. The positive relationship for the number of sources used in gathering market information and the choice of the buyer at the farmgate (H4) was confirmed for maize where 'Regio' was not included as a variable. A positive relationship between the (stated) preference for an outlet and the use of that outlet was confirmed for maize (H5).

A positive relationship was assumed for the number of markets in the evoked set and the choice of market as an outlet (H7). For beans (1990/91 and 1991/92), we found a negative relationship between the number of markets in the evoked set and the choice of farmgate as an outlet. This is a confirmation of the hypothesis (H7), meaning that fewer markets in the evoked set are significantly related to the choice of the buyer at the farmgate. A high number of markets in the evoked set are related to the choice of market as an outlet.

Only one hypothesis was clearly rejected: the relationship between 'Regio' and choice of outlet (H9). It was assumed that in Borgou Province the buyer at the farmgate would be used more often as an outlet, while in Mono Province the market would be chosen more often. Contrary to expectations, we found that for beans (year 1991/92), the probability of selling at the farmgate was even higher in the Mono region than in the Borgou area.

In conclusion, we may say that the main research result is that 'choice of the previous year', 'acreage cultivated with the crop', 'the number of sources used for market information', and 'the preference for the farmgate as an outlet' had a positive influence on the probability that peasant farmers would choose buyers at the farmgate. A negative relationship was found between the 'number of markets in the evoked set' and the probability of choosing buyers at the farmgate.

References

ELLIS, F. (1993) *Peasant Economics: Farm, farm households and agrarian development.* Second Edition. Cambridge: Cambridge University Press.
FANOU, K.L. (1994) 'Analyses des performances du système de commercialisation des produits vivriers au Bénin'. Thèse de l'Université Nationale de Côte d'Ivoire.
HAIR, J.F., R.E. ANDERSON & R.L. TATHAM (1992) *Multivariate Data Analysis.* Third edition. New York: Macmillan Publishing Company.
KOOL, M. (1994) 'Buying Behavior of Farmers'. Dissertation Wageningen Agricultural University, The Netherlands.
KOTLER, P. (1997) *Marketing Management, Analysis, Planning, Implementation, and Control.* Ninth edition. Prentice-Hall International, Inc.
LUTZ, C. (1994) 'The functioning of the maize market in Benin; spatial and temporal arbitrage on the market of a staple food crop'. Dissertation University of Amsterdam, The Netherlands.
WEBSTER, F.E. & Y. WIND (1972) *Organizational Buying Behavior.* Englewood Cliffs (N.J.): Prentice-Hall.

9

Horticultural Marketing in Kenya
Why Potato Farmers need Collecting Wholesalers

Tjalling Dijkstra

Abstract

Collecting wholesalers play a vital role in the marketing of horticultural commodities in Kenya, as in many other parts of Sub-Saharan Africa. They bridge the gap between small-scale producers who live in often isolated rural areas on the one hand, and distributing wholesalers who reside in large urban centres on the other. Farmers and politicians tend to judge the activities of these middlemen unfavourably, but their opinion is usually preconceived. This chapter shows that collecting wholesalers contribute to the efficiency in marketing channels to the benefit of both farmers and distributing wholesalers. The analysis is based on the example of Kinangop potatoes grown for the Nairobi market.

    For potato farmers in Kinangop, selling potatoes at the farm gate is more profitable than taking them to Nairobi with the attendant high initial costs, especially in relation to transport, information and financing. A farmer's total average marketing costs would, by taking his crop to Nairobi, exceed his average marketing revenue. Collecting wholesalers have lower average costs because of substantially higher turnovers which allow them to level out their initial costs.

    Even if farmers' costs in relation to transport, financing and information were reduced through credit and improved market information, the majority of farmers would be still better off selling their produce to collecting wholesalers. Their supply is simply too small. Only when acting as a group could they hope to reach the same scale of operation as collecting wholesalers.

    Collecting wholesalers operate in such a way as to allow distributing wholesalers to focus entirely on their urban clientele. This is important in large urban centres where wholesale and retail markets are operational six days a week. For such distributing wholesalers, being absent results in lost revenue and poor customer relations.

9.1 Introduction: Horticultural marketing channels in Kenya

Kenyan smallholders produce the bulk of the vegetables, fruits and tubers (horticultural commodities) for the domestic market. The few large-scale horticultural farms in the country concentrate on production for export (Dijkstra & Magori, 1995a), but horticultural exports are outside the scope of this chapter.

The horticultural commodities are collected from producers and distributed to consumers by private traders. The marketing channels in which these traders operate are embedded in a marketing environment. The Kenyan environment is in many aspects quite similar to the environment of horticultural marketing channels in other Sub-Saharan African countries. Three points deserve attention. The political and legal environment is weak. Government intervention, which until recently characterized the marketing of grains, is absent in the case of horticultural commodities. Vegetables, fruits and tubers are not regarded as strategic. Moreover, their perishability makes intervention risky, and requires cold store facilities in the event of (off-season) storage. The demographic and economic environments have a greater impact on the horticultural marketing channels than the political and legal environment has. The size of the urban population, the degree of self-sufficiency of rural households, and the purchasing power of rural and urban households are all determinants of the size of the potential consumer population.

The physical environment (infrastructure) determines whether consumers can actually be reached, and affects the quality of the commodities offered for sale. Market places and roads in production areas are often in a poor state. Lack of sheds, concrete floors and proper drainage adversely affect the quality of the fruits and vegetables sold in rural market places. The commodities, generally highly perishable, are displayed on the ground without protection from the sun or rain. Trade flows to urban centres are affected by the state of the roads. Bumpy dirt roads reduce quality, increase produce losses and raise transport costs. During the rainy season, when most of the commodities are harvested and offered for sale, many a rural access road is recurrently impassable, and many a vehicle gets stuck on its way to or from the production area.

A wide variety of traders operate in the channels. Farmer traders and professional retailers serve local consumers in periodic retail markets in rural areas. Farmer traders and assembling traders sell in rural assembly markets to wholesalers from elsewhere (Dijkstra, 1996). Professional wholesalers in daily urban markets sell to professional retailers, who in turn sell in the same or in another daily urban market to consumers. The professional wholesalers may collect the produce themselves or act as distributing wholesalers, using collecting wholesalers as intermediaries.

By far the majority of horticultural traders are women. Male traders appear only when remunerations are relatively high, as is the case in wholesale trade, or in retail trade carried out in the daily retail markets of large urban centres (Dijkstra, 1997).

In addition to traders, marketing intermediaries who do not take title to the produce operate in the channels. Purchasing agents are the most common. They work in the production areas on behalf of collecting wholesalers. They reduce collection costs by identifying produce for sale, carrying out the negotiations and streamlining the process. In return they receive a commission.

The most common facilitators in the marketing channel are transporters (in the broadest sense of the word). Porters are usually for hire for short distances. They carry bags, baskets and boxes on their head or back, from the farm to the road or from the bus stop to the market place. In addition to porters, transporters with donkeys and tractors may be available for short-distance transport in rural areas, and transporters with handcarts are to be found in urban areas.

For longer distances buses can be used. Minibuses (*matatus*) traverse rural areas and link up production areas with urban centres.[1] They carry both passengers and their cargo; the cargo is strapped to a roof rack. Unsophisticated entrepreneurs use *matatus* to get their merchandise to the market. The cargo on top of the minibus is therefore at least as important for the driver as the people inside. This is reflected in the payment system: a passenger pays a fee for each bag, basket or box carried. In addition, he/she has to buy a ticket to accompany the cargo.

Instead of using a *matatu*, a trader may hire a truck to transport his/her produce. Transport companies that hire out trucks are usually located in cities. Most truck owners who live in rural areas are not primarily transporters but traders: they only rent out their trucks when they do not have business themselves. They own one or a few trucks, whereas urban truck companies may own a whole fleet of vehicles.

In addition to transport facilitators, financial facilitators are important in the domestic horticultural trade. They are 'informal' money lenders, and savings and credit associations. Commercial banks are relatively unimportant because they are reluctant to issue loans to horticultural traders because of their lack of collateral and their high trade risks.

Marketing research companies are unimportant as facilitators. Traders get their information while buying and selling in the market places. Up-to-date price information is a problem for horticultural farmers in isolated production areas without assembly markets. They depend for their sales on collecting wholesalers who come to the farms, while receiving their price information from these same traders (Dijkstra & Magori, 1995b).

Collecting wholesalers play a vital role in the marketing system because they bridge the gap between the small-scale producers who live in often isolated rural areas and the distributing wholesalers who reside in large urban centres. Nevertheless, many farmers tend to judge the activities of these traders unfavourably, and many African politicians question their rationale.

The collecting wholesalers' motives for going into business are clear: they want to make money and they have found a way to do so. Within a capitalistic system that is a legitimate reason. The question of whether their activities are not only beneficial to themselves but also to other actors in the marketing chain remains. This will be discussed in the coming sections. The hypothesis is that collecting wholesalers tend to improve the efficiency in the marketing channel to the benefit of farmers and distributing wholesalers.

---

[1] Large buses (coaches) are only used to connect major cities.

9.2 The efficiency rationale of collecting wholesalers: the farmer's perspective

To show the efficiency rationale of collecting wholesalers with regard to farmers we take the example of Kinangop potatoes grown for the Nairobi market. Kinangop is situated some 100 kilometres to the north-west of Nairobi, and is one of the main suppliers of potatoes to the Kenyan capital. Ninety-two per cent of the farmers in the area sold potatoes during the main harvesting period of 1990. As few as 2 percent of these farmers took their produce to Nairobi to sell to distributing wholesalers. All the others (98 per cent) relied on collecting wholesalers who came to their farms to buy. Calculations will show that they made the right decision: selling at the farm gate was more profitable than going to Nairobi. The analysis is based on information collected in 1990 during a survey among 150 farmers in Kinangop (of which 138 were potato farmers) and supplemented by interviews with 24 collecting wholesalers of potatoes operating in the area.

Marketing strategies
A potato farmer in Kinangop can choose between three marketing strategies:
(a) selling the produce at the farm gate;
(b) selling the produce in the Nairobi wholesale market:
    (b1) using a hired truck, or
    (b2) using a public minibus (*matatu*).
If he chooses the first alternative, he does not perform any marketing functions.[2] He receives a lower price, however, than if he sells the potatoes in Nairobi. The difference between the farm-gate price and the Nairobi price is here called the marketing revenue (the money the farmer receives on top of the farm-gate price). The farmer's marketing revenue must be compared with his marketing costs. If the average marketing costs exceed the average marketing revenue, selling at the farm gate is more profitable.

    The marketing costs of the farmer are related to the marketing functions that have to be performed. These marketing functions include: transport, packing, physical handling, storage, financing, risk taking, information, negotiation, ordering, payment and title.[3] Two pairs of functions are synchronous. A successful negotiation process will lead to the immediate placement of an order, and titles change hands when payments are made (due to the practice of 'cash-on-delivery'). Thus, only nine marketing functions have to be discussed (Table 9.1).

    Table 9.1 shows the average costs of each function in relation to the marketing strategy chosen by the farmer. In column 1 the farmer does not perform any marketing functions when selling at the farm gate. Therefore all costs are zero. When the farmer takes his

---

[2] In Kinangop both men and women are involved in potato production and selling. References to male farmers in the present chapter also apply to female farmers.
[3] Kotler (1997) delineates nine functions: information, promotion, negotiation, ordering, financing, risk taking, physical possession, payment and title. When dealing with horticultural trade in Africa, physical possession can be subdivided into packing, physical handling, transport and storage. Promotion can be omitted because it is of minor importance.

potatoes to Nairobi all nine marketing functions are essential and he has to face the costs involved. Some of the functions show considerable initial costs. When the farmer increases his sales, the initial cost can be levelled out and his average costs will decrease. Three functions show particularly high initial costs, notably transport, financing and information.

Table 9.1 Average marketing costs per bag, incurred by potato farmers in Kinangop in 1990 under different marketing strategies

Marketing functions	Strategy a (farm gate)	Strategy b1 (hired truck)	Strategy b2 (matatu)
transport	zero	decreasing*	constant
packing	zero	constant	constant
physical handling	zero	constant	constant
storage	zero	zero	increasing
financing	zero	decreasing*	decreasing
risk taking	zero	constant	constant
information	zero	decreasing*	decreasing*
negotiation	zero	decreasing	constant
payment	zero	decreasing	constant

Source: data collected by author.
* decreasing from a high initial cost.

The composition of each function-related cost will be discussed in brief. Readers who are interested in the detailed cost specifications are referred to Dijkstra (1997).

Marketing costs in relation to the transport function
Seven-tonne trucks are for hire in Nairobi, and are best suited to the job. They are commonly used by collecting wholesalers of potatoes in Kinangop. By hiring a 7-tonne truck, the farmer can carry 60 bags per trip. To get hold of such a vehicle, he faces what I call indirect transport costs. He has to travel by public transport to Nairobi to meet transporters. During his stay in Nairobi he has to pay for food and lodging. The first time he goes to Nairobi he needs at least two and a half days to travel to the city, find a willing transporter, and return with the truck (and driver). Subsequent trips can be made in one and a half days because the farmer knows where to go. During his absence his part of the work on the farm either has to be postponed or casual labour has to be hired. This too incurs costs.

Once the hire of the truck has been arranged, the farmer faces direct transport costs. The transporter who agrees to hire out his truck for a trip to the production area and back charges the farmer a lump sum that includes petrol, a driver, and two 'turn boys' (assistants). The first time the farmer deals with the transporter, he has to pay more than regular customers. Only when the transporter gets to know the farmer better will he lower the price to the regular-customer level.

The farmer can sit in the truck on the journey from the farm to the urban market at no extra cost. He has, however, to travel back home by *matatu* (an indirect transport cost). The entire trip takes one and a half days, including half a day to load the truck and travel to

Nairobi, and one day to sell the produce and return home. The farmer does not spend the night in a hotel but remains in the truck to make sure his potatoes are not stolen. The truck is parked in the queue with other produce trucks in front of the wholesale market. Since he has no lodging costs, only food costs remain. On top of the travel and food costs, the opportunity costs of the farmer's labour have to be counted as indirect costs again. All direct and indirect transport costs are summarized in the first column of Table 9.2 (strategy b1).

Instead of hiring a truck, the farmer can use a *matatu* to get his produce to Nairobi. The farmer then carries his bags to the road and waits for a *matatu* to pass. He does not have to make a separate trip to Nairobi to organize transport and does not incur the indirect transport costs involved but he can only take 3 bags at a time. *Matatu* drivers do not normally allow more bags, to avoid excessive overloading.

The farmer pays the *matatu* driver a transport fee for carrying his produce. In addition, he has to buy a ticket to accompany the produce. He also has to buy a ticket to get back home. Both tickets are indirect transport costs. The entire trip will take one and a half days. The farmer will travel during the afternoon and night, and return the next day after selling the potatoes. All direct and indirect costs are summarized in the second column of Table 9.2 (strategy b2).

Table 9.2 **Direct and indirect transport costs, incurred by potato farmers in Kinangop in 1990 under different marketing strategies**

Transport costs (TC)	Strategy b1 (hired truck)	Strategy b2 (matatu)
Direct TC	- lump sum incl. petrol, driver and 2 turn boys	- transport fee per bag
Indirect TC		
obtaining the vehicle	- *matatu* ticket to Nairobi - food and lodging - opportunity costs labour	
accompanying the produce	- food - *matatu* ticket back home - opportunity costs labour	- *matatu* ticket to Nairobi - food - *matatu* ticket back home - opportunity costs labour

Marketing costs in relation to the packing function
A farmer who wants to take his potatoes to Nairobi incurs packing costs. Both when using a truck and a *matatu*, he has to purchase gunny bags to pack the potatoes and hire young men to extend (top up) filled bags with twined sisal. The sisal also has to be bought. If the farmer had sold his potatoes at the farm gate, the collecting wholesaler would have supplied the bags and sisal, and would have employed the men to top up the bags.

Bags have to be extended because the entire wholesale trade is based on extended bags. The cause is the system of market fees in the Nairobi wholesale market. Traders who bring produce into this market are charged a fixed fee per bag regardless of its size. It is therefore more economical to have a truck load of 60 bags weighing 120 kg each than one of 72 bags weighing 100 kg each.

Marketing costs in relation to the physical handling function
In addition to transport and packing, the physical handling of the potato bags entails costs. When using a truck, the extended bags have to be loaded onto the truck by hired help. On arrival in Nairobi, market fees have to be paid at the entrance to the Nairobi wholesale market. Once in the market, men have to be hired to unload the truck. The farmer would not have had to concern himself with these details if he had sold his potatoes at the farm gate.

Marketing costs in relation to the storage function
A farmer who sells in Nairobi faces storage costs. They may consist of interest and depreciation on investments in a store, or may be costs arising from storage losses. To start with the first: most farmers in Nyandarua do not have a sophisticated vegetable store and use their house or a low-budget general farm store instead. Therefore, their investments with regard to storage are nil, and so are their interest and depreciation costs.

This leaves costs in relation to storage losses. Such losses are related to the storage period, i.e. the interval between harvest and sale. If a farmer hires a 7-tonne truck, all the bags from one plot can easily be accommodated in one truck.[4] The potatoes are harvested one or a few days before hiring the truck. As a consequence the storage losses are nil.

If a farmer travels to Nairobi by *matatu* the potatoes harvested from a plot are transported and sold over a period of time. The maximum storage period depends on the size of the harvest and the number of trips the farmer is able to make per week.[5] He has to combine his travels with his farm work, and is therefore able to travel to Nairobi twice a week at the most.

With a substantial harvest, the interval between harvest and sale will be much longer when using a *matatu* than when hiring a truck. The interval will also be much longer than when selling to a collecting wholesaler. This trader, or his agent, usually announces in advance which day he will come to collect produce. The farmer can thus harvest his potatoes a few days beforehand. His storage losses are nil, as is the case when hiring a truck.[6]

Marketing costs in relation to the financing function
A farmer who sells in Nairobi will not receive money until he has reached the urban market and sold the produce to a distributing wholesaler. He has to finance the transport costs from his own resources or by a loan, which entails interest costs. The money requirements are

---

[4] According to the farm survey, a maximum of 42 bags were sold per plot. Different plots could be harvested simultaneously or one after the other.

[5] All potatoes from one plot are normally harvested at the same time. There are two reasons for this. First, land preparation for the next crop has to start soon after the harvesting of the previous one. Second, harvesting is often done by hired labour groups. They are in high demand and only come if a job is worth doing.

[6] Storage losses occur when the collecting wholesaler does not turn up and no other collecting wholesalers are around to buy. Usually this happens when access roads are impassable after heavy rain. In such a situation none of the three marketing strategies will work: hired trucks and *matatus* cannot pass either.

especially high for hiring a truck. As explained above, the farmer will need money to travel by *matatu* to Nairobi and for food and lodging while there. The transporter who hires out the truck will, in the beginning, ask for advance payment to cover the entire rent because he does not know the farmer and does not yet trust him. Finally, the farmer will need money to buy gunny bags and sisal twine and to pay casual labourers for the topping-up, loading and unloading.

The period during which the money is needed is limited since hiring a truck to sell one truckload of potatoes only takes a few days, and offloading the entire harvest will take two months at most. Nevertheless, organizing a loan may be costly. Commercial banks do not like to deal with horticultural farmers who want to go into trade. Such farmers therefore have to rely on informal money lenders who do not require collateral but charge higher interest rates. The expensive prefinancing of transport, packing and handling costs may be a decisive element in the farmer's decision not to hire a truck.

If the farmer takes a *matatu* instead of hiring a truck, the required prefinancing is much lower, including only the packing and physical handling costs, and the transport fees and ticket to Nairobi. In addition to this, the farmer faces the limited financial costs of storing the potatoes.

Marketing costs in relation to the risk-taking function
Kohls & Uhl (1990) mention two types of risk in marketing: physical and market risks. In the case of the potato trade in Kenya, the market risks are small compared to the physical risks. Potato prices in Nairobi fluctuate considerably, due mainly to seasonal cycles (Durr & Lorenzl, 1980). Such cycles do not cause large market risks because there is no seasonal potato storage between harvesting and selling in the urban market.

Road and weather conditions account for the fact that the physical risks are much larger than the market risks. Transport as such does not cause quality deterioration but the potatoes are often longer in transit than intended. Tarmac roads are non-existent in the production areas of Kinangop, and vehicles break down regularly due to the rough roads. Moreover, the high precipitation of over 800 mm per annum causes regular floods that block roads and leave vehicles stuck in the mud for days. When such problems occur, the quality of perishable goods like potatoes deteriorates quickly, especially because the load is not protected from the sun and rain. If a farmer sells his produce at the farm gate to a collecting wholesaler, the latter bears the costs of such quality losses. The farmer who transports his own potatoes to Nairobi carries the risk himself.[7]

Marketing costs in relation to the information function
A farmer who bypasses collecting wholesalers to sell his potatoes to distributing wholesalers in Nairobi has to acquire a knowledge of the Nairobi market. He has to know who the

---

[7] If he has a substantial harvest and decides to transport the potatoes to Nairobi by *matatu* he also has to run the risk of excessive quality deterioration during storage. The chances of such excessive quality deterioration are unpredictable. They are especially high if the farmer does not store the potatoes properly. The losses involved come in addition to the 'normal' storage losses discussed earlier under 'marketing costs in relation to the storage function'.

distributing wholesalers are, who their brokers are, and how such traders should be approached. In addition he needs to know what price he can expect on the day he brings his potatoes to the market. Such knowledge can only be gained through experience. Traders in the market do not have a signboard, and prices are neither fixed nor announced in the market. Only when the farmer brings potatoes to the market regularly will he gain knowledge of the trading practices, trader strategies and price developments.

Due to his lack of information, the farmer receives a lower price than collecting wholesalers would on his first trips to Nairobi. These lost revenues can be defined as the farmer's information costs. On subsequent trips the farmer's knowledge increases and he will earn a better price for his produce.

Marketing costs in relation to the negotiation function
Prices in the Nairobi wholesale market are determined by negotiation. The results of the negotiations depend on two factors. The first is knowledge of the market system and price developments. The costs of the negotiation function coincide here with those of the information function. The second factor is the number of bags of potatoes offered for sale. Collecting wholesalers always arrive in Nairobi with a fully loaded truck, both to reduce their average transport costs and to have a strong bargaining position *vis-à-vis* distributing wholesalers. The more bags the latter can buy at one go, the shorter their average negotiating time per bag, and hence the greater their willingness to offer a higher price per bag. This is a matter of concern to a farmer who hires a truck but is not able to fill it completely, and even more so for one who brings only three bags of potatoes by *matatu* to the market. The latter will never be able to get the same price as a collecting wholesaler, even if he frequents the market as often as the wholesaler.

Marketing costs in relation to the payment function
To bypass the collecting wholesalers, the farmer takes the potatoes to Nairobi himself. In theory the farmer might also ask somebody who is going to Nairobi for other purposes to accompany the produce and do the selling for him. However, he will prefer to travel to Nairobi himself for two reasons. First, knowledge about the market system and price developments will only accumulate when the same person does the selling all the time. Second, the distributing wholesalers pay cash on delivery and the farmer will only trust himself (or his close relatives) when it comes to bringing the money back home. He will therefore accompany the produce as part of the payment function. The costs of accompanying the produce were already identified as indirect transport costs (see Table 9.2). Thus, the costs of the payment function partly coincide with the costs of the transport function.

Marketing costs and marketing revenue: the break-even point
When the farmer takes his potatoes to Nairobi all nine marketing functions have to be performed. To derive the farmer's total average marketing costs, the average costs of all the functions have to be worked out. The result is visualized in Figure 9.1. The figure shows the total average cost curves in relation to the number of potato bags a farmer trades when hiring

a 7-tonne truck and when using a *matatu*. The curves reflect the costs for fully loaded trucks (60 bags) and for the maximum number of bags allowed when travelling by *matatu* (3 bags).

It also shows the marketing revenue per bag, defined as the difference between the farm-gate price and the Nairobi price. This revenue was Ksh 156 during the period under consideration. The farm-gate price in Kinangop during the main harvesting period of 1990 was on average KSh 180 per bag, and the buying price of distributing wholesalers at the Nairobi wholesale market was KSh 336. Both prices fluctuated but the gross margin of KSh 156 appears to have stayed more or less constant during the observation period because there was sufficient competition at the buying and selling stages and no speculative storage at any level of the marketing chain.

We can conclude from the figure that, when using a *matatu*, the farmer's marketing costs were always higher than his marketing revenues. In other words, it was more profitable for a farmer to sell his potatoes to a collecting wholesaler than to take them to Nairobi by *matatu*, regardless of the number of potato bags he had for sale during the harvesting period. When hiring a truck, the farmer's break-even point was 8 truck-loads or 480 bags. If the farmer had more than 480 bags for sale, hiring a truck was more profitable than selling to collecting wholesalers at the farm gate.

Figure 9.1 Average marketing costs and marketing revenue per bag for Kinangop farmers taking potatoes to Nairobi market

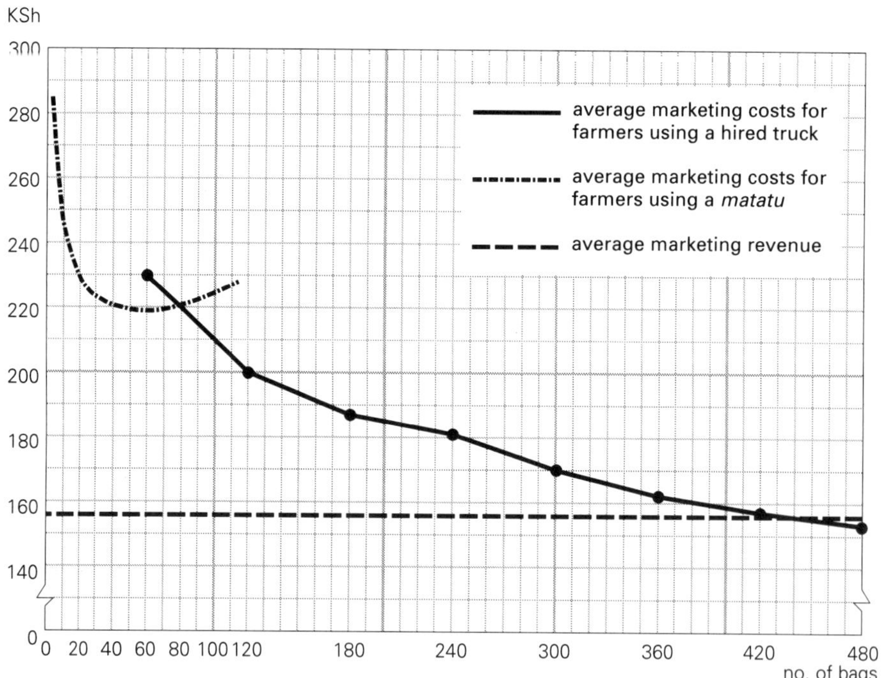

Source: see text.

We can compare these findings with the actual sales per farmer during the period under consideration. Table 9.3 shows that none of the interviewed potato farmers in Kinangop sold more than 300 bags of potatoes, and only 7 per cent sold over 60 bags. It can therefore be concluded that, on the basis of our calculations, collecting wholesalers were the best method of selling for all potato farmers in Kinangop.

Table 9.3 Potato sales by potato farmers in Kinangop during the main harvesting period of 1990 (n=138)

No. of bags sold	No. of farmers	% of farmers	Cumulative % of farmers
1 to 3	13	9	9
3 to 10	35	25	34
11 to 20	39	28	62
21 to 40	29	21	83
41 to 60	12	9	92
61 to 120	8	6	98
121 to 300	2	1	99

Source: data collected by author.

According to the survey, 98 percent of the potato farmers in Kinangop sold their potatoes to collecting wholesalers. Three respondents took their potatoes by truck to Nairobi, and none did so by *matatu*. Two of the farmers who went to Nairobi carried not only their own potatoes but also those they had bought from other farmers, thus acting primarily as collecting wholesalers. The third farmer reported sharing a hired truck with other potato farmers. It was the only case of group marketing found during the survey.

It can be concluded that virtually all potato farmers in the survey acted as was expected on the basis of the analysis of marketing costs and marketing revenues. Selling to collecting wholesalers at the farm gate was more profitable than taking their potatoes to the Nairobi wholesale market by hired truck or *matatu*. The farmers' supplies were too small to make hiring a 7-tonne truck attractive. High initial costs in relation to transport, information and financing could not be levelled out. Collecting wholesalers were, however, able to do just that. Those in business on a full-time basis handled over 25 truck-loads of Kinangop potatoes (1,500 bags) in one harvesting season.[8]

It is not argued here that all farmers in the sample based their marketing strategy on proper cost-benefit calculations. They may also have decided to sell at the farm gate for non-economic reasons such as a language barrier or stories about unscrupulous bargaining methods in the Nairobi market. The analysis shows, however, that collecting wholesalers increase the efficiency of the marketing channel for all farmers.

---

[8] A collecting wholesaler can easily make three trips a week, and sometimes even four to five. In the case of four or five trips a week, however, he has to use purchasing agents who also have their price (in the case of three trips or fewer he does not have to use their services).

The future role of the collecting wholesalers
The position of the collecting wholesalers will only be undermined when in the (near) future the average scale of production increases substantially, or group marketing is adopted. The first situation is not very likely to happen because of rising population pressure and a high level of land utilization. The second alternative is often mentioned by policy makers, but most farmers in Kinangop shy away from group marketing. The reason lies, at least partly, in the past. Group marketing of potatoes was tried by the Kinangop Agricultural Cooperative Society in the 1980s, but the initiative failed due to mismanagement and the lack of a successful marketing strategy. With regard to its strategy: the society just copied the activities of the collecting wholesalers, but without their knowledge of the marketing system. It had an especially hard time selling members' produce during regional harvesting peaks. The number of collecting wholesalers supplying produce to the Nairobi wholesale market multiplied and competition reached a cut-throat level. The society had to realize peak sales, but failed. In the end, many members still had to sell their produce to collecting wholesalers.[9] Ever since, horticultural farmers in Kinangop have been reluctant to participate in any group marketing initiative.

All in all, it is not expected that the position of collecting wholesalers in Kinangop will change in the near future. Even if marketing costs were reduced by means of a credit scheme and an improved market information system,[10] it could be expected that collecting wholesalers would stay in business (Dijkstra, 1997). Selling in Nairobi would become profitable for a small group of large potato farmers, but the majority of the farmers in Kinangop would still be better off selling their potatoes at the farm gate. Their supplies are just too small to make hiring a 7-tonne truck feasible.

9.3 The efficiency rationale of collecting wholesalers: the distributing wholesaler's perspective

Collecting wholesalers of potatoes improve efficiency in the marketing channel to the benefit of both the Kinangop farmers from whom they buy and the distributing wholesalers in Nairobi to whom they sell. The second point will be argued in qualitative terms on the basis of observations in the Nairobi wholesale market and interviews with some of the distributing wholesalers.

A potato wholesaler who continuously operates in the Nairobi wholesale market has three alternative buying strategies:
(a) buying from collecting wholesalers who come to Nairobi;
(b) buying from farmers in the production area,
    (b1) travelling to the production area himself, or
    (b2) sending an employee or agent on his behalf.

---

[9] For more details, see Dijkstra (1997).
[10] In Kenya, the radio has failed to be an appropriate medium for a horticultural market information system (Dijkstra, 1997). Other methods have to be tried.

Observations revealed that strategy (a) was the most common. It resulted from three factors: the daily character of the wholesale market (operational 6 days a week), supervision problems and distrust.

When a wholesaler goes to Kinangop to buy potatoes (strategy b1), he is away for at least one full day. He will be able to get cheaper supplies but he will not sell anything during his absence.[11] His absence from Nairobi will also weaken his relationship with customer-retailers. Many urban horticultural retailers come to buy produce from wholesalers every day of the week, early in the morning before starting their own trading. For each commodity or group of related commodities they prefer to deal with one wholesaler who they can trust in terms of price and quality. They therefore choose a distributing wholesaler who is available throughout the week rather than a part-time wholesaler, unless the latter offers substantially lower prices.

To avoid losing customers, a wholesaler could send an employee (or agent) to the production area to do the buying, while he himself stays in Nairobi (strategy b2). This is not very common because of a combination of supervision problems and problems of trust. Standardized buying units and grades do not exist in the Kenyan potato trade, and communication between a wholesaler in Nairobi and his employee in the field is not possible. The wholesaler is therefore not able to supervise the employee properly. This is a problem as a lot of money is at stake and the wholesaler is not sure whether he can trust his employee. The employee has to take a substantial amount of money to the production area because most farmers have to be paid cash on delivery. Wholesalers recount stories of an employee who absconded with all the money, and another who paid farmers half the price and promised to pay the rest within a few weeks. By the time farmers started to complain of lack of payment, the employee had disappeared. Whether the stories are true or not is not important. They show wholesalers' perceptions of the possible financial risks when sending an employee or agent to the production area with large sums of money. Even when an employee is given the benefit of the doubt, a wholesaler cannot verify everything the employee tells him. If the employee says farm-gate prices have suddenly gone up, the wholesaler either has to accept this or travel to the production area to check prices himself. To reduce all these financial risks, wholesalers prefer to pay farmers personally. An employee or an agent may conduct the negotiations, but the wholesaler finalizes the transaction.[12]

From the point of view of distributing wholesalers, then, the use of collecting wholesalers can be explained in efficiency terms: the benefits are thought to exceed the costs. Such costs would be lower if roads in the production areas were in better shape (less collection time), standardized buying units and grades existed (no visual inspection required), the banking system were better developed (no cash payments required), and

---

[11] There will be no revenue but the rent of the stall will still have to be paid (stalls are rented out on a monthly basis).
[12] Similarly, wholesalers also prefer to finalize transactions personally with customers in the wholesale market. Employees (or brokers) may open negotiations but the wholesaler comes to supervise the transactions and to collect the money. In retail trade the situation is different. It is not uncommon for retail traders to look after each other's businesses. The amount of money involved, however, is much smaller than in the wholesale trade.

farmers and employees had telephones (easier communication). In other words, the existence of collecting wholesalers is at least partly due to the poorly developed marketing environment.

9.4 Conclusion

The present chapter deals with collecting potato wholesalers in Kenya. Farmers and politicians tend to judge the activities of these and other horticultural middlemen unfavourably. Collecting wholesalers, however, improve the efficiency in marketing channels to the benefit of farmers and distributing wholesalers.

Our case study has shown the efficiency rationale of the traders. For potato farmers in Kinangop, selling to collecting wholesalers at the farm gate is more profitable than taking their produce to Nairobi. The marketing costs of the latter strategy would exceed the marketing revenue (the money received on top of the farm-gate price). To distributing wholesalers in Nairobi buying from collecting wholesalers results from the daily character of the urban wholesale and retail markets. Absence from Nairobi has its costs in terms of lost revenues and poorer customer relations.

The potato farmers in the case study have a much smaller scale of operation than the collecting wholesalers. This is also the case for other horticultural commodities in other parts of Kenya, and for that matter in many parts of Sub-Saharan Africa. Farmers can never operate as efficiently as professional traders, now or in the near future. Only if farmers entered *en masse* into group marketing would collecting wholesalers become less important, but this will not easily happen. Policies to reorganize and improve the collecting stage of horticultural trade in Sub-Saharan Africa should therefore focus on a better bargaining position for farmers towards collecting wholesalers (e.g. access to market information), the ability of collecting wholesalers to operate more efficiently (e.g. improved rural roads and rural assembly markets), and increasing competition among collecting wholesalers (e.g. the removal of entry barriers with regard to finance and transport).

References

DIJKSTRA, T. (1996) 'Food Assembly Markets in Africa: Lessons from the Horticultural Sector of Kenya'. In *British Food Journal*, Vol. 98, no. 9, pp. 26-34.

DIJKSTRA, T. (1997) *Trading the Fruits of the Land: Horticultural Marketing Channels in Kenya*. Aldershot: Ashgate.

DIJKSTRA, T. & T.D. MAGORI (1995a) 'Flowers and French Beans from Kenya; A Story of Export Success'. In S. Ellis & Y. A. Fauré (eds) *Entreprises et entrepreneurs africains*. Paris: Karthala, pp. 435-444.

DIJKSTRA, T. & T.D. MAGORI (eds.) (1995b) *Horticultural Production and Marketing in Kenya; Part 5: Proceedings of a Dissemination Seminar at Nairobi, 16-17th November 1994*. Nairobi & Leiden: Ministry of Planning and National Development & African Studies Centre, Food and Nutrition Studies Programme, Report no. 53.

DURR, G. & G. LORENZL (1980) *Potato Production and Utilization in Kenya*. Nairobi, Berlin & Colombia: University of Nairobi, Technical University Berlin & Centro Internacional de la Papa.
KOHLS, R.L. & J.N. UHL (1990) *Marketing of Agricultural Products*. Seventh edition. New York: Macmillan.
KOTLER, P. (1997) *Marketing Management: Analysis, Planning, Implementation, and Control*. Ninth edition. Upper Saddle River, NJ: Prentice Hall International.
PORTER, M.E. (1980) *Competitive Strategy: Techniques for Analyzing Industries and Competitors*. New York & London: The Free Press, Macmillan.

10

Cattle Marketing in Zambia, 1965-1995
Policies, Institutions and Cattle Owners
in Western Province

Henk A.J. Moll and Désirée C.E. Dietvorst

Abstract

Increasing the offtake from cattle grazed on natural rangelands has been the policy of many African governments for reasons of (a) natural resource management, (b) improving farmers' welfare, and (c) increasing overall productivity. This chapter focuses on (a) the Zambian government's policies in cattle marketing over the period from independence in 1965 to 1995 and (b) the marketing behaviour of cattle owners in Western Province. In this period the policies shifted from supporting monopolistic public marketing institutions to allowing private traders to take over all marketing functions with the discontinuation of the ailing public institutions. Attention is also paid to other factors affecting cattle marketing, such as infrastructural development and outbreaks of disease.

Marketing policies and other factors are compared with Western Province data on (a) registered offtake, i.e. the sale of animals for the urban consumers' market, and (b) herd growth. The analysis shows a fluctuating, but significantly rising annual registered offtake rate, reaching 4.4 per cent in 1995. The provincial or macro perspective on cattle marketing is complemented by a study of the cattle owners' views on the sale of cattle. Data collection through a survey of 122 households took place in 1991. The analysis shows that people are only selling cattle if they have urgent requirements for substantial amounts of cash. One variable affects the propensity to sell: household self-sufficiency in crop production. The herd size does not affect the cattle owner's propensity to sell.

Finally, conclusions are drawn regarding the long-term effects of government policies on cattle marketing at a provincial level and on the sales behaviour of cattle owners. The combination of the two research perspectives provides an illuminating comparison. Apparently, the time horizon of the research affects the conclusions: micro data, collected at a certain point in time, suggest a widespread reluctance to sell cattle among cattle owners, while macro data, covering a period of thirty years, show an increasing propensity to sell.

10.1 Introduction

In many African countries the national policies dealing with cattle grazed on natural rangelands cover two main fields: veterinary services and marketing. After gaining independence in the 1960s, national governments, especially in Southern Africa, continued to support the dominant role of public organizations in both fields. In the 1980s, a change occurred, first in cattle marketing where private traders were allowed to enter the market, and later in veterinary services, which became the subject of much debate. Zambia is no exception to this general pattern as cattle marketing policies shifted from supporting public marketing institutions in monopoly positions to allowing private trade to compete with them. The redefinition of public and private sector roles in veterinary services, which started later, is outside the scope of this chapter.

Policies in cattle marketing generally try to stimulate the sale of cattle. They may result from: a) a concern for the sustainable use of the rangelands; b) the wish to improve rural welfare; c) a desire to increase the supply of meat to the urban population; and d) the need to earn foreign currency. The effect of marketing policies depends on the possibility of shifting the balance between keeping cattle and selling cattle in the direction of sales. Whether it is possible to affect this balance is subject to debate: one school of thought maintains that cattle keeping is so closely connected with many aspects of rural life that policies are bound to fail; the other school argues that cattle owners are as much subject to policy inducements as other economic agents (Motel-Combes, 1996; Moll & Heerink, 1998).

The objective of this study is to contribute to the debate on the effectiveness of cattle marketing policies. The study employs two supplementary perspectives. The macro perspective is formed by an overview of marketing policies and institutions, and the overall supply reactions of cattle owners in Western Province over a period of 30 years. An analysis of the sales behaviour of selected individual cattle owners forms the micro perspective. The analysis starts in Section 10.2 with a description of the pull factors: the cattle marketing policies and the consequences for the institutions in cattle marketing. In Section 10.3 we consider the cattle owners' response by analyzing developments in herd size and in registered offtake rates in Western Province. Sections 10.2 and 10.3 cover the period from independence to 1995. Section 10.4, where the micro perspective begins, provides an analysis of the cattle owners' views in order to gain an insight into the push factors: what makes them sell or retain cattle? This section is based on a survey carried out in 1991. All findings are brought together and discussed in Section 10.5.

The data used in the analysis are exceptionally accurate for African conditions because of the geographic isolation of Western Province, the strict veterinary control of all cattle movements out of the province, and the presence of successive Dutch bilateral cooperation projects dealing with veterinary services and cattle production in the province since the early

1980s.[1] This chapter owes much to studies carried out by the staff of these cooperation projects.[2]

10.2 Policies and market structure from 1965 to 1995

National policies and institutions
The national policy objectives for beef remained constant over the period under review: increasing beef production, especially among small-scale cattle owners; increasing per capita consumption of beef; and expanding the export of beef. The objectives with regard to cattle marketing in the traditional sector were: increasing the offtake rate and improving the marketing facilities. These policy objectives were pursued through government participation in marketing through public institutions, and market regulation. The changes in these two strategies and the effects on types and numbers of participants and market structure are reviewed below.

The Cold Storage Board (CSB) continued operating after independence as the sole, parastatal buyer of cattle and processor of meat until 1972. Then, the government transformed the CSB into the Cold Storage Board of Zambia (CSBZ), a statutory board with the ultimate objective of providing the Zambian population with more protein at reasonable prices. The tasks of the CSBZ remained the same as those of the CSB: the purchase and slaughter of cattle and the sale of beef and beef products to wholesale and retail outlets. Prices of animals and the retail price of meat and by-products were regulated by the government under the Prices Act.

Less then satisfactory performance of the parastatals operating in the agricultural sector later resulted in deregulation of the market. In 1980 the government transferred the marketing functions of the national agricultural marketing board (Namboard) to provincial cooperative unions. One year later, the CSBZ's monopoly position was abolished and cooperatives and private traders were allowed to engage in cattle buying. These policy changes towards opening up the markets were accompanied by new and substantial government and donor support for the cooperatives in Zambia.

In 1986, the CSBZ lost its independent status as a statutory board, and the Zambia Cold Storage Corporation Limited (ZCSC), a subsidiary of the parastatal ZIMCO conglomerate, took over cattle marketing and meat processing in the country. The reorganization did not, however, result in improved performance and in 1995 the ZCSC Ltd was earmarked for sale to private parties by the Zambia Privatisation Agency (ZPA). In the course of the privatization process, ZCSC had to close down operations due to mounting debts. This meant the end of parastatal involvement in cattle marketing.

---

[1] The Animal Disease Control Programme, from 1982 to 1987; The Livestock Development Projects Phases I and II, from 1988 to 1996; since April 1996 the Livestock Development Programme.

[2] The contributions and support of the staff of DRSS (Department of Research and Specialist Services) and the Department of Agriculture in data collection are gratefully acknowledged. Thanks are also due to M.M. van den Berg for assistance with the statistical analysis in Section 10.4.

In June 1989, the marketing of beef and cattle products was decontrolled, as part of the general liberalization of the economy. Since then both producer and consumer prices for cattle and beef products have been determined by market forces. Liberalization did not bring major changes as the involvement of private trade in cattle and meat – actually from the late 1970s onwards and officially since 1981 – has made enforcement of price regulations impossible.

The poor performance of the successive parastatals and the abolition of their monopoly positions provided new opportunities for private trade and cooperatives. Private trade gradually increased its market share and the demise of the ZCSC in 1996 did not have a major impact on the purchase of cattle and the supply of meat to urban consumers.

National policies and cattle marketing in Western Province
The reorganization of the CSB into the CSBZ gave a new impetus to cattle marketing in Western Province. New sales yards were established throughout the province. In 1975 their number had increased to over 90 from the 16 that were present in 1964 (MacLean, 1965). With the assistance of foreign donors, the CSBZ built an abattoir with a slaughter capacity of 100 head per day and freezing facilities in Mongu, the provincial capital, in 1975. The objectives were to increase the value added in Western Province and to reduce transport costs. In the same year, the tarmac road between Mongu and Lusaka (600 km) was opened, which meant a substantial reduction in transport costs. Despite the new abattoir and improved transport possibilities the performance of the CSBZ was never satisfactory and the number of cattle slaughtered in the abattoir never exceeded 30 per cent of its slaughter capacity.

After the abolition of the parastatal's monopoly position, the Western Province Cooperative Union (WPCU) was registered in 1981 as a multi-functional enterprise engaged in the supply of agricultural inputs and marketing. Supported by foreign donors the WPCU started cattle marketing and became the second large-scale buyer in the province after the CSBZ. The WPCU purchased animals through the Primary Cooperative Societies (PCSs), newly established and re-established cooperatives at district and sub-district level, and directly from private traders. The PCSs did not operate successfully and private traders supplied the WPCU with most of their cattle. In July 1991, the WPCU underwent a reorganization. The various departments were transformed into limited companies, whereby the Cattle Development Department became Westcoop Livestock Limited (WLL). The WLL, however, did not develop into a viable enterprise and operations ceased in 1993.

The involvement of private traders in the marketing of cattle dates back to the late 1970s when the sole cattle buyer, CSBZ, failed to cope with the increasing volume of animals being offered for sale by cattle owners throughout the province. Private trade filled this gap and mediated between cattle owners and the CSBZ. After 1981, when marketing by private trade was officially allowed, private trade developed its own channels to buyers in urban areas.

Three types of private cattle traders can be distinguished: a) local traders; b) registered traders, and c) private butchers. Local traders operate within the province at a low rate of 1 to 15 animals purchased per quarter. (The designation 'cattle trader' is in fact not fully correct as they are also involved in other occupations, which demand most of their time.) They reside in the villages, buy directly from cattle owners and sell animals to butchers, registered traders, parastatal or cooperative buyers.

Registered traders buy in the province and sell mostly outside it, in Lusaka and the Copperbelt. They need a licence. In 1991 approximately 40 traders were registered. Registered traders handle larger numbers of animals, usually above 15 per batch. A few have their own transport fleet while the rest hire lorries. The traders buy animals throughout the cattle areas through their own buying teams, or they buy from local traders who have trekked the animals to centrally located sites.

Butchers form a third category of private traders. They buy their cattle from local traders or directly from cattle owners. Butchers generally pay less attention to the health and condition of the animals than local traders, which is understandable as animals are almost immediately slaughtered.

The private traders, local as well as registered ones, have established the Western Province Cattle Marketing and Producers Association (WPCMPA) with its headquarters in Mongu. The association has a membership of 300 (in 1996) and was recently successful in acquiring the Mongu abattoir from the defunct ZCSC through the ZPA. The WPCMPA registered a limited company under the name Mongu Meat Corporation and started operating in late 1996 under a management lease agreement with the Lusaka-based Kembe Meat Packers.

Table 10.1 Registered cattle purchases in Western Province by type of buyer, 1985-1995 (head of cattle)

	Local butchers	Registered traders	ZCSC	WPCU	Total
1985	5740	5755	7150	3165	21810
1986	6120	8080	7590	4500	26290
1987	4147	16992	5824	1981	28944
1988	4302	12261	4532	1987	23082
1989	3967	13326	4306	2333	23932
1990	4597	14786	5830	1834	27047
1991	4665	13218	3804	1701	23388
1992	8405	11030	5169	n.a.	24604
1993	4450	16030	2430		22910
1994	2026	7611	1009		10646
1995	5347	17682	565		23494

Sources: DVTCS, WPCU, ZCSC (in Mwafulirwa & Moll, 1991; Muneku, 1996).

The data in Table 10.1 refer to registered purchases and show the changing shares of the various types of buyers. Veterinary inspection takes place before animals are purchased by local butchers. The inspection is carried out by staff of a government department, which was first called DVTCS (Department of Veterinary and Tsetse Control Services) and later

DRSS (Department of Research and Specialist Services). The local government departments also keep records of animals slaughtered by butchers because of the fees to be paid. The registered traders, ZCSC, and WPCU 'export' cattle out of the province. All these animals are inspected because of veterinary regulations. The data thus provide an accurate record of the purchases of cattle for slaughter and consumption, either within or outside the province.

Table 10.1 shows that the share of private traders has increased considerably at the expense of the parastatal and the cooperative. Local traders sell to all four types of buyers and their purchases are included in the figures.

Conclusion

The government participated in cattle marketing in Western Province through a series of organizations. Despite considerable investment by government and donors in purchase facilities, transport, abattoir and freezing facilities and numerous organizational changes, the operations of the Cold Storage Board and its successors never reached commercial sustainability. As a result, the market position of the parastatal organization declined after competition was allowed.

Since the cooperatives in Western Province, with an official status as independent business enterprises, received massive support from the government and several foreign donors, they should also be considered as public enterprises. Unfortunately, this financial and managerial support did not result in sustainable operations and the cooperatives followed the same disappointing track of reorganization and restructuring as the parastatal organizations.

The private cattle trade has gradually acquired a dominant role in Western Province. The recent purchase of the abattoir by the WPCMPA completed the take-over of cattle marketing by the private sector, a process that took a period of approximately 15 years. With this purchase, part of the earlier donor and government support ended up in the private sector. The dominant position of the private sector has been built up without external support and under business conditions that made entry into the market difficult: limited access to financial services from the banks; high inflation; and poor road and telephone communications within the province.

Reviewing the roles of all market parties, we conclude that despite the poor performance of parastatals and cooperatives as business enterprises, they have both played a useful initiating role in cattle marketing in Western Province. The development of marketing infrastructure by the Cold Storage Board and later also the cooperatives facilitated the entrance of commercial buyers located in the urban centres. Within the province, the cattle purchases of the CSB and WPCU enabled individuals to enter the cattle trade on a small scale and gradually acquire the information and financial resources required for growth. Whether these useful roles of the CSB and WPCU and their successors are in balance with the public resources spent remains doubtful.

10.3 Herd development and registered offtake

Data and definitions
Monitoring and analysis of herd dynamics is an essential component of livestock policies. In this section, data from various sources on herd size and registered offtake over the past 31 years are presented. But first a brief sketch of the province in relation to data reliability is given.

Western Province is geographically isolated from the rest of Zambia by the Kafue National Park on the eastern border of the province. Three roads connect Western Province with the rest of Zambia: the main Mongu-Lusaka road leads through the park; one dirt road north of the park leads via a ferry to the Copperbelt, and a partly surfaced road south of the park connects the southern part of the province with Livingstone. In the west, the province is bordered by Angola where lack of effective control results in outbreaks of contagious bovine pleuro pneumonia (CBPP) and other cattle diseases. This has led to the creation of a buffer zone and other measures to reduce the risk of these diseases spreading to Western Province and the rest of Zambia. As a result, live cattle are only allowed to be transported out of Western Province for immediate slaughter on condition that (a) the traders register with the DRSS; (2) they have all cattle tested for CBPP prior to departure; (3) such cattle are escorted by DRSS staff to the approved abattoir, where they witness their slaughter; and (4) cattle held in the buffer zone bordering Angola can only be slaughtered in the Mongu abattoir. Geographical isolation enables an effective enforcement of these measures. This explains the high quality of the DRSS data on cattle leaving the province. In addition to these data, the institutional buyers like the ZCSC and the WPCU have kept records of their turnovers.

Registered offtake is defined as the registered purchase of cattle by the four types of buyers shown in Table 10.1. Offtake in the form of slaughter by the cattle owners themselves because of old age, sickness or death of animals or because of own consumption requirements, is not included. The 'unregistered' offtake has been estimated at 4 per cent of the herd annually, based on herd growth, reproduction rates, and registered offtake (Mwafulirwa & Moll, 1991).

Data on the provincial herd are collected annually through a livestock census by the DRSS. The data collection for this census has been, and still is, linked to free inoculation campaigns and this forms an incentive for cattle owners to provide reliable information.

Herd development and registered offtake
The development of the herd and the registered offtake are depicted in Figure 10.1 together with the estimated trends.

The provincial herd size shows a steady growth from just under 300,000 to over 500,000 over a 31-years period. Linear regression analysis shows an estimated annual herd growth of 8,600 head over the total period (line a), which means that relative herd growth has declined.

Figure 10.1 Herd size and registered offtake in head of cattle in Western Province, 1965-1995

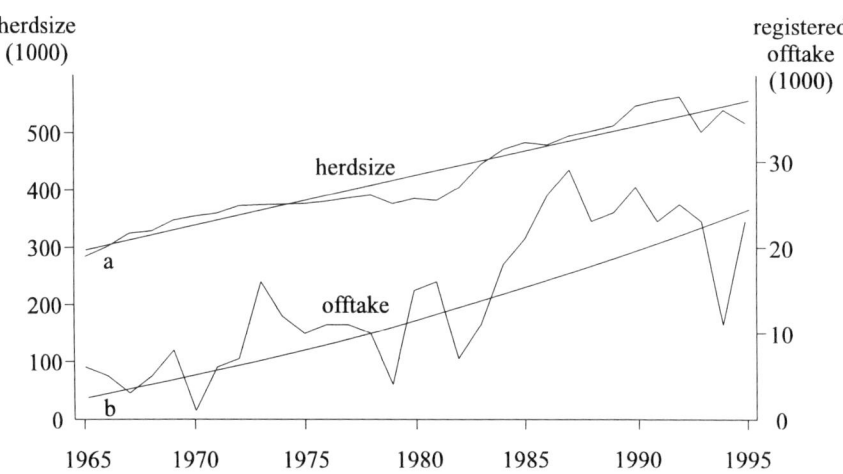

Sources: DVTCS, WPCU, ZCSC (in Mwafulirwa, Moll & Mumbuna, 1992; Muneku, 1996).

The annual registered offtake shows a gradual increase, as well as high fluctuations from year to year. The estimated trend is depicted by curve b, which shows an increasing slope due to a steady increase in the registered offtake expressed as a percentage of the (gradually increasing) provincial herd (Table 10.2, column 3). Linear regression analysis of the offtake percentage results in an estimated annual increase in the offtake percentage of 0.11 per cent, from an estimated 1.40 per cent in 1965 to 4.73 per cent in 1995 ($R^2 = 0.57$).

The increase in registered offtake cannot be entirely explained by marketing policies, as offtake is probably influenced by several other factors: the national economic situation, climatic conditions, outbreaks of disease inside and outside the province, and farmers' preferences. The last factor is discussed in Section 10.4; the other factors are reviewed here.

Annual rainfall is assumed to influence offtake in the sense that following a year with low rainfall, offtake tends to be above normal levels. Dry years (i.e. with less than 800 mm of rain during the season) in the period reviewed were 1966/67, 1972/73, 1976/77, 1981/82, 1983/84, and 1986/87. Comparison of these seasons with the sales in either the rest of the calendar year, or the following year, does not indicate a direct relationship between dry years and higher offtake rates. The generally assumed relationship may possibly be obscured by other factors, but the data for the province do not confirm this.

Outbreaks of disease had a direct impact on offtake as cattle movements were restricted or completely forbidden. Two major events must be mentioned: the CBPP outbreak in Western Province from 1970 to 1972, and the outbreak of 'corridor disease' in

Southern Province, followed by foot-and-mouth disease in 1987. The first resulted in reduced offtake rates as stock movement restrictions almost halted cattle marketing.

Table 10.2 Cattle herd size and registered offtake in Western Province, 1965-1995

Year	Cattle herd	Offtake		
		Total	As proportion of provincial herd	5-year moving average
	(1000 head) (1)	(1000 head) (2)	(%) (3)	(%) (4)
1965	284	6	2.11	-
1966	301	5	1.66	-
1967	324	3	0.93	1.71
1968	328	5	1.52	1.34
1969	347	8	2.31	1.34
1970	354	1	0.28	1.53
1971	359	6	1.67	2.08
1972	372	7	1.88	2.26
1973	374	16	4.28	2.74
1974	375	12	3.20	2.98
1975	376	10	2.66	3.18
1976	380	11	2.89	2.83
1977	386	11	2.85	2.41
1978	391	10	2.56	2.65
1979	376	4	1.06	2.91
1980	385	15	3.90	2.69
1981	382	16	4.19	2.67
1982	404	7	1.73	3.22
1983	445	11	2.47	3.31
1984	471	18	3.82	3.56
1985	483	21	4.35	4.39
1986	479	26	5.43	4.81
1987	495	29	5.86	4.98
1988	503	23	4.57	5.09
1989	513	24	4.68	4.84
1990	547	27	4.94	4.55
1991	556	23	4.14	4.55
1992	563	25	4.44	4.03
1993	502	23	4.58	3.93
1994	540	11	2.04	-
1995	518	23	4.44	-

Sources: column (1) DVTCS; column (2) DVTCS, WPCU, ZCSC (in Mwafulirwa, Moll & Mumbuna, 1992); Muneke, 1996.

After the lifting of the restrictions, a peak of 16,000 head was achieved in 1973. The second event resulted in increased offtake as national traders switched their attention from Southern Province to Western Province. This resulted in the highest offtake rate ever recorded for Western Province, indicating that increased coverage by traders and higher prices persuaded farmers to sell their animals.

The national economic situation directly after independence was favourable and the 1960s show an average registered offtake of 1.3 per cent with an increase towards the end of the decade. This increase was probably caused by increased demand from major urban areas, slightly higher prices and more active purchasing by the Cold Storage Board. The increased offtake may also have been due to an earlier higher rate of provincial net herd growth (Wood, 1989).

The Mongu-Lusaka tarred road, opened in the 1970s, made Western Province much more accessible than before. In addition, goods from urban areas became more easily available and this also may have stimulated sales. With the establishment of the ZCSC abattoir in Mongu in 1975 the infrastructure, as far as roads and cattle marketing facilities were concerned, reached a level which has not basically changed since. The main additional public facility that became available was the telephone system between the district centres in the province and the urban centres along the 'line of rail'. The improvements in infrastructure resulted in the creation of relatively good marketing conditions. The registered offtake rate varied between 2 and 3 per cent in this period.

The economic situation in Zambia from the 1980s onwards has declined or at best has been stagnant. Continuous pressure on the government budget has resulted in a general fall in the standards of the infrastructure and services provided in the 1970s. Charges for public services in health and education were introduced and this increased farmers' needs for cash, and thereby created the incentive to sell more cattle. The government's dwindling funding of the DVTCS/DRSS during the late 1970s and early 1980s led to poorer veterinary services. But bilateral assistance from the Netherlands from 1982 onwards improved services with positive effects on herd growth and increased possibilities for selling outside the province because veterinary standards could be met most of the time. Registered offtake rates reached 4 to 5 per cent in this period.

Conclusion
The natural conditions and institutional factors summarized above had different and, to some extent, contradictory influences on the registered offtake. Peaks and dips in the offtake rate can be related to outbreaks of disease inside and outside the province. The upward trend in offtake combined with a constant average herd growth are more difficult to relate to specific factors. Our review, however, shows that increased offtake rates and herd growth took place under conditions of infrastructural improvement, initially declining and thereafter improving veterinary services, and the gradual incorporation of Western Province into the national economy.

10.4 The cattle owner's perspective

Data collection
Cattle owners' views on the sale of animals were studied in 1991 by a team from the Livestock Development Project, composed of two Zambian staff members and the senior

author of this chapter. Their research findings are presented in Mwafulirwa, Moll & Mumbuna (1992). The three main cattle districts in Western Province, Kalabo, Mongu and Senanga, together accounting for 68 per cent of the provincial herd, were selected for the study. (In the remaining three districts cattle have a much less prominent role in the agricultural system.) Within each district one veterinary camp (a geographical area used by the DRSS for the cattle census) was selected and within the camp area one or two cattle posts (sub-areas) were chosen for sampling respondents. The selection procedure of areas was purposive and the five cattle-post areas selected reflect the existing differences with regard to the accessibility to urban centres, farming systems, and ethnic affiliation. The main characteristics of the study areas are given in Table 10.3.

Table 10.3 Main characteristics of study areas, 1991

District	Kalabo	Mongu	Senanga
Veterinary camp	Ngombe	Imalyo	Lukanda
Cattle population (head)	1974	873	4171
Accessibility	good	poor	very good
Production cash crops	rice	rice	-
Cattle marketing by	private trade, WLL, ZCSC	private trade	private trade WLL, ZCSC

Source: Mwafulirwa, Moll & Mumbuna, 1992.

Within each area, 20 kraals were selected at random from the livestock census list of 1990. A kraal is a management unit with approximately 80 head of cattle owned by one or several owners. Each kraal has a kraal keeper, a senior cattle owner who is consulted by the other cattle owners in cases of illness and the sale and purchase of animals. For each kraal, two respondents were selected at random, preferably the kraal keeper and one other cattle owner. However, in the absence of the kraal keeper, two cattle owners in one kraal were interviewed; only the kraal keeper was interviewed if he was the sole owner of cattle in the kraal, or if the other owner(s) were not available.

Random selection of 110 cattle owners resulted in just over 20 owners who had sold one or more animals over the previous twelve months. Since this number was considered too low to allow an insight into sales behaviour, another 20 cattle owners who had sold cattle during the past twelve months were added to the sample. 'Sale' is defined as the disposal of animals against cash payment to cattle traders, and sales thus refer to the registered offtake as defined in the previous sections. The data of 122 cattle owners[3] were used in the analysis; together they owned 1,452 head of cattle at the time of the survey. Out of the 122 cattle owners, 40 had sold one or more head of cattle during the previous twelve months, with total sales of 80 head of cattle, an average of two per cattle owner. The other 82 persons, the majority of the cattle owners, had not sold cattle during the previous twelve months.

---

[3] The data of eight cattle owners were incomplete and therefore not used.

Besides data on cattle sales, the general characteristics of the cattle owner's household, its asset position, and data on revenues in monetary form and crop production were collected through a structured questionnaire. Additional information was obtained by field observations and discussions with cattle owners and office and field staff of the DRSS and the Department of Agriculture.

Cattle owners and their households
Rural households in the selected districts are all engaged in crop production, mainly for their own consumption. Approximately 50 per cent of the households combine crop production with cattle keeping. Cattle are kept in kraals near the villages and herded during the day. The kraals are moved frequently, once every two to three weeks, and crops such as millet and maize are afterwards grown on the land used for the kraals. The main characteristics of the households of the cattle owners are shown in Table 10.4.

Table 10.4 Household characteristics, mean values

Household characteristics	Mean values	Binomial probit model		
		Coefficient	Significance	Marginal effect at mean
General Characteristics				
Head household,				
male = 1; female = 0	0.84	0.3261	0.4345	0.1128
Age of head of household, years	52	- 0.0011	0.8903	- 0.0004
Education of head of household,				
no formal education = 0				
formal education = 1	0.57	- 0.0897	0.7487	- 0.0310
Dependents, number	6.0	0.0720	0.1080	0.0249
Dependents, school-aged				
children, number	1.6	- 0.1125	0.2037	- 0.0389
Asset position				
Cattle, number	11.9	0.0100	0.3931	0.0035
Assets other than cattle,			0.1279	0.0000
in Kwacha	7990	0.0000		
Revenues				
Recurrent revenues				
cattle, in Kwacha	700	0.0001	0.2725	0.0000
Recurrent revenue				
other livestock, in Kwacha	80	0.0002	0.6153	0.0001
Off-farm revenues, in Kwacha	1240	- 0.0001	0.3529	- 0.0000
Crop production				
Labour hire,				
no = 0, yes = 1	0.32	0.3471	0.2376	0.1201
Produce sold,				
no = 0, yes = 1	0.34	- 0.2532	0.4634	- 0.0876
Self-sufficiency,				
no = 0, yes = 1	0.46	- 0.6426	0.0435 *	- 0.2223
Constant		- 1.0011	0.0796	- 0.3464

Source: Mwafulirwa, Moll & Mumbuna, 1992.
* significant at .05 level.

The general characteristics show that 84 per cent of the households are male headed; the majority of the heads of household have formal education ranging from a few years of primary school to secondary school or college; and the average household size is 7 with a range from 2 to 15 and a standard deviation of 3.

The asset position of the households covers in principle capital assets, land and labour resources. However, land is free as a household may use the area they can cultivate, and therefore land is not included as a characteristic. Houses show few differences and offer no basis for a classification of wealth either. Hence, cattle and capital assets such as equipment like ploughs, scotch carts and sledges, and durable consumer goods like sewing machines and kerosene lamps form the main components of the asset position. The average cattle herd of 11.9 head per household has an estimated value of K 71000 and cattle form the main asset making up on average about 90 per cent of the total asset value. A more detailed insight into the ownership of cattle is provided in Table 10.5.

The largest group of households owns 1 to 5 head of cattle or 12 per cent of the total number of cattle in the sample. At the other end of the scale is the small group (17%) of owners of large herds, 21 head and more, who together own about 50 percent of the total number of cattle. The average size of herd per household shows considerable differences among districts: the cattle owners in Senanga on average own 18 head, whereas cattle owners in Kalabo and Mongu on average own 10 and 8 head respectively. The difference in herd size between female- and male-headed households is striking, 6 against 13 head, confirming other studies (Beerling, 1986).

Table 10.5 Households by herd size and gender of household head

Herd size class	Households	Average herd size per household per class	Proportion of all cattle	Gender of household head	
				male	female
(head)	(number)	(number)	(%)	(number)	
1-5	53	3.2	12	40	13
6-10	25	7.9	14	20	5
11-15	14	12.6	12	14	-
16-20	10	19.6	13	8	2
21-25	6	22.8	9	6	-
26-30	8	29.1	16	8	-
>30	6	57.3	24	6	-
Total	122		100	102	20
Average		11.9			

Source: Mwafulirwa, Moll & Mumbuna, 1992.

Revenues, other than from the sale of cattle, are mainly from the sale of milk; the hiring out of oxen; the sale of meat from animals that need to be slaughtered because of accidents, sickness or old age; the sale of livestock products such as eggs and chickens; and off-farm employment.

Crop production in the research area is primarily for home consumption, and when any produce is sold, the quantities are small. The average values of the characteristics show that less than half of the households are self-sufficient; most of the households thus need to buy food.

Sales behaviour

From the 122 respondents, 40 had sold one or more head of cattle during the past twelve months with a total sale of 80 head. The probability of the sale of cattle by a household as a function of the household characteristics was estimated through a binary probit model. The results presented in Table 10.4 show that only one characteristic, self-sufficiency in crop production, is significant at the 0.05 level, and negatively related to the probability of selling one or more animals. This relationship is logical as food self-sufficiency removes the need to sell cattle to purchase food. The marginal effect of the significant variable on the sales decision is small and the predictive power of the model is low, see Table 10.6. The proportion of correctly predicted decisions is 78 per cent, with 93 per cent of the cases without sales, and 48 per cent of the cases with sales correctly predicted.[4]

Table 10.6 Sales decisions, actual and predicted by the binomial probit model

Actual	Predicted No	Predicted Yes	Total
No	76	6	82
Yes	21	19	40
Total	97	25	122

The variable 'number of cattle owned' has no significant effect on the sales behaviour of cattle owners. This finding is noteworthy because it means that there is no positive relationship between the volume of animal production (directly related to the number of animals) and sales. As a consequence the offtake, the ratio between animals sold and animals owned over a certain period, is lower for the owners of large herds than for the owners of small herds.

To obtain qualitative explanations the respondent cattle owners were asked about their decision making and reasoning. Cattle owners primarily consult family members and relatives before taking the decision to sell. Usually this is a matter of 'informing', rather than of seeking approval. Consultation with the kraal keeper is the second step when the

---

[4] The unequal number of cases with and without sales, 40 and 82 respectively, does not negatively affect the overall predictability; if the cases without sales are randomly split into two groups and if each of these groups is combined with the 40 cases with sales, the proportion of correctly predicted cases in the two new models drops to 68% and 74%.

composition of the total herd of the kraal is taken into account. As a result the prospective seller may replace one of his/her animals with an animal in the kraal which is no longer productive and thus can be sold without impairing recurrent production. No respondent in the sample refrained from selling an animal as a result of the advice received from those consulted.

The reasons given for selling cattle during the last twelve months are listed in Table 10.7, under the two headings 'consumption' and 'production and investment'. Most of the reasons classified under 'consumption' refer to urgent requirements, if not calamities. The need to buy food, clothes and blankets is a major reason for selling cattle. (This confirms the negative relationship between the sale of animals and self-sufficiency in food production found in the probit model.) Production and investment purposes are mainly related to education and the purchase of capital goods. All answers reveal that selling an animal is directly linked to the immediate utilization of the money received.

Table 10.7 Respondents' reasons for selling cattle

	Frequency
a) Consumption	
to buy food, clothes and blankets	12
to pay hospital fees for a child	2
to clear credits	2
to pay a witch doctor who treated a sick child	1
to pay a fine because son impregnated a girl	1
to solve problems resulting from the death of a child	1
to send money to a sister who had lost her job	1
to send money to a daughter with problems in Lusaka	1
Sub-total	22
b) Production or investment	8
to send children to school	4
to pay *lobola* (bride price)	2
to replace unproductive stock	1
to send a son on a mechanics course	1
to support a nephew training as a driver	1
to buy fishing nets	1
to build a house	1
to buy fertilizer and seeds and to hire labour	2
to pay people to harvest rice	1
Sub-total	20
Total	42

Source: Mwafulirwa, Moll & Mumbuna, 1992.
Note: Some respondents mentioned reasons in more than one category.

Table 10.7 is complemented by Table 10.8 which lists the answers of the cattle owners who did not sell during the previous twelve months.

Table 10.8 Respondents' reasons for not selling cattle

	Frequency
I have very few animals; I want the number to increase	53
Recently some of my animals died	9
No reason to sell at present	9
I have alternative sources of income	3
If I sell there is nothing I can buy	2
Total	76

Source: Mwafulirwa, Moll & Mumbuna, 1992.
Note: Some respondents mentioned reasons in more than one category.

The answers suggest a strong propensity to maintain, and if possible to increase, the number of cattle owned.

The sales behaviour of cattle owners can be explained by the various roles cattle play in the rural economy of Western Province. Firstly, cattle form the main asset in the household and have a high liquidity. The ownership of cattle thus provides the capacity to meet financial emergencies. Secondly, cattle present a convenient form of saving in an environment where people do not have access to financial institutions. Elsewhere the option exists of selling cattle at the optimal moment from a bio-physical viewpoint or in periods of high prices, and of subsequently depositing the revenues with a bank until required. Here this option is not available. The sale of animals whenever the household faces substantial requirements of cash is thus a rational strategy. Moreover, saving is part and parcel of cattle keeping as the weight gain of individual animals and/or an increase in numbers means investing in herd value. Thirdly, cattle provide recurrent production in terms of milk, manure and draught power, part of which can be sold. The three roles can be summarized as insurance, financing and recurrent production respectively (see Bosman et al., 1997 for a quantitative assessment of these roles). These three roles are, to some extent, mutually exclusive: the sale of an animal results in one large sum of money, but it ends recurrent production as well as the capacity to meet future requirements. In an environment with no other accessible options for financing or insurance than cattle, the sale of an animal thus requires a careful assessment of present and future, expected and unexpected, household requirements.

Conclusions

The reasons given by the cattle owners for selling and not selling cattle lead to the conclusion that cattle are only sold when there are serious requirements for substantial amounts of cash. This conclusion is supported by our statistical analysis which on the one hand indicates that self-sufficiency in crop production decreases the propensity to sell cattle, and on the other hand shows that there is no relationship between herd size and sales.

The results of our study are in line with earlier reports by Fielder (1973) and Beerling (1986). Beerling gives a vivid impression of the ideas cattle owners have about being rich in cattle and states that the borderline between rich and not rich seems to be drawn at about 50 head of cattle. Considering the actual herd size shown in Table 10.5, there were very few households who could be considered rich according to this criterion, while the majority of the households can sell an animal only once in a few years if they want to maintain their herd.

10.5 Discussion

Our review of cattle marketing in Western Province over the past 30 years shows a continuous search for viable marketing institutions. This search is part of the wider and continuous search for the demarcation of the roles of government and private sector in society. Since the initial justification for government intervention was a lack of essential services, public organizations seemed the logical answer. A generally poor performance of public organizations on the one hand, and rising economic opportunities in cattle marketing on the other, removed the justification for government participation. In the early 1990s the conclusion was that support for public organizations be terminated and cattle marketing left to the private sector. The search for effective institutions has, however, not ended. Private trade is just beginning to develop its own voluntary, independent institutions. The history of intervention and support by government and donors should result in extreme caution regarding interference in this process of institutional development.

The longitudinal, overall analysis of cattle marketing in Western Province shows a gradually increasing proportion of the cattle herd entering the marketing channels. This finding seems to contradict the conclusion that 'cattle are only sold if there are serious requirements for substantial amounts of cash' found in our micro study of the sales behaviour of the individual cattle owners. The same contradiction appears from studies of the sales behaviour of cattle owners carried out in Western Province in 1973 and 1986. The apparent conflict between the longitudinal analysis and the micro studies can be resolved by the perspective that, firstly, increased sales opportunities offer cattle owners the possibility to sell their cattle in order to deal with serious requirements and, secondly, that the cattle owners' definition of 'serious requirements' changes over time. This perspective on pull and push factors determining cattle sales is supported by observations during several episodes when cattle marketing in Western Province was affected by external factors: a) the ban on cattle sales due to outbreaks of disease in the province was, for instance, followed by increased sales after the lifting of the ban; and, b) increased activity of cattle traders due to temporary marketing restrictions in other Zambian provinces led to an increased offtake.

The positions in the debate on the effect of marketing policies on the sales decision of cattle keepers mentioned in the introduction are apparently dependent on the time perspective of the analysis. Studies dealing with sales decisions over a short period suggest a static picture[5] and may easily result in the conclusion that cattle owners are not affected by market conditions created by marketing policies. However, our longitudinal analysis of cattle marketing in Western Province (over a period of 30 years) shows a distinct positive supply response of cattle owners towards increased marketing opportunities, created directly by marketing policies and indirectly by policies dealing with infrastructure. The changing requirements of cattle owners and their household members apparently provide strong incentives to make use of the increased marketing opportunities.

References

BAARS, R.M.T. & M.M. MUMBUNA (1991) 'Grazing management systems, a supplement to "Farming in Western Province, A.R.P.T., 1988."' Mongu: Department of Veterinary and Tsetse Control Services, Livestock Development Project.
BEERLING, M.L. (1986) 'Acquisition and alienation of cattle in Western Province, Zambia.' Mongu: Department of Veterinary and Tsetse Control Services, Livestock Development Project.
BEERLING, M.L. (1991) 'The advantage of having cattle, distribution of cattle and access to benefits in the Western Province of Zambia.' Mongu: Department of Veterinary and Tsetse Control Services, Livestock Development Project.
BOSMAN, H.G., H.A.J. MOLL & H. UDO (1997) 'Measuring and interpreting the benefits of goat keeping in tropical farm systems.' In *Agricultural Systems*, Vol 53, pp. 349-372.
CENTRAL STATISTICAL OFFICE (1983 to 1990) *Zambia in Figures*. Lusaka: Government of the Republic of Zambia.
CHIZYUKA, W.G.B., D. ZWART & S.F. POSTMA (1987) 'Cattle in Western Province, The Animal Disease Control Project and related aspects.' The Hague: Government of the Republic of Zambia and Ministry of Development Cooperation.
CORTEN, J.J.F.M. (1989) 'Productivity of cattle in Western Province, Zambia.' Mongu: Department of Veterinary and Tsetse Control Services, Animal Disease Control Project, Western Province.
DEPARTMENT OF REGIONAL PLANNING (1974). 'Regional study and plan of Western Province.' Lusaka: Development Planning Division, Ministry of Planning and Finance.
FIELDER, R.J. (1973) 'The role of cattle in the Ila economy - a conflict of views on the uses of cattle by the Ila of Namwala.' In *African Social Research*, no. 15, pp. 327-361.
GULHATI, R. (undated) *Impasse in Zambia: The Economics and Politics of Reform*. Washington D.C.: The World Bank.
LOW, A. (1986) 'Agricultural development in Southern Africa: farm-household economics and the food crisis.' In *Books in African studies*. London: Currey, pp. 217
LUTKE-ENTRUP, J. (1971) 'Limitations and Possibilities of Increasing Market Production of Peasant African cattle holders in Western Province.' University of Zambia, Institute for African Studies, communication no 7.
MACLEAN, H.A.M. (1965) 'An Agricultural Stocking of Barotseland.' Lusaka: Government of Zambia.
MOLL, H.A.J. (1997) 'Livestock keeping and missing markets.' Working paper, Wageningen: Wageningen Agricultural University.
MOLL, H.A.J. & N.B.M. HEERINK (1998) 'Price adjustments and the cattle sub-sector in Central West Africa.' In: *Livestock and the Environment, Proceedings of the International Conference on Livestock and the Environment*, Ede/Wageningen, June 1997 by World Bank/Food and Agriculture Organization and the International Agricultural Centre. pp. 72-87.

---

[5] Incidental external shocks may, however, temporarily disturb the static picture – temporarily because the rate of reproduction is limited. For evidence from Western Province, see above. For evidence from West Africa, see Moll & Heerink (1998).

MOTEL-COMBES, P. (1996) 'Les déterminants de l'offre de bétail dans les pays sahéliens.' In *Révue économique*, Vol. 47, no. 5, pp.1103-1109.
MUNEKE, F.M., (1996) 'Private sector cattle marketing networks in Western Province'. Working Paper 96/1, Mongu: Livestock Development Programme.
MUWAMBA, J.M. (1989) 'Identification of cattle sellers, status and implication on livestock development as an alternative cash source.' Mongu: Department of Agriculture, Research Branch, Adaptive Research Planning Team.
MWAFULIRWA, C. & H.A.J. MOLL (1991) 'Economics of cattle and crop sub sectors of Western Province.' Mongu: Department of Veterinary and Tsetse Control Services, R.D.P. Livestock Services.
MWAFULIRWA, C., H.A.J. MOLL & MWENDA M. MUMBUNA (1992) 'Cattle marketing in Western Province.' Mongu: Department of Veterinary and Tsetse Control Services, R.D.P. Livestock Services.
NATIONAL COMMISSION FOR DEVELOPMENT PLANNING (1989) *New Economic Recovery Programme, Fourth National Development Plan 1983-1993*. Vol. 1, Lusaka.
PROVINCIAL PLANNING UNIT (1991) 'Western Province Medium Term Development Plan 1991-1996.' Mongu.
PROVINCIAL PLANNING UNIT (1983) 'Statistical handout for Western Province.' In N.N. Mongu (1987) 'Report of the tripartite mission to Western Province Co-operative Union.' The Hague, Helsinki.
SCHOONMAN, L. (1990) *Census Figures 1990*. Department of Veterinary and Tsetse Control Services, Mongu, Livestock Development Project.
TAPSON, D.R. (1991) 'The overstocking and offtake controversy reexamined for the case of Kwazulu.' London: ODI Pastoral Development Network.
VAN KLINK, E.G.M., M.M. KAWAMBWA & D.M. KALOKONI (1990) 'The cattle population of Western Province, Zambia on the basis of the annual livestock census 1987, 1988, 1989.' Mongu: Department of Veterinary and Tsetse Control Services, R.D.P Livestock Services.
WOOD, A.P. (1988) 'A socio-economic analysis of cattle keeping for planning sustainable extension and service provision through the Livestock Development Project, Western Province.' Huddersfield: Royd House, Houses Hill, Kirkheaton.
WOOD, A.P. (1989) 'Cattle development in Western Province'. ODI Pastoral Development Network, London, Agricultural Administrative Unit.
WORLD BANK (1990) 'Zambia: Issues and options in livestock development.' Draft working paper No.11 Agriculture Operations Division, Southern Africa.

11

Cross-border Cattle Marketing in Sub-Saharan Africa since 1900
Geographical Patterns and Government-induced Change

Leo de Haan, Paul Quarles van Ufford and Fred Zaal

Abstract

This chapter aims to study the impact of government policies on cross-border cattle marketing in Africa. It analyzes the geographical patterns of cattle trade in the pre-colonial, colonial and post-colonial periods and examines the main reasons for the increase, decline or diversion of cross-border cattle trade paying specific attention to government policies.

The volume of this trade in Sub-Saharan Africa, which is often long distance trade, became significant when the colonial economy developed. Population growth, export production and increased incomes triggered demand for meat in newly emerging consumption areas. Whereas in West Africa colonial trade policies contributed little to this expansion, government interventions in East and Southern Africa had more impact. However, despite the stronger grip of the state on cattle marketing in East and Southern Africa, much of the cross-border cattle trade in these regions was in the hands of private traders as in West Africa. In the post-colonial era, government interventions increased through the creation of cattle and meat marketing boards. In West Africa many of these boards never functioned properly but in East and Southern Africa their impact was substantial. Most were nevertheless dismantled under structural adjustment programmes.

The chapter concludes that changes in supply caused by (civil) wars and droughts, and changes in demand caused by rising and falling economic prosperity have had the most significant impact on cross-border cattle trade. Notwithstanding the differences between West Africa on the one hand and East and Southern Africa on the other, government policies aiming at intervention in cattle marketing have only temporarily and marginally affected cross-border trade. Slightly more important have been the general economic policies causing, for example, changes in the value of the national currency. Private cattle traders are acknowledged for their remarkable responsiveness to both short- and long-term opportunities which the cross-border cattle trade, legal or illegal, offers them.

11.1 Introduction

This chapter aims to study the impact of government policies on cross-border cattle trade in Sub-Saharan Africa. In its analysis, it follows the debate on the *espace céréalier* (common food grain market) in West Africa which discussed the effects of borders and different national trade policies on the efficiency of the macro-regional food market. Particular attention will therefore be paid to geographical patterns of cross-border cattle trade and national trade policies. Our aim is to determine to what extent this often long distance trade in Sub-Saharan Africa has been influenced by different national (trade) policies and the existence of political boundaries.

In the debate on the *espace céréalier* in West Africa (De Haan et al., 1995), discussion focused primarily on the extent to which cross-border trade is influenced by government policies and whether harmonization of government policies, i.e. regional integration, is needed to ensure a more efficient functioning of food grain markets. It was noticed that discrepancies in national trade policies were creating cross-border trade. For example, rice was re-exported in large quantities from countries permitting, in the absence of a significant national rice production, cheap imports from the world market to countries protecting their national rice production with high producer prices. In addition, cross-border trade occurred between countries where differences between the real value of the national currency and the official value, the so-called overvaluation, could be exploited resulting in attractive profits. Due to official regulations, which often restricted or even banned cross-border trade, most of it was illegal (De Haan et al., 1995, 69).

Egg et al. (1988) and Egg & Igué (1990) have demonstrated the importance of these factors in the food grain trade in post-colonial West Africa. Although they consider comparative advantages in food production as the major determinant of cross-border trade flows, they point in particular at disparities in economic, notably monetary, policies to explain the numerous examples of cross-border trade they found. They further mention the cultural bonds between people who live on both sides of a border as a factor that facilitates this trade. In addition, Grégoire (1986, 136-144) describes the strategies of Hausa traders from Niger who imported cigarettes and textiles from Europe through the Cotonou harbour in Benin,[1] whereby they used the services of NITRA, the Niger government transit organization, to fulfil all formalities. Cigarettes and textiles were subject to prohibitive import restrictions in Nigeria but the Niger Hausa traders made use of extensive trade networks to bring the merchandise to Nigeria through Niger. These types of transactions generated enormous profits for the traders involved (ibid.).

One of the questions in the debate was whether harmonization of these national policies would result in an increase or decrease of trade. Some argued that if trade was liberated from regulations, the free market would generate more trade. Others maintained that once traders

---

[1] Benin has always had a liberal import policy. Thus, all kinds of goods are imported through its port and subsequently illegally re-exported to neighbouring countries (Nigeria in particular) where import policies are more restrictive. Igué & Soulé (1992) have aptly described this as the 'warehouse' function of Cotonou.

could no longer exploit price differences caused by government policies, trade would shrink. The concepts used in this debate, like trade creation and trade diversion, were derived from Viner (1950). Viner only paid attention to trade between countries, i.e. cross-border trade. He advocated free international trade as the most efficient and thus optimal kind of trade, and considered the establishment of customs unions as suboptimal because it implies discrimination against other possible trading partners. According to Viner (see Aalbersberg, 1996) two kinds of intercountry substitution would result from the establishment of a customs union. Trade creation would occur if sources of supply shift from domestic to foreign inside the customs union. Trade diversion would occur if sources of supply shift from a foreign country outside the customs union to a foreign country inside the customs union.

To analyze cross-border cattle trade in Africa we will make use of these concepts of trade creation and trade diversion. However, we will not use them to evaluate the establishment of customs unions but rather as a tool to relate geographical patterns of cross-border cattle trade to trade policies and other government policies. Therefore, we should not overlook trade contraction as a third possibility. Contraction might simply be the result of failing demand, but in the case of customs unions, harmonization of policies might result in a decline in interest in the foreign market because exploiting differences between the real and official value of currencies would no longer be attractive.

We think that the creation of boundaries during the colonial epoch, with corresponding tariffs and other trade barriers such as quarantine measures and export bans have caused a similar, suboptimal restructuring of cattle trade patterns. Trade flows may have contracted or been diverted because of new policies. However, new trade flows may have resulted from this as well.

In summary, in this chapter we will extend the analysis of changes in trade flows as a consequence of government policies, known primarily from the food trade and trade in export products, to cross-border trade in cattle. We have tried to cover the whole of Sub-Saharan Africa. However, the bulk of our argument stems from field observations in Kenya and the central part of West Africa, supplemented by literature surveys for the whole of West and East Africa. We will discuss cross-border cattle trade in Southern Africa only in general terms. In addition, we will demonstrate that cattle trade, as far as it was influenced by colonial and post-colonial policy, was influenced differently in the various parts of Africa. In East and Southern Africa, settler dominance shaped cattle marketing, while in West Africa, cattle trade remained an African activity throughout the colonial period. The explanation for these different marketing environments lay in their different production structures. Cross-border cattle trade is often synonymous with long distance trade, especially where pre-colonial and early colonial cattle trade is concerned, because it links production and consumption areas with one another even though they are sometimes situated more than a thousand kilometers apart, such as in West Africa. However, cross-border trade is not always long distance trade and our analysis concerns cross-border trade over shorter distances too.

In the next section, we will present a sketch of pre-colonial and early colonial geographical patterns of cattle trade. In Sections 11.3 and 11.4 we will examine the changes that occurred in these patterns, first in the colonial period and then after independence, and their link with government policies and other interventions. The final section will summarize our main conclusions.

11.2 Initial patterns of the cattle trade

In a recent study, Kerven (1992) points to the existence of long distance livestock trade flows in pre-colonial Sub-Saharan Africa. Many historians seem to have neglected this trade, perhaps because they were more interested in export goods like ivory and slaves. Most livestock was traded in networks of which the core business was oriented towards luxury products such as gold or cloth rather than towards livestock. Nevertheless, livestock and livestock products such as skins, hides and leather featured in these trading caravans.

In his pioneering economic history of West Africa, Hopkins (1973, 58-73) explains that for centuries products were traded between the complementary ecological zones of this region. In the northern parts of West Africa, extensive livestock rearing took place, while the southern parts were not suited to stock breeding due to trypanosomiasis caused by the tsetse fly. Thus, livestock products from the Sahel and salt from the Sahara were exchanged for slaves, ivory and kola nuts from the forest zones. According to Kerven (1992, 50), the urban areas of the Hausa-Fulani emirates, situated within the livestock zone, were important outlets too. In the nineteenth century, West African pre-colonial long distance trade was monopolized by Hausa and Dyula traders. The Hausa transported leather, textile and salt from Hausaland to Ashante in large caravans of porters and donkeys, and brought kola nuts back home. Their caravan routes traversed present-day Benin and Togo. Norris (1984, 170) reports that 10 per cent of the value of products traded by the caravans traversing Togo was made up of cattle and other livestock. Dyula traders dominated the western parts of the sub-region and were involved, among other things, in the dried fish trade from the Niger inner delta southwards. Generally, trade patterns were determined by the location of prosperous regions such as Ashante and Hausaland as well as the region around Kankan in north-east Guinea. Because of high transportation costs, long distance trade was mainly limited to luxury products which only the high-income elite could afford.

In Eastern Africa long distance trade developed from the early nineteenth century onwards and was mainly dominated by the Swahili and Arabs from the coast. With respect to this region as well as to Southern African patterns, Fage (1995) mentions gold, in addition to ivory, slaves, cloves and only occasionally skins, as the major trade products. All of these were considered to be export products because African communities themselves were not widely diversified (Fage, 1995, 323). Kerven (1992, 16-17), however, taking a closer look at East African pastoral economies, not only presents evidence of local trade between pastoralists and peasants but also of long distance trade. Due to the relative proximity of ecological gradients in East Africa, the exchange of food grains and livestock products between peasants and pastoralists was usually short distance trade. However, long distance cattle trade took place as well. After the devastating pandemics of the late nineteenth century, the Maasai demand for stock was such that present-day Kenya and Tanzania were included in the long distance livestock trade from Somalia and southern Ethiopia. Somali traders would barter camels for heifers and young bulls in the northern rangelands of Kenya. These animals would be taken to the Maasai area and exchanged for mature bulls, which were sold in the emerging consumer centres.

In general, the direct intervention of African authorities in trade is judged as minimal. Authors such as Lovejoy (1980) considered this of prime importance for long distance trade to flourish. Even so, some pre-colonial states did meddle with trading caravans within their own territories. This usually involved substantial taxation in exchange for physical protection.

11.3 The colonial era

Geographical patterns
From the early stages of colonial occupation, flourishing export crop economies in West Africa led to a significant increase in demand for meat.[2] Transformation and intensification of pre-colonial trade patterns in West Africa therefore occurred in the early colonial era. This was particularly true for southern Ghana, Nigeria, and Senegal (Quarles van Ufford, 1999).

For example, the rise of cash incomes in the cocoa region of Ghana and the oil-palm region of Nigeria raised demand for meat and consequently stimulated livestock trade from the Sudan and Sahel belts to the coast. In German Togo, the savannah region already supplied cattle to the coastal export production zone of Togo and Ghana from the turn of the century onwards (De Haan, 1993, 65,109). Norris (1984, 181) and De Haan (1993, 108) make clear that the importance of northern Togo as a transit area for the long distance trade in kola nuts declined at the beginning of the twentieth century. Instead of traveling to Ghana directly through Benin and Togo, traders now traveled first to Gourma and Mossi areas in present-day Burkina Faso in order to trade textiles for cattle. The cattle were then transported on the hoof to the coast and sold at considerable profit. Next, kola nuts were bought and, due to their perishability, transported straight to Hausaland. By then, the Hausa traders were increasingly making use of regular, modern ocean-going shipping connections in the kola nut trade (Hopkins, 1973, 248), thus shifting their trade routes to the coastal ports. The kola nuts were shipped from one port on the coast to another and then again inland. In 1904 and 1905, present-day Ghana imported some 16,000 head of cattle from present-day Burkina Faso, a number that had quadrupled by 1950 (Skinner, 1964). This example reflects the restructuring of pre-colonial trade patterns as well as the first steps towards the

---

[2] The provisioning of military garrisons was an important contributing factor in increasing trade. Notably during the First and Second World Wars, this demand required specific regulatory policies in order to satisfy the meat provision of the various garrisons spread over West Africa. In a careful account of the war-time policies of the French authorities in Dahomey (Benin), d'Almeida Topor (1995, 227-235) shows how the latter tried to control commercial movements of livestock to fulfil not only local demand (population and garrisons) but also demand in France and its other colonies, notably from troops garrisoned in Cameroon. Again, local traders themselves organized the supplies. After 1917, the livestock trade reverted to 'pre-war' patterns.

modernization of means of transport, although livestock was to be transported on the hoof for a long time to come.

Livestock exports to southern Nigeria, especially to the booming cities of Lagos and Ibadan, rose from 8,000 in 1906 to around 200,000 animals per year in the 1930s (Hopkins, 1973, 248), an estimated 125,000 originating from the French territories to the north (Kerven, 1992, 56). In contrast to this, the northward trans-Saharan trade slowly collapsed because of taxation by the French and increased competition from commodities imported through the coastal ports (Kerven, 1992).

Meat was imported from Europe into West Africa in considerable quantities as well. In the late 1950s, about 19,000 tons of mostly frozen and canned meat were brought into the region annually (Mittendorf & Wilson, 1961). Total imports from Europe into North and West Africa had risen from 23,000 tons in 1950 to 65,000 tons in 1959.[3] Because these are considerable quantities, frozen meat will not only have been sold to Europeans and African higher income groups. However, it is difficult to determine to what extent imported meat was in competition with indigenous cattle production.

In East Africa the pre-colonial patterns of cattle trading were much more disrupted. Sales from African livestock producers in Kenya were generally hampered by veterinary quarantine restrictions. Trade between indigenous producers and white settlers or with the newly established consumer markets was only allowed when demand for local stock was high. This was the case when settlers needed stock to start their ranches, or when demand for meat was high such as during the First World War. During the droughts of 1918-21 and the late 1920s, increasing numbers of animals came on the market, causing massive slumps in prices due to the limited sales possibilities. Illegal trade took place between cattle-producing areas and areas of emerging African small-scale agriculture and the developing urban centres. Cattle were brought illegally from Kenya to Tanzania as well, where they caused problems with diseases at the time when the Tanzanian government had been paying a lot of attention to the eradication of disease among their local herds. In fact, here we witness the continuation and extension of a trade flow already established in the pre-colonial period. In the mid 1930s, double the number of animals were marketed in Kenya compared to during the 1920s (Kerven, 1992). By then, producers were being encouraged to sell to emerging African consumer markets. Official figures indicate an increase in sales from 8,000 to 24,000 head of cattle and from 14,000 to 48,000 head of small stock annually in the 1930s. During the Second World War, 25,000 head of cattle a year were sold by Maasai producers to supply meat to the armed forces.

The pattern that developed in the 1950s was more complex. White settlers in Kenya marketed most of their livestock through the Kenya Meat Commission, established in 1950. KMC served mostly the settler population, as well as exporting to Europe. Considerable numbers of African livestock came from Northern Kenya and Somalia to the coast, from the

---

[3] Assuming a slaughter weight of 150 kg per animal, 1 metric ton of carcass is the equivalent of 6.7 animals. The 125,000 animals exported from French West Africa into Nigeria would yield 18,750 tons in cold dressed weight. Carcasses from European animals weighed from 250 to 265 kg (Mittendorf & Wilson, 1961, 12).

southern rangelands to both Nairobi and Tanzania, and from the western part of Kenya, mainly the Rift Valley, to Nyanza Province and Uganda. In 1957-58, for example, official records suggest that between 50,000 and 63,000 head of cattle were marketed to Nyanza and Uganda from Rift Valley producers and Trans Mara Maasai (Republic of Kenya, 1959). Some cattle came from southern Sudan to Uganda as well. Cattle would also come from the central parts of Tanzania to the coastal town of Dar es Salaam. However, in the late 1950s, meat prices in Kenya had risen so much that cattle started to come from Tanzania to the north into Nairobi (Mittendorf & Wilson, 1961). Overseas exports were important as well, mainly from Kenya and Tanzania to the UK, Germany, and Mediterranean countries. Low quality animals from African producers, processed by the Liebig Company under the supervision of the KMC, were exported as corned beef. In the late 1950s, this amounted to 13,000 tons from Kenya, and almost 10,000 tons from Tanzania.

In Southern Africa by that time, the important industrial and cash crop producing areas in Zambia, Zimbabwe and South Africa had generated demand for huge numbers of animals for slaughter, as the labour force in the towns had grown rapidly during the colonial period with the development of mines and industry. In the late 1950s, 10,000 head of cattle were exported annually from Botswana to Zimbabwe, 12,000 from Swaziland to South Africa, and a staggering 270,000 head from Namibia to South Africa. Most of these animals came from the ranches of settlers, not from African producers (Mittendorf & Wilson, 1961).

Trade and other policies
The overall picture of geographical patterns of cattle trade described in the previous section points at a clear distinction between West Africa on the one hand and the so-called settler and mining colonies of East and Southern Africa on the other. In the former, the colonial *économie de traite* (trade economy) was based on export production by African peasants dominated by European trading firms, while the indigenous food trade was left relatively untouched. In the latter, European settlers dominated, resulting in a different structure of production, giving rise to different trade policies. The indigenous livestock economy in East Africa was curtailed in access to both grazing areas and market outlets in favour of white settlers' ranches from the beginning of the twentieth century. High quality rangeland was closed to African pastoralists and reserved for settlers. Strict quarantine regulations prevented the former from marketing their livestock at traditional and new markets. Overall policy remained unchanged in the colonial period and if changes did occur, it was merely to address problems which were created originally by disrupting indigenous trade and confining pastoralists to low quality areas. For example, during the 1930s overstocking of these African areas threatened because a loss of grazing areas to settlers, marketing restrictions and quarantine measures had caused overgrazing. This explains the subsequent encouragement of sales to emerging African consumer markets. By that time pastoralists' willingness to sell had increased too. It is also worthwhile mentioning that during the First World War cattle sales to meet the military demand had to be enforced upon pastoralists, not only because the prices offered were low, but because pastoralists' cash needs were too. During the Second World War the prices set were more favourable and pastoralists' cash needs were also higher, which explains the striking supply response of the Maasai. Other

examples are the slaughtering and canning facilities built by Liebig's. British colonial preoccupation with the conservation of African grazing areas threatened by overstocking resulted in the permanent skimming of cattle surpluses in areas considered to be overstocked. Liebig's facilities played an important role in this strategy enabling the surplus to be marketed, and exported as corned beef.

In Southern Africa, where the comparative advantage of Tswana livestock production in Botswana was acknowledged in an early stage, marketing development oriented towards African producers was much more important. Bore-hole development facilitated grazing in heretofore unexploited areas. Large stock owners became the principal suppliers for the markets of the mining areas in neighbouring colonies. Although the first marketing board was set up in 1932 in South Africa, it was in the final stages of colonial rule that state intervention in cattle production and trade became more pronounced. The rationale behind these policies was veterinary improvement, and consequently, quarantine camps were widespread.

In contrast to West Africa, marketing boards were established, representing state involvement in marketing. The Cold Storage Commission (CSC) in South Africa, the Botswana Meat Commission (BMC) and the Kenya Meat Commission (KMC) have been influential state enterprises. Kenya may serve as an example. Established in 1950,[4] the KMC was initially given a monopoly on virtually all stages of the livestock marketing process (purchase, slaughtering, wholesaling and the export of meat). However, it could not enforce its monopoly for the country as a whole and for African slaughter stock in particular. As a result, private trade occurred depending on fluctuations in demand. For the purpose of destocking, the African Livestock Marketing Organisation (ALMO) was set up in 1952. This organization, which formed part of the Veterinary Department, was responsible for the purchase of African livestock at fixed, low prices, part of which had to be resold to the KMC. However, ALMO experienced severe competition from private Maasai and Somali livestock traders who operated at lower costs and could bypass quality controls and quarantine restrictions (Republic of Kenya, 1959). In the early 1960s, European settlers marketed their cattle without competition to the KMC (Azarya, 1996, 61), but the whole trade in slaughter stock in African areas was in the hands of local traders (Republic of Kenya, 1959, 7). State intervention was also reflected in the organization of cattle markets. In many cases, these were auction markets at which minimum prices were set by the authorities along the lines of a weight and grade system. The most extreme form of public control was found in the 1950s when the Ugandan government attempted to enforce compulsory sales quotas on pastoral areas (Mittendorf & Wilson, 1961).

In West Africa the rapid increase of the cattle trade from the Sahel to the coast at the beginning of the colonial era indicates an African traders' response to new opportunities. They were able to do so because state control over the indigenous food trade was minimal (Dijkstra, 1995). Furthermore, infrastructure development in general and the construction of railways in particular proved to be a major impetus to the cattle trade and added to its

---

[4] The Kenya Meat Commission succeeded the Meat Marketing Board which was established just after the Second World War.

southward expansion.[5] Thus, although even in the early colonial days borders were established and import duties levied (Norris, 1984), the cattle trade, as trade in general, was stimulated rather than hampered. In contrast, the northward trans-Saharan trade by Tuareg had become increasingly under pressure and dwindled. Until the 1920s the Tuareg resisted French rule and presented a threat to the small and ill-financed French military presence, to which the French responded by systematically undermining Tuareg economic and military power. Trade was easily taxed because northbound routes were few in number and all had to pass certain oases. After the nation-wide revolt against the French in 1916 a large number of Tuareg fled to Nigeria and the trans-Saharan trade pattern was disrupted (Kerven, 1992, 77-78). In addition trans-Saharan trade started to experience increased competition from commodities imported through the coastal ports.

Apart from customs and taxation, colonial policies in West Africa affected the cattle trade in another indirect way, i.e. through veterinary measures. French colonial policy in West Africa was mainly oriented towards increasing meat production by traditional pastoralists (De Haan, 1997, 100). This *politique de la viande* (meat policy) invested a great deal of effort in the training of veterinary personnel and the setting up of a network of veterinary posts where medicines were distributed, livestock vaccinated and the health of slaughtered animals certified. French research was primarily concentrated on disease control, the production of vaccines and the breeding of trypano-tolerant cattle. In addition, new grazing areas were opened up by the digging of wells, and trekking routes to market outlets were provided with watering points, kraals and passages. British colonial policy in West Africa improved trekking routes as well. It focused on veterinary measures among which were attempts to eradicate rinderpest and control tsetse fly. As a consequence, cattle numbers increased.

Both colonial powers imposed taxes on cattle, which resulted in increased sales over the colonial era. The *jangali* cattle tax which the British took over from the Hausa in Nigeria is the best known. Since the colonial powers quickly recognized the economic importance of cross-border cattle trade, attempts were made to cream off some of its wealth. Whereas French taxation of the Saharan trade added to its downfall and diverted trade flows to the south, the British caravan toll on the southward trade did not result in a similar diversion (Kerven, 1992, 78-80). The French policy in Niger to keep livestock trade within French territory and to increase tax revenues was implemented through the introduction of a customs barrier as well as market taxes. Both immediately resulted in cross-border trade, or rather cattle smuggling to Nigeria, where cattle could be marketed tax-free. The customs barrier proved too expensive and was soon abandoned (ibid.). The French policy did not prevent an increase in livestock marketed towards coastal areas.

The only direct and meaningful trade involvement of a colonial power in West Africa was the British attempt to control the export of hides and skins. Adebayo (1992)

---

[5] Initially, the Nigerian railways provided a new opportunity for groundnut exports. Afterwards, the railways became increasingly used for the transport of livestock. On the eve of independence, some 160,000 cattle were transported annually from the northern territories towards Ibadan and Lagos (Mittendorf & Wilson, 1961).

demonstrated the importance of hides and skins as export products for British colonial enterprises. African hides and skins supplied the European and later also the American leather industries. At the turn of the century, the Royal Niger Company (RNC) was given exclusive rights to these exports. In keeping with developments in other export sectors, several local traders engaged as agents for the RNC at the expense of their previously independent businesses. The export of hides and skins constituted the only area in the cattle trade sector which the colonial powers sought to regulate and control. It was not until the late colonial period that British policy in Nigeria tried to persuade Fulani livestock owners to market more cattle in order to provide urban consumers in the south with a regular meat supply to improve the nutritional quality of their diet (Kerven, 1992). Contrary to this, French policy towards trade regulation became more relaxed around 1950.

Analysis
The previous sections clearly demonstrate that cross-border cattle trade in Sub-Saharan Africa experienced a tremendous impetus in the colonial era because of the growing demand for meat caused by increased incomes in those regions which became integrated into the colonial export economy from the turn of the century onwards. It is clear that some pre-colonial patterns of livestock trade were extended, just as others contracted or were diverted. In West Africa, pre-colonial geographical patterns increased generally in volume but hardly changed in direction. Colonial trade policies contributed little to this expansion. Measures such as infrastructure development and the *pax colonial* certainly enabled the cattle trade to expand, but more as a side effect because trade policies were primarily oriented towards exports for the world market. If measures were oriented directly to the cattle trade they were restrictive and intended to keep produce within the colony thus diverting it from an economically more lucrative direction, such as in the case of the French policy in Niger. However, these measures proved to be only temporary and, given large-scale smuggling, hardly effective.

In East Africa, on the contrary, the restriction of African pastoralists to native reserves and the imposition of quarantine regulations had much more influence. However, most flows continued to exist illegally to some extent through the actions of private traders, such as the cross-border trade from Kenya to Tanzania. Due to the illegal character and the risks involved, marketing costs were probably higher than in a free-trade situation. Later on, the direction of this cross-border trade reversed because of growing demand in the urban areas of Kenya. But again, trade was in the hands of private, African traders. Nevertheless, government interventions in physical infrastructure for cattle marketing, such as sales yards, dips and trekking routes, as well as in the organization of auctions seem to have been more important in East than in West Africa.

In Southern Africa, finally, cross-border trade was boosted mainly as a consequence of rising demand in the newly emerging urban mining areas. Here, government intervention was primarily limited to the physical infrastructure of cattle marketing.

11.4 The post-colonial era

Geographical patterns

In post-colonial West Africa, direct state involvement in the cattle trade was as limited as it had been in the colonial era. Trade itself remained primarily north-south orientated, since the major consumer areas were still located in the coastal zones. However, the growth of Sahelian cities such as Bamako, Ouagadougou and Niamey led to increased demand for meat. Furthermore, as modern means of transportation and communication became available movements by truck have increasingly replaced movements by train and on the hoof. Today, a cattle trader in Pouytenga, the largest cattle market in Burkina Faso, is informed by telephone about market opportunities in Abidjan, the capital of Côte d'Ivoire, and can dispatch a truckload of cattle the very same day which will arrive within 36 hours.

The southward long distance trade experienced some important shifts over the years (Map 11.1). In the 1960s Ghana was the most important market for cross-border cattle trade and the supply mainly originated from Mali, Burkina Faso and Nigeria. In the 1970s Ghana was replaced by Côte d'Ivoire as the main outlet and in the 1980s Côte d'Ivoire was superseded by Nigeria. At the end of the 1990s the original patterns more or less returned, with Mali and Burkina Faso mainly supplying Ghana and Côte d'Ivoire, and Nigeria being supplied by all neighbouring countries.

These shifts were to a large extent determined by three major factors. First, crucial events in the structuring of trade patterns were the extensive droughts that occurred in the early 1970s and 1980s. These droughts eventually caused a major geo-spatial shift of pastoral production systems, i.e. a migratory drift southwards of substantial numbers of herds. A lot of cattle ended up in one of the coastal countries which consequently saw an increase in their rate of self-sufficiency as well as in the magnitude of their internal trade. Second, substantial restructuring of trade flows occurred in reaction to diverging economic development and growth rates in the region's leading economies, Ghana, Côte d'Ivoire and Nigeria. Third, by 1975, after the upheaval caused by the first period of drought, coastal countries began to turn to non-African suppliers of frozen meat on the world market, a policy aimed at providing a regular and stable supply to urban consumers. These beef imports, at first from Argentina and Uruguay, came from the European Union from the middle of the 1980s onwards in the form of substantial imports of subsidized beef. However, it has been demonstrated that these imports were only one reason for the decline in the cross-border cattle trade. The economic recession as well as inefficiencies in regional marketing channels were also contributing factors (Quarles van Ufford & Klaasse Bos, 1996).

Two examples may illustrate the combined effect of these three factors on cross-border cattle trade creation and diversion. At independence, the Ghanaian economy was among the most thriving in the sub-region. As a consequence, the country attracted substantial flows of cattle from various origins. Cattle even reached Accra from north-eastern Nigeria. In 1960, some 20,000 head of cattle were transported from Maiduguri/Kano to Lagos by train and then by truck to Accra (Mittendorf & Wilson, 1961). At the same time, about 74,000 head of cattle were imported from Mali and Burkina Faso (ibid.). These geographical patterns

Map 11.1 Main geographical patterns of cross-border cattle trade in West Africa since 1960

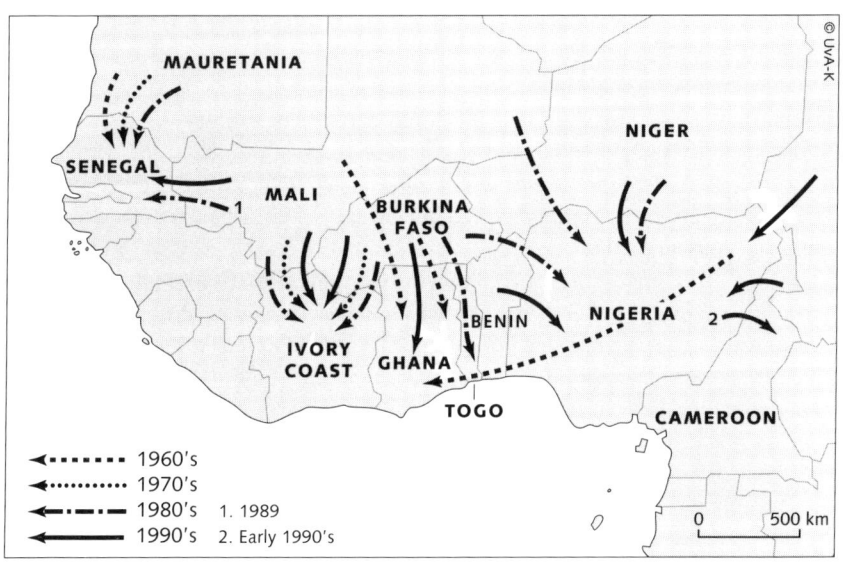

Map 11.2 Main geographical patterns of cross-border cattle trade in East Africa since 1960

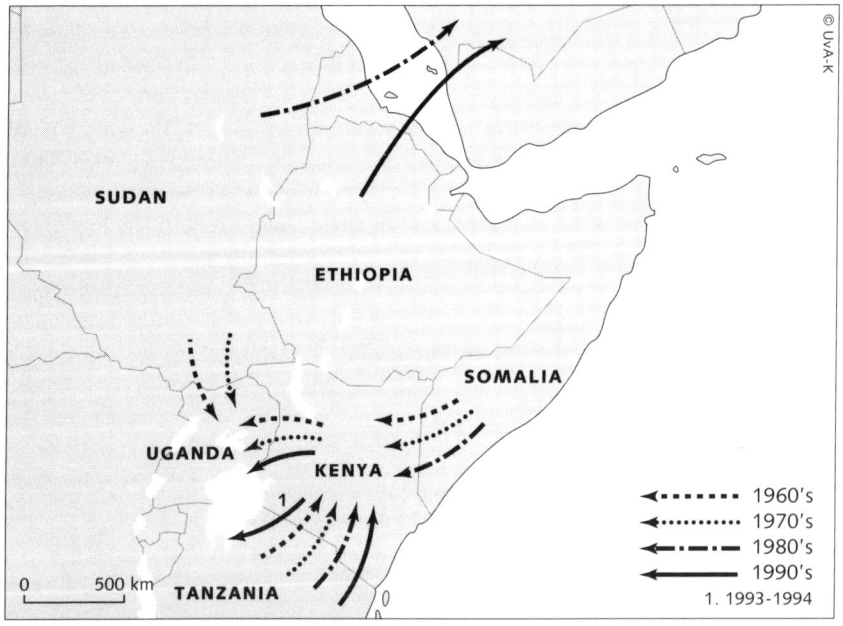

changed, however, when in the early 1970s the Ghanaian economy collapsed and the Nigerian economy experienced significant growth due to increasing oil revenues. Cattle from as far away as Mauritania were brought to the booming Lagos and Ibadan consumer centres.[6] Côte d'Ivoire's economy experienced a similar growth. Consequently, cattle exports from Burkina Faso to Côte d'Ivoire went up from 49 per cent of total Burkinabé exports in the 1960s to 72 per cent in the 1970s. During the same period, Ghana's share in these total exports had declined to 19 per cent (Josserand, 1990). In addition to these economic trends, currency and exchange rate disparities were equally followed by a restructuring of trade flows. For instance, changes in the value of the Nigerian naira on the black market compared with the relatively stable CFA franc of the francophone West African countries have frequently determined changes in the volume of livestock trade with Nigeria. Whereas the latter had always been a major consumer market for cattle from its neighbouring countries, the deteriorating exchange rate of the naira resulted in a temporary inversion of cross-border trade at the beginning of the 1990s. Nigerian cattle were observed at consumer markets in Cameroon.

In 1994 the CFA franc underwent a sudden devaluation of 50 per cent and, as a consequence, unfavourable terms of trade with Ghana, where the cedi had been progressively devalued because of the Structural Adjustment Programme of the 1980s, were implicitly rectified. Analyzing the impact on cross-border cattle trade one year after the devaluation, Quarles van Ufford & Klaasse Bos (1996, 14) pointed at increased numbers of livestock exported from Sahelian countries to both Ghana (up 380 per cent to a total of around 50,000 head annually) and Côte d'Ivoire (up 15 per cent to a total of 105,000 head a year). This rise was partly due to declining imports of frozen beef. In Côte d'Ivoire, these imports halted completely because of a doubling of prices after the devaluation and a reduction of European Union export subsidies on its frozen meat. This reduction caused a drop of frozen meat imports into Ghana too. As a consequence of the increased exports, slaughterhouses in the Sahel experienced a relative scarcity in supply for several months after the devaluation. In Benin, trade flows were modified comparably and the first few months following the devaluation witnessed a steep increase in exports to Nigeria. When the value of the naira further decreased, however, trade declined to its usual level.

Only on rare occasions have trade flows been diverted or contracted by political tensions. For instance, as a result of the political conflict between Senegal and Mauritania in 1989, the geographical patterns as well as the actors involved changed significantly (McCorkle, 1995, 56). Senegalese imports from Mauritania were partly replaced by imports from Mali. Today, the old cross-border cattle trade has largely been restored and Mauritanian traders have returned to the scene. Similarly, after many Fulani were expelled from Ghana

---

[6] A similar sequence of increased oil revenues and growth in livestock imports occurred in the early 1980s when the Shagari regime maintained favourable currency exchange rates. However, when Shagari was succeeded by Mohamed Buhari in 1984, the latter immediately introduced severe monetary measures such as a drastic devaluation of the naira and restrictions on the circulation of the CFA franc. These measures slowed down livestock imports very rapidly.

following the so-called *Operation Cow Leg* in 1988, internal geographical patterns were restructured since the availability of animals decreased in some regions.

As in post-colonial West Africa, geographical patterns in most East and Southern African countries did not change much in the first years after independence. Trade flows, being basically dependent on slowly changing supply and demand, continued to be directed from the drylands to the main consumer areas in the various countries. In Southern Africa, Namibia continued to rely on South Africa for its exports which declined in the early 1960s due to drought, but then picked up from 170,000 head of cattle to 250,000 head in the late 1960s to 500,000 head in the early 1970s. In the late 1970s, exports went down again and than fluctuated between 130,000 and 200,000 head of cattle throughout the 1980s and 1990s (FAO Statistics, 1990-1997). About half of the cattle are exported to South Africa, with most of the rest being exported as meat to the European Union on favourable 'Lomé' conditions. The bulk of these animals come from commercial ranches in the southern part of Namibia which were traditionally supported financially and fiscally by successive Namibian colonial governments. They still enjoy this support and their highly controlled produce is accepted by the European Union and the three main meat-processing corporations in South Africa (Christian Aid, 1997).

Exports from Namibia and Botswana to South Africa have decreased because of the political upheavals and the subsequent general disruption of trade and industry in South Africa. Moreover, cheap meat imports from the European Union increased to 55,000 tons in 1997 (Christian Aid, 1997). As a consequence cross-border trade of cattle and meat from Botswana to South Africa dropped from 50,000 head of cattle and 30,000 tons of processed meat to a few thousand head of cattle and about 20,000 tons of processed meat (FAO Statistics, 1990-1997).

The situation in East Africa is more complex, for the larger part due to the various wars and economic upheavals in the region. Cross-border cattle trade has been seriously affected because of this. Nevertheless the overall picture has remained stable, with Kenya as the main consumer market and Somalia and Tanzania as its main foreign suppliers (Map 11.2). An interesting example is Somalia, where in recent years wars have seriously affected the population and the economy. Cross-border cattle trade, mostly to Kenya, was high during the drought periods of the early 1970s (around 70,000 head) and 1980s (150,000 head), but since then it went down to about 20,000 head in 1990. Finally, due to the civil war and a complete avoidance by Kenyan traders of Somalia and the neighbouring region of Kenya, cross-border trade stopped completely in 1992 (Zaal, 1997).

Official figures on cross-border cattle trade from Sudan and Kenya to Uganda have shown a steady decline over the years, with peaks during drought years. In the late 1980s this trade became negligible, although it has recently re-emerged in an illegal form. In addition, following the ups and downs of civil war and conciliation, exports from Sudan to Saudi Arabia in the 1980s have presently been replaced by exports from Ethiopia. However, this mainly concerns sheep and goats.

Officially, cattle trade from Tanzania to Kenya has been small since the early 1990s. However, fieldwork by Zaal (1997) proves that thousands of head of cattle cross the border unofficially, attracted by the high prices in nearby Nairobi.

In all, although underestimated in official statistics, cross-border cattle trade in East Africa is relatively insignificant when compared to internal flows. Both in Kenya and in Tanzania roughly two million head of cattle have been traded annually in the 1990s. The same goes for Namibia and Botswana where internal trade and consumption exceed exports (FAO Statistics, 1990-1997).

Trade and other policies
The early post-colonial policies of the West African francophone countries continued to pay attention to veterinary issues but the focus gradually changed towards the development of ranching schemes and the allocation of grazing rights. From the 1980s onwards, the approach to livestock development has shifted first to large cattle projects and then to pastoral groups and natural resource management (De Haan, 1997). The cattle marketing policies of the newly independent states, on which we will elaborate below, remained remarkably stable for an extended period of time.

Government intervention in cattle marketing differed substantially from its intervention in other agricultural sectors. In addition to the colonial marketing boards for commodities such as coffee, cocoa and cotton, many countries established cereal marketing boards just after independence in order to guarantee national food security, a task governments did not want to entrust to the private sector. Several of these boards received considerable financial support from western donors (Lele & Christiansen, 1989). However, the new boards refrained from trading perishables because of the risky nature of the operations that required a high degree of flexibility, and the limited availability of cold storage and processing facilities (Dijkstra, 1995, 29). Nevertheless, some Sahelian governments, however small and unsuccessful their efforts, took some initiatives in this domain. Their policies were initially geared to the construction of slaughterhouses, cold-store facilities and the encouragement of meat marketing from Sahelian areas to the coastal countries.[7] To accomplish these objectives, organizations such as ONERA (Burkina Faso), SODEPRA (Côte d'Ivoire), SONARAN (Niger) and SODERA (Benin) were established in the 1970s.[8] They made some efforts to control particular stages of the marketing channel. Besides the construction and management of slaughterhouses they engaged for instance in milk production, and attempted to set consumer prices and regulate cattle markets according to a weight and grade system. However, they never tried to monopolize all the stages of the marketing process. Private traders have been operating parallel to these marketing boards and sometimes even benefited when the board engaged them to purchase cattle for state ranches.

The Meat Marketing Board in Ghana provides an illustration. The Ghanaian government set up this board just after independence in 1960. It invested heavily in slaughterhouse facilities and a canning plant on the border with Burkina Faso where cattle were bought directly from Burkinabé traders. Domestic marketing was carried out by the private sector (Sullivan, 1984). The MMB also possessed a monopoly on extra-African meat

---
[7] Chad and Niger exported considerable quantities of meat to the French colonies in Central and West Africa respectively, but these operations, which started in the 1950s, came to an end in the early 1970s.
[8] Note that some specific organizations were founded in order to regulate the hides-and-skins export sector.

imports and determined official consumer prices which were frequently circumvented by the private sector. However, the scale of its activities steadily declined, like many of its sub-regional counterparts, due to poor management practices. Today, the MMB has mainly a distribution function, purchasing meat from private butchers and selling it subsequently through a few MMB cold stores.

Finally, the case of Niger's marketing board SONARAN is worth mentioning. In the early 1980s, SONARAN (*Société Nationale des Ressources Animales*) engaged in official livestock and meat trade with one of the few private industrial meat canning companies in West Africa, the Nigerian Food Company (NFC). On the basis of yearly contracts, a significant financial turnover was achieved. However, it was the government of Niger itself which was responsible for SONARAN's failure to fulfil its contract obligations, since it established regional export quotas in 1986 in order to re-establish cattle herds (Soulé, 1993). At the end of the 1980s, SONARAN's relations with the NFC suffered increasingly from the deteriorating exchange rate of the naira and operations were suspended accordingly.

Post-colonial policies in Southern and East Africa were very much an extension of colonial policies as marketing boards continued to play a role. However, in the course of the 1970s and 1980s, quite a number of these boards ran into financial problems. A notable exception was the Botswana Meat Commission, described by Abbott (1987, 165) as a highly professional undertaking and an outstanding model of cattle marketing in a difficult environment. Operating in a competitive international market the BMC, supported by government investments for example in cordon fences, provided an attractive outlet for Botswana's larger cattle owners to South Africa and the European Union.

In other countries, livestock and meat marketing boards were either temporarily dissolved and repeatedly reinstated, or finally privatized with the introduction of economic structural adjustment. In Kenya, for example, the KMC continued to buy cattle from ranches in limited numbers, while ALMO was responsible for purchasing cattle from pastoral areas. With the Kenya Livestock Development Project in 1968, a new department took over from ALMO, the Livestock Marketing Department (LMD). Providing holding grounds, stock routes, price information and various other services, it became a service-oriented organization, and no longer bought cattle from producers, a task which proved too costly. Like the KMC, high running costs have pushed ALMO out of the market. The KMC, as other livestock related services,[9] extended its clientele to include small-scale African producers (Heyer, Maitha & Senga, 1976). However, as private slaughterhouses slowly took over the market in the late 1970s, the two enormous slaughterhouses owned by the KMC deteriorated and were finally closed in 1992 (Zaal, 1998).

In Tanzania, a similar situation occurred. The *Ujamaa* philosophy required the implementation of government policies to control the cattle trade. However, the livestock sector was not adequately controlled by the livestock and meat marketing boards due to their unfavourable fixed prices. In addition, cattle producers made only a token contribution of

---

[9] Such as the national agricultural research station at Kiboko, the Veterinary Department, the Agricultural Finance Corporation (AFC) and the Livestock Marketing Department of the Ministry of Agriculture and Livestock Development (LMD).

animals to cooperative farms and to state-controlled dairy units. As a consequence, the cattle sector experienced a fairly high degree of competition between official and parallel markets, the Tanzania Livestock Marketing Company (TLMC) holding a market share of 20-40 per cent in the 1970s and even less in the 1980s (De Wilde, 1984).

General economic policies explain the sudden change in cross-border cattle trade between Tanzania and Kenya in 1993. While economic restructuring in Tanzania slowly strengthened the Tanzania shilling in the early 1990s, high inflation, a loss of donor support due to the slow implementation of the structural adjustment programme, and political unrest slowly weakened the Kenyan shilling. In late 1993, the flow of cattle suddenly changed direction. Instead of going northwards from Tanzania to Nairobi, cattle were traded from Kenya to Tanzania (Zaal, 1997). After March/April, when the economic situation in Kenya returned to normal, the Kenyan shilling appreciated and the cross-border cattle trade turned northwards again.

Analysis
Although the patterns of the cattle trade remained roughly the same, the structure of the marketing channels underwent modifications once the colonial era came to an end. Government interventions increased as development strategies of that period expected the state to plan and to take the lead in economic development. Governments accordingly tried to strengthen their grip on internal and cross-border cattle trade by founding state-controlled marketing boards. Particularly in West Africa, these organizations hardly deserve being labeled as such. They mainly concentrated on the processing part of the *filière* (marketing channel) and they soon became marginal because of their poor performance. In East Africa, livestock marketing boards date back to the late colonial period when they controlled a larger percentage of the cattle marketed. They were mainly oriented towards the marketing of cattle from large (settler) producers. After independence they had to extend their services to new regions with small African producers, which caused a sharp and disproportionate increase in running costs. This eventually contributed to their withdrawal from marketing or total demise in the early 1990s.

Though livestock trade policies had only a minor influence on trade patterns, economic policies in general were important. A number of changes that occurred throughout Sub-Saharan Africa, both in geographical patterns of trade and in numbers of animals involved, appear to be linked with local fluctuations in demand. These fluctuations either discouraged the cross-border cattle trade, as in Ghana in the 1970s and in Nigeria and South Africa in the 1980s, or stimulated it, as in Côte d'Ivoire in the 1970s, and could be attributed to national economic policies on the one hand and to more general economic circumstances related to the country's position on the world market on the other. Policies related to currency exchange rates have especially influenced geographical patterns and volumes of cross-border cattle trade as was illustrated by the temporary reversal of trade flows between Tanzania and Kenya in 1993/94, and the changes in trade following the CFA franc devaluation in early 1994. The former only corresponds to a temporary modification of a familiar geographical pattern. The latter seems to have partially restored a colonial trade flow to Ghana, clearly linked with this country's successful economic recovery. The question as to whether trade was created or diverted in this particular case is more difficult to answer. Declining imports of frozen meat from the European Union into Côte d'Ivoire as a result of higher import prices increased demand for Sahelian meat and resulted in the creation of cross-border trade. However, the temporary shortage from which slaughterhouses in the Sahel suffered at the same time leads to the hypothesis that trade was at least partially diverted from local to more remote markets across the border. In addition to the CFA franc devaluation, the reduction of subsidies by the European Union, under the pressure of European public opinion, on its exports of frozen meat to West Africa contributed to declining imports.

Notwithstanding the above, general economic policies were not the only cause of post-colonial changes in cross-border cattle trade. In the whole of Sub-Saharan Africa, political tensions, wars and civil wars on the one hand and recurrent droughts on the other have been influential factors. Political tension and war seem to be the only events that can really stop traders from transporting and selling cattle in places where prices are profitable. In East and Southern Africa, droughts have caused major reductions in the supply of cattle and the consumption of meat. However, after every major drought, a steady growth to new highs followed. In West Africa, if not a permanent than at least a long-lasting migratory drift of pastoralists caused a shift in the location of cattle production areas. In the post-colonial era many pastoralists have moved from the Sahel to the northern regions of the West African coastal countries. Consequently, trade routes have been shortened and cross-border cattle trade has become less significant.

11.5 Conclusions

In this chapter we have shown that the cattle trade in Sub-Saharan Africa, as it existed in pre-colonial times, received an important impetus as the colonial economy developed. Population growth, specialization and increasing incomes in export production areas caused a growing demand for meat in many parts of the continent. Several of the ancient trade routes were gradually diverted towards these emerging areas and new cross-border cattle trade was created. At the same time, the volume of the cattle trade expanded substantially. Thus, the foundations for most contemporary patterns of cross-border cattle trade were laid in the colonial era. Drastic and long-term changes have rarely occurred since then. It appears that only events such as civil wars, like the one in Somalia, and droughts, as those in West Africa in the 1970s and 1980s, have had a long-term impact on cattle trade patterns. Questions remain about how structural these changes are. For instance, the case of West Africa demonstrates how, as a consequence of two extensive drought periods, the pastoral production system was dislocated and its centre of gravity moved southwards. This had a long-term impact on the cattle trade which from then on increasingly originated from new areas where pastoral producers had settled. Because some of these new areas are located within the boundaries of the coastal countries, traditionally the most important consumer markets, this change had a contracting effect on cross-border cattle trade, which was, however, neutralized by a general increase in demand. Other droughts had short-term consequences only, when the effect of herds being decimated and rebuilt resulted in sharp but temporary fluctuations in cross-border cattle trade.

We may also conclude that, in contrast to these long-term shifts, the geographical patterns of cross-border cattle trade were much less or only temporarily affected by government policies. Throughout the colonial and post-colonial eras, cross-border cattle trade remained an African, private traders' affair. Still, a number of cases were identified in which general economic policies, causing changes in the value of the national currency, and temporary changes in demand, contributed to the diversion and to a lesser extent to the creation and contraction of cattle trade flows, as illustrated by the shift of demand in West Africa, from Ghana to Côte d'Ivoire and then to Nigeria. Admittedly, these cases make it clear that general economic circumstances such as a country's position on the world market matter as well. Effects of currency value changes were clearly shown in the examples of the CFA franc devaluation in 1994 and the temporarily reversed cross-border trade between Kenya and Tanzania in 1993/94.

It was also demonstrated that private cattle traders have responded extremely well to short-term opportunities or *rentes frontalières* (border rents) as Grégoire & Labazée (1993, 10) have called them. With respect to government interventions which were directly targeted at cross-border cattle trade, such as import or export taxes and trade restrictions, the responsiveness of cattle livestock traders has been remarkable too. Especially with regard to West Africa we have noticed that traders organize themselves in multiple cross-border trade networks resulting in a continuation of most trade flows, albeit unregistered and illegal. Traders in general do not seem to be bound by a legal exchange sphere, demarcated by import prohibitions, regulations and taxes. On the contrary, their actual exchange sphere extends largely beyond it, taking into account every opportunity, in terms of optimal outlet, that is provided. Furthermore, the continuing possibility to transport cattle on the hoof across the borders, which is still often made use of in the case of smuggling, gives traders a head start on government controls.

With respect to direct state intervention in cattle trade, however, considerable differences were observed between West Africa and East and Southern Africa. In West Africa, governments only marginally intervened in the cattle trade and most efforts were geared towards the meat processing part of the marketing channel. In East and Southern Africa though, the influence of governments was not restricted to meat processing alone, since policies attempted to organize cattle markets, to facilitate the marketing of cattle from large-scale ranches and to control the sale of cattle by indigenous livestock producers in order to reduce grazing pressure. These interventions did not so much change the geographical patterns of trade but rather affected its structure. As a result of embargoes and quarantine regulations, at least part of the growing demand for meat was supplied by settlers thus partially hampering trade from pastoral areas. The analysis showed that both in East and in Southern Africa marketing boards played a much more important role than in West Africa.

In this chapter we have extended the analysis of trade-flow changes as a consequence of government policies, known primarily from the food trade and the trade in export products, to the cross-border trade in cattle. We have tried to relate geographical patterns of this type of trade to trade policies and other government policies. To analyze these patterns we made use of the concepts of trade creation, trade diversion and trade contraction. We conclude that war and drought, and not government policy, most affect cross-border trade. War and civil wars obstruct the movement of trade, even if demand and supply remain unchanged, and result in contraction. Droughts reduce the supply, after a temporary increase by distress selling, and thus cause the cattle trade to contract. Rising economic prosperity, generally as a result of a combination of world market-related developments and government policies, leads to cross-border trade creation and diversion. Declining economic prosperity has the opposite effect.

Finally, the impact of government policies is apparent when the value of currencies is concerned. Relative changes in currency value gradually create external demand and cross-border cattle trade as a consequence. A devaluation will abruptly cause a contraction or diversion of this trade.

11.6 Epilogue

In the continuous debate on the sustainable management of African rangelands, on the possible risk of exceeding carrying capacities, and on the supposed need for destocking, the creation of marketing outlets is often indicated as a solution to overstocking by those researchers who think African pastoralists overexploit their rangelands. The advocates of this solution thus assume that a large surplus of cattle, ready to be tapped, exists in the production areas. This supply would be able to satisfy effective demand if this demand rose or (marketing) costs diminished. However, in our analysis of the last two decades, we have not encountered spectacular supply increases which were more than temporary. The cattle trading system with its African private traders is too effective in connecting supply and demand for an untapped surplus to develop. Consequently, we cannot support the hypothesis that large surpluses of livestock are kept by pastoralists because of lack of opportunities to sell.

References

AALBERSBERG, M. (1996) *The Way Of Maize. The role of public food trade policy in the functioning of interstatal maize trade between Ghana and Burkina Faso.* M.A. thesis. Amsterdam: Department of Human Geography, University of Amsterdam.
ABBOTT, J.C. (1987) *Agricultural Marketing Enterprises For The Developing World.* Cambridge: Cambridge University Press.
ADEBAYO, A.G. (1992) 'The production of hides and skins in colonial northern Nigeria, 1900-1945'. In *The Journal of African History,* Vol. 33, pp. 273-300.
D'ALMEIDA TOPOR, H. (1995) *Histoire Economique du Dahomey (Bénin), 1890-1920.* Vol. 2, Paris: l'Harmattan.
ANDERSON, D. (1988) 'Cultivating pastoralists. Ecology and economy among the IlChamus of Baringo, 1840-1980'. In D. Johnson & D. Anderson (eds) *The ecology of survival.* London: Croole Green Academic Publishers, pp. 141-261.

AZARYA, V. (1996) *Nomads and the state in Africa: The political roots of marginality*. Leiden: Avebury/African Studies Centre, Research Series no. 9.
BREUKERS, G. (1991) 'The common tragedy of Hardin's tragedy of the commons: livestock development policies in the pastoral areas of Sub-Saharan Africa'. The Hague: Institute of Social Studies, Management Regimes For Common Pool Natural Resources Discussion Paper no. 8.
CHRISTIAN AID (1997) 'Out of Joint. Report on research into European Union beef dumping in South Africa'. London: Christian Aid.
DE HAAN, L. (1993) *La Région des Savanes au Togo. L'Etat, les paysans et l'intégration régionale (1885-1985)*. Paris: Karthala.
DE HAAN, L., A. KLAASSE BOS & C. LUTZ (1995) 'Regional Food Trade and Policy in West Africa in Relation to Structural Adjustment'. In D. Simon, W. van Spengen, C. Dixon & A. Närman (eds) *Structurally Adjusted Africa. Poverty, Debt and Basic Needs*. London: Pluto Press, pp. 57-79.
DE HAAN, L. (1997) 'Stockbreeding in Western Africa'. In T. van Naerssen, M. Rutten & A. Zoomers (eds) *The Diversity of Development. Essays in Honour of Jan Kleinpenning*. Assen: Van Gorcum, pp. 95-105.
DE WILDE (1984) *Agriculture, marketing and pricing in sub-Sahara Africa*. Los Angeles: ASC/ASA, University of California.
DIJKSTRA, T. (1995) *Food trade and urbanization in Sub-Saharan Africa. From the early stone age to the structural adjustment era*. Leiden: African Studies Centre, Working Paper no. 22.
DOUMA, P., M. DIOP & L. DE HAAN (1994) *Les Association Pastorales et la Gestion des Ressources Naturelles, Raport Final*. Amsterdam: Université d'Amsterdam, Commission des Communautés Européennes.
EGG, J., J. IGUÉ & J. COSTE (1988) *Echanges régionaux, Commerce frontalier et Sécurité alimentaire en Afrique de l'Ouest. Méthodologie et premiers résultats*. Paris: INRA/UNB/IRAM.
EGG, J. & J. IGUÉ (1990) *Espaces régionaux d'échanges et politiques agricoles en Afrique de l'Ouest*. Montpellier: CIRAD/Club du Sahel/OCDE.
FAGE, J. (1995) *A History Of Africa*. Third Edition, London: Routledge.
FAO (1990-1997) FAOSTAT database collections on-line. Rome: FAO.
GRÉGOIRE, E. (1986) *Les Alhazai de Maradi (Niger): histoire d'un groupe de riches marchands sahéliens*. Paris: Editions de l'ORSTOM.
GRÉGOIRE, E. & P. LABAZÉE (1993) *Grands commerçants d'Afrique de l'ouest; logiques et pratiques d'un groupe d'hommes d'affaires contemporains*. Paris: Karthala.
HEYER, J., J.K. MAITHA, & W.M. SENGA (1976) *Agricultural Development in Kenya, an economic assessment*. Nairobi: Oxford University Press.
HOLTZMAN, J. & N.P. KULIBABA (1992) *Livestock marketing and trade in the central corridor of West Africa*. Washington: USAID.
HOPKINS, a. (1973) *Economic History of West Africa*. London: Longman.
IGUÉ, J.O. & B.G. SOULÉ (1992) *L'état entrepôt au Bénin*. Paris: Karthala.
JOSSERAND, H.P. (1990) *Systèmes ouest-africains de production et d'échanges en produits d'élevage: aide-mémoire synthétique et premiers éléments d'analyse régionale*. Paris: CILLS/Club du Sahel.
KERVEN, C. (1992) *Customary Commerce. A historical reassessment of pastoral livestock marketing in Africa*. London: Overseas Development Institute, Agricultural Occasional Paper no. 15.
LELE, U. & R.E. CHRISTIANSEN (1989) 'Markets, Marketing Boards, and Cooperatives in Africa; Issues in Adjustment policy'. Washington: The World Bank, MADIA discussion paper no. 11.
LOVEJOY, p. (1980) *Caravans of kola, the Hausa kola trade 1700-1900*. Zaria: Ahmadu Bello University Press/University Press Ltd.
MCCORKLE, C. (1995) *Cross-border trade and ethnic groups in West Africa*. Cambridge Massachusetts: USAID, Abt. Associates.
MEILLASSOUX, C. (1971) *L'évolution du commerce africain depuis le XIXeme siècle en Afrique de l'ouest*. London: Oxford University Press.
MITTENDORF, H.J. & S.G. WILSON (1961) *Livestock and Meat Marketing in Africa*. Rome: FAO.
NORRIS, E. (1984) 'The Hausa Kola Trade Through Togo, 1889-1912: some quantifications'. In *Paideuma*, Vol. 30, pp. 162-184.
QUARLES VAN UFFORD, P. & A. KLAASSE BOS (1996) 'Distorted beef markets and regional livestock trade in West Africa'. In *Tijdschrift voor Sociaalwetenschappelijk onderzoek van de Landbouw*, Vol. 11, no.1, pp. 5-20.
QUARLES VAN UFFORD, P. (1999) *Trade and Traders. The making of the cattle market in Benin*. Amsterdam: Thela Thesis.

REPUBLIC OF KENYA (1959) *The marketing of African Livestock. Report of an enquiry made by Mr. P.H. Jones into the whole problem of the marketing of African Livestock.* Nairobi: Ministry of Agriculture, Animal Husbandry and Water Resources.
REPUBLIC OF KENYA (1980) *National Livestock Development Policy.* Nairobi: Ministry of Livestock Development.
REPUBLIC OF KENYA (1995) *Economic Survey 1995.* Nairobi: Central Bureau of Statistics.
SKINNER, E. (1964) *The Mossi people of Upper Volta. The political development of a Sudanese people.* Stanford, California: Stanford University Press.
SOULÉ, B.G. (1993) 'Les échanges agricoles entre le Niger et le Nigéria et leurs déterminants'. In Egg J. (ed.) *L'économie agricole et alimentaire du Niger: vers une intégration au marché du Nigéria?* Paris: INRA/UNB/IRAM, pp. 31-59.
SULLIVAN, G.M. (1984) 'Impact of government policies on the performance of the livestock-meat subsector'. In Simpson & Evangelou (eds.) *Livestock development in Sub-Saharan Africa: constraints, prospects, policy.* Boulder Colorado: Westview Press, pp. 143-159.
VAN DER LAAN, L. (1981) 'Modern Inland Transport and the European Trading Firms in Colonial West Africa'. In *Cahiers d'Etudes Africaines,* Vol. 84, no. 21-4, pp. 547-575.
VINER, J. (1950) *The Customs Union Issue.* New York: Carnegie Endowment for International Peace.
ZAAL, F. (1997) *Livestock traders in Kajiado District, Kenya.* University of Amsterdam, MDP report no. 9.
ZAAL, F. (1998) *Pastoralism in a Global Age. Livestock marketing and pastoral commercial activities in Kenya and Burkina Faso.* Amsterdam: Thela Thesis.

About the Authors

Arhin Brempong, Nana K. (Ghana)
Dr. Nana Arhin Brempong is a sociologist and anthropologist who obtained his BSc and PhD in London and his BLitt in Oxford. He has done research on economic, political and social transformation in African institutions. He was formerly Professor and Director of the Institute of African Studies, University of Ghana, Legon, and Chairman of the Board of Directors of the Ghana Cocoa Board. At the symposium in November 1997 he discussed the papers by Van der Laan and Pelupessy.

Bassolet, Boubié (Burkina Faso)
Boubié Bassolet is a lecturer at the Faculté des Sciences Economiques et de Gestion (FaSEG) and researcher at the Centre d'Etudes, de Documentation, de Recherche Economique et Social (CEDRES) at the University of Ouagadougou in Burkina Faso. His research deals with the institutional aspects of underdevelopment, with particular emphasis on information and transaction costs. He is doing his PhD research on the organization and the performance of cereal markets under liberalization in Burkina Faso. He is a participant in the research network 'Commerce, Infrastructure and Food Security' at the foundation of Sustainable Food Security in Central West Africa (SADAOC).

Bryceson, Deborah Fahy (UK)
Dr. Deborah Bryceson is a research fellow at the African Studies Centre, Leiden. She received her training in economic geography at the University of Dar es Salaam and Oxford University. Her work has primarily focused on East Africa and spans a wide range of topics within the field of rural development, namely: food marketing, agricultural policy, famine prevention and rehabilitation, rural transport and mobility patterns and the impact of public investment on rural welfare. In addition she has worked on women's employment patterns, urbanization in developing countries and urban food supply. She is currently coordinating a collaborative research programme on rural employment involving research teams in Ethiopia, Nigeria, Tanzania and South Africa.

De Haan, Leo (The Netherlands)
Dr. Leo de Haan is Professor of development studies at the Catholic University of Nijmegen. He has worked extensively throughout West Africa. At present he is involved in studies on rural livelihood strategies, resource management by pastoral associations, resource conflicts between peasants and pastoralists, and cross-border trade in grains and cattle in West Africa. In addition, he is directing a research programme on oasis revitalization in the Magreb and a programme on scientific cooperation between Dutch universities and the National University of Benin. The chapter he has contributed to this book details the results of a research programme he supervised.

De Jong, Ali (The Netherlands)
Dr. Ali de Jong is a lecturer at the Institute of Development Studies Utrecht (IDSU) in the Faculty of Geographical Sciences, and specializes in rural development problems in Africa. She is the coordinator of the joint research programme MUCAM (Mutations socio-économiques en milieu rural du Cameroun) run by IDSU and the Department of Geography of the University of Yaounde I, which is studying the production and marketing of cocoa, palm oil and food crops. In addition, she is engaged in research in Mali. Together with Annelet Harts-Broekhuis she carried out her PhD research in the Mopti region of Mali.

Dietvorst, Désirée C.E. (The Netherlands)
Désirée Dietvorst studied animal production and health at Larenstein International Agricultural College and then at the Centre for Tropical Veterinary Medicine in Edinburgh. She worked with the ODI Pastoral Development Network in London before moving to Western Province in Zambia in 1993 where she was engaged in applied research in the bilateral Livestock Development Programme. She is currently living in Harare where she is working as a consultant in the biophysical and socio-economic aspects of livestock keeping.

Dijkstra, Tjalling (The Netherlands)
Dr. Tjalling Dijkstra is a research fellow of the African Studies Centre. From 1988 to 1995 he did research on agricultural marketing in Kenya, the first two years focusing on cotton, and the subsequent six years on horticultural commodities. He wrote his PhD thesis on the structure and development of horticultural marketing channels in Kenya. Since 1998 he has been involved in research on export diversification in Uganda and Kenya, looking at non-traditional agricultural exports. In 1999 the commercial edition of his PhD thesis, *Trading the Fruits of the Land: Horticultural Marketing Channels in Kenya*, was awarded the John Abbott Prize.

Hamming, Inge (The Netherlands)
Inge Hamming graduated in agricultural economics at Wageningen Agricultural University in 1996. Her graduation theses focused on development economics and marketing in developing countries and dealt with maize marketing in Ghana and rice marketing in north-west Sierra Leone. The latter was a statistical analysis of the degree of commercialization and the choice of outlet of 372 rice-growing households. Between 1996 and 1998 she worked for several firms on a part-time basis and she recently moved to Yemen, where she is currently doing research on women's marketing activities and their economic contributions to farm households, a project financed by the Netherlands Embassy in Yemen.

Harts-Broekhuis, Annelet (The Netherlands)
Dr. Annelet Harts-Broekhuis is a geographer with experience in research, training and consultancy work related to development problems in Africa. At present she is a lecturer at IDSU, Faculty of Geographical Sciences, Utrecht University. For her doctorate she carried out research in Mali and together with Ali de Jong she co-authored the book *Subsistence and Survival in the Sahel* about the responses of rural and urban households and enterprises to

deteriorating conditions, and development policy in the Mopti region of Mali. Besides her academic interest and research in West Africa, she is involved in a research project in Zimbabwe. From 1989-1996 she was a member of the Board of the African Studies Centre in Leiden.

Klaasse Bos, Andries (The Netherlands)
Andries Klaasse Bos specializes in development economics. He is a lecturer at the Faculty of Economics and Econometrics of Amsterdam University, the Netherlands. His research interest is in the economics of agricultural development in countries of Sub-Saharan Africa and especially in the underlying causes of food insecurity of rural households. His other interest is agricultural and food policies. After several years in agricultural planning with the government of Surinam, he worked in the planning of rural water development with the Kenyan Ministry of Agriculture. He has undertaken various short-term economic consultancies in West African countries.

Kormawa, Patrick (Sierra Leone)
Dr. Patrick Kormawa is a staff member at the policy research unit of the International Institute of Tropical Agriculture (IITA), Ibadan, Nigeria. He is carrying out studies on food demand structures of IITA-mandate crops as well as their market potential. Nigeria and Uganda have been targeted for these studies. His professional interests have been agricultural policy and price analysis, modelling resource use and agricultural productivity, as well as interregional trade modelling. At the symposium in November 1997 he discussed the papers by Klaasse Bos, Lutz and Bassolet, Van Tilburg and Hamming, and Bryceson, Seppälä and Tapio-Biström.

Lutz, Clemens (The Netherlands)
Dr. Clemens Lutz is a lecturer in marketing at the Faculty of Management and Organization, Groningen University, the Netherlands. His research interest focuses on the performance of food markets in developing countries. Food security, the organization of marketing channels, market integration and market information are key issues in his research. From 1986 until 1990 he was a lecturer at the Faculty of Agricultural Sciences (FSA) in Benin. In 1994 he defended his PhD thesis on the functioning of the maize market in Benin. Nowadays he is involved in research on food marketing in Benin, Burkina Faso, Eritrea, Rwanda and Vietnam.

Meilink, Henk (The Netherlands)
Henk Meilink is a senior economist at the African Studies Centre in Leiden. His main research areas include the socio-economic impact of structural adjustment programmes (SAPs) in Africa and issues of food security at different levels of African societies. Other research topics under study are the far-reaching and challenging implications for Africa of the rapid global changes in trade, aid, investment and debt conditions which appear to be contributing to Africa's further marginalization in the world economy.

Moll, Henk A.J. (The Netherlands)

Dr. Henk Moll studied horticulture in Utrecht and joined the Organization of Netherlands' Volunteers to work in Zambia in the cooperative movement. He then studied development economics at Wageningen Agricultural University. He worked with the Food and Agriculture Organization and the Netherlands Ministry of Development Cooperation in Tanzania, Sri Lanka, and Indonesia until 1982. Since then he has been a lecturer in development economics in the Department of Economics and Management of Wageningen Agricultural University where his main interests in teaching and research are rural institutions, and the economics of crop and livestock production. His PhD research focused on rural financial institutions.

Pelupessy, Wim (The Netherlands)

Dr. Wim Pelupessy is a lecturer in development economics at the Faculty of Economic Sciences of Tilburg University, the Netherlands. He is also a senior research fellow at the Development Research Institute in Tilburg. He is the author of *The Limits of Economic Reform in El Salvador, Perspectives on the Agro-Export Economy in Central America* and *Economic Maladjustment in Central America* (all edited by Macmillan, London). He has also written *El Mercado Mundial del Café: El Caso de El Salvador* (DEI, San José).

Quarles van Ufford, Paul (The Netherlands)

Paul Quarles van Ufford is guest researcher at the Amsterdam Institute for Global Issues and Development Studies (AGIDS) at the University of Amsterdam. His main topic of study is the livestock trade in West Africa. He has done research on livestock exports from Burkina Faso to Ghana and Côte d'Ivoire, as well as on the impact of frozen beef imports on consumption patterns in Accra and Abidjan. He will defend his PhD thesis on the cattle trade and cattle traders in the Republic of Benin in December 1999 at the University of Amsterdam. His PhD research was funded jointly by the European Union (STD3 programme) and the University of Amsterdam.

Rutten, Marcel M.E.M. (The Netherlands)

Dr. Marcel Rutten is a geographer and research fellow at the African Studies Centre, Leiden. He has conducted research in Kenya among Turkana and Maasai pastoralists and is the author of a book on the individualization of land ownership among Maasai pastoralists. In addition to a continuous monitoring of this process he is currently involved in research on sustainable water projects (i.e. shallow wells) combining indigenous and modern technical knowledge, and in a survey comparing drought-planning strategies among Maasai, Bedouin and Turkana pastoralists. At the symposium in November 1997 he discussed the papers by De Haan, Quarles van Ufford and Zaal, and Moll and Dietvorst.

Seppälä, Pekka (Finland)

Dr. Pekka Seppälä is a research fellow at the Institute of Development Studies, Helsinki University. He is an anthropologist with extensive research experience on rural development in Eastern Africa. His main issues of analysis are microenterprises, rural trade, and the interfaces between state and rural citizens. Seppälä has recently edited a volume entitled *Liberalised and Neglected? Food Marketing in Eastern Africa* published by UNU/WIDER.

Tapio-Biström, Marja-Liisa (Finland)
Marja-Liisa Tapio-Biström studied agricultural economics and agronomy. She is a research fellow at the Institute of Development Studies, Helsinki University. Her research interests are food security from the global to local level, food aid and its impact on recipient countries, food policy analysis, sustainable farming systems, nutrition, traditional diets and changes in food habits (especially the spread and acceptance of yellow maize in Sub-Saharan Africa). She specializes in Tanzania, Kenya, Zambia and Ethiopia.

Van Bruggen, Lineke (The Netherlands)
Lineke van Bruggen graduated from Wageningen Agricultural University in 1984. Her main subjects were sociology, extension education and research methodology of the social sciences. She worked for Erasmus University in Rotterdam and Wageningen Agricultural University in the Netherlands in various positions and has also worked as a consultant. She gained experience in Benin, Togo, Kenya and Mali and is currently finishing her PhD concerning the relationship between crop choice and market behaviour of larger peasant farmers in Benin for the Department of Marketing and Marketing Research at Wageningen Agricultural University. Her contribution to this book is based on this study.

Van der Laan, H. Laurens (The Netherlands)
Dr. Laurens van der Laan studied economics at the universities of Rotterdam and Madison, Wisconsin. He taught economics at the University of Sierra Leone from 1959 to 1969 and then joined the African Studies Centre in Leiden where he worked as a senior researcher until his retirement. At first he specialized in marketing boards and in 1983 he was one of the organizers of an international conference on African marketing boards. From 1986 to 1997 he helped teach the course on agricultural marketing in developing countries at the Agricultural University in Wageningen.

Dr. Van Tilburg, Aad (The Netherlands)
Dr. Aad van Tilburg graduated in econometrics from Erasmus University Rotterdam in 1971. He joined Wageningen Agricultural University in 1974 where he now holds the post of senior lecturer. His PhD thesis was entitled 'Consumer choice of cut flowers and pot plants'. His research covers several topics in agricultural marketing, particularly the analysis of the structure and performance of food marketing systems in developing countries, notably in Africa. He has published widely on this subject in journals and has co-authored several books.

Zaal, Fred (The Netherlands)
Dr. Fred Zaal is a staff member at the Amsterdam Institute for Global Issues and Development Studies (AGIDS) at the University of Amsterdam. He has worked on food aid studies, natural resource management issues and NGO development strategies in West

Africa. In November 1998 he defended his PhD thesis on the influence of the food grain and cattle markets on household food security and commercial strategies of pastoralists in Burkina Faso and Kenya. Presently he participates in research projects studying the effects of climatic change in the Sahel and the transition towards sustainable dryland agriculture in Kenya.

Index

Abbott, John C., 12,
agriculture, *ad passim*
ALMO [Kenya], 212, 220,
Angola, 191,
anthropology/anthropologist, 7,
ARA (Annual Rice Account), 131-151,
arabica, 111-2, 123-6. *See also* coffee
Arabs, 31, 208,
arbitrage (regional/seasonal), 70, 77-9, 84,
Ashante/Ashanti, 87-106, 208,
assembling, 2-3, 8, 170. *See also* collecting
auction(s), 13, 81-4, 212, 214,

bags (jute), 9, 50, 53, 55, 59, 100, 140, 171, 173-9,
bananas, 5, 16, 19,
banks [commercial], 29, 102, 171, 176, 190, 200,
bargaining [position/power], 10-11, 109, 121, 123, 128, 177, 179, 182,
beans, 49, 59, 153-168,
Benin, 153-168, 206, 208-9, 217, 219,
Borgou [Benin], 153-168,
Botswana, 211-2, 218-20,
Botswana Meat Commission, 212, 220,
brand (name), 3, 9, 16, 120-1, 123,
brokers, 24, 77, 177,
Burkina Faso, 67-85, 209, 215, 217, 219,

Cameroon(ian), 87-106, 116, 209, 217,
can(ning), 6, 119, 210, 212, 219-20,
CARDER [Benin], 156,
cash crop, 12, 24-5, 79, 88, 96, 195, 211. *See also* cocoa, coffee and cotton
cash-on-delivery, 14, 172, 177, 181,
cassava, 5, 19, 27, 59, 137-8, 140-2, 154,
cattle, 185-202, 205-224,
Central Province [Cameroon], 87-106,
cereals. *See* food grains,
CICC [Cameroon], 97,
climate/climatic, 2, 19-20, 26, 31-2, 34, 36, 39, 67, 192,
CMC (Cocoa Marketing Company) [Ghana], 99,
cocoa, 87-106, 114-7, 219,
Cocobod. *See* Ghana Cocoa Board,
CODESRIA, 16,
coffee, 90, 93, 98, 109-128, 219,
Cold Storage Commission [RSA], 212,
collect(ing)/collection, 2-3, 77, 82, 87, 96, 98, 138, 170. *See also* assembling
commodity chain (global/national), 109-10, 114-20,
consumers, *ad passim*

cooperative(s), 4, 7-8, 10, 24-7, 29, 33, 55-6, 76, 94-6, 98, 102-4, 113, 117, 187-90, 221,
Costa Rica, 109-128,
Côte d'Ivoire, 109-128, 215, 217, 219, 221-3,
cotton, 7, 154, 156, 219,
credit, 7, 14, 49, 51, 60, 78, 81, 83-4, 95, 97, 101, 104, 115-6, 121, 138, 141-2, 144, 147-50, 169, 171, 180, 199,
credit, pre-harvest, 14,
crops. *See* cash crops, domestic crops, export crops and food crops
cross-border (trade/transport), 205-24,
CSB(Z) [Zambia], 187-8, 190, 194,
CSRP (Cereal Sector Reform Programme) [Kenya], 55-6,
CSSPPA [Côte d'Ivoire], 115-6, 118-9, 128,
currency, national, 46-7, 117, 205-6, 223-4. *See also* exchange rate
customs union, 207,
CUT (Cooperative Union of Tanganyika), 24,

dalali, 29-30,
Dar es Salaam, 21, 25-7, 29-35, 37, 39, 211,
devaluation, 26, 46-7, 101-3, 105, 116-8, 217, 221-4,
development, agricultural, *ad passim*
development, export-oriented, 5, 13,
distribute/distribution, 2, 16, 27, 35-7, 67, 77, 80, 82-3, 85, 93, 95, 120-2, 132,
domestic crops, 9, 12-3, 16,
donor (country/organization), 28, 36-9, 44, 55-7, 70, 72, 187-8, 190, 221,
drought, 5, 24-6, 28, 30, 34, 39, 47-8, 52, 56-8, 71-2, 76, 79, 133, 140-1, 146-7, 150, 205, 210, 215, 218, 222, 224,
DRSS [Zambia], 187, 190-1, 194-6,
drying, 6, 9,
durable, 3, 5-6, 8-9, 120, 197,
DVTCS [Zambia], 189, 194,
Dyula, 208,

early warning (system), 29, 37, 67, 84-5,
empower(ment), 94-5,
entitlements, 67-8, 70-2, 75-6, 83-5,
Ethiopia, 36, 209, 218,
European Community/Union (EU), 20, 55-6, 120, 123, 125, 215, 217-8, 220, 222,
exchange rate, 26, 45, 70, 117-8, 217, 220-1,
export crops, 5, 7-10, 12-3, 24, 88, 93-4, 96-7, 101, 209. *See also* cocoa, coffee and cotton
export revenues, 116,
exporter(s), 5, 7, 13, 96-7, 114, 116, 121, 124, 127,
extension (services), 24-5, 98, 103, 148-9,

famine, 22, 37-9, 67, 70-2, 75, 80, 84,
famine relief, 22, 26, 36-9, 71,
FAO, 12, 16, 21, 28, 32, 37, 70,
farmer, *ad passim*
farmers' organizations, 12, 76, 81-2, 95, 97-8, 103,
farmgate, 8, 51, 59, 153-169, 172, 174-6, 178-82,
fertilizer, 7, 27, 32-3, 47, 58, 92, 103, 105, 148-9, 199,
finance/financing, 8-11, 49, 100, 169, 172-3, 175, 179, 182, 200,

food aid, 27-8, 36-8, 72, 80, 84,
food crops, 25, 29, 90, 93, 102,
food-for-work, 83,
food grains, 5-6, 8-11, 14, 19-41, 43, 67-85, 170, 206, 208. *See also* maize, rice, millet and sorghum
food insecurity (chronic/transitory), 5, 67-8, 71-2, 76, 78, 83-5,
food marketing, 3-4, 16, 19-41, 44, 55,
food policy, 22,
food security, 21-2, 25, 28, 38-9, 43-8, 55-8, 61-2, 67-85, 219,
food self-sufficiency, 20, 23, 39, 48, 51, 68, 75, 81, 83-4, 170, 185, 196, 198-200, 215,
food shortages, 5, 11, 22-5, 34-5, 37-9, 54, 56, 58, 68, 70, 74, 83,
food system, 45, 68-70,
foreigner, overseas, 7, 13,
forward (contract/selling), 14, 121,
France, 122-7, 209,
fruit, 6, 138, 170,
Fulani, 208, 214, 217,
functions, marketing, 1, 4, 8, 172, 177, 185, 187,
fungicides, 90, 92, 103,

geography/geographers, 5, 7-8, 15,
Germany, 36, 121-7, 211,
Ghana, 87-106, 209, 215, 217, 221, 223,
Ghana Cocoa Board, 90, 98-9, 102,
government, *ad passim*. *See also* state
grade/grading, 3, 9, 94, 102, 127, 181, 212, 219,
grain banks, 76, 82-4,
grain(s). *See* food grains
grazing areas, 211-3,
Great Scarcies (River), 131-51,
GSD (Grain Storage Department) [Tanganyika], 23-4, 39,
Guinea, 208,
Guinea corn. *See* sorghum

handling (physical), 9, 31, 172-3, 175-6,
harvest(ing), 2, 4, 6, 10, 20, 22-30, 33-9, 47-8, 50, 56-8, 60, 67, 70, 72-4, 77-9, 82-4, 92, 98, 100, 105, 113, 131, 135-47, 153-4, 170, 172, 175-6, 178-80,
Hausa, 206, 208-9, 213,
hides and skins, 208, 213-4, 219,
hoard(ing), 11, 72, 84,
horticultural/horticulture, 154, 169-72, 176, 180-2,
household, 5, 20, 22, 39, 44-7, 61, 67-85, 90, 93, 153-68, 170, 185, 196-8, 200-2. *See also* rice farming household
humidity, 6,
hunger, 37, 70-2, 75,
husk rice. *See* paddy

IBRD. *See* World Bank
ICAFE [Costa Rica], 116-7,
illegal (trade), 54, 205-6, 210, 214, 218, 223,
IMF (International Monetary Fund), 26-7, 39, 43-5, 55, 62, 88, 93, 117,
imperfect information, 80-1,

incomplete markets, 81,
indigenous knowledge, 15,
information provider, 162,
infrastructure/infrastructural, 30, 47, 60, 90, 92, 94, 102, 105-6, 109, 115, 121, 127, 131-2, 148, 159-60, 170, 185, 190, 194, 202, 212, 214,
inputs (farm/agricultural), 7, 25, 27, 35, 47-9, 51-2, 58, 87, 90, 92-5, 97-8, 101-5, 111-2, 148-9, 151, 188,
intensification [of agriculture], 7, 105-6,
inter-African trade, 13. *See also* cross-border
Ivory Coast. *See* Côte d'Ivoire

KANU [Kenya], 54,
Kenya, 11, 36, 43-62, 169-82, 207-12, 214, 218-21, 223,
Kenya Meat Commission, 210-2, 220,
kolanut, 9, 13, 140, 208-9,

labour [agricultural], 2, 71, 112, 115, 139, 144-5, 148-51, 173-6, 196, 199,
labourer, 20, 22,
LBC (Licensed Buying Company) [Ghana], 99-100, 102,
Lekie [Cameroon], 90, 96-7,
liberalization [of trade/market], liberalize, 22, 27-9, 31-5, 38-9, 43-62, 67-8, 80-1, 83, 87-8, 97-105, 114, 116, 127, 188,
licensed buying agent (LBA), 55, 96. *See also* trader, licensed
Liebig, 211-2,
literacy, 15,
livestock, 2, 6, 191, 195, 198, 208-14, 217, 219-21, 223. *See also* cattle
Lomé Agreement, 125, 218,
long distance trade, 13, 205-9,

Maasai, 208-12,
maize, 5, 13-4, 19-41, 43-62, 68, 72, 75, 79, 93, 137-40, 143, 153-68, 196,
Malawi, 36, 47,
Mali, 47, 215, 217,
market, physical, 4, 7-8, 13-4, 153-68,
market, rural, 8, 43, 47, 51, 53-4, 59, 62, 170, 182,
market, urban, 8, 10, 47, 174-80, 182,
market environment, 153-4, 156-7, 161, 163, 170, 207,
market failures, 68-9, 72,
market imperfections, 68, 81, 83-4,
market information/intelligence, 8, 10-1, 14, 29-30, 77, 79-84, 153, 156-69, 171-3, 176-7, 179-80, 190,
market integration, 34, 79, 81,
market reforms, 87, 96-8, 101,
marketing, *ad passim*
marketing board, 7, 10, 14-5, 43-4, 46, 50, 54, 61, 94-6, 102, 105, 110, 205, 212, 219-21,
marketing chain, 4, 25, 29-30, 97, 99, 171, 178,
marketing channel, 4, 10, 12-4, 16, 47, 59, 71, 76-7, 169-71, 179-82, 215, 219, 221, 223,
Mauritania, 217,
Mbam and Kim [Cameroon], 90, 93, 97,
meat, 6, 120, 143, 186-8, 197, 205, 209-11, 213-5, 217-23,
Meat Marketing Board [Ghana], 219-20,

merchants, 24. *See also* wholesalers
milk, 6, 197, 200,
millet, 5, 13-4, 19-20, 27, 59, 68, 72-3, 75, 79, 137-8, 140, 143, 154, 196,
mill(ing) [grain], 30-1, 43, 54, 60-1, 132, 140, 145-6, 151,
Mongu [Zambia], 188-9,
Mono [Benin], 153-68,
monopsony, 14, 87, 96, 98,
Mozambique, 36,

naira, 217, 220,
Namboard [Zambia], 187,
Namibia, 211, 218-9,
NAPB (National Agricultural Products Board) [Tanzania], 24-5, 39,
NCPB (National Cereals Produce Board) [Kenya], 43-62,
Nestlé, 114, 121,
NGO (non-governmental organization), 36, 67, 75, 102, 104,
Niger, 206, 208, 213-4, 219-20,
Nigeria, 116, 206, 209-10, 213-5, 217, 221, 223,
NMC (National Milling Corporation) [Tanzania], 25-31, 34, 39,
NPMB/ONCPB [Cameroon], 96-8, 101,

OAU (Organization of African Unity), 16,
off-farm, 196, 198,
offtake rate, 185-7, 191-4, 198, 201,
OFNACER, 76, 79-80, 84,
ONCC [Cameroon], 97-8,
ONCPB [Cameroon]. *See* NPMB/ONCPB
on-farm, 2, 35, 98,
open market, 19, 29, 33, 56,
osusu, 135, 138-9, 142, 147, 149, 151,
outlet [market(ing)], 57, 61, 93, 146-7, 153-68, 187,
overland trade/transport, 13. *See also* cross-border

pack(ag)ing, 9, 47, 98, 172-6,
paddy (rice), 131-51,
parastatal, 25-6, 41, 46, 50, 54, 187-90. *See also* marketing board
pastoral(ist), 208, 211-5, 220, 222-4,
PBC (Produce Buying Company) [Ghana], 98-100,
peasant farmer, 153-68,
perishable/perishability, 2-3, 5-6, 9, 170, 176, 209, 219,
pesticides, 7, 90, 92, 105,
plantains, 5,
plantation(s), 3, 20, 22, 93, 105, 111, 115,
politique de la viande, 213,
posho, 50, 52, 54, 60, 62,
potatoes, 59, 169-82,
practices [commercial/trade], 7, 15, 177,
preserve/preservation, 2, 6,
price(s), *ad passim*
price control, 23, 27, 44,
price formation, 14, 46, 51, 97,
price risk, 10, 116-7, 123. *See also* risks, commercial
prices, observed, 8, 14,

prices, official, 14, 51-2, 79-80,
prices, panterritorial, 24-6, 32-3, 94,
prices, retail, 23, 47, 120, 122-7,
private sector, 27, 30-1, 38, 46, 60, 93-8, 186, 190, 201,
processing, industrial, 8, 16, 30-1, 47, 61, 93, 113-4, 116, 119, 121, 128, 221, 223. *See also* milling
processing, artisanal, 8-9, 31,
producer prices, 23, 25-6, 31-5, 44, 46-54, 58-9, 87, 94-5, 97, 101-2, 105, 115-8, 135, 147, 188, 206. *See also* prices, official
producers, *ad passim*
pro-farmer (feelings), 4, 7,
public sector, 30, 46, 117-8, 186,
public works, 22, 36,

quality (control), 2, 9, 95-9, 105-6, 109, 114-6, 121, 123-4, 127-8, 139, 143, 170, 176, 181, 211-2,
quarantine, 207, 210-2, 214, 223,

radio broadcasts, 81. *See also* wireless
rain(fall), 26, 32, 35, 37-8, 51, 57, 78, 90, 137, 139, 141, 170, 175-6, 192,
ranches, 211, 218-20, 223,
refrigeration, 6,
relief. *See* famine relief
research, *ad passim*
retail(er), 9, 23-4, 29, 47, 52, 54, 57, 59, 77, 82, 120, 127, 160, 169-70, 181, 187,
rice, 5, 13, 19-20, 27, 68, 131-51, 195, 199, 206,
rice farming household, 131-51,
rice transaction, 131-51,
risks, commercial/market/trade, 8, 10, 156, 171, 176,
risks, physical, 8, 10, 176,
robusta, 97, 111-2, 123-8. *See also* coffee
Royal Niger Company, 214,
roots/root crops, 5, 140,
rural institutions, 135, 148-51,

Sahel(ian), 5, 70, 75-7, 208, 212, 215, 217, 219, 222,
sales behaviour, 185-6, 195, 198, 200-1,
savannah, 209,
season(al)/seasonality, 2-3, 6, 10-1, 33-5, 53, 62, 70, 72, 74-5, 77-8, 80-1, 133, 136, 138-41, 154, 176, 192,
seed(s), 27, 35, 37, 49, 70, 73, 135-6, 138-43, 149, 199,
selling unit, 158,
sembe, 26-7, 30,
Sen, A.K., 5, 70-1,
Senegal, 209, 217,
settler farmers, 11, 20, 52, 207, 210-2, 221, 223,
SGR (Strategic Grain Reserve) [Tanzania], 21, 27-9, 33, 36-9,
Sierra Leone, 4, 8, 131-51,
slaughter(house), 187-91, 197, 212-3, 217, 219-20, 222,
SLPMB (Sierra Leone Produce Marketing Board), 132, 147,
smallholders, 43, 49-51, 62, 90, 93, 103, 112, 115, 170,
social security [informal], 131, 136, 141, 143, 150,
sociology/sociologist, 3, 7,

SOCOODER [Cameroon], 96,
SODECAO [Cameroon], 96-8, 101, 103-4,
soils, 2, 90, 92-3, 139,
Somali(a), 36, 209-10, 212, 218, 222,
SONAGESS, 76, 80, 83-4,
SONARAN [Niger], 219-20,
sorghum, 5, 19-20, 23, 27, 59, 68, 72-3, 75, 78-9, 137-8, 140, 143, 154,
sorting, 2-3, 9, 127. *See also* grading
South Africa, 211, 218, 220-1,
Southern Rhodesia, 11. *See also* Zimbabwe
spatial integration [of markets], 14,
stabilization fund [for prices of export crops], 94-5, 97, 101, 116,
staple food (crops), 3, 5-6, 11, 19-41, 43-4, 131-2,
starvation, 70,
state, *ad passim. See also* government
stocks [of agricultural products], 3, 9-11, 28, 30, 33, 38, 70, 72, 74, 79, 81, 84, 123, 147,
storage, 2-3, 6, 8, 10-1, 28, 30-1, 35, 47, 51, 60, 78, 81-2, 98, 102, 136, 142, 147, 172-3, 175-6,
structural adjustment (programme) (SAP), 7, 27, 41, 43-7, 51, 55, 58, 60, 67-8, 76, 80, 83, 87-8, 93-6, 101-5, 110, 116-9, 128, 205, 217, 220-1,
subsidize/subsidy, 11, 20, 25-8, 32-3, 38, 44, 46, 50, 52, 56, 58, 60-1, 87, 102, 105, 115-7, 215, 217, 222,
subsistence, 12-3, 50, 131-3, 136, 140-1, 146, 150-1,
Sudan [country], 211, 218,
sustainable/sustainability, 110,
Swahili, 208,
Swaziland, 211,

Tanganyika/Tanzania, 19-41, 47, 59, 208, 210-1, 214, 218-21, 223,
tax(ation), 5-6, 46, 70, 79, 94, 101, 109, 116-7, 122, 125-8, 160, 209-10, 213, 223,
thin(ness) [market], 50, 72, 78-82,
Togo, 208-9,
trade associations, 4, 7,
trade contraction, 207, 224,
trade creation, 207, 215, 224,
trade diversion, 207, 215, 224,
trader, *ad passim*
trader, collecting, 3, 7-8, 10, 14, 160,
trader, licensed, 15, 23-4,
traders, African, 13, 38-9, 212, 214, 223-4,
traders, Asian, 24, 31, 39,
traders, local, 38, 51, 80, 188-90, 212, 214,
traders, private, 21, 23-4, 27-9, 32, 35, 39, 43, 46, 54-8, 60-2, 76, 80-1, 83, 94, 101, 104, 170, 185-90, 205, 214, 219, 223-4,
traders, overseas, 10, 97,
tradition(al), 13, 133, 136, 138, 147, 151, 161-2, 187,
trans-oceanic (crops), 13, 15-6,
transport(ation), 5, 8, 13-4, 20, 22-3, 25-32, 34, 36, 38, 49-50, 55, 59-60, 80-1, 90, 93, 96, 98, 100, 113, 120, 127, 145, 156, 159-62, 169-77, 179, 182, 188-91, 208-10, 213, 215, 222-3,
trans-Sahara trade, 210, 213,
trekking routes [cattle], 213-4,

trust, 14, 95, 181,
Tuareg, 213,
tubers, 5, 154, 170,

Uganda, 36, 59, 111, 211-2,
UNCTAD, 16,
UNECA, 16,
urbanization, 20, 22, 81,

variety [botanical], 2, 20, 90, 92, 112, 123-4, 128, 138-40, 148-9, 165,
vegetables, 6, 143, 154, 170, 175,

weighing/weight, 9, 15, 94, 175, 200,
Western Province [Zambia], 185-202,
WFP (World Food Programme), 28, 36-8,
wholesalers, 24, 29-31, 33, 77, 81, 160, 169-182,
wireless, 10. *See also* radio broadcasts
WLL [Zambia], 188, 195,
World Bank, 19, 31, 33-4, 39, 43-5, 50, 52, 55-6, 62, 71, 76, 80, 88, 93-5, 104, 110, 116-8, 149,
World War II, 22, 209-11,
WPCMPA [Zambia], 189-90,
WPCU [Zambia], 188-91,

yams, 5, 142,

zakat, 136, 143, 150,
Zambia, 185-202, 211,
ZCSC [Zambia], 187-91, 194-5,
Zimbabwe, 47, 211,
ZIMCO [Zambia], 187,

Research Series of the African Studies Centre, Leiden, The Netherlands

1. Dick Foeken & Nina Tellegen 1994 — Tied to the land. Living conditions of labourers on large farms in Trans Nzoia District, Kenya

2. Tom Kuhlman, 1994 — Asylum or Aid? The economic integration of Ethiopian and Eritrean refugees in the Sudan

3. Kees Schilder, 1994 — Quest for self-esteem. State, Islam and Mundang ethnicity in Northern Cameroon

4. Johan A. van Dijk, 1995 — Taking the waters. Soil and water conservation among settling Beja nomads in Eastern Sudan

5. Piet Konings, 1995 — Gender and class in the tea estates of Cameroon

6. Thera Rasing, 1995 — Passing on the rites of passage. Girls' initiation rites in the context of an urban Roman Catholic community on the Zambian Copperbelt

7. Jan Hoorweg, Dick Foeken & Wijnand Klaver, 1995 — Seasons and nutrition at the Kenya coast

8. John A. Houtkamp, 1996 — Tropical Africa's emergence as a banana supplier in the inter-war period

9. Victor Azarya, 1996 — Nomads and the state in Africa: the political roots of marginality

10. Deborah Bryceson & Vali Jamal, eds, 1997 — Farewell to farms. De-agrarianization and employment in Africa

11. Tjalling Dijkstra, 1997 — Trading the fruits of the land: horticultural marketing channels in Kenya

12. Nina Tellegen, 1997 — Rural enterprises in Malawi: necessity or opportunity?

13. Klaas van Walraven, 1999 — Dreams of power. The role of the organization of African Unity in the politics of Africa 1963 - 1993

14. Isaac Sindiga, 1999 — Tourism and African development. Change and challenge of tourism in Kenya

15. H. Laurens van der Laan, Tjalling Dijkstra & Aad van Tilburg, 1999 — Agricultural marketing in tropical Africa: contributions from the Netherlands

Copies can be ordered at: Ashgate Publishing Ltd.
Gower House
Croft Road
Aldershot
Hampshire GU11 3HR
England

African agriculture has always had a strong appeal for the people of the Netherlands. This is due to (1) a long-established interest in tropical agriculture going back to the days when Indonesia was a Dutch colony; (2) a broad-based desire to help the Third World; and (3) the view that Tropical Africa is highly dependent on agriculture.

As practical expertise in Africa and systematic research on African agriculture grew, specialization became both possible and necessary. This volume reflects the specialization in marketing which has been welcomed by economists, geographers and scholars of agricultural marketing. In addition to a general introductory chapter, this book includes five contributions on staple food grains, two on export crops, two on cattle and one on horticulture. Nine of the chapters are country-specific, covering Benin, Burkina Faso, Cameroon, Côte d'Ivoire, Ghana, Kenya, Sierra Leone, Tanzania and Zambia.

Laurens van der Laan and **Tjalling Dijkstra** are research fellows of the African Studies Centre. **Aad van Tilburg** is senior lecturer at the Marketing and Consumer Behaviour Group, Wageningen Agricultural University.

AFRICAN STUDIES CENTRE LEIDEN

PO BOX 9555
2300 RB LEIDEN
THE NETHERLANDS
E-mail: asc@fsw.leidenuniv.nl
Website: asc.leidenuniv.nl